What Do Mothers Need?

Motherhood Activists and Scholars Speak Out on Maternal Empowerment for the 21st Century

Edited by

Andrea O'Reilly

DEMETER

DEMETER PRESS

Published by:
Demeter Press
c/o Motherhood Initiative for Research and
Community Involvement (MIRCI)
140 Holland St. West, P.O. 13022
Bradford, ON, L3Z 2Y5
Telephone: 905.775.9089
Email: info@demeterpress.org
Website: www.demeterpress.org

Demeter Press logo based on Skulptur "Demeter" by Maria-Luise Bodirsky <www.keramik-atelier.bodirsky.edu>

Cover Artwork: Leesa Streifler in collaboration with her son, Daniel Bell. Chromira print, 2007.

Printed and Bound in Canada

Library and Archives Canada Cataloguing in Publication

What do mothers need? : motherhood activists and scholars speak out on maternal empowerment for the 21st century / edited by Andrea O'Reilly.

Includes bibliographical references.
ISBN 978-1-927335-07-9

1. Motherhood. 2. Mothers—Social conditions—21st century. 3. Parenting. 4. Feminism. I. O'Reilly, Andrea, 1961–

HQ759.W43 2012 306.874'309051 C2012-908265-1

For the women of room 1418 — Debbie Bryd, Tracey Carlyle, Renée Knapp, Fiona Green, and Regina Edmonds.

Table of Contents

Acknowledgements

This volume shows that what mothers most need is a culture that believes in and supports motherwork; and that for motherwork to be done well it must be shared and sustained by many. I am blessed as a mother and as a writer to have so many people in my life that believe in and support the work that I do, particularly as I prepared this book for publication. Thank you to the contributors of the volume for making the public forum "What do Mothers Need?" the huge success that it was and for their passionate and visionary work in making the world a better place for mothers.

Thank you as always to the Demeter team who once again made order out of chaos: Tracey Carlyle, Melissa Nurse, Angie Deveau, Randy Chase and, in particular, Luciana Ricciutelli. A special thank you is due to the Social Science and Humanities Research Council of Canada (SSHRC) for their funding of this public forum "What Do Mothers Need?" from which the volume is developed. Thank you to my MIRCI family for providing the safe and sustaining "homeplace" that makes possible my maternal scholarship.

And as always, and forever, thank you to my partner of thirty years, Terry Conlin, and my three children Casey, Erin and Jesse for giving me what I need.

Introduction

What Do Mothers Need?

ANDREA O'REILLY

In MAY 2012 the *Motherhood Initiative for Research and Community Involvement* hosted a one day public forum entitled "What Do Mothers Need?": Motherhood Activists and Scholars Speak out on Maternal Empowerment for the 21st Century. We invited 31 of the leading motherhood activists and scholars from across North America and asked them to answer this question: "What Do Mothers Need?" The motherhood organizations represented at the forum included the Canadian and Ontario Native Women's Association, Hip Mama, LGBTQ Parenting Network, National Association of Mother Centres, Mothers & More, Welfare Warriors, Mocha Moms, and Sister Song. Motherhood scholars included Patrizia Albanese, Paula Caplan, Pamela Stone, Gina Wong, Jasjit Sangha, Jewelles Smith, Heather Hewett, Melissa Maldonado-Salcedo, Kim Anderson, Jennifer Brant, Susan Boyd, Fiona Green, Andrea O'Reilly, Barbara Katz Rothman, Amber Kinser, Wanda Thomas Bernard, Andrea Doucet, Margaret K. Nelson, Jocelyn Elise Crowley, Judith Warner, and Lynn O'Brien Hallstein. The speakers, who were from diverse academic disciplines and activist agencies, were asked to position their research and community involvement from what may be termed a social relevance or "results driven" perspective; that is, presenting specific strategies for the betterment of mothers' lives within the family, the workplace, and the larger society.

At the conclusion of the conference the speakers came together for a three-hour roundtable discussion to identify common themes of the forum, and to develop strategies for the empowerment of mothers today. Grounded in a long history, in which women activists, writers, and feminists focused much effort on strengthening the social, personal, and political

Andrea O'Reilly

power of mothers, the forum explored what mothers in twenty-first century North American society need in order to adequately care for their children while living full and purposeful lives. Overall, the aim of the forum was to explore what changes were needed in public/social policy, health, education, the workplace, maternal support/advocacy, and the family in order to afford full and lasting gender equity for mothers in the twenty-first century. More specifically, the event sought to explore how best to broker, leverage, mobilize and implement scholarship on maternal empowerment in order to effect real change in the lives of North American mothers, and to deliver models, strategies, and practices of maternal empowerment that are of relevance and, most importantly, are "of use" for activists, service providers, and policy makers who work for, and on behalf of, mothers. That being said, the forum was informed by a view of academic research that, in both theory and practice, defines good scholarship as—to borrow from the noted scholar and activist Angela Davis—that which has social relevance and use, and the worth of which is measured by its impact on society and the achievement of a just and equitable world.

The 26 chapters in this book have been developed from the forum presentations. The chapters are organized under six themes: "Redefining Motherhood," "Empowering Mothers," "Mothers, Children and Families: Health and Well-Being," "Mothers, Education and Social Change," "Mothers, Partners and Parenting," and "Mothers and Work." The themes and issues explored are many: midwifery, intensive mothering, food allergies, workplace flexibility, family meals, childcare, education, popular culture, "opting out," maternal empowerment, fathers, maternal activism, poverty, shared parenting, and work/life balance to name but a few. These themes and issues are examined from a wide range of perspectives including Aboriginal, Latina, African American/Canadian, military, single, poor, young, at-home, waged mothers, as well as mothers with disabilities.[1] However, although the chapters explore diverse issues and offer various strategies, they agree and emphasize that all mothers in patriarchal societies are disadvantaged and disempowered, albeit in different ways. Likewise, they all demonstrate that if mothers are to achieve maternal empowerment in and for the twenty-first century, as the book's subtitle proclaims, they need social and political change which is developed from and in response to their specific identities and work as mothers. The introduction will present the diverse issues and strategies as discussed in each chapter. Following this, it will explore common themes as considered and identified in the roundtable that closed the forum in an attempt to answer the larger question of the forum and this volume: What do mothers need for maternal empowerment in the twenty-first century?

INTRODUCTION TO THE CHAPTERS

The first section of the book, "Redefining Motherhood," opens with Fiona Joy Green's chapter, "Moms Under Surveillance: Noticing and Challenging the Idea of the 'Good' Mother." In her chapter Green examines the influence of celebrity media, reality TV, and mommy blogs on the continual surveillance of moms. She offers concrete examples of how, once they have an understanding of the complexity of the situation, mothers and others can trouble and challenge this damaging and hurtful practice through individual and collective action. Likewise, in the chapter that follows, "Rebelling Against 'Mom:' Finding Fulfillment Beyond the Media's Myths of Motherhood," Estelle Sobel Erasmus argues that while the media offers a plethora of hollow platitudes touting that motherhood is the "best job in the world," they are the first to generalize, sensationalize and try to create division between mothers in the never ending hunt for headlines. She demonstrates this by citing examples of how companies and the media have used recent news items to recreate "the mommy wars," and offers solutions and step by step methods on how activists can harness the power of social media to do good and help support mothers.

In the next chapter, "What Mothers Need: For Parenting to Get Under Control," Margaret K. Nelson argues that the critique of what has

Heather Hewett, Jewelles Smith and Barbara Katz Rothman, Session on Mothers, Family, Children and Family: Health and Well-Being, "What Do Mothers Need?" Public Forum.

been called "Helicopter Parenting" misses the major issues associated with hyper-vigilance on the part of parents. Drawing on her research in "Parenting Out of Control: Anxious Parents in Uncertain Times," she argues that the turn towards extensive engagement with the well-being of their own children has left professional middle class parents with little free time to develop their own interests. Moreover, she argues that the phenomenon (which she calls "parenting out of control") has lead to an erosion of community engagement and has allowed the reproduction of class privilege to go unchecked. Judith Warner, similar to Nelson in her chapter, "Bait and Switch: Moving on From 'Mommy Madness'," writes on how the American culture of motherhood has changed from the point, ten years ago, when she wrote "Perfect Madness: Motherhood in the Age of Anxiety," when Lisa Belkin's article, "The Opt-Out Revolution," defined the times (for the *New York Times Magazine*), and when all the talk was of staying home and "surrendering" to motherhood. She describes the feeling of being left holding the bag that so many mothers—particularly those who did everything "right" in losing themselves in their family lives—now have as they contemplate moving forward. It's an exploration of why too much "intensive motherhood" isn't good for you—and of whether the time is now ripe to open up a new space in our cultural conversation in which to reposition working motherhood as an inherent good, rather than a necessary evil. O'Reilly builds upon Nelson and Warner's critique of intensive mothering in her

Jasjit K. Sangha speaking at Session on Empowering Mothers, "What Do Mothers Need?" Public Forum.

chapter, "Outlaw(ing) Motherhood: A Theory and Politic of Maternal Empowerment for the 21st Century," by asking that scholars and activists alike rethink received or accepted notions of how and why motherhood functions as an oppressive institution for women. When asked, students, mothers, and researchers readily describe the exhaustion, guilt, boredom, anxiety, loneliness, and so forth of contemporary Western motherhood, but are less forthcoming on why this is so. O'Reilly argues that gender essentialism and the resulting naturalized opposition of the public and private spheres is the reason why modern motherhood, despite forty years of feminism, remains a patriarchal institution that is resistant to change. According to O'Reilly, only by unearthing and severing the ideological underpinning of patriarchal motherhood—gender essentialism—can we develop a politic of maternal empowerment and a practice of outlaw motherhood for the twenty-first century.

In the final chapter of section one Gina Wong explores the transformative and revolutionary process of matroreform. Through this process, the way that mothers come into their own way of mothering is conceptualized apart from the way they were mothered and the way in which society defines motherhood. Matroreform is an act of resistance and empowerment on a personal level to refuse the replication of our mother's oppression; it also captures the process of collective resistance against the subjugation of mothers in the broader social sphere. In outlining what mother's need, Wong emphasizes the centrality of matroreform: a feminist

From left to right, Andrea O'Reilly and Lorri Slepian

process to engender new motherworlds. At the same time, she delineates matroreform to involve an interpersonal and intra-psychic process whereby mothers choose to reform mothering from her own experiences of being mothered that may or may not be prompted by a deliberate feminist consciousness.

Section Two, "Empowering Mothers," opens with Paula J. Caplan's chapter "Mothers and the Military: What It's Like and How It Needs to Be." The chapter examines the ways that three groups of mothers, who are related to the military in different ways, are affected by the impossible standards set for all mothers and the psychopathologizing of both mothers' work and the emotional and moral consequences of war. The three groups are mothers who serve in the military, mothers who have adult offspring who return from military service and need care, and mothers whose partners are in or have returned from the military. Caplan also addresses what these mothers need to lighten their heavy burdens, including but not limited to demythologizing motherhood and challenging the psychopathologizing of the effects of trauma.

In the following chapter, "What More Do You People Want? The Unique Needs of Aboriginal Mothers in a Modern Context," Lavell-Harvard and Corbiere-Lavell, an Ojibway/Odawa mother and daughter, describe the traditional role of Aboriginal women, the impacts of colonization, and the resulting legacy. Drawing upon a collective 70 years of expe-

Welfare Warriors T-shirt

rience working with Aboriginal women at all levels—grassroots activism to international human rights forums—the authors share their insight and recommendations for the empowerment of contemporary Aboriginal mothers. In "What Do Mothers Need? Money," Pat Gowens argues that motherwork is crucial, complex, but unpaid work. As such motherwork often throws many mothers into an exhausting double workday, or into poverty, and even into crime which deprives children of their most precious necessity, a mother, and consequently of a secure, healthy childhood. She explains why mothers need access to economic resources, what countries provide financial support to mothers and children, and who is organizing for recognition and pay for motherworkers. Jasjit K. Sangha, in the final chapter of section two, "What Do South Asian Mothers Need? Negotiating Culture, Family and Selfhood" argues that South Asian cultural constructions of motherhood can both be a source of constraint as well as power for South Asian mothers. She shows that although specific cultural practices such as upholding *izzat* (honour) or arranged marriage can be limiting for mothers, they are not passive transmitters of dominant South Asian cultural ideals. Rather, they express their agency and resist their marginality through both subtle and overt means.

Section three, "Mothers, Children and Families: Health and Well-Being" opens with Barbara Katz Rothman's chapter, "What Do Mothers Need? Midwives!" Her chapter has a simple answer to what mothers need: midwives. In an interesting comparison to the growing food movement, she argues for the re-valuing of midwifery skills, not just the 'kindness' and 'warmth' we are encouraged to think about, and the patience to go with the natural, but the very specific and quite impressive skills

Demeter Press banner

and craftsmanship they bring to birth. The following chapter, "DisAbled Mothers in the 21st Century: Finding Empowerment Through Activism" by Jewelles Smith, outlines the author's journey as a single mother, an activist, and a differently abled individual. She stressed the need for all disadvantaged women, but especially differently abled mothers, to stand strong against the implicit and explicit prejudices and discrimination that seems entrenched in our governmental system. Her hope is that through sharing her story, and some of the practicalities that it has taught her, she can assist other women facing similar struggles to succeed in attaining the assistance that is theirs by right. Section three concludes with Heather Hewett's article "Toward a Feminist Analysis of Motherhood, Family and Food Allergies." Hewett examines the psychological advice that a "necessary" amount of parental anxiety is required for raising children with life-threatening food allergies and explores the gendered dimensions of this emotional labor. She develops a feminist framework for analyzing the difficulties of managing this anxiety and fulfilling the cultural expectations of being a "good mother" to children with severe chronic conditions at a moment when institutions vary widely in their ability to keep food-allergic children safe.

Section four is on the topic of "Mothers, Education and Social Change;" it opens with Melissa Maldonado-Salcedo's chapter "(Cheesy) Mami Issues and Representations." In her chapter, Maldonado-Salcedo explores her political and personal experiences of being a Latina, scholar, daughter, and mother. She argues that Latina women can become empowered to be

Audience at "What Do Mothers Need ?" Public Forum

their best possible selves through an education. Her argument is contextualized against the conditions of this post-9/11 world in which popular representations of Latina mothers and daughters are in conversation with dominant discourses of sexuality, immigration, and education reform. These then inform the personal choices Latina mothers and daughters make in regard to their futures. She concludes that Latina mothers need to have access to an education in order to break the cycles of poverty that silence their histories and futures.

In their chapter, "Influencing Evolution Through an Evolving Revolution," Lorri Slepian and Laurie Sylla argue that in order for mothers to address their needs and wants they need to meet together in a nurturing, non-judgmental, ethical culture where the maternal experience and the maternal perspective is highly respected; where mothers can safely speak the truth to each other and to themselves. They point out that this culture already exists within the mother centers (of the USA, Europe, and South America) and that the spread of this kind of environment would aid mothers in experiencing a process of empowerment, and an appreciation for themselves and each other as women. Within such a culture women can come to realize that they are powerful enough to make the important changes needed to shape a world where care work and healthful mothering is valued and supported; where with consciousness and intention, mothers take actions, ever strengthening the evolving mother revolution that will bring about a transformed society and a more highly evolved humankind.

Jennifer Brant and Kim Anderson in their chapter "In the Scholarly Way: Making Generations of Inroads to Empowered Indigenous Mothering" write about the connections they share with a larger web of Indigenous women who are reclaiming empowered Indigenous mothering in the academy. The paper describes the inroads they have made within their own journeys that led them to discover the power of "eachother." The role of Indigenous based maternal pedagogy in inspiring and empowering generations of Indigenous women is also explored through an overview of the Gidayaamin Aboriginal Women's Certificate Program. In her chapter, "Ripe for Revolution," Gwen Lewis discusses the food system, agricultural/water pollution, energy depletion, corporate greed/government corruption, and overpopulation as some of the key threats to life and society as we know it, particularly the quality of life our children will experience. She discusses these issues and provides a framework to understand the web of connection between them. She argues that what mothers need most is the guarantee of a good, livable future for all our children and that the best way to address these problems is to educate the public, promote discussion on these issues, and to keep an open mind to a better future while advocating for major social change.

Susan Boyd's chapter, "Shared Parenting and Challenges for Maternal Autonomy," opens section five, "Mothers, Partners and Parenting." Boyd explores the tensions between autonomy and expectations of mother-caregivers in the context of trends in child custody law. Do mothers have appropriate scope for autonomy in the face of socio-legal norms that prioritize shared parenting? Feminism has been centrally concerned with freeing women to shape their own lives, rather than accepting a male-dominated definition of their lives. Yet the very relationship between mother-caregivers and children illustrates the important connection between relationships and autonomy: the caregiving that mothers provide enables children to become autonomous persons, yet this relationship simultaneously constrains maternal autonomy. In the current normative

Participants at "What Do Mothers Need?" Public Forum

climate, the potential for maternal autonomy is further compromised—even when mothers choose to live apart from a child's biological father. A responsible mother is expected to nurture a child's relationship with the father, unless he is proven to be harmful. The dominance of the heterosexual and patriarchal family—always a challenge for women's autonomy—is reproduced in this imposition of equal parenting. Given this, how can autonomous motherhood be promoted in the face of normative shared parenting?

The following chapter, "What do Mothers Need? Not to Give up on Their Own Ambitions and Persistence in Securing Partner Participation in Family Life," by D. Lynn O'Brien Hallstein, argues that mothers must re-remember the rallying cry of our second-wave feminist foremothers: "the personal is political." She does so because O'Brien Hallstein believes that, as contemporary women's public lives are becoming more and more similar to men's, many contemporary mothers seem to have "forgotten" that our personal lives and family relationships are also political and, often but not always, deeply implicated in patriarchy and patriarchal relationships. As a result, O'Brien Hallstein contends that we must re-remember just how much the personal is political in two specific ways: first, we must re-focus on both our right to and need for our own personal ambitions and, second, we must refuse to engage in normative wife roles in our private lives and family structure. O'Brien

Hallstein concludes that if we fail to do so, maternal empowerment in the twenty-first century will continue to elude contemporary mothers, even though contemporary women's lives are more similar to men's lives in the public sphere.

In her chapter, "Beyond Baby Mama Drama: What Single Black Mothers Expect from the Fathers of Their Children," Wanda Thomas Bernard questions the notion of Baby Mama Drama from the perspective of young African Canadian single mothers. She invites readers to understand what these mothers say they need from the fathers of their children, and at the forefront is less "drama" for the sake of their children. Bernard concludes with a discussion of how we might engage in more meaningful dialogue to help bring about change. Andrea Doucet's chapter focuses on the dilemma of gender "equality" in care work in her chapter "'Blurred Lines and Grey Flecks': Breadwinning Mothers, Caregiving Fathers and a Dilemma of Gender 'Equality' in Care." Drawing on a twenty-year research program with breadwinning mothers and caregiving fathers, she interrogates this concept of gender *equality* in care work as well as the *concept of care* itself. She argues for a more nuanced approach of "blurred lines and grey flecks" that begins with an ontologically relational conception of care, that integrates gender equality with gender differences in care work across diverse spaces and times, and she suggests that symmetry in care may be a more apt feminist response to the question "what do mothers need?"

The final section "Mothers and Work" opens with Pamela Stone's chapter, "Thoughts on the Implications of 'Opting Out' for Motherhood and Mothers' Movements." Stone argues that professional women, having been effectively shut out of their careers rather than "opting out," cope with both the loss of their professional identity and their assumption of the new and less valued identity of at-home mother through a variety of strategies involving what she calls the "professionalization" of motherhood and domesticity. While sounding a cautionary note about the potential for women in the privileged small group of "opt-outers" to perpetuate classist notions of motherhood, she also sees in them the potential to develop a dual consciousness which, together with their skills and resources, positions them for a leadership role in movements that advocate for women and families across the socio-economic spectrum.

In the following chapter "Mothers on a Tightrope: Finding Balance with Everything on the Line," Kuae Kelch Mattox discusses the delicate balancing act waged by today's mothers, particularly stay at home

African American mothers. She outlines how the stakes are high for the future of these mothers and their children, devastated by the effects of a global recession and an erosion of jobs that have upset the family balance and taken away the safety nets that these mothers could once rely upon.

In her chapter, "At the Core of the Work/Life Balance Myth: Motherhood and Family Dinners," Amber Kinser critiques the exclusion of mothers in over a decade's worth of research on correlations between the frequency of shared meals within families and a host of physical and mental health and social issues. Citing numerous findings showing that mothers continue to carry the load for meal provision, and arguing that frequent meal provision is a complex undertaking that warrants institutional support, Kinser works to redirect intervention efforts away from individual families (and mothers in particular) and toward societal-level solutions and forms of support. Kinser concludes the chapter with seven recommendations for facilitating shared family meals.

In the next chapter, "What Mothers and Early Childhood Educatiors Need But Don't Always Get: Competing(?) Voices on Childcare in Rural Communities," Patrizia Albanese, Megan Butryn, Louisa Hawkins and Courtney Manion present findings from two interrelated studies that include first-hand accounts from mothers and child care providers living and working in rural Ontario and Quebec—two related but distinct policy jurisdictions. The chapter draws on interviews that outline some of the daily experiences and challenges connected to caring for young children. It also shows that at times, especially in neo-liberal times, the interests and needs of these key stakeholders—mothers and childcare providers—appear to be or are made to seem at odds with one another. That said, by highlighting some of these seemingly competing interests and needs, they hope to move closer to providing recommendations that may help shed light on the importance of having state-funded child care as part of Canada's (currently weak) family policies.

In the chapter that concludes section six, "What Mothers Want: Workplace Flexibility," Jocelyn Elise Crowley uses survey data from women who are members of five mothers' organizations located across the United States in order to understand their views on how workplace flexibility would operate in their "ideal jobs." She finds that across groups and regardless of whether a mother is currently staying at home or working for pay, there is a remarkable consensus on the importance of workplace flexibility. Crowley also demonstrates that the majority of these mothers share strong views that the government could be doing more right now to advance this goal of flexibility, at least in the areas of employer education and incentives.

THE ROUNDTABLE DISCUSSION: CENTRAL FINDINGS AND COMMON THEMES

The forum, as noted above, concluded with the speakers coming together for a three hour roundtable conversation to discuss the central findings of the forum. The purpose of the conversation was to identify common themes and to explore how best to move the findings of the forum forward by way of future research, activism, and programming, with the specific aim of developing recommendations for new maternal empowerment policies and practices in the family, workplace, education, and the larger society. Significantly, the topic that opened the roundtable, and was emphasized throughout the discussion, was the importance and centrality of difference. While the participants agreed that motherhood disadvantages and disempowers all mothers in patriarchal societies, the experience and meaning of such is determined by the specific societal position and positioning of each individual mother. For example, one participant observed: "A poor black woman in the Bronx has different needs than a professor somewhere else." Given that the cultural location of the mother determines how patriarchal motherhood is experienced and how it may be resisted, participants emphasized that motherhood activists and researchers must challenge and move beyond the "one size fits all" approach and work from a theory and model of intersectionality to both understand and counter the oppression of mothers. As one participant commented: "We need to situate ourselves and recognize that diversity exists, and then ask what do we do about it." In other words, there is not and can never be one definitive answer for the question "What do mothers need?" The answers will be as varied as the mothers themselves.

Another central theme that emerged in the roundtable discussion was that things are worse for mothers now than they were twenty to thirty years ago. Participants identified two reasons for this: the rise of neo-liberalism over the last two-plus decades, and what Sharon Hays has termed intensive mothering. Under neo-liberalism, as one partici-

Roundtable discussion, "What Do Mothers Need" Public Forum.

pant commented, "women are increasingly asked to take on a burden of care and such cuts across class. People are discharged early from hospitals: women and especially mothers are expected to take that on." Indeed as another participant observed, "assumptions are that things have slowly gotten better but we have seen with the neoliberal shift, that even in progressive places, we are two steps back: while we have moved forward on some things, we have moved back with others." As neo-liberalism has resulted in far more work being downloaded onto mothers, from community work, schooling, education, health and carework, "the bar of what is expected of mothers," in the words of one participant, "is so much higher than it used to be." The forces of neo-liberalism and intensive mothering, the participants agreed, have created the perfect storm situation for twenty-first century motherhood, as mothers today must do far more work with far less resources. Therefore, what mothers need, the participants emphasized, are new models of care and family that challenge the privatization and intensification of modern motherhood.

The participants discussed possible models at length or what one person called "new framings" of mother work to challenge the current privatization and intensification of motherhood. One participant suggested the feminist ethic of care model while another discussed the practice of other-mothering found in African Canadian/American and Aboriginal cultures. Others discussed the need to de-gender motherwork and to position the word mother as verb rather than a noun; as a practice that can be undertaken by any individual committed to the care of children to include fathers, co-mothers, other-mothers, fictive kin, and extended family. Overall the participants stressed the need to begin what one person called a new "cultural conversation" on how best to raise children and support families. Indeed, the participants emphasized that what mothers need is what our societies need: a radical re-visioning of community and family; care and love.

In the introduction to my edited volume, *The 21st Century Motherhood Movement: Mothers Speak Out On Why We Need to Change the World and How to Do It*," I argued that mothers need a theory and politic of feminism for mothers, what I termed 'matricentric feminism.' This was not to suggest that a matricentric feminism should replace traditional feminist thought; rather, it is to remind and emphasize that the category of mother is distinct from the category of woman, and that many of the problems mothers face—socially, economically, politically, culturally, psychologically and so forth—are specific to women's roles and identity as mothers. Indeed, mothers are oppressed under patriarchy as women *and as mothers*. Consequently, mothers need a mother-centred or matricentric mode of feminism organized from and for their particular identity and work as mothers. Indeed, if mother activists and scholars agree on anything, it is that a mother-centred feminism is urgently needed and long overdue because mothers, arguably more so than women in general, remain disempowered despite forty years of feminism. In late 2012, as I conclude the introduction to this volume, the need for a matricentric feminism has become all that much more apparent. In 2011, the world witnessed a movement for social justice arguably unparalleled in the last 40 years: the Occupy movement. Significantly, while wealth inequity was the focus of this movement, the voices and concerns of mothers, who do the bulk of unpaid work globally and who are underpaid in waged work, were completely absent in the movement's agenda and activism. In my view, the Occupy Movement's failure to involve mothers or include their concerns, underscores the urgent need for mother-centred research and activism: a matricentric feminism for and by mothers.

CONCLUSION

So what do mothers need? What would this matricentric feminism lobby for? The forum participants ultimately were unable, or perhaps more accurately, unwilling to answer this question. Instead of answers, what emerged from the conversation was a call, to quote the participants again, for a new "cultural conversation" on and "a reframing' of motherhood; one that is appreciative of the diversity of mothers' lived experiences, attentive to the specific social context of twenty-first century motherhood, and audacious enough to imagine radical and transformative ways to mother and be mothered. It is my hope that, in exploring what mothers need from a multitude of perspectives, in presenting innovative strategies for empowered mothering, each in a specific twenty-first century context, this volume will begin this much needed conversation on what mothers need for maternal empowerment in the twenty-first century.

I would like to acknowledge the support of The Social Science and Research Council of Canada (SSHRC) and the funding they provided to host the public forum "What Do Mothers Need?" from which this book is developed.

[1]Regrettably, representatives from two motherhood organizations—LGBTQ Parenting Network and Sister Song—who presented at the Forum did not submit their papers for inclusion in this volume.

WORK CITED

O'Reilly, Andrea, ed. *The 21st Century Motherhood Movement: Mothers Speak Out on Why we Need to Change the World and How to Do It.* Bradford, Ontario: Demeter Press, 2011.

I. Redefining Motherhood

Moms Under Surveillance

Noticing and Challenging the Idea of the "Good" Mother

FIONA JOY GREEN

People are always staring. I always feel singled out or something—when I'm going shopping, especially. I always feel like I have to buy certain stuff just so they don't think less of me.[1]

THE EXPERIENCE THAT RAVEN PRINCE, a 26-year-old single mother of two living in Vancouver, BC, describes above is not particularly unusual. Susan Douglas and Meredith Michaels argue in *The Mommy Myth* that "motherhood has become a psychological police state" because "everyone watches us, we watch ourselves and other mothers, and we watch ourselves watching ourselves" (6). Today, many mothers feel that they are under scrutiny, are judged for their parenting abilities, and fear being (considered) a "bad mother." It's not difficult to understand why they may feel this way, given the assortment of parenting practices or types of mothers that women may identify with, aspire to, try to avoid, or dread being labeled. Some of these include, in no particular order: "Good Mom," "Bad Mother," "Helicopter Parent," "Hyper-Parent," "Extreme Mother," "Tiger Mom," "Attachment Parent," "Slow-Parent," "Soccer/Hockey Mom," "Stay-at-Home Mom," "Working Mom," "Welfare Mom," "Teen Mom," "Celebrity Mom," "Yummy Mummy," "MILF" (Mother I'd Like to Fuck), "Slummy Mummy," "Slacker Mom," "Momzilla," "Mommy Blogger," "Momager," "Momoirist," and "Mompreneur."

Scrutinizing mothers has been a centuries long project, possibly beginning with the publication of Jean-Jacques Rousseau's *Emile* in 1762, which describes, prescribes and proscribes the ways in which mothers are to be devoted to their children, and judges them to be "evil or monstrous" if they are not (Podnieks 2012a: 8-9). By the nineteenth century, mostly male experts, such as doctors, priests, philosophers, professors, and writers were telling Western women how to be proper mothers, while simultaneously monitoring them to ensure that they were not dreadful parents. The rise of Freudian psychology after the First World War solidified and promoted the stereotype of the castrating and devouring monstrous mother and has continued to feed the "new momism," which came about in the mid-1980s with "the explosion of motherhood in the media," and perpetuates the "good" mother/ "bad" mother dichotomy first introduced by Rousseau 250 years ago (Podnieks 2012a:11).

I begin this chapter by explaining the concept and practice of surveillance, the current ideals of motherhood in the Western world, how women are judged to be "good" or "bad" mothers, and some of the expectations placed on women to conform to various types of mothering ideals and practices. I then explore some of the ways in which mothers are closely watched, monitored and evaluated by others, particularly through celebrity media coverage and reality TV, and how surveillance can be hurtful to mothers. I conclude by proposing ways in which these damaging practices can and are being contested by mothers.

UNDERSTANDING SURVEILLANCE AND SOME OF THE WAYS MOTHERS ARE SCRUTINIZED

The French word "surveillance" means watching over, and is understood to entail monitoring the behaviour and activities of people for the purposes of influencing, managing, directing, and/or protecting them (Lyon). Today our behaviour is monitored through surveillance cameras in most public places, including, but not limited to: elevators, schools, shopping malls, boats, buses and taxis, train and bus stations, and the street. We are trained to view others and ourselves on security screens in banks, hospitals, universities, sports and community centers, restaurants, and stores; in photos on Facebook; in videos on YouTube; on Google images; or on other Internet sites.

Increasingly, we see images of regular folk and celebrities living their everyday lives on televised news, documentary, magazine and reality shows, on the Internet, and in electronic and print newspapers and magazines. More and more, we expect and accept the use of computers, cameras and phones to document and showcase raw footage of natural disasters, state violence and war, personal and political conflict, and local and global uprisings. Computerized monitoring and tracking of people's movements and interpersonal connections are frequent at places of employment, where the monitoring of phone calls and keyboard key strokes and the testing for drugs are more common and acceptable to some, and of great concern to others (Regan 21; Langer and Sussman; Rickwood).

According to Michel Foucault, individuals and groups who are knowingly subjected to surveillance and scrutiny often bring the effects of the power of inspection upon themselves through acts of self-policing, self-evaluation, and/ or self-monitoring (cited in Wong 39; Henderson, Harmon and Houser 234-236). Mark Poster argues that today's "reliance on new communication technologies," such as mobile phones with cameras, text messaging and Internet uploading/downloading capabilities, "has made possible the emergence of a superpanopticon" surveillance system that "continuously, systematically and surreptitiously" works to collect information and data, as well as compile profiles about individuals and groups (cited in Wong 38).

The goal of this type of surveillance is "the normalization of individuals" through monitoring and censoring their own personal behaviour (Wong 38; Henderson et al. 235). Folks often engage in the act of relentless self-surveillance because they believe that someone can always be watching and judging them according to their appearance and behaviour. This self-monitoring encourages people to mould themselves according to mainstream norms so that they fit in and are not marginalized for being deviant or abnormal (Wong 39; Henderson et al. 234-236). While surveillance encourages the scrutiny of our own and other people's behaviour, it may also, according to Foucault, offer people an opportunity to bring together their ideas, agency, and power in ways that can open up self-study and prospective social change (Wong 34, 37, 40).

CURRENT IDEALS OF MOTHERHOOD AND THE GOOD/BAD MOTHER DICHOTOMY

As I have noted in *Practicing Feminist Mothering*, motherhood scholars recognize the distinction between two tightly overlapping and defining elements of motherhood originally identified by Adrienne Rich in *Of Woman Born*. Motherhood entails mothering—the interpersonal relations and work involved in raising children that is generally taken up by women—and the prescribed ideals of mothering, which are often experienced as oppressive because of the narrowly constituted and institutionalized patriarchal rules and expectations that dictate and regulate familial and child rearing roles, responsibilities and relationships among women, children and men.

Central to understanding women's experiences of mothering is recognizing that motherhood is not restricted to merely bearing and/or caring for children—which themselves take enormous amounts of energy and commitment—but that motherhood also includes the culmination of social structures and meanings that create conditions under which women are expected to parent and, thus, prescribe and shape the circumstances of women's lives. Simply put, women are not at liberty to mother in ways they may consider suitable or appropriate for themselves and their children. Rather, they are pressured to parent within socially and culturally prescribed and supported ideals and conditions that are often restrictive and damaging (Green 2011: 67).

While there is no universal practice of caring for children, because it is "an ongoing process that is negotiated and re-negotiated by mothers and their support systems," within the current early twenty-first century Western context there is an assumption and expectation that mothers are responsible for providing the basic needs of food, clothing, and shelter for their children, as well as protecting their children's innocence and their emotional, psychological, physical and spiritual well-being (Henderson et al. 233; Hays). Mothers are also expected to "acquire professional-level skills such as those of a therapist, paediatrician, consumer products safety inspector, and teacher," and to practice the unobtainable and unrealistic "new momism" standard of mothering perfection that promotes motherhood as the best and most important prescribed activity a woman can do because it is a devotion that is eternally fulfilling and rewarding (Douglas and Michaels 3-5).

The ideals and pressures to be a perfect mother come from various sources, including formal social institutions, such as health care (pediatricians and nurses), government and social service agencies (political figures, policy writers, social workers, civil servants, unemployment officers), the media (news, popular magazines, reality TV shows, celebrity stories), as well as from informal interpersonal interactions with family, friends, other mothers, salespeople and strangers (Henderson et al. 231, 234, 238; Podnieks 2012a: 15-18). Integral to our beliefs about the appropriate, if not perfect, practice of mothering, and hence about mothers themselves, is that childcare and housework are the primary responsibility of women, which some argue has intensified over the past sixty years and "puts the intensive mothering practices of the 1950s to shame" (Douglas and Michaels 6). As in the past, these beliefs and pressures also contain an evaluation and judgement of women's maternal practices.

The success of a "good" mother is judged by her ability to meet the mainstream Western standards of intensive mothering and new momism. Should she fail in her duties, she is quickly reminded of the legitimacy of the ideal mother and the righteous downfall of the "bad" mother by other mothers, medical professionals, and faith/religious leaders.[2] As Jacques Donzelot notes, "social workers, public schools, the courts, and law-enforcement all contribute to training mothers and children at the same time that they serve government interest in 'policing the family'" (qtd. in Hays 162). A woman's family, friends, peers, co-workers, and acquaintances also perpetuate the dominant expectations of motherhood through their attention/surveillance and unsolicited suggestions, and the good woman/mother standard is presented and normalized through their voluntary remarks, advice and/or personal judgments.

MOMS UNDER SURVEILLANCE: CELEBRITY MEDIA, REALITY TV AND MOMMY BLOGS

Elizabeth Podnieks argues in the introduction to *Mediating Moms: Mothers in Popular Culture* that mothers are "more visible and vocal today than ever before" and that "media related to entertainment, advertising, politics, law, medicine, and the economy are dramatically revising and refashioning the way we consider and practice mothering" (14).[3] Twitter, Facebook, YouTube, and blogs also have a fundamental role in capturing, recording and distributing images, attitudes and judgments about mothers and their ability to care for children.

Feminist scholars have written about the influence celebrity moms have on the mothering ideals and mothering practices of everyday women. For instance, Lynn O'Brien Hallstein posits that celebrity moms are the quintessential "yummy mummies" and that their popular images suggest to readers that they, "too, can be a 'yummy mummy' if only she has the discipline to work out" (125). O'Brien Hallstein maintains that "the new postpregnant quickly slender, even bikini-ready, body is being integrated as a key rhetorical element of the new momism, which continues to develop as the accepted hegemonic ideology of 'good' mothering," to contribute to feelings of guilt and failure, and to construct "an unencumbered body that communicates a symbolic statement about how quickly postpartum women can and should return to their public unencumbered self" (128-9). This latest scrutinized maternal body sets up a new standard for moms; the images of "the quickly slender celebrity mom profiles now suggest that empowered, sexy, young and unencumbered women now need also to be empowered, sexy moms postpartum" (125).

Tanja Tudhope warns that although "it would be easy to dismiss the stories of Hollywood mothers as irrelevant fantasy lives, doing so would be to completely deny the impact of Hollywood and celebrities within contemporary North American culture." She cautions that "regardless of how distasteful it may be, people such as [Julia] Roberts, [Halle] Berry, and [Elle] McPherson (and their peers) are role-models to countless numbers of women who want to be like them and because of this women-as-mothers take their cues from these celebrities about what the maternal should look and feel like, essentially mimicking the stars who are passing as representations of a fetishized notion of the maternal experience" (11).

Elizabeth Podnieks, too, reminds us that while media depictions of celebrity moms, particularly those in entertainment journalism, "airbrush the realities of mothering," they also "simultaneously delight in pulling back the dreamy veil coating (of) these images, supposedly exposing mothers as incompetent at best, dangerous at worst" (2012b: 90-91). This distinction between, and battle of, the "good" versus the "bad" mother continues to contribute to this age-old narrative, and to the policing of mothers by modeling the restrictive mainstream standards, as well as to ways of evaluating and judging the appearance and behavior of mothers. It also alerts us all that celebrities, too, are not immune from the surveillance and judgment imposed upon all mothers.

A recent example is the palpable outrage and disgust expressed by news reporters regarding 35-year-old American actor Alicia Silverstone's video posting to her website *The Kind Life* in March 2012, which shows Silverstone sharing her pre-chewed food with her ten-month-old son directly out of her mouth. The video sparked a huge controversy on TV and the Web over whether or not the practice of premastication, or pre-chewing solid food for an infant, was appropriate or not ("Alicia Silverstone defends pre-chewing"). Captions such as "feeding her baby like a bird" in

Fiona Joy Green

the media set the critical tone and judged Silverstone for being "unhygienic" because, according to the Centers for Disease Control, in some cases the practice may pass on disease and bacteria such as "HIV strep and tooth decay," and for looking like a "'mouth-kissing-thing' that makes some people feel uncomfortable" ("Alicia Silverstone baby feeding").

The trend of scrutinizing mothers seen in entertainment and celebrity media is also popular in reality TV programing and its approach of combining the everyday experiences and struggles of parenting with the myths constituted by the idealized mythology and discourse of motherhood.[4] Shows such as *Bubble Wrap Kids*, *Pregnant and 16*, *Supernanny*, and *Wife Swap* involve the surveillance and guidance of mothers to ensure that they and viewers are able to distinguish between "good" and "bad" mothering practices and to also learn the appropriate intensive mothering and new momism techniques that ensure correct parenting. The popularity of mommy reality TV is evidenced in the much acclaimed international *Supernanny* series that was nominated for an Emmy Award in 2005, has been broadcast in at least 18 countries, has published how-to parenting books in various languages, and has developed a smart phone application to assist parents in "getting the best from their children."[5]

Angela Henderson, Sandra M. Harmon and Jeffrey Houser note that mother-to-mother interaction among middle-class mothers is particularly harsh and infused with criticism because they surveil other mothers on an interpersonal level (231, 234). Mother-blame is everywhere; it's in the media, on the Internet, in our families, in the theories and practices of educators, childrearing experts, as well as ingrained in medical, judicial and religious institutional practices. It's also a pervasive and powerful mothering ideology that often governs and highly influences mothering practices, and is quickly learned and internalized by mothers and others (Henderson et al. 233, 240, 241). Janet Taylor believes that there's a lot of "insecurity," "confusion" and "resentment" about being a mother and, at times, moms feel they have to be better than other mothers. She posits that mothers feeling this pressure sometimes attempt to prove it by "writing negative things" as a way of not being supportive of other mothers (qtd. in Wild).

Emma Donoghue speaks to the increasing pressure that mothers find themselves having to deal with regarding surveillance and the often-accompanying criticism in her article "I'm sick of all this mutual surveillance—Let's put a stop to the Mummy Wars," where she questions the hugely judgmental attitudes and practices toward motherhood and suggests we can chose to conduct ourselves differently "without forming hostile tribes among and between mothers." She aptly notes "when it comes to motherhood, our culture has a strange tendency to slide from the descriptive, to the prescriptive, to the proscriptive. From 'Ah, look at that baby happily nursing', to 'breast is best', to 'if you put that bottle in your baby's mouth you'll damage his IQ'" (2).

MOMS PUSH BACK: CONTESTING THE DAMAGING PRACTICE OF SURVEILLANCE

Susan Douglas and Meredith Michaels urge us to "turn the surveillance cameras away from ourselves and instead turn them on the media that shaped us and that manufactured more of our beliefs and practices than we may appreciate, or want to admit" (25). While this is often difficult, given that folks are commonly unaware of and dismiss the power of popular culture to influence their attitudes because "it seems so ordinary, so unexceptional; it is 'just what we do'" (Podnieks 2012a: 7), mothers are pushing back against the climate of surveillance we are all living in. For instance, Elizabeth Podnieks attempts to expose and discuss the presence and influence of surveillance in conversations with her pre-teenage daughter, who loves to read and engage with celebrity tabloids, news and media, by asking her to think about *what* it means when a magazine is calling someone a "bad" mother, rather than why a celebrity such as "Unfitney" Britney Spears is labeled a bad mom (2012a: 101).

Some moms find that cyberspace, particularly the mommy blog, offers them an opportunity for engaging in the radical act of counteracting the harmful myths and expectations of motherhood (Lopez; Friedman and Calizte 21-36). According to digital marketing and media research company eMarketer, there are currently an estimated 3.9 million mothers writing and updating a blog at least once a week, and project there will be 4.4 million mommy bloggers by 2014 (Digital Mom). Blogging involves a live audience that has the ability to comment, support, contest, complicate and trouble the construction of motherhood and to articulate the fluid experiences and practices of mothering (Powell 41). While there are serious instances of bullying between mommybloggers on the mommasphere, mommy blogs "also present multiple subjectivities, interrupt their self-made dichotomies and resist the good mother/bad mother discourse" (Donoghue; Howell; Wild; Powell 49). For some, blogging is a place where moms are "developing their own voices for discussing (mothering and) motherhood" and "expanding their own personal narratives of struggle and challenge into interactive conversations with other mothers, and in so doing are beginning to expand our notion of motherhood, women bloggers, and mother's place within the public sphere" (Lopez 733-744).

A number of mommy blogs are taking on this task of encouraging critical dialogue and discourse about motherhood and also supporting alternative perspectives. For Heather Cox, Founder of femomist.com, the purpose of her site is twofold: it's "to support mothers" and also "a call to arms" because mothering and revolution are exhausting and lonely. She acknowledges that "some items are strategically not included in publishing, because they are gossipy, sensationalist or just all-around bummers where no action can be taken, no letters can be written, no calls can be made." Cox developed the title "Femomist" for the site, which "began as a contraction of *femme, mom* and *terrorist,*" because she thought they sounded "powerful," "like fist," and "like the answer to a question: Are there such things as feminist mothers?" Catherine Conner, author of herbadmother.com has written and posted a manifesto on her site that candidly unmasks new momism and intensive motherhood where she overtly turns surveillance upon itself in her acknowledgment that she has engaged in a number of activities that are deemed "bad," including "leaving her children in the bathtub alone," putting her "own needs first," and having moments of "resenting" her children, which she lays "bare for the world to see" in her blog.

The power of the activities of moms on the Internet can be seen in the political action that has been organized and then showcased through this medium. For instance, mothers responded to a Motrin advertisement for the relief of pain, allegedly brought about by the "new fashion trend" of "babywearing," by launching a grassroots attack against Motrin on Twitter, blogs and YouTube, leading the company to remove the ad (Podnieks 2012a: 6-7). Breastfeeding moms, too, have been successful in organizing and talking back to the surveillance and judgments passed by others about their parenting practices. In September 2010, lactivists promoted the boycotting of Old Navy, along with its sister stores Gap and Banana Republic, after it introduced an infant onesie with a logo of a baby bottle surrounded by the slogan "Formula Powered." The mom activists successfully argued that the message was "empowering to the formula industry" (Feministing), which resulted with Old Navy issuing an apology (Podnieks 2012a: 6-7).

Mother Outlaws, which has been active since 2004 in Toronto, Canada, and more recently in London, UK, has established itself as a "cultural signifier of how mothering against the institution of motherhood can be envisioned and experienced as empowering for women" that works to "challenge normative discourses of motherhood and bridge the divides between 'lived mothering' (personal experiences and activism) and 'examined motherhood' (academic scholarship)."[6] The group's outreach initiatives include: "a Toronto Feminist Mothers' discussion group, a continuing Mother Outlaws' Speakers Series, special events, activist activities, media coverage, T-shirt sales, and assisting with the start-ups of Mother Outlaws groups elsewhere."

A collective of young moms living in Toronto, with the support of Toronto based non-profit organization Literacy for Life, have developed *Yo' Mama Magazine* as an alternative discursive space that is written by and for teen aged moms to reject "the dominant, exclusive and elitist discourse" on motherhood and speak to "a host of issues that are specific only to them" (O'Connor 185-190). The title *Yo' Mama* means "Young Mama" and reverses the connotation of the catcall "Yo' Mama" used by men on the street to harass young moms with their babies into "a positive expression" used by young mamas to "call out" to other teenage moms (O'Connor 191). The magazine addresses "the empowerment of young mothers', "offers a resistant, renewed definition of beauty," and redefines "the very term 'good mother'" (O'Connor 192-193). *Yo' Mama* is "not only talking back" it allows teenage mothers to "speak as experts on their own lives" (O'Connor 190, 197).

Brain, Child: The Magazine for Thinking Mothers, was founded by two friends who were mothers of young children and had backgrounds in journalism. Wanting a magazine with "smart writing that delved into the meatier issues of the life-altering experience (of) motherhood," Jennifer Niesslein and Stephanie Wilkinson published the first edition in 2000, which has since won numerous awards and has a "circulation of 36,000" and "subscribers from every state and as far away as Sweden, Egypt, and Hong Kong" (Niesslein). An article published in the Spring 2011 edition addresses the influences of parents within personal networks and explores the influence of social network theory in assisting mothers in making sense of and being open to the many diverse mothering approaches, as well as changing them (Niesslein).

CONCLUSION

Without a doubt, moms are under more and more surveillance and scrutiny than ever before; their pregnant and postpregnant bodies are more closely monitored and analyzed, as are their child rearing attitudes and their mothering decisions and practices. Yet, individually and collectively moms are able to strongly influence, and at times determine how popular or unsuccessful products may be, and to also rebuff certain maternal myths or norms of the "good mother" by demonstrating through their voices and actions that mothering is a dynamic and fluid lived experience that is not limited by the mainstream patriarchal institution of motherhood.

[1]These are the reflections of Raven Prince, quoted in a 2007 interview addressing the income decline of single mothers (Smith).

[2]"The code of the bad mother stands in for real confrontations with serious problems of society and avoids looking at poverty, racism, and colonialism, the lack of access to affordable daycare, anti-feminism, devaluation of mothering, and work structures that don't recognize families and childrearing (Ladd-Taylor and Umansky 23). Richard Friedman, Professor of Psychology, notes in a 2010 *Globe and Mail* article that mental health professionals have been trained over time to see a bad mother behind the bad behaviour of children."

[3]*Mediating Moms* is an excellent collection that addresses this observation in detail.
[4]For further discussion, see Green 2007, 2012.
[5]The 18 countries that *Supernanny* has broadcast in include Australia, Canada and the USA, Belgium, Brazil, China, France, Greece, Holland, Indonesia, Israel, Italy, Germany, Malaysia Romania, Singapore, Spain and Sweden.
[6]See the Mother Outlaws website: <http://www.motherhoodinitiative.org/motheroutlaws.html>.

WORKS CITED

"Alicia Silverstone baby feeding mouth-to-mouth video." ABC News. 29 March 2012. Web. Accessed 04/28/2012.

"Alicia Silverstone defends pre-chewing food for son Bear." *US Magazine* 27 April 2012. Web. Accessed 4/28/2012.

"Actress Alicia Silverstone feeds her baby like a bird." *Daily Telegraph* 28 March 2012. Web. Accessed 4/25/2012.

Brain, Child Magazine. Web. Accessed 4/30/2012.

Conner, Catherine. "The Bad Mother Manifesto." June 8, 2009. Web. Accessed 4/29/2012.

Cox, Heather. "Editor's Letter and Response to some FAQs." Femomist. Web.

Digital Mom. 2011. "How many moms are blogging?" Digital Mom Blog. October 13, 2011. Web. Accessed 04/29/2012.

Donoghue, Emma. "I'm sick of all this mutual surveillance—Let's put a stop to the Mummy Wars." *The Guardian* Saturday 23 April 2011. Web. Accessed March 26, 2012.

Douglas, Susan and Meredith Michaels. *The Mommy Myth: The Idealization of Motherhood and How It Has Undermined Women*. New York: Free Press, 2004. Print.

Feministing. "Breastfeeding activists boycott Old Navy." Web. Accessed 4/30/2012.

Friedman, Richard. "When bad eggs happen to good parents: When a child's misbehaviour is chronic, we tend to blame mom and dad, but even the best nest can produce toxic offspring." *The Globe and Mail* 16 July 2010: L5. Print.

Friedman, May and Shana L. Calizte. "Introduction." *Mothering and*

Blogging: The Radical Act of the Mommyblog. Eds. May Friedman and Shana L. Calizte. Toronto: Demeter Press, 2009. 21-36.

Green, Fiona Joy. "Real(ity) TV Practices of Surveillance: Evaluating Mothers in Supernanny and Crash Test Mommy." *Mediating Moms: Mothers in Popular Culture*. Ed. Elizabeth Podnieks. Montreal: McGill-Queen's University Press, 2012. 69-86. Print.

Green, Fiona Joy. *Practicing Feminist Mothering*. Winnipeg: Arbeiter Ring Publication, 2011. Print.

Green, Fiona Joy. "*Supernanny*: Disciplining Mothers through a Narrative of Domesticity." *Storytelling: A Critical Journal of Popular Narrative* 6 (2) (2007): 99-107. Print.

Hays, Sharon. *The Cultural Contradictions of Motherhood*. New Haven: Yale University Press 1996. Print.

Henderson, Angela C., Sandra M. Harmon and Jeffrey Houser. "A New State of Surveillance? An Application of Michel Foucault to Modern Motherhood." *Surveillance and Society* 7 (3/4) (2010): 231-247. Print.

Howell, Elizabeth. "Why All the Hate? The Dark Side of Mommy Blogging." Unpublished paper presented at the *Popular Culture Association-American Culture Association* 42nd Annual Conference, Boston Marriott Copley Place, Boston, Massachusetts, April 11-14, 2012. Print.

Ladd-Taylor, Molly and Lauri Umansky, eds. *"Bad" Mothers: The Politics of Blame in Twentieth-Century America*. New York: New York University Press, 1998. Print.

Langer, Gary and Dalia Sussman. "Phone-Records Surveillance Is Broadly Acceptable to Public." *ABC News* May 12, 2006. Web. Accessed 4/20/2012.

Lopez, Lori Kido. "The Radical Act of 'Mommy Blogging': Redefining Motherhood Through the Blogosphere." *New Media & Society* 11 (2009): 729-747. Print.

Lyon, David. *Surveillance Studies: An Overview*. London: Polity, 2007. Print.

Motherhood Initiative for Research and Community Involvement (MIRCI). Web. Accessed 4/40/2012

Momrising. Web. Accessed 4/40/2012

Mother Outlaws. Web. Accessed 5/02/2012.

Niesslein, Jennifer. 2011. "The Village: How Other Parents Influence Your Parenting." *Brain, Child Magazine*. Spring 2011. Web. Accessed 4/30/2012.

O'Brien Hallstein, Lynn. "She Gives Birth, She's Wearing a Bikini: Mobilizing the Post-Pregnant Celebrity Mom Body to Manage the Post-Second Wave Crisis in Femininity." *Women's Studies in Communication* 34 (2) (2011): 111-138. Print.

O'Connor, Beth. "'You Have to Take it and Own It': *Yo' Mama Magazine* as a Space of Refusal for Teenage Mothers." *Mediating Moms: Mothers in Popular Culture.* Ed. Elizabeth Podnieks. Montreal: McGill-Queen's University Press, 2012. 185-203. Print.

Podnieks, Elizabeth. "Introduction: Popular Culture's Maternal Embrace." *Mediating Moms: Mothers in Popular Culture.* Ed. Elizabeth Podnieks. Montreal: McGill-Queen's University Press, 2012a. 1-32. Print.

Podnieks, Elizabeth. "'The Bump is Back': Celebrity Moms, Entertainment Journalism, and the 'Media Mother Police'." *Mediating Moms: Mothers in Popular Culture.* Ed. Elizabeth Podnieks. Montreal: McGill-Queen's University Press, 2012b. 87-107. Print.

Powell, Rebecca. 2012. "Good Mothers, Bad Mothers and Mommy Bloggers: Rhetorical Resistance and Fluid Subjectivities." *MP: An Online Feminist Journal.* 2012. Web. Accessed 4/30/2012.

Regan, Pricilla. "Genetic Testing and Work Place Surveillance: Implications for Privacy." *Computers, Surveillance, and Privacy.* Eds. David Lyon and Elia Zureik. Minneapolis: University of Minnesota Press, 1996. 21-46. Print.

Rich, Adrienne. *Of Woman Born: Motherhood as Experience and Institution.* London: Virago Press, 1986. Print.

Rickwood, Lee. "Surveillance by Design: Government Rules, Business Practices Threaten Canadians' Personal Privacy." What's your Tech.ca. January 30, 2012. Web. Accessed 4/20/2012.

Smith, Charlie. "Mothers Under Siege." Straight.com. June 7, 2007. Web. Accessed March 2, 2012.

Tudhope, Tanja. "Escaping the Fetish: Understanding the Maternal." Unpublished paper presented at the *Popular Culture Association-American Culture Association* 42nd Annual Conference, Boston Marriott Copley Place, Boston, Massachusetts, April 11-14, 2012. Print.

Wild, Anna. "Grown Up Mean Girls: Mom on Mom Cyberbullying." ABC News. April 28, 2010. Web. Accessed 4/28/2012.

Wong, James. "Here's Looking at You: Reality TV, Big Brother, and Foucault." *Canadian Journal of Communication* 26 (2001): 33-45. Print.

Rebelling Against "Mom"

Finding Fulfillment Beyond the Media's Myths of Motherhood

ESTELLE SOBEL ERASMUS

TODAY'S MEDIA IS FULL OF HOLLOW PLATITUDES that we do not have to be perfect mothers. But why then does the "role" of mother become confused with the "housework" of raising a family? Mothers are still inundated by media messages that suggest we are the ones ultimately responsible for all of the family's care giving needs. Why do we as mothers so easily embrace this depiction and take on all the responsibility?

Proctor & Gamble, a corporation noted for their support of moms ,sponsored a very popular television advertisement lauding the "work" of mom in honor of the 2012 London Olympic Games.[1] While I watched, I admit the advertisement's tales of self-sacrificing moms did cause me to tear up a bit. But, right after I wiped away my tears, I found myself plagued with frustration. Why?

The admittedly heart-tugging ad shows mothers from several continents doing the everyday work of mothering, that every parent is familiar with—waking the kids, cooking for and feeding them, getting them out of the house on time to get on the bus. These children are different; however, these children are destined to be Olympic champions. So we see them through early childhood, later teen years and finally achieving their (and their moms) dream of being an Olympic athlete.

The tagline of the ad reads:

> *The hardest job in the world is the best job in the world.*
> *Thank you, mom.*

This Procter & Gamble commercial honors everything that all moms do to help their children succeed by showcasing the amazing moms behind Olympic athletes at the London 2012 Olympic games. Okay, the support and nurturing part I get. But the role of mother to support, nurture, well, isn't that also the role of parenting—*so where is the father in this whole scenario*? Off somewhere to the side or not there at all; definitely not involved in the "work" of parenting or even co-parenting.

The company also has an official Thank You, Mom Facebook Page—with over 772,897 likes and counting.[2] The page allows its fans to read about Procter & Gamble products, see notes from athletes, and learn about the latest London Olympic games news. The page also includes an app where you can thank your mother using pictures, words or even videos. As a part of the Procter & Gamble Thank You Mom promotion, Procter & Gamble has committed to raise $5 million to support local youth sports programs in many countries, through a portion of sales and donations from the company's brands.

Here's the point: Procter & Gamble is definitely doing the right thing by bringing to light and acknowledging mothers' work They are admitting that it is hard to be a caretaker and the sacrifices of a mother can ultimately result in a child becoming a star—i.e., an Olympic athlete. But, still I must ask: why isn't the work of mothering separate from the role of mother? Cooking, cleaning, laundry is expected. It is just what moms do.

Now Corporate America, I'm putting you on notice that I don't want to see more of these "mother is the best" ads. Procter & Gamble did it and did it well. Instead, put your money where your ad is, and work to get mothers resources; support us for fair wages, paid family leave, paid sick time, affordable pre-school, support for women who lose out in retirement because they have been out of the workforce. We can let go of the sentiments; we can't let go of the need for progress.

CENSUS BUREAU-CRACY

"Since over 80 percent of women in our nation have children by the time they're 44 years old,[3] this means the majority of women in our nation are disadvantaged by discrimination at some point in their lives," says Kristin Rowe-Finkbeiner, Executive Director, CEO and Co-Founder of the advocacy organization Mom'sRising.org, on her blog.[4] She was referring to the financial discrimination women face. One often-cited study showed that mothers (even if their resumes and job experiences were equal to that of women who are childless) were offered $11,000 lower starting salaries.[5] The same study showed that unlike mothers, fathers were rewarded for their role, and were offered $6,000 more in starting salaries than men who weren't fathers.

I was surprised to see discrimination from our own U.S. Census Bureau, which sent out a media release with their latest report *Who's Minding the Kids*.[6] The report states that when moms watch their children it is called "caretaking," but when dads watch their children (if, let's say, the mom is working), it is called "babysitting." *The New York Times* Motherlode blog[7] said what most people (mothers and fathers) thought:

> *I mean, seriously, Census Bureau? How hard is it to have a "designated parent" question? "Which parent is the designated/primary parent (i.e. the parent that provides the majority of child care)?" That is literally one question, Census Bureau. I am sure you can ask one more question in order not to erase men who provide the primary care for their children, and not to paint fathers as glorified babysitters.*

If on the next *Who's Minding the Kids* media report, the Census Bureau listens to the outpouring of indignation from parents, and decides to include the second question, it will prevent the media from being misinformed and spreading misinformation about who is really doing the caregiving (not babysitting) in America. Hopefully, the U.S. Census Bureau and the media will both realize that when a father is watching his kids, he is parenting them, not being a babysitter (like the teen you pay $10 an hour to watch your child).

As mothers we need to continue to put pressure on the census bureau to lift themselves out of the dark ages. So if the report on "Who's Minding the Kids" disturbs you, write to the Census Bureau Twitter @uscensusbureau and on Facebook www.facebook.com/uscensusbureau or email Lynda Laughlin (Lynda.L.Laughlin@census.gov) at the Census Bureau's Fertility and Family Statistics Branch.

MEDIA AND THE MOMMY WARS REDUX

Perhaps one of the sharpest swords in the gauntlet being thrown down by the media in their depiction of "mom" was the Hilary Rosen and Ann

Romney fracas. After Hilary Rosen made an inappropriate comment on CNN about Ann Romney, "never working a day in her life," the politicos and media brought up the old and tired Mommy Wars, which pits stay-at-home moms against moms who work outside of the home for income. Yes, as human nature would have it, a few women jumped into the media manipulation and joined the fray.

But for the most part instead of getting divisive women changed the conversation. We changed the conversation to the one that really matters: the policies that support mothers, whether they work in the home (because caretaking is still work, albeit invisible work), or work out of the home to make an income. Most mothers realize that there should not be a different perception of a mother who works from a mother who stays home. We are all mothers and must stand together, lest we be divided. And we all know that a house divided will fall.

We demanded that government take note that women are 50 percent of the electoral vote and asked them to stop treating us as a special interest group; we insisted that policies be enacted to support women and mothers; to provide paid family leave, paid sick days, quality and affordable child care, fair wages and to end the war on women.

And make no mistake: this is a war on women. If we don't see and shout our value to the world, we will remain invisible, and our work of caretaking and supporting society and our communities will remain invisible. In the meantime, there is much work to be done, and we can start by making sure that the media doesn't make our situation any more difficult than it already is.

HOW THE MEDIA GETS IT WRONG

The misrepresentation of women and mothers in the media is rampant. According to The National Organization for Women, the largest organization of feminist activists in the United States:

> Media stories on women, work and family often are incomplete, because the stories report only on the experiences and attitudes of small or elite groups of mothers. Reporters often use these small groups to convey their stories as common to all mothers.

Clearly, generalizing gender roles can result in even more discrimination

Estelle Sobel Erasmus

for women and mothers. Other ways the media gets it wrong:

•Framing the difficult options facing a mother as being a personal choice, rather than a result of public policy.
•Rehashing the Mommy Wars; the truth is that most women go in and out of the workforce during the course of their lives, and also while their children are growing up.
•By not recognizing that mothers who want to work, find less opportunities because of the inflexible and archaic structure (set on a 1950s model of the man being the primary breadwinner and the wife and mother at home) of most of corporate America, which still believes that face time is key to getting ahead, even though most parents say the key to work satisfaction is the ability to have flexibility. Unfortunately, there is a gap between policy and practice because the concept of the "perfect" worker does not reflect the realities of modern family (enmeshed in caregiving for both children and aging parents) and society.
•Corporations like to talk about work/life/balance, and the media picks up on that; but that is not the case, especially in this economy.
•Confusing the "work" of mothering (the activities that take care of a family) with the role of mother.
•Using the word mothering instead of the word parenting.

According to the Women's Media Center, the underlying, unspoken themes of mainstream media coverage on women, work and family encourage gender discrimination by reinforcing existing cultural biases, such as the belief that women are more caring and less competitive than men and are less willing to make the personal sacrifices required for success.

HOW CAN WE ADDRESS (OR FIGHT BACK) AGAINST BLATANT MISREPRESENTATION?

Framing the problem correctly is a first step to policy change. As previously mentioned, the real focus of the media should be the issues of public policy for mothers: childcare, healthcare for children, the inequality of pay, flexible jobs, and the struggles and challenges of real everyday life for mothers and caregivers.

Mothers need to be involved in their own advocacy, and find one or many communities to provide support and encouragement as they seek to create change. To that end:

- If you read misleading portrayals of mothers in the media, including trend stories based on anecdotal accounts that are presented as facts, contact organizations like The Women's Media Center (http://www.womensmediacenter.org), or MISREPRESENTATION (http://www.missrepresentation.org), NOW (http://www.now.org)
- Create a petition on Change.org
- Call, write or email the media outlet or company with your concerns.
- If you feel that companies are off base in how they represent mothers, post your comments on their Facebook walls or Twitter. Use the immediacy of social media to support your cause.
- To find community, join Mothers & More (http://www.mothersandmore.org), a national non-profit organization which touts the value of a mothers work whether paid or unpaid, provides opportunities to connect with like-minded women, and offers chances to give back to the community and economically disadvantaged women through advocacy efforts like Power of the Purse, where gently used and new purses are collected and provided to shelters.

• Check out www.MomsRising.org, a group that is aligned with Mothers & More which highlights the issues and provides links to letters you can sign that go straight to policy makers.
•Pay attention to bills on the table (check out www.USA.gov) that will take away your rights and write to your local congressperson via writing to the United States House of Representatives (http://www.house.gov/representatives/find/)
•Write about the situation on your blog, or raise the situation to the attention of popular mom bloggers, whose community is one of the most powerful and influential online communities on the Internet.

I believe it is the bloggers who will bring forth a new generation of politically involved women (and we have to be involved, it's a matter of our survival). Bloggers are giving motherhood and the invisible work of motherhood a voice heard like never before in the history of our culture (since Gloria Steinem, my idol, created *Ms.* magazine).

Case in point: The Susan G. Komen Backlash. In early 2012 when the Susan G. Komen foundation was going to withdraw their financial support from Planned Parenthood (the money went to fund breast cancer screening for low-income women) the blogosphere got into action. A Google search for blogs with keywords, Susan G. Komen, Planned Parenthood, delivered 63 million sources (from all types of media).

The bloggers blogged and people's voices rang out against the foundation and Nancy Brinker (its founder) on a variety of social media including Facebook, Twitter and Google +. The combined media onslaught was enough to get the foundation to reverse their decision.

THE CREDIT CRUNCH FOR STAY-AT-HOME PARENTS

In another example, this year there was a petition on Change.org along with MomsRising.org to the Consumer Financial Protection Bureau to change a ruling to a credit card act that adversely affected stay-at-home-moms. Mothers & More, the national non-profit education and advocacy organization is proud to have gotten the ball rolling on this issue, by writing a letter in 2011 to Dr. Elizabeth Warren at the Consumer Financial Protection Bureau expressing the organization's concerns about the ruling. The letter was also sent to the Board of Governors of the Federal Reserve.

The new ruling was meant to protect consumers from misleading credit card practices. What it actually did though, was prevent a woman from getting a credit card in her own name based on her partner's salary, even if she had a good credit rating prior to making the decision to stay at home. The rule stated, "credit card applications generally cannot request a consumer's 'household income' because that term is too vague to allow issuers to properly evaluate the consumer's ability to pay. Instead, issuers must consider the consumer's individual income or salary." Which meant that instead of filling in your "household income" you could only note your own income. So what happened if you didn't have an income?

Then, if you wanted a credit card the partner making the income would need to co-sign for it for you. Shocking, right? This set women back one hundred years. This also meany that women and mothers in abusive relationships had one more layer of control to fight against (and one more way they could be made to feel unequal in the relationship). And this applied even if the woman made 95 percent of the financial purchases in the home and had a fantastic credit rating prior to staying home. The ruling unfairly diminished a mother's "equality to her partner" further and made her feel like a second-class citizen.

What's apparent is through the work of Mothers & More, Mom's Rising and Change.org, the Consumer Financial Protection Bureau was able to overturn the ruling without going through a long, painful Congressional process. This is the power of social media in action.

A SHIFT IN CONSCIOUSNESS

Clearly, society needs to shift its thinking. I believe that if enough people shift their thinking, the zeitgeist will change, and society will reflect those changes as the norm. We each have a role in this journey. We can create the change in our lives that we want to see in the world one activist, journalist, blogger, mother at a time.

Over the next few years, women should be starting up new foundations to give women a voice in "corporate America" policy, government and the national stage. We are in a revolution; at stake is our value. So let's sound the clarion call to action and rise up and be heard. Because as we have always said and continue to say at Mothers & More: "Together, mothers are powerful."

[1]<http://www.youtube.com/watch?v=NScs_qX2Okk>. Viewed 8/31/2012.

[2]<https://www.facebook.com/thankyoumom>. Viewed 8/31/2012.

[3]<http://www.census.gov/hhes/fertility/data/cps/2010.html>.

[4]<http://www.momsrising.org/blog/its-not-a-mommy-war-its-a-war-on-moms>.

[5]<http://www.news.cornell.edu/stories/Feb07/SS.Focus.Correll.html>.

[6]<http://www.census.gov/prod/2010pubs/p70-121.pdf>.

[7]<http://parenting.blogs.nytimes.com/2012/02/08/the-census-bureau-counts-fathers-as-child-care>.

What Mothers Need

For Parenting to Get Under Control

MARGARET K. NELSON

ALMOST EVERY WEEK—and probably every day if I looked more closely—a new article appears in the media about what has often been referred to as helicopter parenting. Many of these articles get picked up by, or appear on, blogs so that often, on a single day, the same item actually will show up in numerous places scattered around the world. And no matter where they appear—in the U.S., Canada, Japan, Australia, or England—these articles are critical of the practice of helicopter parenting.

But what exactly is helicopter parenting anyway—and why do so many people want to write (and read) about it? According to the not-so-reliable Wikipedia, the term "helicopter parenting" was originally coined by Foster W. Cline, M.D. and Jim Fay in their 1990 book *Parenting with Love and Logic: Teaching Children Responsibility*. Helicopter parents, Wikipedia continues, "are so named because, like helicopters, they hover closely overhead, rarely out of reach, whether their children need them or not." Beyond the initial definition, subsequent articles have come to define different "types" of helicopter parents according to their style and degree of intervention. One piece describes five categories: "consumer advocate," "only want what's best for my child" parents, "helopat," "entitlement advocate," and "vicarious college student" ("Mom Needs an 'A'"). Others list different categories including hovercrafts, lawnmowers, and snowplows (those who smooth everything out so their children have no bumps or falls). In Sweden, I've heard, they are called "curling parents."

Whatever they're called, or however it's defined, helicopter parenting, the articles say, is bad for the children subject to this style of parental control. What's the problem, you might ask, of having a parent deeply involved in a child's life? Well, the presumed problems are legion. Chief among these (based on my analysis of over 100 different articles) is the claim that the children of helicopter parents will fail to develop into independent, self-reliant, autonomous adults, but instead will learn how to be soft and weak individuals ("wimps") who will act immaturely. A second concern is that the children of helicopter parents will have mental health problems, including low self-esteem, inadequate social skills, and unhealthy relationships. Some items link what are defined as problematic behaviors ("binge drinking, experiments with drugs and sex and self-cutting") to helicopter parenting, insisting that students who have been hovered over their entire lives now "need to have an authentic experience that is truly their own" (Aspen Education Group). There also is a moral element here, especially in the U.S. where the rugged, self-sufficient individual is a national icon and where reliance on welfare is seen as a defect of character. The worry about the lack of independence within the next generation has a decidedly ethical component. This ethical message is reinforced when mention is made, as well, of a failure to respect boundaries, discipline, and one's elders.

Several issues about these claims of harm might be noticed. First, to a large extent the assertion of harm resulting from helicopter parenting depends on standards that are presented as if it they are absolute when they are necessarily variable. The central issue of maturity itself is a good example: what is considered immature behavior in one time period or place might be seen as age-appropriate in another. Second, and closely related, normative terms are treated as if they too have universal applications: for example, articles claim that the children of helicopter parents will be unable to "form healthy relationships," or have "proper job skills," implying that the basic standards for assessing relationships and job skills are immutable. Third, most of the items offer no data whatsoever, but rely instead on unsubstantiated assertions by people like human resource personnel and college deans who draw on their own experience to make their claims; sometimes they don't even substantiate their assertions at all. Fourth, the studies that do exist rely on correlations and don't prove causation. Take the frequently cited study of 300 college freshmen by Neil Montgomery, a psychologist at Keene State College, which found that students with helicopter parents (ten percent of those surveyed) were more dependent, more neurotic and less open than other students. Although this study works from correlations (the association between helicopter parenting and "neurotic behaviour") without adequately demonstrating causation, it is widely interpreted as if the association alone is sufficient proof that helicopter parenting has problematic consequences (Rettner). Another report, by my colleague Barbara Hofer, a psychologist at Middlebury College, found a connection between how frequently students communicate with their parents and how dependent they are on their parents (Hofer and Moore); once again, cause and effect are obscure (and the measure of "dependency" is arbitrary).

Finally, I want to note that the harm attributed to helicopter parenting is linked to a specific notion of what should constitute a childhood. The discussions explain that children are "rarely left to their own devices for hours at a time," a parental action which, when it is part of the parenting style that Annette Lareau calls the "accomplishment of natural growth" among the working class and poor arouses some concern. It may indeed be because helicopter parenting is associated with the elite (a point I address more fully below) that the critics worry that these children have a "hurried" childhood, that they don't enjoy "leisure," and that they don't have the enriching and creativity-building activity of "play." When referring to the elite, solitary activities, leisure and play are no longer considered to be problematic (or even evidence of laziness), but are viewed as the necessary preconditions for the development of the whole self. One recent article, for example, quotes Peter Gay, an evolutionary psychologist, as saying "free play is a marvelous biological solution to the big problem that human beings have, which is that we are both selfish and social. We depend on cooperating with other people, and yet we are also looking out for number one. Children are constantly negotiating that balance in their play" (qtd. in Ozment).

So what does this all have to do with the title of my chapter? Am I just raising another voice against Helicopter Parenting under the guise of saying that mothers need to get parenting under control? No. The phrase "parenting out of control" is one I came up with when I compared the parenting styles among professional middle-class respondents with those of their less privileged peers (Nelson). Among the former, parenting includes a long perspective on children's dependency without a clear launching point for a grown child, a commitment to creating "passionate" people who know how to find a "proper" balance between working hard and having fun, personalized and negotiated guidance in the activities of daily life, respectful responsiveness to children's

Margaret K. Nelson

individual needs and desires, a belief in boundless potential, ambitious goals for achievement, and an intense engagement with children who in previous generations might have been encouraged to begin the process of separation.

In some ways these characteristics make for an approach to parenting that is filled with tensions and enduring dilemmas. For example, professional middle-class parents want both to "protect" their children from growing up too quickly and to push them to high achievement at an early age. The latter impulse often leads to treating their children as peers and to claiming that those children can be trusted to make decisions on their own; the former impulse often leads to hovering and to concealed surveillance. And while the contemporary style of parenting rests on an approach that has been found among privileged parents for some time—an emphasis on being permissive rather than authoritarian or even authoritative, a reliance on internalized constraint rather than punishment and external control—the intense negotiation that often results from a commitment to loose reins and to trust takes place along with what appear to be relatively new patterns of vigilance and connection.

All of this makes for the much noticed distinction between the current parenting style and that which characterized child rearing among the elite as recently as 20 or 30 years ago. These distinctions are commented on by the parents interviewed for this study who see themselves as forging a new model and as breaking with the past.

My findings of intimacy and hovering combined with elastic constraint and covert surveillance are central to my dubbing the professional middle-class approach "parenting out of control." Clearly intimacy and hovering lay the groundwork for control in the commonsense meaning of the word: parents are carefully guiding, shaping, and determining the contours of their children's actions. Moreover, much of teenage children's daily lives is subject to observation, discussion, and negotiation; those who are subject to this kind of involvement in their activities and personal lives may experience their parents as being "out of control." (There is another meaning I address below.)

By way of contrast, the working-class and less elite middle-class parents are more concerned with skills that will ensure self-sufficiency than they are with passion and fun. Working-class and middle-class parents are less interested in intimacy and engagement than they are in clear rules of authority within the family. They do not believe they need to be involved in making every decision about their children's lives and they welcome shortcuts that can ease their burdens. And although they too view themselves as being more alone in responsibility for their children's safety than were *their* parents, limited resources shape day-to-day decisions and strategies. Taken as a whole, they experience fewer internal contradictions in their parenting approach. Middle-class and working-class parents are also less conscious of carving out a new mode of parenting that differs radically from that of their own parents. Although they understand that more isolation for individual families and what are seen to be greater dangers might require more intense vigilance, they refer more often to continuity than to difference. Both attention to external constraints of limited financial resources and limited time, and attention to having children who obey family rules, are central to my dubbing this approach "parenting with limits."

My concern, when I say that parenting has to get under control, is that the former style—that practiced by the professional middle class—has two sets of negative consequences. The first has to do with the parents; the second has to do with the broader society.

Parents first. Quite simply, what some call helicopter parenting and I call parenting out of control is, to put it mildly, more time-consuming and more emotionally demanding than other parenting styles. And much of its work falls (as the work of parenting always has) on women. Since 1965, the amount of time mothers spend on all child-care activities has risen, even though the majority of mothers are now in the labor force; the increase has been particularly sharp among highly educated mothers (Bianchi, Robinson and Milkie). So it's not just that today's professional mothers are holding down what would, in the 1960s, have been two separate jobs—one inside the home, the other outside it. It's that the first of those jobs is a lot more taxing than it used to be. Mothers who try to live up to the new parenting standards of the professional middle class seem to have few options: They can overwork themselves, or they can leave the workforce.

Although women don't opt out of employment as often as is sometimes supposed, those who do tend to give two main explanations (Stone). The workplace is still not particularly flexible or family-friendly, they say, and parenting has become more intensive and more demanding than ever. But these women may find themselves trying to justify their decision; approaching child-rearing as a full-time, totally consuming job provides such a justification. At this point, the cycle becomes self-perpetuating: Professional women bring considerable skills to raising children, and because they do it so conscientiously, they may set trends for other parents.

For those helicopter mothers who don't leave the workplace, personal relationships seem to be the first thing to go. Working a demanding job while paying painstaking attention to one's children leaves little time for maintaining a marriage. A study by Robin Wilson of the Washington and Lee University School of Law reports that women with MBAs get divorced or separated more often than those who have only a bachelor's degree, while women with law or medical degrees are more likely to divorce or separate than their male counterparts (Wilson). Meanwhile, according to sociologists Suzanne Bianchi, John Robinson and Melissa Milkie, adults in 2000 spent less time with their spouses than adults did in 1975, as they spent more time at work and more time with their children. University of California at San Diego economists Valerie and Garey Ramey report that between 1990 and the early 2000s, college-educated mothers came to spend an average of nine hours more per week with their children than their own mothers had spent with them; fathers spent an average of five more hours. Whatever they were doing (and much of it apparently involved coordinating their kids' extracurricular activities) they weren't devoting it to themselves, their communities, or their relationships. Indeed, the higher divorce rate among women with high-pressure careers could therefore be both a cause and a consequence of intense devotion to one's children: These mothers may find that the only reliable, and persistent, relationships are those with their kids.

When people turn inward to their families, their communities also pay a high price. In a series of studies, sociologists Naomi Gerstel, Sally Gallagher and Natalia Sarkisian (Gallagher and Gerstel; Gerstel and Sarkisian; Sarkisian and Gerstel) have shown that, parenting practices notwithstanding, marriage is a greedy institution. Compared with singles, married people are less likely to visit relatives, less likely to take care of elderly parents and are less involved with neighbors and friends. I suspect that the tendency to turn inward must be even more intense among hyper-vigilant parents. And this withdrawal may extend to parents' broader social and civic engagement. These days, we don't just bowl alone, as the political scientist Robert Putnam famously argued; we devote less energy to the PTA, to local politics, to charity. And to friendship. The time married parents spend visiting with friends and relatives outside the nuclear family has declined dramatically: Married fathers spent almost 40 percent less time and married mothers spent almost a third less time socializing in 2000 than they did in 1965, according to Bianchi, Robinson and Milkie. I can't help but think that the new intensity of daily life is part of the problem. Parents seem to have few opportunities to pursue friendships unless they are friendships that take little extra time (as with co-workers or other parents on the sideline of a child's sporting event). Many of the helicopter mothers I've spoken to have told me, often with pride in their voices, that their daughters are their best friends. At first, I wondered why these women—some of them in their late 40s or 50s—wouldn't prefer to spend their free time with people their own age. But as I looked more closely at the way they are tackling parenthood, I understood: They have no free time.

Moreover, we might note that even as the practices of helicopter parenting are mocked in the press and on the blogs, that mockery never mentions the very real issues of social class privileges that are part and parcel of what it is that some parents do to ensure success for their children. In fact, the practices of helicopter parenting are *precisely* designed to maintain and reproduce elite status. But, the discussions of helicopter parenting rewrite class reproduction *only* as bad parenting. In this rewriting although some aspects of class reproduction are acknowledged as being problematic, many more of them are ignored. For example, in a Doonesbury cartoon, parents are mocked for wake-up calls to college students or for knowing a student's daily schedule. But parents are not chided for helping students write papers or for using their networks to help college graduates get job interviews. Indeed, in some articles students are encouraged to call on their parents for this latter type of assistance. And there is no mention of the vast array of other *material, social and cultural* advantages available to the children of the elite. That is, the focus is *not* on the practices that most challenge meritocracy—and I mean here practices like private school educations, classes and training in a range of educational activities, and the resources to take on interesting unpaid internships. These advantages are all ignored when attention is focused on the possibility that the children of the contemporary elite (who should be preparing to lead) won't be able to handle modest adversity.

Thus when I say that what mothers need, then, is to get parenting under control, what I mean is that parents should back off—not because they are creating depressed, substance abusing, wimps—but because mothers are exhausting themselves, undermining their communities, and reproducing (and even intensifying) the extreme inequality in our society. For all these reasons, it's time to play the parenting game differently—and with a more level field.

WORKS CITED

Aspen Education Group. "A Generation Tethered to Their Helicopter Parents: Over Protective Childrearing Ruining Kids Lives." Blog. July 28 2010. Web. May 15, 2012.

Bianchi, Suzanne M., John P. Robinson, and Melissa A. Milkie. *Changing Rhythms of American Family Life*. New York: Russell Sage Foundation, 2006. Print.

Cline, Foster W. and Jim Fay. *Parenting with Love and Logic: Teaching Children Responsibility*. Colorado Springs: Pinon Press, 1990. Print.

Gallagher, Sally K. and Naomi Gerstel. "Connections and Constraints:

The Effects of Children on Caregiving." *Journal of Marriage and Family* 63 (1) (February 2001): 265-75. Print.

Gerstel, Naomi and Natalia Sarkisian. "Marriage as a Greedy Institution." *Contexts* 5 (4) (2006): 16-21. Print.

"Helicopter Parent." *Wikipedia, The Free Encyclopedia.* Wikimedia Foundation. August 30 2010. Web. August 30, 2010.

Hofer, Barbara, and Abigail Sullivan Moore. *The iConnected Parent: Staying Close to Your Kids in College (and Beyond) While Letting Them Grow Up.* New York: Free Press, 2010. Print.

Lareau, Annette. *Unequal Childhoods: Class, Race, and Family Life.* Berkeley: University of California Press, 2003. Print.

Mom Needs an "A." University of Texas at Austin. 2007. Web. April 12, 2008.

Nelson, Margaret K. *Parenting Out of Control: Anxious Families in Uncertain Times.* New York: New York University Press, 2010. Print.

Ozment, Katherine. "Welcome to the Age of Overparenting: How I Learned to Let My Kids Be Kids." *Boston Magazine* December 2011. Web.

Putnam, Robert D. *Bowling Alone: The Collapse and Revival of American Community.* New York: Simon and Schuster, 2001. Print.

Ramey, Garey, and Valerie Ramey. "The Rug Rat Race." *Brookings Papers on Economic Activity* Spring (2010): 129-76. Print.

Rettner, Rachel. "'Helicopter' Parents Have Neurotic Kids, Study Suggests." *Live Science* June 3 2010. Web. May 15, 2012.

Sarkisian, Ntalia and Naomi Gerstel. "Till Marriage Do Us Part: Adult Children's Relationships with Their Parents." *Journal of Marriage and Family* 70 (May 2008): 360-76. Print.

Stone, Pamela. *Opting Out: Why Women Really Quit Careers and Head Home.* Berkeley: University of California Press, 2007. Print.

Wilson, Robin Fretwell. "Keeping Women in Business (and Family)." *Social Science Research Network* April 1 2008. Web. April 10, 2008.

Bait and Switch

Moving on from "Mommy Madness"

JUDITH WARNER

IT IS HARD FOR ME TO BELIEVE that enough time has passed that I can look back to the period when I published my book on the American culture of motherhood, *Perfect Madness: Motherhood in the Age of Anxiety,* and say that it belonged to a distinct era, one that has started to retreat into the past. And yet, that period—the beginning of the 2000s when I'd just moved to Washington, DC, from Paris, and come in for the shock of competitive, high stakes, all-Mommy-all-the-time American parenting—was a very different time. It was a very different time in life for me, having a baby at home and a preschooler, rather than the 12- and 15-year-olds I have now, and it was a very different time for our country politically—and economically above all.

It was also a very different moment in the American culture of motherhood. The 1990s had just ended. It had been a decade of cultural obsession with all the ways that mothering could go wrong, that bonding could go bad, that babies—even (especially) middle class or upper middle class children with no greater degree of life challenge than that of having a working mother—could end up in a state of "failure to thrive" that would cost them their emotional and cognitive wellbeing for a lifetime. We had spent a decade worrying about incompetent nannies, dangerous day care centers, and murderous au pairs. These fears related to working motherhood were then greatly inflamed by the discovery of infants and toddlers in horrific circumstances in the post-Ceausescu Romanian orphanages in the late 1980s. The example of these severely deprived children, many of whom were living in filth and even tied to their cribs, had been instrumentalized in the U.S. by the opponents of working motherhood as a cautionary tale for all mothers who might underestimate the daily cost to a baby of such ostensibly comparable experiences of deprivation and loss as seeing his or her mother blithely walk out the door or having a babysitter come and go. The conservative columnist George Will, for one, made the link between the psychological devastation of "maternal deprivation" and the lived reality of modern motherhood all too clear when, in the then mass-circulation news magazine *Newsweek*, he warned of "gilded ghettos" whose "residents include 'privileged' children of parents too affluent for their children's good, parents able and eager to give children anything but attention, measuring out what these parents are pleased to call 'quality time' in dribs and drabs" (80).

All of this terror coincided with the coming-into motherhood of a generation of women who had largely rejected the get-out-and-work rhetoric of second wave feminism; a generation whose adult identity, forged in the 1980s, had been largely based on a sense of limitless possibility, and all-but-unlimited personal potential. This was a generation that had been raised to believe they could do it all—that nothing would stand in the way of their dreams. A generation who, encountering the powerful tug of motherhood, and a new cultural imperative to "surrender—as a 1997 book by Iris Krasnow famously put it (9)—did whatever they could to give their all to their children. Those who could afford to dropped out of the workforce. Those who couldn't guiltily labored on, piling on shift after shift of high-intensity paid and unpaid work, striving to live up to the promise of being all that they could be, even when doing so exhausted and unhinged them, and ultimately—when the experiment in superhumanness eventually, necessarily failed—eroded their sense of self-worth.

This experiment in being more perfect, more complete and whole and high-performing than the most self-exacting 1950s housewife was called the "New Traditionalism." It was celebrated as the highest form of freely chosen selfhood by a generation blessed by a panoply of unrestricted choices. Leaving the workforce for home in particular was hailed as the pinnacle of modern liberation, as the headline *New York Times Magazine* editors chose for journalist Lisa Belkin's 2003 cover story, "The Opt-Out Revolution," made perfectly clear.

It all happened in a clear narrative arc: the decade that began with panics over the satanic ritual abuse of children, ended with a historical reversal of the 40-year trend toward women's increasing participation in the workforce. A new development—however limited to women at the very top and the very bottom of the income distribution curve, as later research would make clear—that set off a firestorm of attention by the media. "60 Minutes"[1] dedicated a much-talked about segment to Leslie Stahl's encounter with a group of extremely high-achieving women, representatives of a generation who, she said, was "the first to achieve success without having to fight for it," and who were "now walking away willingly and without regrets." A *Time* magazine cover story made "The Case for Staying Home"—as did countless women's magazines, making the argument that, for many families, women's work just didn't pay.

Never mind that, as countless feminist scholars like the Pamela Stone and Joan Williams have argued, these women really didn't "opt-out," they were pushed out—by inflexible workplaces, inhospitable bosses, and, indirectly, by a generation of husbands who, feeling beleaguered themselves, were unwilling to take on their fair share of work at home (Williams, Manvell and Bornstein; see also Stone). That story—which necessarily led to discussions of (America's virtually nonexistent) family policy—was nowhere nearly as sexy as the one of women who Had it All giving it all up. And so—for a while at least—the fairy tale of free choice and personal liberation, of a generation finding itself in the glorious pursuit of ideal motherhood—become the story of motherhood in our time.

Fast-forward to now. In the wake of the Great Recession, which began with a "Mancession" and has wound down with men reclaiming the lion's share of work, as jobs slowly return, no one's talking about "opting out" anymore. Women want *in* to the workplace, and they're not finding the way in to be easy. In 2010, the Center for Work-Life Policy in New York found that 73 percent of women trying to return to the workforce after a voluntary period of time out were having significant problems finding a job. Those who did return came back to work to find they'd lost 16 percent of their pre-opting out earning power. More than 25 percent saw their management responsibilities decline, and almost a quarter had to accept a lower job title (Hewlett, Sherbin, Shiller and Sumberg).

In the wake of the Great Recession, the economic facts of American family life have changed in ways yet-unseen in the booming, "New Traditionalist" 1990s. Most notably: women's financial contributions to their households are more important than ever before. Forty percent now are either single working moms or married mothers who earn as much or more than their spouse. Only 23 percent of American families with children under age 15 now have a wage-earning dad and a stay-at-home mom: a historic low. And as has always been the case, behavior change, driven by economics, has brought attitude change: in 2010, according to the General Social Survey, which has collected data on social trends and attitudes since 1972, fully 75 percent of Americans agreed that "a working mother can establish just as warm and secure a relationship with her children as a mother who does not work." Sixty-five percent of the public even now believes that preschool children are not likely to suffer if their mothers work outside the home. By comparison, in 1977, more than half of respondents felt that mother's working was harmful to children, and while by 1994 that percentage had fallen to 30 percent, by 2000—when I moved back to America from France—it had crept back up to 38 percent.

Undoubtedly, as a result, discussion of the evils of working motherhood are all but absent now from the media. It is just irrelevant—not to mention offensive, to too many people. For the sake of scoring political points in the U.S. presidential election this past year, both the Democratic and Republican parties tried, at various points, to stoke the "Mommy Wars" for their advantage, chiefly by rallying women for or against Ann Romney, as the symbol of idealized, mid-twentieth century, stay-at-home motherhood. The media rose up to take the bait—yet reader responses showed many women pushing back, expressing impatience with what many saw as a worn-out and outdated debate, and wanting to get on with the business of figuring out how to best live their over-busy lives.

Which brings us to family policy, which in the United States, after a half-century of women's vastly increasing workforce participation, remains all but non-existent. The change that has come since I wrote *Perfect Madness* is distressingly limited. *And yet.* There have been some real shifts in attitudes. Back when I published *Perfect Madness,* in 2005, people laughed at me (if they weren't shaking their heads in rage) when I talked about looking abroad to learn from successful societal approaches to the problems of things like day care and early childhood education. "Do you want the government raising your children?" is what I was often asked.

That general attitude I truly believe subtly started to shift. A number of the Democratic candidates in the 2006 Congressional elections made a point of talking about the difficulties of contemporary family life. All the Democratic Presidential candidates in 2008 made helping families a cornerstone of their campaign platforms. President Obama, very early in his presidency, swore, time and again, to make improving the quality of

Judith Warner. Photo: Jean-Louis Atlan

life of middle-class families the anchor of his domestic policies. And the country seemed to applaud him. In the early days of his Presidency, he created the White House Council on Women and Girls to convey that family issues would remain at the center of his agenda. His Administration sponsored a White House conference on workplace flexibility. Until the full reality of the economic crisis—and of Republican obstructionism—hit home, at least, there was a whole new sense of possibility in Washington.

And out in the states (which have typically been the crucible of new social policy in America, liberal or conservative), there has been some actual—albeit limited—progress. Politically conservative states like Georgia and Oklahoma have established universal voluntary free preschools. Three states—California, Washington, and New Jersey—have instituted paid family and medical leave; only Washington state, because it had no previously existing funding mechanism in place, had to delay implementation after the economic downturn began, and utilization rates in California have been very low, as most workers have been not made aware of their right to paid leave. Three cities—San Francisco, Washington, DC, and Seattle—now have laws on the books guaranteeing workers the right to paid sick days (a right that, shockingly, nearly 40 percent of private sector workers in the U.S. do not share). One state—Connecticut—recently passed a paid sick day law as well, though it applies only to service workers—and a bill that would bring paid sick days to New York City has been languishing in the City Council, held up by political concerns in a mayoral election year.

Most interestingly, national polls now show very strong support for paid family and medical leave, and for paid sick days. Indeed, a 2007 poll from the National Partnership for Women and Families in Washington, DC, showed 61 percent of women and 53 percent of men said they "strongly favored" legislation guaranteeing paid family leave for American workers, at a minimal cost to both employer and employee, and an additional 18 percent of women and 20 percent of men favored it "not so strongly." Another poll showed that 77 percent of respondents—liberals and conservatives combined—showing support for the idea that "business should be required" to provide paid family leave to workers. And yet another showed 96 percent of liberals and 68 percent of conservatives supporting paid sick leave as a "basic worker's right." Promisingly, in an American political context, Evangelical Christians were among the strongest supporters of these sorts of pro-family programs (Kunin).

So the culture is changing.

And, I find, the way women are talking and writing about motherhood is changing, too. In the 1990s and early 2000s, the talk on motherhood was breathless, worshipful. The idea that motherhood was woman's highest calling—practically her one and true calling—was back, in quasi-religious terms both utterly anachronistic and uniquely modern. Then came an extended *Bad Mother* phase—a kind of rebellion against the hyperventilating hyper-vigilance of the recent past that included Ayelet Waldman's book of that name, and also books about, say, Free-Range Parenting, Three-Martini playdates and the like. Most recently, the books that have shaped our cultural discussion of motherhood (*Battle Hymn of the Tiger Mother* and *Bringing Up Bébé*) actually tap into an undercurrent of hostility toward children, an almost punishing impulse, and a desire to get them into line and undo the over-indulgent parenting of the past couple of decades. What I think this is really about, on a deep, semi-conscious level, is bitterness and disenchantment with where the extreme child-centeredness and maternal self-sacrifice practiced by so many mothers in the 1990s and aughts eventually leads.

After a decade or two of all-consuming, high-intensity motherhood, the chickens are coming home to roost, so to speak, for America's mothers. Many are exhausted, personally depleted. Many who did everything "right" now find themselves with the sense that the rules have changed and they've been left holding the bag; almost as though they'd been victims of a sort of bait and switch. Many with children now entering their teens or perhaps even entering college are finding themselves returned to themselves and facing the question of: what's next? What's left of one's self after years and years of devoting yourself to the putatively selfless pursuit of perfect motherhood? After having "given your all" for so long, what resources do you have left for yourself to move forward into the next phase of your life?

For the past year or so, I've been talking to as many women as were interested about the challenges of encountering midlife today. (A topic of earth-shattering importance because I was wrestling with it), and I've seen a very clear pattern emerge from what these women say. The women who most completely made their children the center of their lives, really submerging themselves in the pursuit of ideal motherhood, are very often, now kind of lost. Their children need less and less of them. They have more time to themselves and yet—they don't quite know what to do with themselves anymore

"Is this it? Is this who I was supposed to be?" an Ivy League educated former lawyer in Washington put it to me in one talk, as she reflected on her life of school volunteering and driving through the suburbs.

She told me of having gone to an event billed as a way to remove anxiety and anger from your life, she continued. It came down, she was told, to following your dream—visualizing it so that you could get it. "What if I can't get as far as even being able to see what I want?" she said. "I want to follow my passion, but I don't know what my passion is anymore."

Those who sailed through their earlier motherhood years powered by the sense that they were doing the very best thing for their kids through their endlessly intensive devotion now often feel quite disempowered as the life path they'd imagined for themselves—off-ramping and on-ramping at will, as the women's magazines had promised them, just doesn't work out. The re-entry route back into the workforce—to the extent that it ever really existed—has pretty much dried up. Stay-at-home mothers give up their financial freedom, and with it many feel their sense of agency slip away. Their position of equality with their husbands is by necessity somewhat eroded. They lose the sense of strength that comes from knowing that, come what may, they can keep themselves and their children afloat economically.

Unfortunately, what I see very often now in this cohort in response to this unhappiness is the very sort of self-blame I found so epidemic back in the early aughts. Just as back then women blamed themselves if they couldn't, seamlessly, be absolutely all for their children, absolutely all the time, many of these same women now look back and blame themselves for somehow not being the women they'd always—in a previous, pre-children life—believed they would grow up to be. What I hear often these days is the expression of a mournful sort of bait and switch. It's not so much a complaint of having been ripped off by someone, or something, external; it's more a sense of self-betrayal, that somehow they got things all wrong while living their lives believing they were perfectly following all the rules and now were left holding the bag. They should have known better, done more, seen the future more clearly. Been a better role model for their daughters.

Surveys and social science research have shown on a larger scale what I've encountered anecdotally: the group of mothers who—either by choice or necessity—made exclusive motherhood the center of their lives, leaving the workforce to stay home full-time, is considerably less happy than working mothers, and less contented than part-time working mothers in particular. In 2011, for example, researchers at the University of North Carolina/Greensboro surveyed more than 1,300 mothers in the United States and found that women with jobs—especially part-time jobs—were both less depressed and in better overall health than those whose lives were devoted full-time to their homes and their kids (Stein). In 2012, a Gallup poll made headlines when it found that mothers who don't work outside the home were far more likely to be depressed—and plain old angry, sad, stressed and worried—than mothers who were engaged in professional activities (Mendes, Saad and McGeeney). Also this year, University of Mary Washington professors Holly Schiffrin and Miriam Liss compiled survey data comparing the mental health of women who more or less profoundly ascribe to a philosophy of "intensive mothering" and, in an article published this year in the *Journal of Child and Family Studies*, reported finding that women who believe that they are the "essential" parent, naturally endowed with a sense of calling for motherhood, show decreased life satisfaction and greater stress. Women who believe that motherhood is the "hardest job in the world" (to paraphrase both from their survey and from Ann Romney) also report less life satisfaction and more depression and stress. And those who practice an assiduous form of child-centeredness, they found too, also experience less satisfaction with their lives (Rizzo, Schiffrin and Liss).

These sorts of results should really come as no surprise: they're the basic truths upon which the fight for women's equality, for the right for women to explore and inhabit their "full human potential," as Betty Friedan put it, were waged by the second-wave feminist movement. But somehow, amidst all the good mother messaging of the past couple of decades, they got lost. So much so that when Leslie Bennetts, in her 2007 book, *The Feminine Mistake,* tried to sound an alarm about well-off and highly educated young mothers making a so-called post-feminist choice of stay-at-home motherhood, she was reviled as a bitter old harpie. (She did have some problems with tone.) That this work now does get mainstream press pickup ("Mother is Best?" asked *Time* in 2012 [Rochman]) indicates that there is a change in receptivity to the message that mothers need to lead more balanced, well-rounded and empowering lives.

What I wonder now is whether our changed economic circumstances and changed attitudes stemming both from those circumstances and from the now-widespread awareness that the American pursuit of perfect parenting has simply gotten out of control can now open up a new space in our cultural conversation in which to reposition working motherhood not as a necessary evil but as an inherent good.

What this would mean, though, is an honest and thoroughgoing evaluation of the conditions in America that make working motherhood feel so bad for so many mothers. It would mean, I believe, de-problematizing working motherhood and instead problematizing our culture of work, which is so inimical to women's—or men's—ability to live balanced, "fully human" lives. When the United States is ready to have that conversation—and only then—will we see genuine progress in getting over "Mommy Madness."

[1]Aired October 10, 2004.

WORKS CITED

Belkin, Lisa. "The Opt-Out Revolution." *New York Times Magazine* October 26, 2003: 42ff. Print.

Bennetts, Leslie. *The Feminine Mistake: Are We Giving Up Too Much?* New York: Voice/Hyperion, 2007. Print.

Friedan, Betty. *The Feminine Mystique.* New York: Norton, 2001.

Hewlett, Diana Forster, Laura Sherbin, Peggy Shiller, and Karen Sumberg.

Off-Ramps and On-Ramps Revisited. New York: Center for Work-Life Policy, May 2010. Print.

Krasnow, Iris. *Surrendering to Motherhood.* New York; Hyperion, 1997. Print.

Kunin, Madeleine M. *The New Feminist Agenda: Defining the Next Revolution for Women, Work, and Family.* White River Junction, Vermont: Chelsea Green Publications, 2012. Print.

Mendes, Elizabeth, Lydia Saad and Kyley McGeeney. "Stay-at-Home Moms Report More Depression, Sadness, Anger." *Gallup.com.* May 18, 2012. Web.

Rizzo, Kathryn M., Holly H. Schiffrin and Miriam Liss. "Insight into the Parenting Paradox: Mental Health Outcomes of Intensive Mothering." *Journal of Child and Family Studies* July 5, 2012. Web.

Rochman, Bonnie. "Mother is Best? Why 'Intensive' Parenting Makes Moms More Depressed." *Time Magazine* 7 August 2012. Web.

Stein, Jeannine. "Does working make mothers happier and healthier?" *Latimes.com.* December 13, 2011. Web.

Stone, Pamela. *Opting Out: Why Women Really Quit Careers and Head Home.* Berkeley: University of California Press, 2008. Print.

Will, George F. "Mothers Who Don't Know How." *Newsweek* April 23, 1990: 80. Print.

Williams, Joan C., Jessica Manvell and Stephanie Bornstein. "Opt-Out" or Pushed Out? How the Press Covers Work/Family Conflict." Advance Library Collection. Paper 575. The Center for WorkLife Law, University of California, Hastings College of the Law, 2006. Web.

Outlaw(ing) Motherhood

A Theory and Politic of Maternal Empowerment for the 21st Century

ANDREA O'REILLY

IN HER GROUNDBREAKING BOOK, *Of Woman Born: Motherhood as Experience and Institution*, Adrienne Rich wrote "We do not think of the power stolen from us and the power withheld from us in the name of the institution of motherhood" (275). In the three-plus decades since the publication of Rich's ovarian work, the empowerment of mothers has been a central, if not defining, concern of maternal activism and scholarship. More recently, with the emergence of an international motherhood movement and the development of Motherhood Studies as an academic discipline, maternal scholars and activists have sought to define and develop a politic or theory of maternal empowerment. Maternal activists and researchers today agree that motherhood, as it is currently perceived and practiced in patriarchal societies, is disempowering if not oppressive for a multitude of reasons; among them are the societal devaluation of motherwork, the endless tasks of privatized mothering, and the impossible standards of idealized motherhood. Likewise, maternal activists and researchers have developed a plethora of theories of and strategies for maternal empowerment to contest, challenge, and counter patriarchal motherhood. This chapter will not so much revisit these ideas and strategies as it will request that scholars and activists alike rethink received or accepted notions of how and why motherhood functions as an oppressive institution for women.

When they are asked, students, mothers, and researchers readily describe the exhaustion, guilt, boredom, anxiety, stress, loneliness and so forth, of contemporary Western motherhood, but are less forthcoming on why this is so. Indeed, mothers in North America are overwhelmed, fatigued and guilt-ridden because of the hard work and responsibility that they alone

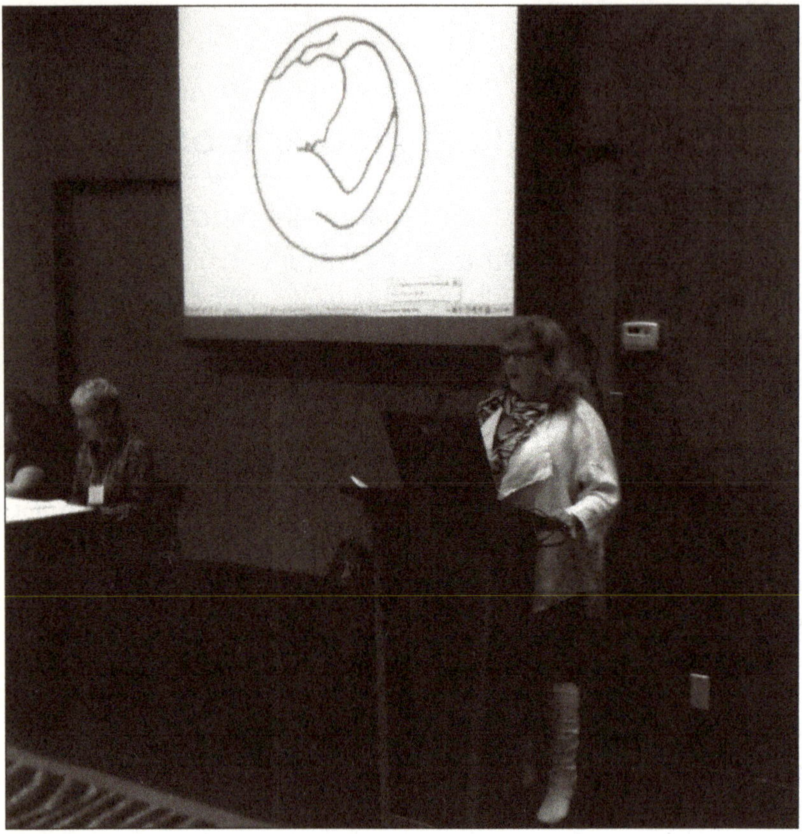

Andrea O'Reilly

assume in motherhood. Yet the larger question remains: why is this so? Despite 40 years of feminism, modern motherhood continues to function as a patriarchal institution, one that remains largely impervious to change. It is my view, and the argument of this chapter, that motherhood remains stuck in this oppressive and disempowering space because it is grounded in gender essentialism, a gender ideology that establishes a naturalized opposition between public and private spheres. This chapter will argue that only by unearthing and severing the ideological underpinning of patriarchal motherhood, gender essentialism, can we develop a politic of maternal empowerment and a practice of outlaw motherhood for the twenty-first century.

In my current work, I argue that patriarchal motherhood is informed and maintained by eight ideological assumptions that cause mothering to be oppressive to women, which I have termed the essentialization, privatization, individualization, naturalization, normalization, idealization, biologicalization, expertization, and intensification of motherhood. While this chapter will focus on the first theme, the essentialization of motherhood, it important to remember and emphasize that such essentialization occurs both as a result of and in response to the other themes, and that all serve to reinforce this essentialization. For example privatization locates motherwork in the reproductive realm of the home, while individualization causes such mothering to be the work and responsibility of one person. Similarly, naturalization assumes that maternity is natural to women and all women are naturally maternal, and normalization limits and restricts maternal identity and practice to one specific mode or form. Biologicalization, in its emphasis on blood ties, positions the birth mother as the 'real' and authentic mother. Finally, the expertization and intensification of motherhood, particularly as they are conveyed in what Sharon Hays has termed intensive mothering and Susan Douglas and Meredith Michaels call "the new momism," causes childrearing to be all consuming for the individual who performs it. Thus, privatization, individualization, naturalization, normalization, idealization, biologicalization, expertization and intensification, together and in unison, all serve to fortify and amplify the essentialization of motherhood that causes motherhood to be oppressive to women.

THEORIZING AND DEFINING MATERNAL EMPOWERMENT

Any discussion of maternal empowerment must begin with the distinction that Rich made in *Of Woman Born* between two meanings of motherhood, one superimposed on the other: "the *potential* relationship of any woman to her powers of reproduction and to children," and "the *institution*—which aims at ensuring that that potential—and all women—shall remain under male control" (13, emphasis in original). It has long been recognized among scholars of motherhood that it was Rich's distinction between mothering and motherhood that enabled feminists to recognize that motherhood is not naturally, necessarily, or inevitably oppressive, a view held by some Second Wave feminists. On the contrary, if freed from motherhood, mothering could be experienced as a site of empowerment and as a location of social change if, to use Rich's words, women became "outlaws from the institution of motherhood." (195). However, while *Of Woman Born* interrupted the patriarchal narrative of motherhood and cleared a space for the development of counter narratives of mothering, it did not generate a discourse of outlaw motherhood or maternal empowerment. Moreover, while much has been published on patriarchal motherhood since Rich's inaugural text—documenting why and how patriarchal motherhood is harmful, indeed unnatural, to mothers and children alike—little has been written on the possibility of empowered mothering or outlaw motherhood. As Fiona Green writes, "a discussion of Rich's monumental contention that even when restrained by patriarchy, motherhood can be a site of empowerment and political activism [is] still largely missing from the increasing dialogue and publication around motherhood" (2004: 31).

In my earlier work I used the term "empowered mothering" to signify non-patriarchal maternity or outlaw motherhood; however, I now think that the term 'maternal empowerment' better describes an identity and practice of outlaw motherhood. While there are similarities and considerable overlap between the concepts empowered mothering and maternal empowerment, there are also significant differences between the two. The term "empowered mothering," constructed as it is from a verb, leaves both the subject and object (in both senses of the word) of the action more or less ambiguous. More specifically, the term fails to address who is doing this? For whom? And why? Moreover, empowered mothering is not synonymous with an empowered mother; a mother may perform empowered mothering, say in the instance of anti-sexist childrearing or maternal activism, without being empowered herself. Anti-sexist childrearing and maternal activism are certainly significant and essential tasks of empowered mothering; however, maternal activism on behalf of children and feminist childrearing for children do not address the needs of mothers in any real manner. Specifically, as I have argued elsewhere, by defining maternal empowerment in this manner it seems that we have, whether consciously or otherwise, discounted and disregarded what should be the first and primary aim of empowered mothering: the empowerment of mothers (O'Reilly 2006b). How and why patriarchal motherhood is oppressive to mothers has been well documented in feminist scholarship; however, when this same scholarship seeks to imagine an empowered mode of mothering, the focus inexplicably shifts from mothers to children (anti-sexist childrearing) and/or to a world apart from the mother (maternal activism). In the feminist critique of patriarchal motherhood the mother and her discontent was our foremost concern; however, as we endeavour to define a non-patriarchal maternity, the mother, while still crucial, frequently becomes instrumental to larger and seemingly more important social change objectives. In other words, mothers are accorded agency to affect social change through childrearing or activism but little attention is paid to what this agency does or means for the mother herself in the context of *her own life*.

Equally as troubling, is the way that the concept of empowered mothering has justified and rationalized shifting the focus away from the mother herself; too often the demand to empower mothers is recast as a strategy for more effective parenting. In her study on empowered mothering Erika Horwitz argues that this practice is characterized by women insisting on "the importance of mothers meeting their own needs," and the realization that "being a mother does not fulfill all of women's needs" (2003: 48). However, in most instances, the mothers' demands for agency and autonomy are repositioned as requirements of the children. As one mother explained, she resisted patriarchal motherhood "to make me a better mother for my children" (qtd. in Horwitz 2003: 52). While I do believe that empowered mothers are more effective mothers, and that anti-sexist childrearing and maternal activism are worthwhile aims, I still worry about why the rhetoric of rationalization has become the strategy of choice among feminist activists and scholars today; I wonder why our campaigns for social change centre on children and not on ourselves as mothers. Why can we not simply demand that motherhood be made better for mothers themselves? Why are mothers' demands for more time, money, support and validation only responded to when they are seen as benefiting children? I realize that this rhetoric is often employed strategically to make gains for mothers that otherwise would not be possible; in other words, patriarchal culture will accord mothers resources if they use them on behalf of children. However, whether or not one agrees with such a strategy, it has become apparent that empowered mothering does not automatically or necessarily mean or translate into a politic of empowerment for mothers or a theory of outlaw motherhood.

Thus, for the reasons noted above, the term "maternal empowerment" better defines a theory and politic of outlaw motherhood. The term "maternal empowerment" is captured as a noun; that is, a state or place in which mothers are or may be empowered, which allows for the mother to be the focal point of the theory and politic. But what do we mean when we theorize upon or lobby for maternal empowerment? It is now understood that maternal empowerment or outlaw motherhood is best understood as an oppositional stance that seeks to counter and correct the many ways that patriarchal motherhood causes mothering to be limiting or oppressive to women. Elsewhere I have argued that contemporary Western patriarchal motherhood may be characterized by eight rules: 1) children can only be properly cared for by the biological mother; 2) this mothering must be provided 24/7; 3) the mother must always put children's needs before her own; 4) mothers must turn to the experts for instruction; 5) the mother must be fully satisfied, fulfilled, completed and composed in motherhood; 6) mothers must lavish excessive amounts of time, energy and money in the rearing of their children; 7) the mother has full responsibility but no power from which to mother; 8) motherwork, childrearing specifically, is regarded as a personal, private undertaking with no political import (O'Reilly 2004a). Patriarchal motherhood causes motherwork to be oppressive to women because it necessitates the repression or denial of the mother's own selfhood, and it assigns mothers all the responsibility for mothering but gives them no real power from which to mother. Such "powerless responsibility," to use Rich's term, denies a mother the authority and agency to determine her own experiences of mothering. As well, it results in most women mothering alone in the isolation of their home, feeling overwhelmed and exhausted. Moreover, since no mother can achieve idealized motherhood, women bring self-recrimination, anxiety, doubt, and guilt into their lived experiences of mothering. In turn, mothers who do not seek to achieve idealized motherhood, either by choice or circumstance, are labeled 'unfit' mothers who will find themselves and their mothering under public scrutiny and surveillance. Finally, in defining mothering as private and non-political work, patriarchal motherhood restricts the way mothers can and do affect social change through feminist child rearing and maternal activism.

Maternal empowerment, whether it be termed feminist (Gordon; Glickman; Green 2004; O'Reilly 2007), outlaw (O'Reilly 2006a, 2006b; Rich), radical (Copper), rebellious (Douglas and Michaels), or hip (Gore and Lavender), seeks to confer to mothers the agency, authority, authenticity, and autonomy denied to them in patriarchal motherhood (O'Reilly, 2004a, 2004b, 2006a, 2006b, 2007, 2008). As Fiona Joy Green has observed (2004, 2006), empowered or outlaw mothers,

> seek to live Rich's emancipatory vision of motherhood and, driven by their feminist consciousness, their intense love for their children and the need to be true to themselves, their families, and their parenting, [these] feminist mothers choose to parent in a way that challenges the status quo. (2004: 130)

Erika Horwitz's study (2003) on empowered mothering reveals that the practice of outlaw motherhood may be characterized by seven themes: The importance of mothers meeting their own needs; Being a Mother does not fulfill all of a woman's needs; Involving others in their children's upbringing; Actively questioning the expectations that are placed on mothers by society; Challenging mainstream parenting practices; Not believing that mothers are solely responsible for how children turn out; and Challenging the idea that the only emotion mothers ever feel toward their children is love. Central to each theme and act of maternal empowerment is a redefinition of motherhood from a feminist-maternal perspective. "Good" mothers in patriarchal motherhood, for example, are defined as white, middle class, married, stay-at-home moms, while "good" mothers from a politic of maternal empowerment are drawn from all maternal identities and include lesbian, non-custodial, poor, single, older, and "working" mothers. Likewise, patriarchal motherhood limits family to a patriarchal nuclear structure wherein the parents are married and are the biological parents of the children, the mother is the nurturer and the father is the provider; conversely, the maternal empowerment perspective embraces a variety of family structures including single, blended, step, matrifocal, same-sex, and so forth.

Further, as patriarchal motherhood characterizes childrearing as a private, non-political undertaking, maternal empowerment foregrounds the political-social dimension of motherwork; specifically, it challenges traditional practices of gender socialization and performs anti-sexist childrearing practices so as to raise empowered daughters and empathetic sons. Finally, for many mothers, maternal empowerment becomes expressed as maternal activism. Mothers, by way of maternal activism, use their position as mothers to lobby for social and political change. Whether it is in the home or in the world at large, or whether it is expressed as anti-sexist childrearing or maternal activism, motherwork is redefined as a social and political act through which social change is made possible from this perspective. Returning to Rich's quote from the beginning of this chapter, simply put, the aim of maternal empowerment is to reclaim the power denied to mothers in patriarchal motherhood.

GENDER ESSENTIALISM AND THE "NEW MOMISM" OF THE 21ST CENTURY

In both motherhood theory and activism the costs of patriarchal motherhood have been well examined and critiqued. However, I would argue that this feminist criticism has been largely limited to the symptomatic manifestations of patriarchal motherhood, failing to examine their root cause: the gender essentialism of modern motherhood. Contemporary Western patriarchal motherhood, though nuanced in its manifestations, is ideologically quite homogeneous and unambiguous; it is defined by a rigid and uniform philosophy of gender essentialism and the resulting binary opposition of the public and private sphere. A central, if not defining, event in the rise of Western Modernity was the emergence of the public/private dichotomy in which the work of production was assigned to the public sphere and the work of reproduction to the private sphere. This dichotomy was, of course, gender coded: a man belonged in the public realm and was to embody the valued masculine traits of the emergent industrial capitalist society, while a woman was to remain in the home domain and serve as the ornamental wife or, in the lexicon of the day, "The Angel in the House." Significantly, this gender polarity resulted in the emergence or, more accurately, the invention of full time motherhood. While this notion of full-time motherhood was largely symbolic—and restricted to middle class mothers—these mothers acquired moral superiority and cultural prestige (though of course not real societal power or respect) in and through their identity as Mother. This gendered schism converged to construct mothering as *essentially* and naturally the identity and purpose of women, and likewise the family as fundamentally a private unit separate and distinct from the larger public, political, social world. Douglas and Michaels have termed the twenty-first-century manifestation of this ideology the "New Momism" which, as they explain, begins with:

> [T]he insistence that no woman is truly complete or fulfilled unless she has kids, that women remain the best primary caretakers of children, and that to be a remotely decent mother, a woman has to devote her entire physical, psychological, emotional, intellec-

> tual being, 24/7, to her children. The new momism is a highly romanticized view of motherhood in which the standards for success are impossible to meet. (4)

However, as Douglas and Michaels go on to explain, "The new momism involves more than just impossible ideals about women's childrearing; it redefines all women, first and foremost, through their relationships to children. Thus, being a citizen, a worker, a governor [and so forth] are supposed to take a backseat to motherhood" (22). "The new momism," Douglas and Michaels continue, "insists that if you want to do anything else, you'd better first prove that you're a doting, totally involved mother before proceeding. The only recourse for women who want careers, or to do anything else besides stay at home with the kids all day, is to prove they can 'do it all'" (22). This type of gender essentialism, whether its conveyed as the "Angel in the House" ideology of the nineteenth century or this century's "New Momism," necessarily naturalizes mothering as "a woman's calling;" this calling is expected to be performed by the biological mother who must be a wife and nurturer in a heterosexual family wherein the father is the provider, and thus is not expected to engage in "mothering."

What is perhaps most distributing about this naturalization of motherhood is the degree to which such is found in purportedly feminist writing. I recently undertook a study of the contemporary motherhood memoir only to find that most of this literature, while highly critical of patriarchal motherhood, was complicit in its gender essentialism and naturalization of motherhood through its allegiance to the New Momism ideology. As I have explored elsewhere, the motherhood memoir reinscribes or, more accurately, naturalizes and normalizes the very patriarchal conditions of motherhood that feminists, including the motherhood memoir writers themselves, seek to dismantle (O'Reilly 2009). At the turn of the last century maternal feminists relied upon the belief in innate gender difference, particularly the alleged moral superiority of mothers, to lobby for and make legitimate their claims for female suffrage. Similarly, be it consciously or otherwise, motherhood memoir writers today draw upon the ethos of the "new momism" to value and validate a public literature on motherhood; in particular, the assumption that children are the all-consuming focus and purpose of a mother's life. This use of maternal feminism and the "new momism" did make significant gender change possible: female suffrage in the last century and a de-privatization of motherhood in this century. However, they also serve to reify gender difference and hence reinforce traditional and patriarchal notions of womanhood and motherhood, most notably, the private/public divide and the gender dichotomy between the feminine/nurturer and the masculine/producer. In the remaining pages I will cite some examples of this genre's compliance and complicity with the gender essentialism found in the "New Momism." Through this, I will illuminate the larger argument of this chapter; namely, that meaningful change only becomes possible when a theory and politic of and for maternal empowerment confronts and counters the gender essentialism of patriarchal motherhood and the feminist writing that continues to conform to it.

While memoir authors do critique the *consequences* of this patriarchal motherhood (i.e., women do all the work of mothering with little or no support), they do not challenge the *assumptions* themselves. Thus, their challenge remains at the level of criticism and not change; this is most evident in the authors' views on childcare. Of the memoirs I have read thus far, none of the authors consider childcare as a possible option for allowing women to develop a selfhood outside of motherhood. For some the reason is financial, though for most it is because they subscribe to the new momism belief in the necessity of full-time, natural, and attachment mothering. They believe that they must be at home 24/7 for the benefit of the child for at least the first three to five years, and to do otherwise would be unwise, if not unnatural, to both child and mother. Indeed, as Ivana Brown notes in her research paper: "While some authors challenge parts of the 'natural mother' myth, all of them are the primary caregivers of their children" (56). She goes on to explain: "Mothers are the main caretakers of the children and fathers are more or less absent, appearing at the time of birth and then having a role in the background in financially supporting the family and helping the mother with certain tasks and responsibilities. The absence of fathers from the daily parenting tasks remains mostly unexplained" (56). Furthermore, as Brown notes, "this approach contributes to the categorical differentiation between men and women [in the motherhood memoir]" (45).

For me the most worrisome part of the new momism, particularly as it is manifested in the motherhood memoir, is that being a stay-at-home mother is constructed as the mother's choice. Again, to return to Douglas and Michaels:

> The mythology of the new momism now insinuates that, when all is said and done, the enlightened mother chooses to stay at home with the kids. Back in the 1950s mothers stayed home because they had no choice. Today having been to the office, having tried a career, women supposedly have seen the inside of the male working world and found it be the inferior choice to staying home, especially when her kids' future is at stake. It's not that mothers can't hack it (1950s thinking). It's that progressive mothers refuse to hack it. The June Cleaver model, if taken as a *choice*, as opposed to a requirement, is the truly modern fulfilling forward-thinking version of motherhood. (23)

While many of the authors expose the concept of choice for what it is—a fiction and a fallacy—they nonetheless see their full-time mothering as inevitable and necessary. However, other memoir writers do deflect and disguise the very real structural and familial inequities mothers face by way of a narrative of choice. For example, a writer in the collection *Breeder* who practices attachment parenting as a college student explains why she decided to quit school when pregnant with her second child: "I was tired every day, tired all over, and the prospect of spending the next several months so impossibly tired was too much for me" (qtd. in Gore and Lavender 83). As she goes on to explain, "Feeling that I faced a *choice* between my future and my present, I withdrew from my classes" (qtd. in Gore and Lavender 84, emphasis added). She later writes, "My education has not been put on hold; on the contrary, I am a full-time student in an accelerated toddler studies program. My three-year-old is experimenting with wet-on-wet watercolours, and the baby will be walking soon. Now that's what I call progress" (qtd. in Gore and Lavender 85).

As someone who gave birth to three children in five years while an undergrad and later a grad student, I can certainly understand being "impossibly tired," but the reasons for such tiredness are as much the result of her adherence to the new momism discourse, which requires her to be the main caretaker of the children 24/7 via attachment parenting, as they are of the demands of academia. Had she used some childcare, insisted upon shared parenting (her partner is mentioned only once), and renounced or reduced her 'natural' and intensive mothering practices, she would have had, in all likelihood, the time and energy to combine motherhood with her studies (this is not to minimize the real need for structural change in education/workplace to enable women to combine work with motherhood). But because of her adherence to the new momism philosophy of mothering, she simply cannot see these as possibilities, and thus must accept societal and familial gender inequities as both inevitable and natural. More troublesome is that all of this is narrated and justified in the language of choice and, even more problematically, as a feminist choice, i.e. when she proclaims, "now that's progress." Most motherhood memoirs, because of their identification with the new momism and its gender essentialism, cannot discern or critique the root causes of mothers' oppression, thus the genre remains one of compliance and not change.

My observations on the motherhood memoir are echoed in the feminist sociology on the family and in everyday conversations with women; simply put, mothers are still doing the bulk of domestic labour and childcare in homes around the world. The necessary work of home and community maintenance is performed by mothers whether they work part- or full-time. Today, however, with the majority of mothers in the paid labour force, we do not have full-time homemakers to do the necessary work of social reproduction; hence the family and work conflict experienced by mothers but not fathers. Although this gender inequity is well documented in feminist scholarship and well experienced in women's own lives, it is strangely absent in much of the activism and thinking on maternal empowerment, and in family and work balance discussions. In order to better illustrate this, I now turn to the following two stories.

In 2005, I attended the Canadian Labour Congress "Balancing Work and Family" Conference as a delegate from my Faculty Union. What struck me first was the "cognitive dissonance" between the topic being discussed and those discussing it. The vast majority of the attendees—it appeared well over 90 percent—were women and yet the terms used were family and parents.[1] From the talks, workshops, and discussions at the conference, the solutions offered for work and family balance seemed to be twofold: a national childcare program and reduced work hours (with a particular emphasis on eliminating overtime). While I would agree that both would go a long way to enable families to do the essential work of social reproduction (from dentist appointments to children's field trips), startlingly absent from the discussion was the recognition that it is mothers who still do the majority of the second shift labour, and that this is unjust, and must be challenged and changed. It is not enough to ask the government for a national childcare program and our employers for reduced work hours, if our partners are not doing their fair share. And while the women certainly complained about this during coffees breaks, not once was it brought up as an official topic of discussion in this two day conference on family and work balance.

More recently, I attended a large motherhood conference that featured talks by the prominent leaders of the North American Motherhood Movement. This conference was attended by close to two hundred mothers who lead or attended mother empowerment groups in the United States. At the close of the conference, a leader from the organization asked the mothers to email pictures of their home when they returned from the conferences to show its complete disarray—laundry undone, kids not bathed, empty pizza boxes about, and a living room littered with children's toys—as a result of their two-day absence. The women laughed uproariously and were soon bragging about and betting upon whose home would be found in the most chaos. No one in my hearing range was asking what should have been obvious questions, particularly at a conference on maternal empowerment: why should the mothers come home and find their house in such a state after a two-day conference? Should fathers not be expected and required to competently run a household in their absence? And why was their "incompetence" or "failure" to do such considered funny? Throughout the weekend, these same women spoke eloquently, passionately, and insightfully on how to empower mothers through support groups, advocacy, and activism and yet, when it came to their own partners they expected and demanded so very little.

I have shared the latter story with mothers and scholars of motherhood and while they were saddened by it, they were not shocked: "after all, what do you expect?" I have spoken extensively on how mothers, even with the involved partners, are the ones who do the maternal thinking: the remembering, worrying, planning, anticipating, orchestrating, arranging, and co-ordinating of and for the household. It is mothers who remember to buy the milk, plan the birthday party, and worry that the daughter's recent loss of appetite may be indicative of anorexia. Although the father may sign the field trip permission form or buy the diapers, in most households it is the mother who reminds him to do so. Delegation does not make equality. However, as this gender inequity may be commonplace, what must be remembered and emphasized, particularly in discussions on maternal empowerment, is that it is neither natural nor inevitable.

WHERE DO GO FROM HERE? A FEMINIST ETHIC OF CARE PARADIGM AND DEGENDERING REPRODUCTIVE LABOUR

In my view, the absence of a sustained analysis on gender inequity in our homes and the ideology of gender essentialism that supports and legitimizes it is the "Achilles' Heel" of the contemporary maternal empowerment movement. While family-friendly government policies and workplace practices are certainly desired and needed, they will only serve to empower mothers if their progress is matched in the private sphere. As the results from my own large qualitative study on mother academics suggest, it seems that gender equity in the home is more often a determinant of employment success than family friendly policies in the workplace. When asked what enabled them to achieve success in academia, the overwhelming majority of respondents identified the support of their partners, not workplace policies: "I couldn't have done it without him" (O'Brien Hallstein and O'Reilly). Or as historian Jodi Vandenberg-Davis remarked: "Women who have reached full professor have shared a common characteristic: husbands who stay at home for part of the child-rearing years, work part time, or at the very least are not in jobs that require a great deal of travel." "These familial adaptations" she continues, "may prove to be more important than the rather minimal institutional adaptations."

Gender essentialism must be recognized as that which underpins modern motherhood and gives rise to its many oppressive practices. But what does all of this mean for a theory and politic of maternal empowerment or outlaw motherhood? The challenge, as I see it, is to determine how best to affirm the necessary work of social reproduction; it must be acknowledged that it is mothers who do this work, often to their own detriment, while insisting that culture, and that includes fathers, must likewise assume responsibility for motherwork and take on its tasks in both thought (i.e., the maternal thinking described above) and action. What is needed, in other words, is a re-positioning of the word "mother" from a noun to a verb so that the work of mothering is rendered separate from the identity of mother, and so that care is divested of biology. In the context of the scholarship and activism on maternal empowerment, such requires that we move from a politic of maternalism to that which Judith Stadtman Tucker perceptively defines as a "feminist ethic of care" framework:

> As with maternalism, feminist care ethic designates caring for others as an essential social function. But rather than valorizing maternal sensitivity and altruism as a vital resource, feminist care ethic aims to liberate caregiving from its peripheral status and reposition it as a primary human activity. (212)

She goes on to explain that, "For proponents of the contemporary mothers' movement, grounding the agenda in an ethic of care opens up the possibility of developing a *gender neutral* approach to social policy and an opportunity to expand the language of care as a public good beyond the maternalist paradigm" (212, emphasis added).

The feminist ethic of care perspective redefines "motherhood issues"—maternity leave, childcare, flextime, workplace discrimination against mothers, and the societal devaluation of carework, to name but a few—as parental and family concerns. In so doing, the "feminist ethic of care" paradigm displaces and dislodges the gender essentialist framework that constructs and constitutes contemporary western motherhood and gives rise to its many oppressive practices. Perhaps this reframing will not automatically result in gender equity in our homes; however, it does make such more probable and achievable. A gender neutral approach makes progressive social policy—from parental leave to flextime—available to fathers, which allows for their active participation in the social reproduction of households. In addition, and perhaps more importantly, it makes carework for men and masculinity normative. In other words, if carework is degendered and if such is reinforced by workplace and governmental policy, the results will be twofold: more men will participate in reproductive labor and this work will no longer be viewed or defined as women's work.

CONCLUSION: OUTLAW(ING) MOTHERHOOD

While the disempowerment of patriarchal motherhood is well known, what is less understood, in my view, is why this institution gives rise to the oppressive practices that it does. Moreover, as I have argued in this chapter, the feminist criticism of patriarchal motherhood has largely been limited to the symptomatic manifestations of patriarchal motherhood, leaving their root cause unexamined, which I contend is the gender essentialism of modern motherhood. The challenge for theorists of and activists for maternal empowerment is to affirm the necessary work of social reproduction, and to acknowledge that it is mothers who do this work (often to their own detriment), while at the same time insisting that culture (which includes fathers) must likewise assume responsibility for reproductive labour.

I have suggested that in order to effectively destabilize patriarchal motherhood we must disrupt and dislodge the gender essentialism that grounds and structures it. Such can be achieved by re-envisioning and repositioning "mother" from a noun to a verb and by creating, in policy, practice and perception, a "feminist ethic of care" paradigm. Paradoxically, as the title of this chapter suggests, we must *outlaw* motherhood to make possible *outlaw motherhood.* Only then will we achieve a truly transformative theory and politic of maternal empowerment for the twenty-first century.

This chapter is a revised version of my chapter of the same name that appeared in 21st Century Motherhood: Experience, Identity, Policy, Agency, *Ed. Andrea O'Reilly, New York: University of Columbia Press, 2010.*

[1]Most anthologies in Motherhood Studies are thematic in focus or discipline specific. Notable exceptions include: Abbey and O'Reilly; O'Barr, Pope and Wyer; Glenn, Chang, and Forcey. These collections, however, are now ten to twenty years old. In 2006, the collection *Motherhood in the Twenty-First Century,* edited by Alcira Mariam Alizade, was published. However, this collection as a title in the "Psychoanalysis and Women series" examines twenty-first century motherhood issues solely from a psychoanalytic perspective.

WORKS CITED

Abbey, Sharon and Andrea O'Reilly. *Redefining Motherhood: Changing*

Identities and Patterns. Toronto: Second Story Press, 1998. Print.

Alizade, Alcira Mariam, ed. *Motherhood in the Twenty-First Century*. New York: Karnac Books, 2006. Print.

Brown, Ivana. "Mommy Memoirs: Feminism, Gender and Motherhood in Popular Literature." *Journal of the Association for Research on Mothering* 8 (1&2) (Winter/Summer 2006): 200-212. Print.

Copper, Baba. "The Radical Potential in Lesbian Mothering of Daughters." *Politics of the Heart: A Lesbian Parenting Anthology*. Eds. Sandra Pollack and Jeanne Vaughn, Ithaca, NY: Firebrand Books, 1987. Print.

Douglas, Susan J. and Meredith Michaels. *The Mommy Myth: The Idealization of Motherhood and How it Has Undermined Women*. New York: New York: Free Press, 2004. Print.

Glenn, Evelyn Nakano, Grace Chang, and Linda Rennie Forcey. *Mothering: Ideology, Experience, and Agency*. New York: Routledge, 1994. Print.

Glickman, Rose L. *Daughters of Feminists: Young Women with Feminist Mothers Talk About Their Lives*. New York: St. Martin's Press, 1993. Print.

Gordon, Tuula. *Feminist Mothers*. New York: New York University Press, 1990. Print.

Gore, Ariel and Bee Lavender. *Breeder: Real Life Stories from the New Generation of Mo*thers. Seattle Washington: Seal Press, 2001. Print.

Green, Fiona. "Feminist Mothers: Successfully Negotiating the Tensions Between Motherhood and Mothering." *Mother Outlaws: Theories and Practices of Empowered Mothering*. Ed. Andrea O'Reilly. Toronto: Women's Press, 2004. 31-42. Print.

Green, Fiona J. "Developing a Feminist Motherline: Reflections on a Decade of Feminist Parenting." *Journal of the Association for Research on Mothering* 8 (1&2) (Winter/Summer 2006): 7-20. Print.

Horwitz, Erika. *Mothers' Resistance to the Western Dominant Discourse on Mothering*. Unpublished dissertation, Simon Fraser University, British Columbia, 2003. Print.

Horwitz, Erika. "Resistance as a Site of Empowerment: The Journey Away From Maternal Sacrifice." *Mother Outlaws: Theories and Practices of Empowered Mothering*. Ed. Andrea O'Reilly. Toronto: Women's Press, 2004. 43-58. Print.

O'Barr, Jean, Deborah Pope and Mary Wyer. *Ties That Bind: Essays on Mothering and Patriarchy*. Chicago: University of Chicago Press, 1990. Print.

O'Brien Hallstein, Lynn and Andrea O'Reilly. *Academic Motherhood In a Post-Second Wave Context: Challenges, Strategies and Possibilities.* Bradford, Ontario: Demeter Press, 2012. Print.

O'Reilly, Andrea, ed. *Mother Matters: Motherhood as Discourse and Practice.* Toronto: ARM Press, 2004a. Print.

O'Reilly, Andrea. *Toni Morrison and Motherhood: A Politics of the Heart.* Albany: SUNY Press, 2004b. Print.

O'Reilly, Andrea. "Between the Baby and the Bathwater: Some Thoughts on a Mother Centered Theory and Practice of Feminist Mothering." *Journal of the Association for Research on Mothering* 8 (1&2) (Winter/Summer 2006a): 323-330. Print.

O'Reilly, Andrea. *Rocking the Cradle: Thoughts on Motherhood, Feminism, and the Possibility of Empowered Mothering.* Toronto: Demeter Press, 2006b. Print.

O'Reilly, Andrea, ed. *Maternal Theory: Essential Readings.* Toronto: Demeter Press, 2007. Print.

O'Reilly, Andrea. *Feminist Mothering.* Albany: SUNY Press, 2008. Print.

Rich, Adrienne. *Of Woman Born: Motherhood as Experience and Institution.* 1976. New York: W.W. Norton, 1986. Print.

Stadtman Tucker, Judith. "Rocking the Boat: Feminism and the Ideological Grounding for the Twenty-First Century Mothers' Movement." *Feminist Mothering.* Ed. Andrea O'Reilly. Albany, New York: SUNY Press, 2008. 205-219. Print.

Vandenberg-Davis, Jodi. Personal communication.

Matroreform

Reforming Mothering / Reforming Motherhood

GINA WONG

MATROREFORM (Wong-Wylie 2006, 2010; Wong 2012) is a transformative maternal practice and is "an act, desire, and process of claiming motherhood power ... a progressive movement to mothering that attempts to institute new mothering rules and practices apart from one's motherline" (Wong-Wylie 2006: 135). In original writings, I describe matroreform as a psychological, spiritual, and emotional reformation of mothering from within that includes removal and elimination of obstacles to self-determination and self-agency as a mother and woman. This chapter explores the transformative and revolutionary process of matroreform, which is the process by which mothers come into their own way of mothering apart from the way she was mothered and apart from the conventional socio-cultural constraints of motherhood. Matroreform is an act of resistance and empowerment on a personal level to refuse replication of mothering oppression. It also captures the process to collective resistance against the subjugation of mothers in the broader social sphere.

In outlining what mother's need and maternal empowerment for the twenty-first century, this chapter focuses on the centrality of matroreform—a feminist process and deliberate enactment to engender new motherworlds. In doing so, further delineating matroreform is necessary to understand the full contours of this praxis and engender mothers to have the language to name an empowering process to re-authoring mothering and motherhood.

Consider the following two fictitious vignettes:

Rosetta grew up in a household where children were seen but not heard. Her mother and father were hardworking people and well respected in their community. They were very strict and critical with the kids and Rosetta always felt like she was doing something wrong. Her mother, in particular, criticized her all the time and compared her to her older sister who always seemed to get better grades and was more naturally athletic and fit than Rosetta. Rosetta's grandmother passed away when Rosetta's mother was three years old, so her mother was raised by her father who was a very quiet and distant man. Rosetta's mother, as a result, was not a warm person. She never hugged or kissed her children and did not say encouraging words because she felt it would be construed as bragging or giving false confidence to the children and they wouldn't work hard anymore. Rosetta always wanted her mother to be proud of her but no matter what she did she always received criticism and harshness. As she grew up the thought of having children of her own did not appeal to her. When she became pregnant unexpectedly at 21 years of age, she decided to have the baby. Rosetta reflected on the kind of mother she wanted to be. She knew at a deep level that she wanted to be a different mother than the mother she had. Rosetta made sure that she praised her child and touched and hugged him often because she knew firsthand the fragility of children's self-esteem. Because she felt such pain about her own difficult upbringing she vowed to herself that she would be the kind of mother that let her child make mistakes and that he know that he was loved and accepted no matter what, which was in direct contrast to her own experience of being mothered.

Nileen grew up in a family where her mother was the one who did all the cooking and cleaning. She was the one who was responsible, or so it seemed, to bear the responsibility of the entire family on her shoulders. Nileen saw the way in which her mother worked hard in her job as a nurse and then hard at home and was always tired and underappreciated. Nileen decided emphatically when she was 16 years old that she did not want to have children. She fought constantly with her mother and looked down on her because her mother could never understand how she felt. She hated how her mother never stood up to anyone and did everything for everyone else. Nileen vowed to never be like her. She wanted to travel and teach abroad and not be tied down to all the things her mother and other women in society seemed to be hinged to. Nileen, over the years stood strong in this position and wore it proudly. She often declared "I am not going to have children" to show what a strong, independent, feminist woman she was. In particular, she felt it let men know that she wasn't that kind of capitulating woman. Years later in her mid-twenties, Nileen met Lucas and after cohabitating for a few years, Nileen began to think about becoming a mother. And when they decided to have children, she was very clear with Lucas that she did not want to become a domestic housewife she saw her mother trapped as. Nileen and Lucas travelled abroad with their children. Lucas was heavily involved in the children's lives and in the household chores as much as Nileen. Although not perfect, Nileen had intentionally become a different mother than her own mother.

The fictitious stories of Rosetta and Nileen represent matroreform as these mothers' change mothering practices apart from their motherliness. These accounts of mothering experiences represent both Nileen and Rosetta experiencing a 'phobia' against mothering. From the original conception, matroreform was derived from the term *matrophobia* first introduced by poet Lynn Sukenick. The concept was more fully developed by Adrienne Rich (1976), who described how matrophobia occurs when girls and women eclipse any part of themselves that wants to become mothers. This is evoked out of fear and is described as a desire to purge themselves of their mothers' bondage, to become individuated and free from expectations of self-sacrifice and pressures to be a perfect domestic housewife (Wong-Wylie 2010), which is exemplified in Nileen's vignette.

Nileen's mother participated in paid work outside the home and was also responsible for most of the domestic chores in the household. Whether a mother has paid works outside of the home or not, mothers are often responsible for the lion's share of domestic labor. Renowned French feminist and author Elizabeth Badinter articulates the continued constraints of marriage and motherhood in her best-selling and controversial book entitled *The Conflict: How Modern Motherhood Undermines the Status of Women*. She writes: "...married life has always come at a social and cultural cost to women, not only in terms of the unequal division of household work and child rearing, but also in its detrimental effect on their career and salary. Today, it is not so much marriage itself that takes its toll on women (marriage no longer being a necessity), but sharing a household and especially after the birth of a child. Sharing a household, which is now widespread, has not brought an end to domestic inequality, even if surveys show that it is more favorable to women than marriage ... [i]t is the arrival of a child that dramatically increases the amount of time women spend on domestic chores...." (16)

Ever present today as it was when Adrienne Rich described the oppressive constraints of motherhood, Badinter expresses the continued toll on women. Rich described: Matrophobia is the fear not of one's mother or of motherhood but of *becoming one's mother*.

> Easier by far to hate and reject a mother outright (as Nileen does) than to see beyond her to the forces acting upon her. But where a mother is hated to the point of matrophobia there may also be a deep underlying pull toward her, a dread that if one relaxes one's guard one will identify with her completely. (193)

This fear of becoming one's mother and experiencing the oppressive bonds of conventional motherhood in matrophobia pushes daughters to deny and denigrate any part of themselves that are similar to those of their mothers in any way. The daughter may enact life choices (like Nileen to be very different than her mother) and create standards of living that are in contrast to what her mother represented in an effort to perform "radical surgery" as Rich depicted (194). There exists a push and pull to her mother nevertheless. In much the same way, a woman in a tenuous and dying marriage may avoid a newly separated or divorced woman, the fear of assimilation and over-identification with that which is most dreaded and feared when one is at the precipice—in a paradoxical push and pull—is what Rich attempts to capture in the concept of matrophobia.

Rich believed that matrophobia is a result of a daughterhood fraught with witnessing the self-sacrificing, capitulating, and self-denial of mother as she attempts to live out the good, sacrificial mother expectations (as with Nileen). These daughters experiencing matrophobia attempt to extricate themselves from anything remotely close to their mother, to do everything possible to avoid the same trap. From a feminist analysis, daughters deconstructing (consciously or subconsciously) their mothers' oppression and the trap of the good and sacrificial mother ideologies, exemplifies empowerment and agency. Nevertheless, the original concept of matrophobia is not derived from feminist approaches, but about the experience of daughters having unrealistic and unfounded fears and thus desiring to project themselves out of the motherline (Wong-Wylie 2010).

When I first introduced the original concept of matrophobia and translated it to matroreform (Wong-Wylie 2006) I used reflective understandings and narrative recounts of journal entries to my daughters. I included seven photographic images to describe my relationship with my mother, layered with first generation Canadian born-Chinese cultural differences between myself and her. I connected reflections and understandings of my relationship as a daughter to my mother and shared how I actively worked to forge a different kind of bond with my two daughters (see also Wong-Wylie 2012). By engaging in this process, I deployed and enacted the active practice of matroreform.

I argue that Rich's conceptualization of matro*phobia* inadequately and inaccurately captures the full experience behind the fear of becoming one's mother. I criticize Rich's use of the term *phobia*, which is defined as an intense and unrealistic fear. Instead, I advance that the concept of phobia fails to capture the real and common experience of feminist girls, women, and mothers and their refusal "to reproduce or [remain] trapped in the oppressive bonds of conventional motherhood" (Wong-Wylie 2006: 142).

Such a process, I argue, is necessary and certainly not borne out of unrealistic fears. In the place of matrophobia, I proposed instead *matroreform*—as "reform" aptly represents an essential feminist model of practice and an empowering process toward claiming motherhood power. More specifically, I translate the experience into one that has the potential to be a transformative maternal practice. In this sense, "matroreform is an act, desire, and process of claiming motherhood power" (2006: 134).

Legitimizing matroreform, Canadian feminist maternal scholar Fiona Joy Green identifies it as a central process in her longitudinal and intergenerational study of feminist motherlines. Through this research and her article, "Matroreform: Feminist Mothers and Their Daughters Creating Feminist Motherlines," and book, *Practicing Feminist Mothering*, Green confirms matroreform as a process that "is not only reforming and reaffirming (but also) a feminist act of voicing up and out of invisibility and silence" (qtd. in Wong-Wylie 2006: 136). Green illustrates how a small group of feminist mothers and their daughters dismantle the patriarchal script and reform their own stories of motherhood and daughterhood. She describes how feminist daughters with feminist mothers can perpetuate an enduring feminist motherline and argues that matroreform is central to this process.

MOTHERHOOD / MOTHERING

Noted by Andrea O'Reilly is the seminal and classic work by Adrienne Rich entitled *Of Woman Born: Motherhood as Experience and Institution* (1976,

Gina Wong

1986). Rich is a forerunner in revealing that maternal experiences and motherhood are chiefly defined through male-centered institutions. Indeed, Adrienne Rich, Sara Ruddick, and Andrea O'Reilly (2006) distinguish between motherhood and the experience of mothering, thereby making it somewhat easier for mothers to thrive amid oppressive forces. They separate *motherhood* (the male-centered institution and ideology, which are oppressive) from *mothering* (the act of mothering and motherwork that has the potential to be empowering).

Extant literature on matroreform has focused primarily on the feminist revolutionary practice of acting up and out of the oppressive constraints of the institution of motherhood. My original writing (Wong-Wylie 2006) was based on delineating the individual and personal process of changing mothering practices from one's own experience of being mothered. Taking this distinction of mothering and motherhood, the concept of matroreform coincides. In my own experience and progression of understanding through nascent research investigations, matroreform is two-pronged. That is, matroreform on the level of "motherhood" is as I have more widely conceptualized in the literature as a feminist acting up and out of the conventional constraints of "motherhood" as in line with Ruddick, Rich, and O'Reilly's distinction of the term from "mothering." Matroreform represents both intentionally standing up to mother*hood* oppression and at the same time, or distinctly, can represent the reforming of mother*ing* at an interpersonal level. Consistent with this perspective, matroreform involves psychological, spiritual, and emotional reformation of mothering from within that includes removal and elimination of obstacles to self-determination and self-agency as a mother and woman. In this way, constraints and limitations within the individual relationship of mother to daughter is reformed in the daughter's own active practice of mother*ing*. This clear distinction renders "reforming mothering" and "reforming motherhood" as relevant processes in the journey in matroreform.

It is important to validate that matroreform is a process for mothers who do not identify as feminist nor resonate with the desire to break free from the conventional bonds of motherhood oppression. Recognizing that matroreform may not always be evoked nor prompted from a deliberate feminist consciousness is an important distinction. In this way, matroreform involves an interpersonal process whereby mothers choose to revise mothering because of her own experiences of being mothered in a way that was psychologically, spiritually, or emotionally damaging. These women say, "I don't want to mother the way my mother mothered me" and not for reasons of feminist uprising, but from an intra-psychic recognition that the way that they were brought up was damaging and/or difficult psychologically, or perhaps abusive. Rather than repeating that pattern of maltreatment and/or dysfunction intergenerationally, she intentionally breaks that cycle in the motherline. As such, she is reforming mothering.

In line with the social ecology of matroreform (see Wong 2012), the level of psychological and spiritual reformation resides in the microsphere level of matroreform where interpersonal and intrapsychic experience of being mothered and the desire to change, revolutionize, and revise the mothering legacy, script, motherline can be realized. Matroreform represents the process for a mother who desires to transform mothering at the intra-psychic and emotional level. There are many women who do not declare or identify themselves as feminist and who want to change mothering from her experience of being mothered. There are also feminist mothers who desire to refuse replication of the motherhood oppression.

The concept, when I first introduced it, was anchored in my own experience of psychological oppression growing up with my mother. Where positive emotionality, fostering self-esteem, confidence, love, and care were generally lacking and absent in the mothering I experienced, I had a desire to revolt against my mother's practices of non-nurturing mothering—replete from emotional caring and encouragement. Reflecting back, my experiences are reflective of Rosetta's vignette. However, as my feminist consciousness grew, my process in matroreform was also informed and prompted by a feminist uprising and my deep desire for reformation of mothering in recognizing the mother's panopticon (see below), which resonates with Nileen's vignette.

MOTHER'S PANOPTICON

In writing about the mother's panopticon (see Wong 2012), matroreform is required in order to be free of this imprisonment. The panopticon (Foucault 1979, 1989) is a figurative embodiment of the imprisonment that keeps mothers under malevolent, omnipresent surveillance. This metaphor captures that an observer (opticon) sees all (pan) prisoners without prisoners knowing whether and when they are being watched. Imprisonment in the mother's panopticon is a result of oppressive ideologies and discourses that regulate mothers' lives (e.g., the *good mother* ideology; *intensive* and *sacrificial mothering* expectations). Likewise, mothers' desire to reform the intra-psychic and interpersonal experience of how she was mothered to foster optimal growth in her children is also a way to counter the forces within the panopticon.

Feminist Elizabeth Badinter's book entitled *The Conflict: How Modern Motherhood Undermines the Status of Women* addresses the mother's panopticon although not from this specific conceptualization. Badinter poignantly articulates what the Motherhood Initiative for Research and Community Involvement (MIRCI) and maternal scholars and activists have known—that unrealistic standards and expectations on modern mothers have increased over time and in fact set mothers further back and to an extent not seen since the 1950s. Badinter describes how attachment parenting, with the same tenets as intensive mothering, tethers mothers to the home and children; and as a result modern mothering ethos have regressed the status of women. She writes that "for a majority of women it remains difficult to reconcile increasingly burdensome maternal responsibilities with personal fulfillment" (2).

In order to release the institution of mothering from the confines of the panopticon, matricentric feminism (O'Reilly 2011) is imperative.

We urgently need a formal and specific theory and politic of feminism explicitly devoted to the emphasis on motherhood and mothering. Through matricentric feminism, matroreform can be fully activated and fully realized as an empowering process that can reform motherhood outside the prison of the mother's panopticon. That is, in order to release mothers, matricentric feminism is imperative to deconstruct ideologies and discourses. And in order to incite change and continued revolution, matroreform is essential to engender new motherworlds. Motherworlds existing outside the panopticon or with the collapse of the mother's panopticon is possible when we enact shifts to reflect on, improve upon, and reform mothering ideologies and practices whether on the personal front or on the political front. In essence, what mothers need in the twenty-first century for maternal empowerment is guidance, mentorship, and facilitation to have the courage to revolutionize mothering for herself and from the oppressive confines of the panopticon.

REFORMING MOTHERING

Reflecting on matroreform involving the process of mothers denigrating and rejecting the way that she was mothered, is problematic in that it focuses on the intra-psychic development of girls and the failure of mothers to foster positive growth. Limitation to this aspect of matroreform is that it does not take into account the other caregivers and adult influences in a child's life. Nicole Letourneau and Gerald Giesbrecht outline the developmental-inadequacy perspective that challenges the view that singularly accuses mothers for all developmental problems in children. Phyllis Chesler discusses women's inhumanity to women and how girls and women treat each other stemming from "envious mother and beautiful high-spirited daughter." It is vital to see women and mothers within the context of her culture and her own upbringing. That is, a mother may be disparaging and critical of her own daughter due to her own issues of feeling 'not good enough' perhaps based on how she was raised and also because of all the pressures that exist for mothers. Considering that "depression, anxiety, self-doubt, low esteem, as well as competition, comparisons, judgment, and regulation of other mothers as well as herself are natural reactions to imprisonment in a panopticon" (Wong 2012: 95), women struggling with empowered and engendered mothering is expected. So, without blaming mothers and intensifying mother-guilt that is already so ubiquitous in our culture, I urge the concept of matroreform and this distinction of reforming mothering to not be construed as reinforcing bad mother myths.

Expanding the concept of matroreform to include recognition of reforming mothering at both these levels (the institution of motherhood and the individual experience and practice of mothering) is an important distinction. Nevertheless, viewing matroreform singularly through this lens reifies maternalism (O'Reilly 2011) and the bad mother ideologies. It is with caution and consideration of these limitations of delineating matroreform in this way that is important to emphasize. Further research investigations are required to understand the process of matroreform, and writings must be sensitive to not depict moms as "bad mothers" and/or further advance mother-blame, which is a challenging balance to find.

In my counselling practice, I ask clients about the influences of all parental figures in her or his life and ask for one gift and one hurt to be named from each parental figure. In this way, positive and negative aspects are highlighted and the culpability of mothers is not a focus. When one or more parental figure influences is determined to have been thwarting, I explore the upbringing and context of life environment and love and support in that figure's life to understand more holistically what impacts that individual's way of being and parenting scripts. The sensitivity when using the concept of matroreform to underscore mother's uprising and revolt against her own mother's practices of mothering is essential. That is to say, this concept is not to be employed as a starting point of conceptions of mothering—to suggest that all mothers want to change mothering because her own mother was inadequate. Rather, it is a concept that captures an empowering process for those women who make an intentional and courageous choice to recreate and revise mothering.

Further research investigations are necessary to confirm these theoretical underpinnings in matroreform. A program of research is underway and at this stage involves a funded study on matroreform conducted through the auspices of Athabasca University in Alberta, Canada entitled *An Evolution of Mothering: Understanding the Experience of Matroreform.* The main impetus for this research study is to gain understanding into the process of matroreform and how it is evolving the institution of mothering. To date, matroreform has been conceptualized mainly from theoretical perspectives. While a growing body of literature is developing in the area of matroreform, conceptualizations informed by the lived experiences of mothers themselves are needed. This investigation will contribute overall to the development and understanding of matroreform and the revolution of mothering.

The purpose of the study is to explore the lived experiences of matroreform from mothers who self-identify as having made the intentional choice to mother her children in fundamentally different ways than how she was mothered. The goal of this research is to gain insight and in-depth understanding into the phenomenon and process of matroreform. Implications for further maternal scholarship in the area, for best counselling practices, and for research directions will be highlighted at the end of the study. Furthermore, mothers who identify themselves as feminists and non-feminists will be explored to further understand the underlying impetus toward matroreform.

Mary E. Bhave demonstrates through her research involving twenty-first century mothers that they shape their own narrative of motherhood in reference to their experience of being mothered. She states that, "these twenty-first century moms engage in a dynamic, intentional selection process of components to develop how they see themselves as a modern mother" (188). The current study on matroreform will shed light on *how* they do this; *why* they choose to mother differently than their own mothers; *what* components, if any, do they maintain; *what* occurs in the moment-to-moment interactions that are different from the way they were mothered; and on a larger scale, *what* affects and fosters women to engage in matroreformic change. These insights will generate greater understanding into how mothers, from micro to macrosphere, engage in an empowering process to reformulate mothering. The findings will be related to the institution of motherhood and specifically elucidate the process, development, and understanding of matroreform and shed light on and further deconstruct the mother's panopticon.

This chapter aims to further conceptualize matroreform to include an interpersonal process whereby mothers choose to revise mothering from her own experience of being mothered that may or may not be prompted by a deliberate feminist consciousness. Indeed, matroreform is a concept that requires further emphasis and research in order to fully understand how it aligns and contributes to the twenty-first century motherhood movement. It is an empowering process of maternal revolution from oppression to empowerment at deeper intra-psychic levels (mothering) and at socio-cultural (motherhood) spheres. What mother's need in the twenty-first century is the creation of new motherworlds where we are released from the mother's entrapment in the panopticon, where we are empowered to be different mothers who can resist and change patterns in our motherline, and have the courage to re-author mothering on our own terms apart from the ideologies and myths of mothers that abound in our culture.

Author's Note: Inquiries about the program of study on matroreform, please contact Gina Wong <ginaw@athabascau.ca>.

WORKS CITED

Badinter, E. *The Conflict: How Modern Motherhood Undermines the Status of Women.* Toronto: HarperCollins Publishers, 2011. Print.

Bhave, M. E. "Burning the Apron Strings: How 21st Century Women Conceptualize Their Mothering in Comparison to That of Their Own Mothers." *An Anthropology of Mothering.* Eds. M. Walks and N. McPherson. Bradford, on: Demeter Press, 2011. 83-101. Print.

Chesler, P. "Envious Mothers, Beautiful High-Spirited Daughters: The First Step Towards Women's Inhumanity to Women." *Moms Gone Mad: Motherhood and Madness, Oppression and Resistance.* Ed. G. Wong. Bradford, ON: Demeter Press, 2012. 219-224. Print.

Foucault, M. *Discipline and Punish: The Birth of the Prison.* Harmondsworth, UK: Penguin, 1979. Print.

Foucault, M. *Madness and Civilization: A History of Insanity in the Age of Reason.* New York: Vintage Books, 1989. Print.

Green, F. J. "Matroreform: Feminist Mothers and Their Daughters Creating Feminist Motherlines." *Journal of the Association for Research in Mothering* 10 (2) (2008): 11-21. Print.

Green, F. J. *Practicing Feminist Mothering.* Winnipeg, Manitoba: Arbeiter Ring, 2011. Print.

Letourneau, N. and G. Giesbrecht. "Postpartum Depression and Caregiving: Beyond the Developmental-Inadequacy Discourse." *Moms Gone Mad: Motherhood and Madness, Oppression and Resistance.* Ed. G. Wong. Bradford, ON: Demeter Press, 2012.165-185. Print.

Motherhood Initiative for Research and Community Involvement (MIRCI). Web.

O'Reilly, A. *Rocking the Cradle: Thoughts on Motherhood, Feminism and the Possibility of Empowered Mothering*. Toronto, ON: Demeter Press. 2006. Print.

O'Reilly, A., ed. *The 21st Century Motherhood Movement: Mothers Speak Out on Why We Need To Change the World and How To Do It*. Bradford, ON: Demeter Press, 2011. Print.

Rich, A. *Of Woman Born: Motherhood as Experience and Institution*. New York: W. W. Norton & Company, 1976. Print.

Ruddick, S. *Maternal Thinking: Toward a Politics of Peace*. Boston: Beacon Press, 1995.

Wong-Wylie, G. "Images and Echoes in Matroreform: A Cultural Feminist Perspective." *Journal of the Association for Research on Mothering* 8 (1,2) (2006): 35-146. Print.

Wong-Wylie, G. "Matro-phobia and Mothering." *Encyclopedia of Motherhood*. Ed. A. O'Reilly. Newbury Park, CA: Sage Publications, 2010. 722-725. Print.

Wong-Wylie, G. "Exploring Motherhood: Heard Through a Child's Lens." *Images and Echoes: Exploring Life with Photography and Writing*. Ed. R. Jevne. Edmonton, AB: Private Publications, 2012. 67-81. Print.

Wong, G. "Matroreform: Toward Collapsing the Mother's Manopticon." *Moms Gone Mad: Motherhood and Madness, Oppression and Resistance*. Ed. G. Wong. Bradford, ON: Demeter Press, 2012. 95-107. Print.

2. Empowering Mothers

Mothers and the Military

What It's Like and How It Needs to Be

PAULA J. CAPLAN

MOTHERS BEAR DIFFERENT, often more onerous or at least more complex burdens than do fathers in relation to the military. This includes mothers who are active duty military or veterans and mothers whose offspring, partners, or parents have been emotionally, physically, or morally wounded because of military service. Both Canada and the United States are war-illiterate nations in which only a tiny percentage of citizens have ever served in the military, never mind having gone to war or served in so-called peacekeeping missions, and thus few civilians know much about war's realities. This lack of knowledge, when combined with the terrible consequences of prevalent—and often unacknowledged—myths about mothers, leads too often to serious isolation of mothers who are servicemembers, veterans, and/or caretakers or partners of either.

In both countries, there are steps that every citizen can take to become both war-literate (knowledgeable about the emotional, physical, and moral effects of war) and literate about the nature and harm caused by myths about mothers. These steps will pave the way for other steps that every citizen can take to reduce harm done to mothers who are variously connected to the military. The steps include wider distribution of the responsibilities of caring for both mothers in the military and mothers otherwise connected to the military and to veterans, as well as dramatically shifting the focus of "treatment" for war trauma away from often-ineffective psychotherapy and often-harmful (and multiple) psychiatric drugs, and instead toward the vast array of alternative approaches that do not involve pathologizing every war-traumatized person as "mentally ill" but do involve providing effective, low-risk help for their suffering.

THE PROBLEM OF INVISIBILITY

It is hard to think about the world of the military and of war. Since North Americans don't much want to think about it, to many civilians the suffering of servicemembers and veterans is invisible. I wrote that statement in my book about war veterans (Caplan 2011), but I was troubled to see that observation borne out as starkly as it has appeared. In March of 2011, I began to write a blog for *Psychology Today* and have posted about 70 essays there, about a dozen of which have been about veterans and servicemembers; the rest have been about a *very* wide array of subjects, including various women's issues, psychiatric diagnosis, and the courts (Caplan 2011-12). With only one exception, every time I have written about veterans, the essays have received between 30 percent and 3 percent the number of views of anything else about which I have written.

War and the military are associated with violence and loss, and since most North American civilians don't *have* to think about them, are not related to anyone involved, often they simply do not do so. In Canada, this is perhaps especially the case. Canada has primarily said it does not fight in wars but only sends its servicemembers on "peacekeeping" missions, so nonmilitary citizens are even less likely even to notice the military and to realize that they have problems that cry out to be addressed. But as L. (Tex) Leugner CD, Warrant Officer (Ret'd), Canadian Army has reported,

> What is called United Nations Peacekeeping often in fact requires soldiers to stand by helplessly, watching the commission of horrific acts of violence against women, children, or others who cannot defend themselves. The helplessness is all the more infuriating and frustrating because UN Peacekeeping rules of engagement will not permit the direct interference by Peacekeepers with local military authorities, armed militias, or savage gangs bent on revenge killings, rapes, or other atrocities, unless Peacekeepers themselves are directly attacked. (Leugner)

Also largely invisible is much of the work of mothering (Caplan 2000), so it is not surprising that little attention has been paid to the suffering and struggles of mothers whose lives intersect with the military in various ways, in their capacities as servicemembers, veterans, or caretakers or partners of either.

THE PROBLEMS OF PATHOLOGIZING

Furthermore, now that North America is intensely psychiatrized, the citizenry and certainly most mental health professionals are quick to call the emotional and moral suffering experienced by members of the military and veterans "mental disorders," most commonly Post-traumatic Stress Disorder.[1] People who are not therapists have often told me that, since they have no mental health training, they believe there is nothing they can do to help servicemembers or veterans, given that they are "probably mentally ill" (Caplan 2011). Often, these civilians are afraid of saying or doing the wrong thing, thereby somehow damaging these "mentally disordered" people or provoking them to violence. Some therapists have, of course, been helpful to servicemembers or veterans, but therapists' guilds have created the impression that professionals—and only professionals—know how to deal with the emotional suffering and moral anguish with which the former often live. As a result, in North America and the United States, the serious needs of servicemembers and veterans are too often left to those who medicalize them, "treat" them primarily with psychiatric drugs that sometimes help but are more likely to damage or kill them than to help them (Whitaker), and intensify their isolation from the communities in which they live, where they are seen as "other," as sick and dangerous (Caplan 2011).

Research has long shown that women are more likely than men to be classified as mentally ill (Caplan and Cosgrove), and my own research and that of others has shown that that is even more true of women who are mothers (Caplan 2000, 2005). This contributes even further to the jeopardy in which mothers who intersect in any way with the military are placed, because any form of strain, suffering, or conflict can be pathologized. And thus, any of these mothers can be made to feel that they should somehow be managing better than they are.

Imagine a mother who is sent to war, leaving behind her young child, and finding unbearable both her longing for the child and her belief that she is a bad mother to have left. Some mothers who have sought help from military therapists have reported being given psychiatric labels for those completely understandable feelings and being prescribed psychiatric drugs to "manage" them (Caplan 2011) and keep them functioning in their military roles. The psychiatric labels can impede their careers, prevent them from getting or cause them to lose security clearance, undermine their self-confidence and trust in their own judgment, and have a wealth of damaging consequences once they are out of the military (Caplan 1995).

A mother serving in the military who is told that her normal reactions to missing her child, to war, and/or to being sexually assaulted are actually proof that she is mentally ill will struggle with the added burden of believing that she should have managed her feelings in some better way, that she should have "gotten over it," that she is broken and may never be fixed. A mother whose offspring or spouse is labelled as, or assumed to be, mentally ill when in fact they are "normally" suffering the despair, terror, shame, guilt, loss of innocence, and moral anguish that any human being would experience because of having been to war, faces the daunting prospect of believing she needs to know how to deal with someone who is mentally ill. Her life is made much harder by the widespread but mistaken belief that drugs and therapies that require extensive training and knowledge are more effective than love, support, and understanding (Caplan 2011). And if she urges the servicemember or veteran to seek help from the traditional mental health system, what guilt she feels when—as happens so often—the therapy is inadequate or wrongly directed, or the medications fail to help and actually cause harm (Caplan 2011).

THE PROBLEMS OF STEREOTYPES AND MYTHS

Nearly every mother is affected by the pervasiveness of two sets of motherhood myths: The Perfect Mother myths involve standards of behavior so high that no human being could ever meet them (e.g., being 100 percent nurturant 100 percent of the time), and the Bad Mother myths involve interpreting virtually anything a mother might do, including something neutral or even good, as evidence that she is deficient or harmful (Caplan 2000). These myths alone are sufficient to arouse fear and shame in any mother who attempts the impossible task of finding ways to act that do not activate the myths and therefore make her look bad in her own eyes and the eyes of others, and this applies to mothers who intersect with the military by being servicemembers or by being caretakers or partners of servicemembers or veterans.

Those mothers who serve in the military, like all military women, are also torn when traditional expectations for women crash up against expec-

Paula J. Caplan

tations for soldiers: Features of traditional socialization of women such as passivity, fragility, and dependency conflict with expectations for servicemembers to be active, strong, independent, and emotionally tough (Caplan 2011). Yet women in the military need to prove that they deserve as much as men to be in the military, even while the vast majority are told they are either dykes or sluts, and at least one-third are sexually assaulted while in service, with, for instance, an estimate of 19,000 such assaults last year in the U.S. military (Caplan 2011; Department of Defense). And military women confront such impossible tasks as trying to act in adult, autonomous ways despite learning through experience to avoid all liquid intake after late afternoon, because if they must venture out to the latrine after dark—especially if they go alone—they are at high risk for being raped (Caplan 2011).

Those servicewomen who are mothers and experience war trauma and/or who are sexually harassed or assaulted while in the military often find when they return home that they are too distracted, upset, or debilitated to do what they feel that good mothers are supposed to do, and the pervasiveness of the myths about mothers only intensifies their anguish about what they regard as failures. Often, they are so ashamed that they cannot bring themselves to talk to anyone, professional or otherwise, about what they are going through, and trying all the harder to be good mothers, they do not feel they ought to take time and energy away from their children in order to seek any kind of help or even respite for themselves.

Mothers whose offspring or life partners have served in the military and been emotionally traumatized or physically harmed are expected, as are mothers across the board, to be able to do endless caretaking and to provide singlehandedly the cures for loved ones' grief, despair, terror, shame, and guilt and solutions for their moral conflicts and religious, spiritual, or existential crises (Caplan 2000). When they are unable to meet these impossible Perfect Mother standards, or even when they are just exhausted from making the attempt, their upset puts them at risk for being diagnosed as mentally ill.

Plaguing all mothers is the expectation that mothers are not supposed to need or want anything for themselves, and the various burdens that mothers connected to the military carry makes it even harder to avoid longing or asking for help, support, or even notice of what they are trying to do. For those who have served in the military, due to the culture shock caused by the rapid move from a military—even combat—setting back to their home, they struggle with having been profoundly changed, when those back at home often expect them to be the same as they were before. These mothers tend to assume that no one outside those with whom they served has any conception of what they experienced and how it has changed them. They often fear that to speak of what they have seen would be to burden a cared-for listener—something no woman and certainly no mother is supposed to do—and/or reveal a chasm between herself and others that cannot be bridged. Many struggle with ongoing guilt for having been away from their children and with the torment of figuring out how, having been trained to be constantly vigilant, constantly on guard, having been scared to death, having witnessed or even committed acts of violence, they can go back to being a serene, loving, nurturing mother who focuses totally on her children while her memories of war haunt her day and night. Imagine how *she* struggles between the Scylla and Charybdis of the Perfect Mother myth and the Bad Mother myths.

Those mothers whose offspring or partners suffer emotionally, physically, or both often struggle with the fear or knowledge that they can never be the perfect nurturers, that nothing they can give will ever be all their adult child or partner needs, that they can never make all the loved one's suffering go away. Many deal in addition with the servicemember's or veteran's anger about their own suffering, limitations, or losses, which—given that mother-blame is rampant in North America (Caplan 2000)—is often taken out on the mother or woman spouse. When these mothers feel drained, unappreciated, even—heaven forbid—angry, they know they are failing to meet the Perfect Mother standards, and a mother who is flawed or inadequate is often immediately categorized as a Bad Mother (Caplan 2000).

THE PROBLEM OF POLITICS

Much of the foregoing is political in various senses, but let us look at some matters that involve politics in the most usual sense. For a number of different reasons, any of the mothers whose lives intersect with the military may wrestle with the question of how they can be involved in the military in any capacity, given that military traditions and war are so strongly associated with much that conflicts with traditional views of women in general and with mothers in particular.

For mothers in any of the three groups described here, what are the consequences if they are opposed to war or to the particular war that directly affected them? Mothers who have served in the military, some of whom joined because their recruiters misleadingly told them they would not see combat and would not be deployed overseas, many of whom joined because they needed the money or were promised higher education or skilled job training, dealing with the traumatic effects of war is hard enough without having to answer questions from people who challenge them about why they joined the military. Mothers who support those wars in which they have served are not infrequently told that one cannot be a good mother if one supports war.

Mothers whose children go off to war and mothers whose spouses are servicemembers have much to do to help themselves and others in the family cope with the terror they feel, knowing their loved one may be seriously injured or killed, while the military and much of the country expects them all to keep their chins up, claim that they are sure their loved one will return and that all will be well, and say they are proud that the loved one is defending their country, liberating other countries, etc. What about those mothers who opposed the loved one's decision to join the military and/or who oppose the particular war or wars across the board? Do they tell the beloved servicemembers how they feel, or do they keep their politics to themselves? Imagine what anguish and distance both speaking up and keeping silent may cause between them. What to do if they hate a war because of what it has done to their loved one, but that loved one who has been in the military fiercely supports that war? What if the suffering adult child or spouse is proud of their military service, but the mother wishes the sufferer had never joined? Will they feel that being a good mother/spouse means remaining silent if they cannot agree with what their suffering child or partner feels about the war that has hurt them? Is silence the only way to be a good woman, a motherly woman?

THE NEEDS OF MOTHERS CONNECTED TO THE MILITARY

All three groups of mothers whose lives intersect with the military need the rest of us to do our part to reduce the invisibility of the realities of servicemembers, veterans, and mothers. As is evident from what has been described here, the expectations placed on all of these mothers are impossible to fulfil. Yet in nations whose populations do not want to think about war, the work of helping servicemembers and veterans to heal is hardly ever shared by the community beyond the immediate family or an all-veterans group of friends. In the war-illiterate nations of Canada and the United States, every civilian should be urged at least to take some responsibility for listening—just listening, with respect and without judgment—to the stories of suffering servicemembers and veterans, whether or not they are mothers, so that all is not left to their mothers and other loved ones (Caplan 2011).[2] And then we can offer to listen to the stories of their mothers and the other family members. All of these people need a chance to speak the truth about how war has affected them and what they need. In a study Heather Milkiewicz and I conducted at Harvard Kennedy School (Caplan and Milkiewicz), we found that having civilians not trained in interviewing but simply instructed to listen with respect and without judgment had a tremendously positive impact on veterans who had not been given the chance to tell their stories. This reminds us that in many cultures and countries, the community understands that trauma changes a person, isolates a person, and that the community must help them heal, must reach out, let these servicemembers, their mothers, and their partners—all of whom have been traumatized in various ways—know they are understood, and listen to what they need in order to break down the terrible isolation, fear, shame, moral anguish, and loss of innocence that torment them, that they suffer far too often in silence and that are the mostly hidden, bitter fruits of war (Caplan 2000).

For all three groups of mothers whose lives intersect with the military, a great deal of respite care is needed. Mothers back from their military service need that support as they make the transition through that culture shock, especially given that the expectations placed on mothers are impossible to meet at the best of times, so how much more help should be given for those who have been traumatized and are now suddenly supposed to be perfect caretakers. Mothers whose offspring or spouses have come back from war need and deserve respite care so that they can have time to sleep, to relax, to play, to study, in fact to do whatever helps reduce the often intolerable strains of trying to provide nonstop care for those who are emotionally and/or physically traumatized by war.

Also essential are far more places where all of these mothers can speak the truth about the impossibility of feeling like a good mother, given the power and pervasiveness of the Perfect Mother Myths and the Bad Mother Myths. For all military-related mothers, all of whom live in a culture in which the myths about mothers only make their lives more difficult, it is helpful to draw their attention purposefully and specifically to the myths about mothers[3] and to point out how the system of myths and the pathologizing of mothers everywhere make their mothering work even more daunting and anxiety-producing than it would otherwise be. Most mothers know at some level about at least some of the myths and about the tendency to blame mothers for anything that goes wrong, but for them to hear someone put this in words and say that it is wrong can provide much-needed support and perspective.

Everyone can help by explicitly addressing—with everyone, often, including in classes and in social settings—the myths and the realities of mothers in general and especially of mothers whose lives intersect with the military. We can talk about them every chance we get, thereby transforming our cultures not only from war-illiterate to war-literate ones but also from ones in which mother myths and the pathologizing of mothers are powerful because they are so often unacknowledged to ones in which these forces lose some of their destructive power.

Author's Note: This chapter is heavily based not only on the books cited in the text but also on the author's listening sessions and discussions with hundreds of mothers who have served in the military or have had offspring or partners who served and/or have been veterans. In just one chapter it is impossible to address more than some of the most common problems they have encountered, and the focus here is primarily on those that solely or disproportionately affect mothers; but many more than those mentioned here affect not only mothers but also women in general whose lives intersect in various ways with the military.

[1]See Caplan (2011) for an extensive critique of the classification of war trauma as "Post-traumatic Stress Disorder" or other kinds of psychopathology.
[2]See simple instructions for the listening sessions as part of The Welcome Johnny and Jane Home Project in a brief video subtitled "Some Solutions" at <http://whenjohnnyandjanecomemarching.weebly.com>.
[3]See Caplan (2000) for a list and description of the dozen or so major myths.

WORKS CITED

Caplan, Paula J. "Science Isn't Golden: Matters of the Mind and Heart." 2011-2012. *Psychology Today* blog. Web.

Caplan, Paula J. *When Johnny and Jane Come Marching Home: How All of Us Can Help Veterans*. Cambridge, MA: MIT Press, 2011. Print.

Caplan, Paula J. "Sex Bias in Psychiatric Diagnosis and the Courts." *Women, Mental Disorder, and The Law.* Eds. W. Chan, D. Chunn and R. Menzies. London: Cavendish, 2005. 115-26. Print.

Caplan, Paula J. *(THE NEW) Don't Blame Mother: Mending the Mother-Daughter Relationship*. New York: Routledge, 2000. Print.

Caplan, Paula J. *They Say You're Crazy: How the World's Most Powerful Psychiatrists Decide Who's Normal.* Reading, MA: Addison Wesley, 1995. Print.

Caplan, Paula J. and Lisa Cosgrove, eds. *Bias in Psychiatric Diagnosis*. Lanham, MD: Rowman and Littlefield, 2004. Print.

Caplan, Paula J. and Heather Milkiewicz. "Listening to Veterans: The Welcome Johnny and Jane Home Project." Unpublished paper, Harvard Kennedy School, 2012. *When Johnny and Jane Come Marching Home*. Web.

Department of Defense. "DoD News Briefing with Secretary Panetta from the Pentagon." 2012. Web.

Leugner, L. (Tex). Personal communication, 2012.

Whitaker, Robert *Anatomy of an Epidemic*. New York: Crown, 2010. Print.

What More Do You People Want?

The Unique Needs of Aboriginal Mothers in a Modern Context

DAWN MEMEE LAVELL-HARVARD AND JEANNETTE CORBIERE LAVELL

WHILE THE CIRCUMSTANCES under which many Aboriginal[1] people are living in Canada are unacceptable, even by the standards of Third World countries, there are disproportionately more Aboriginal women and children living in poverty and facing hunger and homelessness. Sadly, a persistent lack of employment opportunities, safe housing options, proper sanitation systems, or even access to clean water have become an all too common reality for many of our families. Additionally, as evidenced by the disproportionately high number of missing and murdered Aboriginal women in Canada, our indigenous sisters continue to be the most "at risk" of violence and the least likely to receive justice. Given the situation facing Aboriginal mothers as they struggle, often as the sole provider, to raise their children in less than ideal circumstances, the correspondingly disproportionate number of Aboriginal children apprehended by child welfare authorities is not surprising. It is in the context of historical and ongoing persecution of Indigenous nations that we must come to an understanding of the current marginalization of Aboriginal women and children in our society. Although billions of dollars are allocated each year for programs and support services, clearly the funding allocations and priorities have failed to acknowledge, much less actually address, the unique needs of Aboriginal women in a modern context. Something must be done immediately if this dire situation is to change. The following article outlines the traditional role of Aboriginal mothers, as well as the destruction of that role through colonization, and recommendations for the empowerment of Aboriginal mothers based on the work of the authors—an Ojibway/Odawa mother and daughter who share a collective 70 years of experience working with Aboriginal women at all levels from grassroots activism to international human rights forums while raising their own children according to traditional cultural values.

HISTORICAL CONTEXT

As a result of variable historic, geographic, economic, social, and political factors, tribal origins, social classes, and gender identities, there can be no singular universal Aboriginal specific point of view or experience. Indeed, the experience of Aboriginal motherhood is variable, multifaceted, and dynamic. However, this need not be a source of difficulty. As Chandra Talpade Mohanty had suggested, the attempt to identify such ahistorical universals is theoretically unproductive and any analysis of societal inequity should focus instead on the "material and ideological specificities" that constitute particular groups as subordinate in particular contexts (66). Indeed, as Daiva Stasiulis specifically argued, a more complex understanding of oppression and inequality is gained through a focus on "the structural location of particular groups of women in concrete and historically specific social relations and to the accompanying discourses that aid in the processes of denigration, subordination, and exploitation" (290). Clearly, the intersection of multiple forms of oppression that function to constrain Aboriginal women must be understood in their particular historical contexts—which is, in our case, that of a post-colonial settler society—and therefore race, capitalist relations, and patriarchy are all foundational to the creation and maintenance of the current Canadian situation generally, and the circumstances under which Aboriginal women experience motherhood in this society specifically.

Traditionally our women were respected and valued within our communities. Arising out of our role as mothers, as the givers of life, the role of Aboriginal women is specifically to care for and nurture that life once it is brought into the world and, by extension, to care for and nurture our nations (Anderson). Using the teachings of the Dakota nation, Anderson explained that according to our traditions Aboriginal women not only literally "birth the people" they are also given a "lifetime responsibility to nurture the people":

> It's not just women's responsibility to the children—we have a responsibility to all of the people. We have to. We are the life givers. We are the life force of the nation. Our responsibility is

> to everyone; male and female, young or old, because we are that place from which life emanates. And there is nothing greater than that. (Ivy Chaste qtd. in Anderson 169)

Bringing forth and nurturing a new life is understood to be the basis of the creation of our nation and a future for our peoples. Thus, unlike western ideologies that denied women decision-making power in the family and positioned them in a role equivalent to a family servant, traditionally Aboriginal mothers had responsibility for the life they created and, by extension, for the whole family and the entire community. With such responsibility came authority and the "right to make decisions on behalf of the children, the community and the nation" (Anderson 171).

Numerous accounts suggest that prior to colonization most tribes were egalitarian: Aboriginal men and women performed gender specific tasks and although the tasks were different they were considered of equal value (Mihesuah; see also Stevenson; Smith). In comparison to the fundamentally oppressive and sexist nature of the European societies, Aboriginal women in pre-contact communities demanded a tremendous amount of power, respect, and personal autonomy. In the words of Andrea Smith,

> Prior to colonization, Indian societies for the most part were not male dominated. Women served as spiritual, political, and military leaders, and many societies were matrilineal. Although there existed a division of labor between women and men, women's labor and men's labor were accorded similar status. As women and men lived in balance, native societies were consequently much less authoritarian than their European counterparts. (18)

In her 2003 work on Indigenous American women, Devon Mihesuah similarly explained that most Aboriginal groups were egalitarian and "women's and men's roles may have been different, but neither was less important than the other ... none were inferior" (42). The economic contributions of women's labour lead to decision-making authority, and independence in the family and community, while the existence in extended family groupings typically organized around female kinship ties ensured support and protection for the women.

Unfortunately for our people, the Indigenous beliefs in the fundamental equality of all people and the more egalitarian social structures found in many Aboriginal societies, as well as the empowered Aboriginal women therein, were seen as a threat to the patriarchal order of the colonizers. As they were indeed "bearers of a counter-imperial order," the subjugation of Aboriginal women was "critical to the success of the economic, cultural and political colonization" of the new world (Smith 15). The very existence of women who were subject to the authority of neither fathers nor husbands had the potential to throw into question the supposed natural order of patriarchal hierarchies and could therefore not be tolerated. Clearly, as Smith maintained, the subsequent and continued "demonization of Native women can be seen as a strategy of white men to maintain control over white women" (21) and reinforce patriarchy, as well as simultaneously destroying the social structures of Aboriginal nations. Enakshi Dua, Winona Stevenson, Andrea Smith, and Patricia Monture-Angus all described the myriad of ways in which the colonial imagination constructed the "myth" of the Aboriginal woman in order to denigrate, disempower, and dehumanize her, thereby serving a racist and sexist colonial agenda.

According to Dua, departures from the traditional patriarchal nuclear family model were seen as a danger to the social order; fears of miscegenation were intimately mixed with fear of "degeneration" into so-called "primitive patterns of social and family practices" (254). Through their missions the early French colonizers actively worked to replace the functional gender, sexual, and familial relations in Aboriginal communities with patriarchal relationships based on monogamy, discipline, and dependency for women. While such attempts were generally resisted (as the dismayed accounts of missionaries attest), they were not without effect as familial relationships that had served the Aboriginal people well since time immemorial were disrupted. Dua further described how the arrival of British colonizers brought a more destructive attack on Aboriginal societies and their ways of life. While they had initially been seen as important allies in trade and battle, following the War of 1812-1814, when their services were no longer needed, the Aboriginal peoples became a hindrance to the appropriation of land and the creation of a white settler nation.[2] Moving away from the focus (of the French) on replacing our traditional familial relations with those deemed more seemly by Western standards, they began a ruthless attack on Aboriginal families in general, and Aboriginal mothers in particular. Recognizing the importance of mothering in the reproduction of culture, language, and identity, through a succession of legislations culminating in the *Indian Act* of 1876, and a variety of practices and policies thereafter, the colonial government actively worked to eliminate the ability of First Nations women to mother their own children thereby tearing the very hearts from our communities (Allen; see also Milloy; Miller). Generations of children were stolen from their mother's embrace and forcibly confined in residential schools while child welfare policies authorized the abduction of children from our families, thereby breaking critical ties and extinguishing important relationships. One of the key areas of legislative violence inflicted upon Aboriginal women was found in the *Indian Act*:

> For well over a hundred years, beginning in the 1870s and continuing until as recently as 1985, under the provisions of section 12(1)(b), upon their entrance into marriage with a man not possessing Indian Status, the Canadian government stripped tens of thousands of Aboriginal women (and any subsequent children of their Indian Status, and all the rights such status entailed including access to health care, education, and perhaps most importantly the right to live in their own homes and communities. Conversely, under the act, not only did Indian men not lose status upon marriage to a non-aboriginal, their spouses gained status as did their children. (Lavell-Harvard and Corbiere-Lavell 187)

As a result of this forcible removal from their communities many of these women who had previously enjoyed independence and community support found themselves vulnerable and entirely dependent upon their husbands for support, and without recourse in the event of domestic violence, divorce, or widowhood, as the extinguishment of Indian Status was irreversible. Although this discrimination was challenged in the Supreme Court of Canada by Jeannette Corbiere-Lavell, in what would later become known as the Lavell Case, it was not until 1985 when the government of Canada was shamed at the international level for such flagrant violation of human rights that this section of the *Indian Act* was amended. Unfortunately, the amendment did not restore the women to their original status, creating instead a new lesser category of status for reinstates, and imposing a second-generation cut-off that eliminated the ability of any reinstated children to pass along status to their children. Although recent amendments have allowed for the reinstatement of the grandchildren of these women as a recognition of their rights to be treated equal to grandchildren of status Indian men, legal twists and turns continue to allow for the refusal of status to many of our people based on government categorizations.[3]

Many have argued that such policies were specifically designed to destroy family and in so doing breakdown the very foundation of our communities (see Monture-Angus; Dua; McIvor; Stevenson). The simultaneous eradication of our traditional hunting and gathering way of life, and the consequent elimination of our economic independence worked to eliminate what remained of the respect and authority previously accorded to Aboriginal women. The disruption of the traditional social structures and gender balance, along with the deliberate destruction of the vital nurturing relationship between mother and child, has lead to the development of many social ills in our communities including widespread domestic violence, family dysfunction, and substance abuse (Almeida; see also Bowker; Reyhner and Eder) and, consequently, the overall weakening of our nations. The effects of such policies and practices are still being felt today as Aboriginal communities struggle to heal their families and repair their communities (Brant Castellano, Archibald and DeGagne).

A LIFE OF VIOLENCE

Centuries later, in their analysis of the contemporary situation in Canada, the Native Women's Association of Canada (NWAC) found that many Aboriginal women remain burdened by interlocking sources of oppression and the lasting effects of longstanding persecution. As a result, Aboriginal women experience lower levels of education, employment, income, and health than other Canadian women, suffer higher rates of unemployment, poverty, homelessness, and have poorer health than Aboriginal men or non-aboriginal Canadians in general (NWAC). According to the 2010 report on the Sisters in Spirit initiative produced by the Native Women's Association of Canada, documenting the disproportionately high number of missing and murdered Aboriginal women in Canada, Aboriginal women are the most "at risk" of violence, particularly in urban settings. Nationally, Aboriginal women experience violence from either a current or former partner at 3 times the rate experienced by non-Aboriginal women. Aboriginal women are eight times more likely

Dawn Memee Lavell-Harvard, and on the right, Jeannette Corbiere Lavell.

to be abused, and more likely to suffer severe forms abuse: 87 percent of were physically injured and 57 percent had been sexually abused. Aboriginal women are more likely than non-aboriginal women to be assaulted and killed by a total stranger, and as a result of generations of prejudice they are also less likely to receive justice (NWAC; Lamontagne; Brennan). Regional studies have indicated even higher incidences, reporting rates of 75 percent, 80 percent, or as high as 90 percent in some Aboriginal communities in northern Ontario (see OFIFC and ONWA). Tragically, as an overwhelming majority of these women are mothers, Aboriginal children are often witness to, and also victims of, domestic violence. Given societal indifference to the abuse inflicted upon our women many feel they are left with little recourse and often ending up in prison themselves when they eventually fight back against their abusers. The resulting overrepresentation of our women in corrections facilities only exacerbates the already high numbers of our children in the care of child welfare systems. Without appropriate counselling and supports the generational cycles of violence are reproduced.

While it is widely known that poverty, unemployment, and low levels of educational attainment put our women at increased risk of violence, as part of a particularly vicious cycle, the lack of safe and affordable housing options has often meant a lack of opportunity for Aboriginal women fleeing violence, and the resulting increased risk of homelessness lessens the chances of obtaining sufficient education and/or employment. The situation for Aboriginal single mothers is particularly concerning as more than 40 percent of female-lead Aboriginal single-parent families were in core housing need (NWAC). While our communities are the primary source of support, as grandmothers, aunties, cousins and other community members provide assistance, teachings, and guidance for young mothers, many are forced to flee the community to escape violence. Although much of the research tends to focus on the younger female populations, we must also acknowledge the unique needs of elderly Aboriginal women, many of whom are still mothering as they raise grandchildren. Given their comparative financial insecurity, the high rates of physical disability among the senior Aboriginal populations, and a lack of appropriate housing in many communities, many Aboriginal grandmothers find themselves struggling to raise grandchildren on fixed incomes in substandard homes. Clearly, substantive efforts and investments must be made so that all Aboriginal women are provided basic human dignity and the opportunity to live a life free of violence. Indeed, while we are all well aware that education and employment provide access to a better life for our children, and a means of escaping violence, it is often impossible to focus on achieving such goals when living under the constant threat of violence. The eradication of violence against Aboriginal women and girls must therefore be our largest concern and our primary goal.

WHAT DO ABORIGINAL MOTHERS NEED?

Given the legacy of colonization, according to Kim Anderson, "Aboriginal women have had to become practised at resistance" (115) in order to survive in a system that functions to subjugate and oppress both Aboriginal peoples and women generally, and therefore, Aboriginal women particularly. Generations of strong capable Aboriginal women have provided the foundation for such resistance, as Anderson explains, the "guidance that women receive from their mothers, aunts and grandmothers, shapes the way they learn to understand themselves and their positions in the world" (123). Having had to learn how to resist subjugation and how to survive under the weight of oppression, previous generations of Aboriginal mothers have maintained a definition of womanhood premised upon strength and capability that was distinctly different from the negative images and subservient female role offered by mainstream society. Indeed, according to the definition of womanhood cultivated by Western society the so-called "true woman is self-contained within her nuclear family, with specific and separate roles for men and women and with an economic dependence on men, in such a way that motherhood is one's true occupation" (Snorton 57). In contrast, for Aboriginal women the role of wife and mother did not traditionally preclude working outside the home and was certainly not defined by dependency.

In traditional communities, given that the men were often away from the community for long periods, women were not only encouraged, but expected to be independent and self-reliant. Women were therefore neither prevented, nor discouraged from learning tasks that were traditionally seen to be men's work and, moreover, engaging in such work was not seen to take away from one's femininity (Anderson; Berkin; Brown; Landes). Furthermore, as previously mentioned the provision of foodstuffs and resources for the family often relied heavily upon tasks traditionally performed by women, thereby negating any possibility of women being seen as "dependent" upon their husbands and creating instead relationships characterized by "interdependence" and equality (Anderson). For centuries therefore, strength, independence, and self-reliance have defined Aboriginal motherhood, the legacy of which continues to influence our women today. As Anderson explained, generations of "strong, independent female role models provide Native girls with the sense that they can overcome whatever obstacles they will inevitably encounter" (118). It is this belief in one's own ability, like the water, to adapt to and eventually overcome, any obstacle encountered, that inspires resilience and persistence in the face of adversity and such characteristics are unquestionably powerful tools in the struggle for survival.

EDUCATION

Despite the shameful legacy of the residential school experience, most Aboriginal people still view education as a primary means of initiating the social, economic, and political changes necessary if we are to provide a better future for our children. Formal education is absolutely critical for the provision of the skills and credentials necessary for success in contemporary society (Brayboy 2004, 2005; Schissel and Wotherspoon), and conversely the persistent lack of educational attainment translates directly into a lack of opportunity for Aboriginal peoples (Brade, Duncan and Sokal). While it has been noted that Aboriginal women are increasingly achieving better educational outcomes than Aboriginal men, such advances do not necessarily reflect an equality of opportunity. In fact, one might suggest the increase in educational attainment for Aboriginal women is instead the result of a distinct lack of equality of opportunity in contemporary society. The fact that it is easier for Aboriginal men to earn a decent living without higher education in combination with the high proportion of female-lead, single-parent families means that increasingly Aboriginal women are finding they must be better educated in order to provide for their families (Voyageur). When discussing their motivation to pursue post-secondary education many Aboriginal women agreed that without post-secondary credentials the only jobs available were sometimes dangerous, often demeaning, and almost always minimum wage (Lavell-Harvard). With childcare costs eating up a significant portion of an already insufficient wage, making ends meet without an education becomes almost impossible for Aboriginal mothers.

Indeed, an Aboriginal dropout lives an economically marginalized life, yet the Aboriginal male dropout still earns approximately three times the wages of an Aboriginal woman who failed to complete high school. However, income differences based on race and gender lessen with increases in education as women not only earn more individually, they begin to catch up with men, and Aboriginals begin to catch up with non-Aboriginals (Ashenfelter and Rouse; Howe). Shockingly, as Daniel Wilson and David Macdonald demonstrated, with a university degree Aboriginal women have higher median incomes than non-aboriginal women possessing the same level of education. However, with anything less than a university degree, Aboriginal peoples as a group continue to earn much less than non-Aboriginals with equivalent education (Wilson and Macdonald) and Aboriginal women continue to earn less than Aboriginal men. Clearly the potential benefits of educational achievement have greater significance for Aboriginal women as they have much more at stake. Moreover, it is widely accepted that increased levels of education for mothers result in a corresponding increase in educational attainment levels for their children and therefore a larger return for every dollar spent educating Aboriginal women generally, and Aboriginal mothers specifically.

Unfortunately, the intersection of race and gender plays a large role in determining access to funding and financial aid, or the lack thereof, which directly impacts the ability of Aboriginal women to obtain the necessary education. Racist practices within post secondary institutions blatantly discriminate against First Nation students generally, and family circumstances disadvantage Aboriginal women with children specifically (Lavell-Harvard). Moreover, many of these women came from families that were already struggling themselves and were, therefore, unable to offer financial support. Indeed, the lack of funds was the most commonly mentioned barrier for Aboriginal women and better access to financial aid was the most common recommendation for improvement of post secondary access (Lavell-Harvard).

Contrary to popular beliefs, not all Aboriginal peoples receive "free educations" as many of our people are being denied the financial assistance to which they are entitled. According to Shelley Milligan and Evelyne Bougie's analysis of the duly registered and therefore entitled First Nations women, only 58 percent received band funding for their education. The cost of daycare, larger accommodations, transportation, and increased grocery bills created even greater challenges for those who were raising children while attending university. While there are a number of scholarships and awards available, and many specifically for Aboriginal people, Aboriginal women who already have to balance study time with family responsibilities, and perhaps part-time work, are at a disadvantage when applying for awards and bursaries based on academic performance. Unfortunately, centuries of colonial oppression have created such widespread and pervasive poverty in our communities that those most likely to benefit from educational credentials, i.e., Aboriginal women with children, are the least likely to be able to afford to obtain them. Adequate financial support for the pursuit of post secondary education is therefore absolutely critical for the empowerment of Aboriginal mothers and the improvement of outcomes for their children. Providing future generations with a 'better life' is not necessarily only about financial wherewithal and the ability to provide material goods such as food, shelter, and clothing. For many Aboriginal communities, where despair has settled in after generations of persistent crushing poverty, the educational achievement of our women is perceived as a means of concretely demonstrating that a better life is indeed possible for Aboriginal peoples, even in the face of much historical evidence to the contrary.

CHILDCARE

Given the numerous barriers facing Aboriginal women attempting to obtain university credentials, and the high number of Aboriginal women who are the sole support for their families, even though Aboriginal women are in fact outnumbering Aboriginal men in post-secondary institutions, targeted and sustained funding is necessary so that these women can reach a level where equality is even a possibility in Canadian society. Although wanting to provide a better life for their children is a primary motivator, after the increased costs of housing and food are taken into account, for Aboriginal women who are attempting to pursue higher education while simultaneously managing family responsibilities, the lack of affordable childcare spaces is often cited as a significant barrier to educational success (Lavell-Harvard). However, such concern is common to many women in Canada. The childcare system in Canada was ranked last among developed countries in terms of availability of early learning and childcare spaces[4] (OECD).

While clearly the lack of access to quality childcare is a barrier to employment and education for many women in Canada generally, and low income women specifically, according to the Urban Aboriginal Task Force for Aboriginal women living in urban settings particularly, affordable childcare is an absolute necessity if these women are to be able to obtain education, training, and ultimately employment. Moreover, *quality* childcare programs with proper early learning environments and educators have been shown to actually benefit children by encouraging early literacy skills, school readiness, and long term educational performance. However, for women with more than one child, those with less income, or those without a husband to share the financial burden (high rates of female lead single parent families) the exorbitant cost of daycare throws into question the economic feasibility of attempting to work or study as childcare bills surpass university tuition fees (there are no registered savings plans for daycare, and tax credits only benefit those who have the financial wherewithal to wait for annual returns). Regardless of the eventual financial payoffs, and the increased potential for long-term economic security, the short-term costs are often simply insurmountable.

CONCLUSION

Given the disproportionate level of Aboriginal women facing extreme poverty, hunger, homelessness, violence, and other facets of socio-economic stress, rather than continuing to funnel money into social assistance programs, child welfare agencies, corrections systems, and emergency shelters, targeted funding is necessary to provide Aboriginal women with sufficient personal safety and appropriate social supports so that they might begin to take advantage of existing opportunities to obtain the skills needed to be able to provide for their families and improve their circumstances. Ongoing and significant investments in quality childcare options, safe and affordable housing initiatives, and long term violence prevention and intervention programs including the provision of services for children who witness violence must be implemented for the empowerment of Aboriginal mothers. Such funding is not only an investment in individual women, the ripples will be felt in the larger communities and eventually in our nations as a whole: increased opportunity for Aboriginal women and girls will generate stronger healthier families, improved circumstances for future generations of Aboriginal children and grandchildren, and ultimately stronger healthier Aboriginal communities.

[1]For the purposes of this document Aboriginal is to be understood as referring to the First Nations, Métis, and Inuit peoples.

[2]See Allen for more detailed review of circumstances.

[3]See Lavell-Harvard and Corbiere-Lavell for a more detailed explanation of the experience and impact of such legislation.

[4]Due to a severe shortage of regulated childcare spaces available, less than 20 percent of the children under six with working parents could be accommodated (as compared to 60 percent in the UK, 69 percent in France and 78 percent in Denmark). Interestingly, within Canada, Quebec has the highest number of available daycare spaces and all such spaces are subsidized, and therefore as expected, Quebec also has the highest percentage of women participating in post secondary education and the workforce as compared to all other provinces and territories (OECD).

WORKS CITED

Allen, R. *His Majesty's Indian Allies: British Indian Policy in the Defence of Canada, 1774-1815*. Toronto: Dundurn Press, 1992. Print.

Almeida, D. "The Hidden Half: A History of Native American Women's Education." *Harvard Educational Review*, 67 (1997): 757-772. Web.

Anderson, K. *A Recognition of Being*. Toronto: Sumach Press, 2000. Print.

Ashenfelter, O. and C. Rouse. "Schooling, Intelligence, and Income in America." *Meritocracy and Economic Inequality*. Eds. Kenneth Arrow et al. Princeton, NJ: Princeton University Press, 2000. 89-117. Print.

Berkin, C. *First Generations: Women in Colonial America*. New York: Farrar, Straus, and Giroux, 1996. Print.

Bowker, A. (aka Sixkiller Clarke). *Sisters in the Blood: The Education of Native American Women*. Newton, MA: WEEA Publishing Center, 1993. Print.

Brant Castellano, M., L. Archibald and M. DeGagne. *From Truth to Reconciliation: Transforming the Legacy of Residential Schools*. Ottawa: Aboriginal Healing Foundation, 2008. Print.

Brade, C., K. Duncan, and L. Sokal. "The Path to Education in a Canadian Aboriginal Context." *Canadian Journal of Native Education* 27 (2003): 235-248. Web.

Brayboy, B. "Hiding in the Ivy: American Indian Students and Visibility in Elite Educational Settings." *Harvard Educational Review* 74 (2004): 125-152. Web.

Brayboy, B. "Transformational Resistance and Social Justice: American Indians in Ivy League Universities." *Anthropology and Education Quarterly* 36 (2005): 193-211. Web.

Brennan, S. *Violent Victimization of Aboriginal Women in the Canadian Provinces*. Ottawa: Statistics Canada, 2011. Web. Retrieved on October 15, 2012. Print.

Brown, J. "Economic Organization and the Position of Women Among the Iroquois." *Iroquois Women: An Anthology*. Ed. W. G. Spittal. Ohsweken, ON: Iroquois Printing and Craft Supplies, 1990. 182-167. Print.

Dua, E. "Beyond Diversity: Exploring the Ways in which the Discourse of Race Has Shaped the Institution of the Nuclear Family." *Scratching the Surface: Canadian Anti-racist Feminist Thought*. Ed. E. Dua and A. Robertson. Toronto: Women's Press, 1999. 237-260. Print.

Howe, E. "Education and Lifetime Income for Aboriginal People in

Saskatchewan." *Aboriginal Policy Research: Setting the Agenda for Change. Volume 1*. Eds. J. White, P. Maxim and D. Beavon. Toronto: Thompson Educational, 2004. 175-189. Print.

Lamontagne, M. *Violence Against Aboriginal Women: Scan and Report*. Toronto: Canadian Women's Foundation, 2011. Web. Retrieved of October 15, 2012. Print.

Landes, R. *The Ojibwa Woman*. New York: Norton and Company, 1974 [1971]. Print.

Lavell-Harvard, D. M. L. *The Power of Silence and the Price of Success*. Unpublished Ph.D. Dissertation, University of Western Ontario, 2011. Print.

Lavell-Harvard, D. M. and J. Corbiere Lavell. "Aboriginal Women vs. Canada: The Struggle for Our Mothers to Remain Aboriginal." *Until Our Hearts Are on the Ground: Aboriginal Mothering, Oppression, Resistance and Rebirth*. Eds. D. M. Lavell-Harvard and J. Corbiere Lavell. Toronto: Demeter Press, 2006. 184-195. Print.

McIvor, S. "Self Government and Aboriginal Women." *Scratching the Surface: Canadian Anti-racist Feminist Thought*. Ed. E. Dua and A. Robertson. Toronto: Women's Press, 1999. 167-186. Print.

Mihesuah, D. A. *Indigenous American Women: Decolonization, Empowerment, Activism*. Lincoln: University of Nebraska Press, 2003.

Miller, J. *Shingwauks Vision: A History of Native Residential Schools*. Toronto: University of Toronto Press, 1996.v

Milligan, S., and E. Bougie. *First Nations Women and Postsecondary Education in Canada: Snapshots from the Census*. Ottawa: Statistics Canada, 2009. Web. Retrieved on February 28, 2010. v

Milloy, J. *A National Crime: The Canadian Government and the Residential School System, 1879-1986*. Winnipeg: University of Manitoba Press, 1999. Print.

Mohanty, C. "Under Western Eyes: Feminist Scholarship and Colonial Discourses." *Feminist Review* 30 (1988): 61-88. Print.

Monture-Angus, P. *Thunder in My Soul: A Mohawk Woman Speaks*. Halifax: Fernwood Publishing, 1995. Print.

Native Women's Association of Canada (NWAC). *What Their Stories Tell Us: Research Findings from the Sisters in Spirit Initiative*. Ottawa: NWAC, 2010. Print.

Organization for Economic Co-operation and Development (OECD). *Babies and Bosses: Reconciling Work and Family Life*. Volume 4: Canada, Finland, Sweden, and the United Kingdom. 2005. Web. Retrieved March 25, 2010. Print.

Ontario Native Women's Association and Ontario Federation of Indian Friendship Centers (ONWA and OFIFC). *Strategic Framework to End Violence Against Aboriginal Women*. Toronto: OFIFC, 2007. Print.

Reyhner, J. and J. E. Eder. "A History of Indian Education." *Teaching American Indian Students*. Ed. J. Reyhner. Norman: University of Oklahoma Press, 1994. 33-58. Print.

Schissel, B. and T. Wotherspoon. *The Legacy of School for Aboriginal People: Education, Oppression, and Emancipation*. Toronto: Oxford University Press, 2003. Print.

Smith, A. *Conquest: Sexual Violence and American Indian Genocide*. Cambridge, MA: South End Press, 2005. Print.

Snorton, T. E. "The Legacy of the African-American Matriarch: New Perspectives for Pastoral Care." *Through the Eyes of Women*. Ed. Jeanne Stevenson Moessner. Minneapolis: Fortress Press, 1996. 50-65. Print.

Stasiulis, D. "Theorizing Connections: Gender, Race, Ethnicity, and Class." *Race and Ethnic Relations in Canada*. Ed. Peter Li. Oxford: Oxford University Press, 1990. 269-305. Print.

Stevenson, W. "Colonialism and First Nations Women in Canada." *Scratching the Surface: Canadian Anti-racist Feminist Thought* Eds. E. Dua and A. Robertson. Toronto: Women's Press, 1999. 49-80. Print.

Urban Aboriginal Task Force. *Urban Aboriginal Task Force: Final Report*. Toronto: Ontario Federation of Indian Friendship Centers, Ontario Native Women's Association, and Ontario Metis and Aboriginal Association, 2007. Web.

Wilson, D. and D. Macdonald. *The Income Gap Between Aboriginal Peoples and the Rest of Canada*. Ottawa: Canadian Center for Policy Alternatives, 2010. Web. Retrieved May 1, 2010.

What Do Mothers Need?

Money

PAT GOWENS

NO MATTER IN WHAT COUNTRY, what century and what culture, raising children is complex work done primarily by mothers for no pay. The work involves carrying the fetus, giving birth, nursing, feeding, clothing, bathing, educating, training, supervising, counseling, healing, inspiring, loving, serving, disciplining, listening to, shopping for, cooking for, validating, helping, and protecting the child or children. Since this work can occupy a mother's time for 24 hours on some days, and seven days in most weeks for 18 years, it generally leaves moms insufficient time to earn a secure income through paid employment.

Due to the need to engage in unpaid motherwork for years, many mothers are forced into years of an exhausting double workday. This is not only harmful and unfair to mothers. It is also a direct attack on children's security, stability, and spirit. A child whose mother is overworked, absent, or exhausted is a child deprived of the most essential support for a secure childhood.

As a result of children's long-term dependency and the heavy work load that motherwork entails, mothers have traditionally raised children within extended families and paired up with the children's fathers to share the burden of economically supporting the children and helping to raise them. Even with this network of support for children, the primary caregiving burden generally falls on the mother, leaving her minimal time to generate sufficient income to support children while also providing their care.

Of course mothers can and do hire childcare providers to perform some of the motherwork tasks to free them up to do paid employment. But child-rearing responsibilities continue well after the mother's paid workday/workweek ends. And those responsibilities often interfere with a mother's employment, reducing her earning capacity.

Mothers are often impoverished when the fathers fail to remain with the family and then fail to provide child support, though it is legally required in all countries. In other cases it is the mother herself who finds it necessary to separate from the father despite the burden of providing both care and economic support for her offspring.

MOTHERS NEED FOR MONEY IS INVISIBLIZED

Whether raising children in nuclear families, extended families, or single mother families, nearly all mothers need access to cash support. Yet a mother's obvious need for money is minimized, denied, and demeaned in patriarchal cultures. Discussion of money is even taboo in some developed nations.

Popular patriarchal myths maintain that motherwork is no work, anyone can do it, and moms do it for love so economic compensation is unnecessary. Other myths maintain that the single mom who demands child support from the absent dad is a parasite, an anchor, unfairly preying on the children's father who has usually moved on to a new family.

In two-parent families although mom may do the bulk of unpaid motherwork, she is now expected to also work nearly full-time in the paid workforce. Yet her pay is far less than that of non-mothers, both male and female, partly due to her motherwork obligations and partly due to bias against mothers. Ann Crittenden, in her 2001 publication *The Price of Motherhood* found that the gap between men and women's pay is primarily a wage gap between mothers and non-mothers.

Since mothers have traditionally begun bearing and raising children in their late teens or early twenties, they often have less education than non-mothers. This contributes to a further reduction of their wages when in the paid workforce. In addition many mothers seek employment utilizing the skills they perfect while actively engaged in motherwork. But the patriarchal notion that motherwork is no work results in very low pay for all types of employment reflected in motherwork, whether child care which is the lowest paid work in the U.S., or waitress work which is not even required to pay minimum wage in the U.S. These jobs along with home health care, nurses aide work, teachers aide work, maintenance work, and work in the service industry are the jobs with the most growth in the U.S. since 1995. They all pay less than HALF of a livable wage with child care at 29 percent, cashiers at 38 percent, waiters at 43 percent, teachers aides and nurses aides at 45 percent, retail sales at 46 percent, janitors / maids at 46 percent and home health workers at 48 percent of a livable wage (Center on Budget and Policy Priorities; United for Fair Economy). These jobs also provide few if any benefits (paid sick days, vacation pay, maternity leave pay), thus failing mothers, especially single moms, struggling to adequately care for children and to raise their family out of poverty.

WHY DO MOTHERS NEED PAY?

Motherworkers need pay to supplement their reduced wages, whether partnered or single. And motherworkers need pay to provide financial support for children during the periods of necessary full-time caregiving, whether for a sick child, a nursing infant, a troubled teen, or a disabled youngster. Mothers also need money for the periods when they themselves cannot adequately perform the double workday required of full-time caregivers in the paid workforce. There are few supermoms who can work, month after month, year after year the 80 to 120 hour work weeks required of them—without needing time off to properly care for themselves and time off to properly care for their dependent minors.

Although a mother's need for income should be obvious, under patriarchal rule no countries include the unwaged labor of motherworkers in their national budgets. And no countries provide motherworkers a source of income acknowledging this crucial, complex labor.

DO ANY COUNTRIES PAY MOTHERWORKERS?

Some countries do provide a family allowance / child allowance that acknowledge that minor children are dependent and unable to economically support themselves. Unfortunately only the countries in the European Union economically compensate families in this way. In these countries every minor child is entitled to a monthly check regardless of their parent's income. This economic support is not part of a welfare program; there are no income requirements.

Even during recent periods of "austerity" European countries have not been able to dismantle their guaranteed family income support due to its popularity. Unlike welfare programs that base entitlement on harsh income limits, all European families receive the child allowance. This eliminates the resentment and division against welfare beneficiaries that is common in countries where only the severely impoverished are eligible for income supports. Following are some examples of monthly Family Allowance amounts:

Austria pays $154 per child under ten, $180 for children 10–19 and $212 for youth 19–27 years old. France pays $176 each for the first and second child, $202 for each additional child. Germany pays $225 for the first and second child, $261 for the third until age 27 if child is a student. Ireland pays $242 for the first and second child, $296 for each additional child. Luxembourg pays $272 for first child, $644 for two children, $1172 for three children, $1699 for four, $2228 for five, and children ages 6–11 receive an extra $23; children twelve and over receive an extra $72. Norway pays $760 per child; single moms receive the same amount for one more child than actual family size. Sweden pays $159 for the first child, $317 for second child, $476 for the third, and $634 for the fourth child (Clearing House Sec. 1.8, 1.9).

European countries also provide paid maternity leave, paid sick leave, and free health care. They also provide welfare payments to impoverished, unemployed, and disabled/injured individuals. All of these payments to families, combined with the Family Allowances, guarantee moms some supplementary or basic income, which greatly helps to ensure children a safe, secure, and healthy childhood.

Canada paid *all* families a guaranteed Family Allowance indexed to the cost of living until 1998. In 1998 Canada replaced the Family Allowance (FA) with the Canadian Child Tax Benefit (CCTB) and the National Child Benefit Supplement (NCB). Unlike the FA, these benefits are based on a family's income. Families earning less than $45,000 receive cash support. For families with two children and an income less than $24,863 net, the CCTB pays them about $454 per month. Families with income up to $42,707 receive support on a sliding scale. Canada's Universal Child Care Benefit pays *all* families $100 a month for each child under age six and $215 a month for a child with a disability. Canada provides paid maternity leave, paid sick leave and free health care. Welfare payments are available to impoverished families also ("Who Cares?").

WHAT ABOUT COMMUNIST/SOCIALIST COUNTRIES?

Since President Hugo Chavez nationalized Venezuela's oil, that country has created "missions" to provide necessities to struggling families. One of these missions is a monthly paycheck for women who are single homemakers in recognition of the work they perform in the home. *Venezuela is the first country in the world to actually pay women for motherwork.*

China and Cuba are two remaining communist countries. Do they provide income support for motherworkers? Although Cuba provides paid maternity leave, free medical care, free medication, and free education up to and including Ph.D. studies, it does not pay families a child/family allowance. Yet Cuba was named the best underdeveloped country to be a mom thanks to the other cash supports moms receive in that very poor country. China may be vying with the U.S. for the most mother-unfriendly country. It provides no family allowances and few benefits. China's international publication, *Women of China* promotes the martyr-mom economic struggle as hugely praiseworthy. Mothers who work deadly long hours, even at the risk of seriously damaging their own bodies, are cited as heroines and role models.

U.S. ECONOMIC WAR ON MOTHERS AND CHILDREN

Although the U.S. is the wealthiest country on Earth, it wages an ugly economic war on mothers and children. It provides no family allowances, no paid maternity leave, no paid sick days and no free college education. Only the very poor receive free childcare and free health care under a stigmatizing, difficult-to-access welfare program.

Even affordable housing is unavailable to most U.S. families. As a result of this lack of cash support for mothers, millions of mothers and children are forced to live with zero income. In 2010, the *New York Times* found that six million U.S. individuals are struggling to survive with zero income, mostly mothers and children ("Living on Nothing"). These families generally have no access to a home so they double up with family/friends or live from shelter to streets. The children suffer horrible deprivation, moving from school to school and home to home. Many are swept up in the Child Welfare net and forced to live in foster homes with strangers, and often moved from stranger to stranger.

U.S. mothers who are being forced to survive on zero income are primar-

Pat Gowens

ily single moms who 1) are ill or disabled but waiting for disability payments, 2) can't find paid employment because they have inadequate jobs skills to successfully compete in a very competitive job market; 3) have alcohol or drug addictions that interfere with their earning capacity; and 4) have been denied cash welfare support due to having reached an arbitrary time limit (from two to five years depending on the state) during which they were unable to secure employment.

Imagine the lives of children growing up in a country where there is no income supports for moms, little affordable housing, and a severe shortage of jobs, especially living-wage jobs. Children without two employed parents can face a childhood of insecurity, danger, and hopelessness. Often the only people who care for them and believe in them are their heroic moms (and some dads and grandparents) who care for their physical, emotional, spiritual, and mental survival in the face of a heartless, systemic, economic brutality.

WHY DOES MONEY MATTER? ISN'T IT JUST RESPECT THAT MOMS NEED?

Mothers who have access to income supports like a family allowance, affordable housing, free health care, paid maternity leave, paid sick days, and living wages—as well as decent welfare support—have the ability to provide their children with a wholesome, healthy, hopeful and safe childhood. Their children can thrive under the fearless love, supervision, and inspiration of a mom who is able to be there for them physically and emotionally. Their children do not have to care for themselves and each other in a lonely home while waiting hours for mom to return from long work shifts that interfere with motherwork.

Mothers with adequate access to money are able to escape from dangerous partners who hurt them and scare their children. They are able to gain control over their fertility so they do not have more children than they want. They can escape the dangerous neighborhoods where petty criminals congregate and children are not safe. They can protect their children from being snatched by Child Welfare and forced to live with strangers in loveless, and often dangerous, homes.

Finally motherworkers who have access to income supports can escape imprisonment for petty crimes and their children can escape the worse experience in life—that of being a motherless child. U.S. prisons are filled with moms who are convicted of cash crimes: passing bad checks, shoplifting, prostitution, welfare fraud, and staying with a partner who is a drug dealer. Mothers are the fastest growing prison population in the cash-hungry U.S. Eighty-five percent of women in prison are mothers. Lately U.S. moms are being imprisoned for yet one more cash crime, a seemingly bizarre crime that is harshly punished with long prison sentences (Prison Brith Project).

Some moms in poverty place their child in a suburban school by using the suburban address of a family member or friend. Their goal is to get a better education for their child despite their inadequate income. When caught, moms like Tanya McDowell in Bridgeport, Connecticut, are found guilty of "education theft." McDowell must pay back $15,686 for the alleged "educational services" provided to her five-year-old son. And she faced 20 years in prison. In March 2012, she was sentenced to twelve years in prison, ineligible for parole until five years served. Her son, like most children of imprisoned mothers, has become a motherless child (SocialistWorker.org).

AND RESPECT?

Motherworkers need to be acknowledged and respected in their communities, in their churches, in the media, in the workplaces, and by their governments. If this respect were the norm, all of those income supports so desperately needed to keep children safe would automatically be included in every country's budgets. However such respect is not the norm in our patriarchal cultures. In fact we live in a system where money itself defines respect, not the value of the work we do. No matter how crucial a person's work is—whether motherwork, farmwork, carework, earthwork —their paycheck has no bearing on the value of the work. In fact the most essential work is generally the lowest paid.

Under the patri-horde system, the more money a person has the greater respect they "earn." So until we are able to replace our patriarchal rule with a mother-friendly culture, the more money we can legislate for motherworkers, the more respect moms will "earn."

DO A FEW HUNDRED BUCKS MATTER?

Even when motherworkers have access to family allowances and benefits, they may still have a very low income. Their jobs may pay sub-poverty wages. Their periods of unemployment while caring for sick or injured children further erode their income. But the availability of even a small amount of guaranteed monthly income can make a huge difference in family security and health.

The Center on Budget and Policy Priorities in Washington, DC, conducted a study in 2010 to see how much difference an extra $3000 a year made in low-income families. They found that it made a big difference in two areas, their housing security and the children's educational stability. Mothers did not have to keep moving from hovel to shelter during periods of zero income. They did not have to face repeated evictions during periods of sub-poverty paychecks. Regular, small, supplementary cash support was enough to ensure stable housing and, as a result, the children had regular school attendance.

SOLUTION? INVEST IN CARING NOT KILLING

In 1999, Margaretta D'Arcy of Galway Ireland's Women in Media, along with the National Women's Council of Ireland, called for the first Global Women's Strike, demanding "a millennium which values all women's work and all women's lives—an end to no pay, low pay and overwork" (D'Arcy 13). Central to this campaign was the demand that all governments include unwaged work in their economies. They chose March 8, International Women's Day, to inaugurate the campaign and celebrate it yearly. The Strike was quickly made global by London and Philadelphia's International Wages for Housework. The Welfare Warriors in Milwaukee used their publication, *Welfare Mothers Voice*, to publicize the action across the U.S. The goal was to gain recognition and pay for the unwaged work mothers do by striking against mothers' low pay, no pay, and overwork.

Women joined the Global Women's Strike in Australia, Burkina Faso, England, Cameroon, Canada, U.S., Chile, Kurdistan, Mexico, Netherlands, Pakistan, Puerto Rico, Rwanda, Senegal, Sweden, Switzerland, Taiwan, Philippines, Spain, Ecuador, Peru, Pakistan, Ghana, Kenya, Albania, Kosovo and Wales. The Raging Grannies in Kingston, Ontario, Canada, created a Global Women's Strike song to the tune of "Put Your Arms Around Me Baby, Hold Me Tight."

Women of the world
Let us throw off our chains
Let us have a taste of economic gains
Oh, Oh
March 8 we will strike
With all women we'll unite
We want motherwork made a priority
International Women's Day a holiday
Oh Oh
Housework done for pay
Third World debt canceled today
Celebrate the women who are in your life
Mother, sister, granny, auntie, daughter, wife
Oh Oh
Join with the moms fight for peace and pay today

To shore up their arguments about the value of women's unwaged work, U.S. activists shared research showing that women's unwaged work—motherwork, care of elderly and disabled, housework, farming, firewood gathering, work in churches and schools, community organizing, art work, human rights work etc.—contributes at least $11 trillion to the world's economy. Yet this work is unpaid and unappreciated. They pointed out that women do two-thirds of the world's work while earning only five percent of the world's income, leaving most women overworked and poor, struggling to carry out a double work day. As a result children are suffering and communities are disintegrating.

The Philadelphia Wages for Housework group (now called Every Mothering Is a Working Mother) reported on a new national study that found that women caring for ill or disabled family members in the U.S. contribute over $200 billion a year in unwaged work. Researchers Peter Arno, C. Levine and M. M. Memmott used data from five national data banks. They calculated that 25.8 million Americans spend an average of 18 hours a week caring for ailing relatives. If that care was paid for, it would increase health-care costs nationwide by $196 billion a year. The $200 billion contributed by unwaged workers is much greater than the entire home health care industry ($32 billion) and the nursing home industry ($83 billion). And this was just one example of the massive impact of unwaged work on each government's economy.

Indigenous women in Peru used their radio program "Soncco Warmi" (Heart of Women, in Quechua) to promote the strike and lobby for recognition of their work (Economic Value of Informal Caregiving). They announced, "Women of the Andes contribute more than 50 percent of the family income through agriculture—women sow, weed, harvest, take care of the animals—but the state doesn't take into account that we grow and prepare the food. Our work is not included in the national budget. Women also take care of the children and do the housework, but this work is not valued. We are the main producers and keepers of life and culture in the rural areas, and our economic and social contribution is ignored" (*Welfare Mothers Voice* 10-11).

In Spain, women created a two-minute jingle and a radio program interviewing people supporting the strike. Women in Albania and Kosovo translated the radio jingle into Albanian, Macedonian, Serbo-Croatian and Serbian. In the Philippines women lobbied for a Presidential proclamation making March 8 a paid holiday. They announced March 8 a "No Housework Day" and organized women's parties and picnics, sending the message that women had enough of overwork (*Welfare Mothers Voice* 10-11).

Each year, since the 2000 inauguration of the Global Women's Strike, women around the world have been organizing events on March 8 to continue the pressure on governments to include and value unwaged work in their economies and to educate the community about women's unwaged and low-waged work. Women from Trinidad and Tobago, from Ecuador to Ghana, from New Zealand to Nigeria, from Guyana to Korea have been marching in the streets, broadcasting on local and major radio stations, taking kids out of school, invading department stores, reading poetry in the plaza, occupying main streets from midday to midnight, carrying pots on heads and babies on backs while refusing to work, holding four-hour pots-and-pans protests, and lobbying governments to provide payment for caring work via social security payments, land, paid breastfeeding and maternity leave, pensions and other means to compensate and value the unwaged work of women.

Since 2004, the theme of the Global Women's Strike has been "Invest in Caring Not Killing" as U.S. and NATO wars have ravaged the Earth. Women in as many as 64 countries hold Global Women's Strike events each March 8, using that action as a catalyst to carry out ongoing campaigns for everything from clean drinking water to pay equity in the global market to an end to unpaid workfare in welfare programs.[1]

Motherworkers still face a challenging struggle to root out patriarchal contempt for, and exploitation of, caregiving work and the women who do it. But those of us who know our herstory, who remember the tens of thousands of years when mother was god and god was mother—when motherwork was the most valued work and children were loved and helped by all—will never stop fighting for money for mothers.

[1]To join this important campaign to economically empower motherworkers, contact Welfare Warriors at 414-342-6662 / wmvoice@execpc.com.

WORKS CITED

Arno P. S., C. Levine and M. M. Memmott. "The Economic Value of Informal Caregiving." *Health Affairs* 18 (2) (1999): 182-188. Print.

Center on Budget and Policy Priorities. *Off the Charts*. July 13, 2012. Web.

Clearinghouse on International Developments in Child, Youth and Family Policies. Section 1.8, 1.9. Columbia University, New York, November 2004. Web.

Crittenden, Ann. *The Price of Motherhood: Why the Most Important Job in the World is Still the Least Valued*. New York: H. Holt and Co., 2001. Print.

D'Arcy, Margaretta. "Irish Women Call for Global Women's Strike." *Welfare Mothers Voice* (Fall 1999): 13.

Global Women's Strike. Web.

"Living on Nothing." *New York Times* 3 January 2010. Print.

The Prison Birth Project. Web.

Socialist Worker.org. March 7, 2012. Web.

United for a Fair Economy. Web.

"Who Cares? Recent Research on Caregiving-Canada." January 2012. Available from: Beverley Smith, 521-18A St. NW, Calgary, Alberta Canada. <bevsmith@gmail.com>.

Welfare Mothers Voice (Winter/Spring 2000).

Women of China. 2011-12. English Monthly. All China Women's Federation. Beijing Xinhua Printing Company. Print.

What Do South Asian Mothers Need?

Negotiating Culture, Family and Selfhood

JASJIT K. SANGHA

SOUTH ASIAN CULTURE HAS HISTORICALLY revered mothers for providing nurturance, care, and love to the next generation; upholding and preserving family honour; and transmitting and preserving cultural norms and values. Within this context, South Asian mothers are given power in the domestic sphere through their role as dutiful mothers who serve as the bedrock of family life. However, this power has a cost, as mothers must conform to patriarchal constructions of femininity and motherhood in order to wield this power (Krishnaraj). This often results in a negation of their own selfhood, as their wants and needs are intrinsically tied to those of the family. Recent work on South Asian mothering (Sangha and Gonsalves) presents another side of the experiences of South Asian mothers by highlighting how they negotiate culture, family and selfhood, through expressing their agency and their autonomy. In this paper I will attempt to unravel the complexity of South Asian mothering and initiate a dialogue on the question, "*What Do South Asian Mothers Need?*" through a deeper exploration of how cultural norms and values inform, constrain, and empower South Asian mothers.

To clarify, I use the term South Asian with misgivings. Although it is a convenient term that refers to people who have roots in South Asia—i.e. India, Pakistan, Bangladesh, Nepal and Sri Lanka and surrounding areas—it puts a very diverse population of over 1.5 billion people into the same category. It does not capture the heterogeneity of this group of people amongst whom there are differences in language, religion, ethnicity, geography, and cultural practices from region to region within South Asia and transnationally within the diaspora. For example, there are significant ethnic differences between a Tamil mother and a Punjabi mother and stark economic differences between an upper class urban mother from New Delhi and a rural working class Dalit mother. In this way, although the term South Asian is used in this paper, there is a recognition of its limitations. This paper will be divided into three main themes: Reshaping, Reclaiming and Resisting; Mothering, Mental Health and Well-Being; and Complicating Women' Work.

RESHAPING, RECLAIMING AND RESISTING

Within South Asian communities, both in South Asian and in the diaspora, mothers are deemed to be the bearers of culture. They carry the weight of responsibility for ensuring that children—and especially girls—adhere to acceptable expressions of behavior in the immediate family, with extended family, and in greater society. If children stray outside of culturally determined norms, the mother is usually deemed to be at fault. However, despite this pressure, South Asian mothers are not just passive transmitters of dominant cultural ideals. Rather, when mothers are placed in a position of marginality, they rework this position and find power within it by reshaping, reclaiming and resisting cultural expectations that are placed on them. This demonstration of agency can be both subtle or overt, yet still have powerful meaning for mothers.

Rachana Johri deconstructs interviews with upper-class Hindu women in India to show how mothers pass down scripts on acceptable and appropriate forms of womanhood to their daughters. She draws out how mothers underpin the importance of cultural traditions such as *kanyadaan* (giving a virginal bride to her husband's family), and the practice that after marriage a daughter changes from being *apni* (ours) to *parayi* (theirs), and belongs in her husband's home. However, as Johri argues, despite the mothers' adherence to these cultural practices as a way to retain their *izzat* (honour) and status in society, they also resist and question these same practices when their daughters are in crises in their marital homes. For example, mothers assert their resistance through actions such as supporting their daughter through a divorce (despite the backlash they may receive for doing so) and therefore contribute to changing cultural practices that seek to contain and control women.

In her work, "Lessons of Izzat," Mandeep Kaur Mucina focuses her attention on the historical culture practice of *izzat* (honour) as a way of regulating and controlling women's sexuality. This work reveals how

Jasjit K. Sangha

this cultural practice was as relevant for her, living in the South Asian diaspora, as it was for the women in Johri's article who were situated in India. Mucina outlines the vital role played by women—mothers, grandmothers, aunts—in reinforcing the relevancy of *izzat* through the generations, as well as exposing her to ways to resist or undermine oppression stemming from this practice. She contests the moral regulation that is being placed on her as a woman, and concludes that by reclaiming her *izzat*, on her own terms, she is able to find empowerment in this cultural practice.

Tarnjit Johal's work focuses on culture from another perspective, by showing how devout Sikh mothers find solace in religion. She examines the decision by Sikh mothers in Canada and Britain to follow the religious practice of growing their male children's hair (*kesh*), and covering it with a turban. She explains how this decision to keep their *kesh*, as an outward religious symbol, defines their mothering practice. Johal writes that for these Sikh mothers, *kesh* holds deep religious meaning for them, and they seek to impart this meaning to their children through love and understanding.

Writing by Jasjit K. Sangha (2012) offers another vantage point on how faith can be a source of solace for South Asian mothers. She highlights how through her spiritual practice, she was able to attain the inspiration she needed to delve more deeply into herself and overcome tension, anger and resentment she experienced as a new stepmother to two adolescent stepdaughters in a bi-racial stepfamily. While the mothers in Johal's work found meaning in religious traditions, Sangha was compelled to reshape her understanding of South Asian cultural values and traditions because she had married interracially and her stepdaughters resisted the imposition of South Asian culture on their lives.

For other South Asian mothers it is not a question of reshaping, but of resisting South Asian cultural values, because they constrain and undermine their mothering practice. For them, everyday acts of resistance are embedded into their mothering practice. Tahira Gonsalves and Jasjit K. Sangha's interview with South Asian activist mothers exposes the forced vulnerability and constant surveillance they experience due to racism, homophobia and ableism. As a result they must constantly resist judgement on their mothering practices from both within the South Asian community and mainstream society in order to protect their children from ridicule. Rather than trying to preserve or disseminate South Asian culture to their children, their motherwork centres around issues of social justice, critical thinking and resisting marginalization.

As these scholars show, culture, tradition and religion shape and influence the experiences of South Asian Mothers in a myriad of ways, and it is through expressing their agency that South Asian mothers are able to negotiate their relationship with South Asian culture and the constraints it may impose on their lives.

MOTHERING, MENTAL HEALTH AND WELL-BEING

The mental health and well-being of South Asian mothers can be affected for many reasons, stemming from factors such as isolation and poverty related to migration, having a child who is vulnerable due to a disability or illness, or conflict and violence in the home. For mothers facing these challenges, the insularity of the South Asian community, cultural taboos around sharing "family" problems with those outside the family, and limited knowledge of available social services can lead to a decline in the mental health and well-being. This is further exacerbated by their own sense of inadequacy as mothers who are not living up to South Asian cultural ideals of motherhood. However, as scholars outline, through attaining culturally appropriate care and support, South Asian mothers are able to strengthen their sense of self.

In their study of newcomer Tamil mothers in Toronto, Soumia Meiyappan and Lynne Lohfeld outline the factors that contribute to the weakening of the mental health of these South Asian mothers. They show that migration to a new country, stress associated with separation from their family, and a lack of familiarity with the language and culture of mainstream society can be overwhelming. When this was combined with the isolation and exhaustion they felt as new mothers, it lead to changes in their sense of well-being. Unfortunately many Tamil newcomer mothers were either unaware of the social services that were available to support them—such as mother-child drop in centres—and/or unsure about using these services. As a result they were less likely to attain the mental health support that they needed as new mothers and new immigrants.

Research by Satwinder Bains highlights how the stigma attached to having a disabled child adds another layer of complexity to the mental health needs of South Asian mothers. In her study, mothers were often blamed for their child's disability and relatives were not able to provide the necessary support due to their own misconceptions around disability. The pressure of having full responsibility for their children and the lack of empathy for their situation led to stress and depression for some mothers. Like the women, in Meiyappan and Lohfeld's study, they did not have a lot of awareness of social services that were available for their children or for themselves and they were skeptical of going outside the South Asian community for help. However, as Bains asserts, the small group of mothers who did find appropriate services were buoyed by the support they received and tried to reach out to other South Asian mothers whose child had a disability

A short story by Sadia Zaman exemplifies the vulnerability faced by these South Asian mothers through her account of caring for her very sick child. In her work, she shares the pain of watching her tiny son struggle for breath and the transformation she underwent, as a mother, in order to try to protect and support him. Zaman writes about how through donning the metaphorical armour, shield and sword of warrior she was able to reinvent herself from a grieving mother who felt guilt about her son's health condition to a warrior who became a pillar of strength for her son by staying by his side all night, watching his oxygen levels and soothing him with her voice.

In the research by Meiyappan and Lohfeld, and Bains, the mothers also stated that they drew strength from moments of closeness with their children. In this way, there were times when they were able to find meaning and fulfillment through nurturing their children, despite cultural norms that may have led them to feel incompetent as mothers. The work of

Manavi Handa and Baldev Mutta offers innovative solutions to further bolster the agency of South Asian mothers who are experiencing challenges in their lives. They have strived to break through the insularity of immigrant communities and provide culturally appropriate care to South Asian mothers.

In her paper, Handa writes about her work as a midwife in the South Asian community. She delineates how new immigrant mothers in Ontario face constraints as they have to pay hefty fees for health care because they are not covered for the first three months upon arrival in Canada. As a midwife, she intentionally reached out to these women, through means such as leaving relevant information, translated into South Asian languages, in gathering spaces such as mosques, temples and community centres. In this way she was able to serve as a bridge between pregnant new immigrant mothers—who were often living in poverty, isolated and scared—and health care providers. Through her work, she made midwifery accessible and ensured that a diverse group of South Asian mothers, who were at a vulnerable stage of their life, were able to benefit from the informed care that she provided.

Baldev Mutta provides further depth to this discussion of South Asian mothering and mental health through his experiences of providing counseling services for over two decades in Punjabi community. Through his commentary he explains how the cultural socialization of Punjabi mothers to be dutiful, sacrificial and benevolent wives and mothers puts them at risk of over-extending themselves and being susceptible to abuse. He proposes a solution to uplift and empower Punjabi mothers—through an integrated holistic counseling model that involves the whole extended family though parenting classes, a women's program, a senior's program, men's program etc. His commentary discloses how entrenched cultural beliefs and ways of being that may have limited the potential of Punjabi mothers can be altered in order to pave the way for empowerment, leadership and advocacy.

As these researchers illuminate, for South Asian mothers, there are many factors that can impact their mental health. South Asian cultural values in which mothers are deemed to be responsible for their children, contributes to the stress and insecurity they may experience. Within this context, strengthening the agency of South Asian mothers requires health care providers to be more cognizant of the specific contexts of their lives in order to be effective.

COMPLICATING WOMEN'S WORK

Another realm in which South Asian mothers negotiate culture, family and selfhood is in the realm of work. Scholars show how through their work—in realms such as home-based businesses or commercial gestational surrogacy—South Asian mothers are exerting their agency and contesting South Asian cultural interpretations about motherhood, and family life. Although the women may still adhere to South Asian cultural understanding of motherhood and its significance in their lives, the autonomy and power they are accessing through their paid work builds their capacity and lays the ground work for further empowerment.

In Srabani Maitra's study, South Asian mothers chose home-based work, versus work outside the home in a low paying sector, after they experienced deskilling and discrimination in the Canadian workforce. They decided that working at a low paying, precarious job was not worth it because childcare would be very costly. Instead, they decided to set up home-based businesses so they could fulfill their roles as mothers and wives, yet also have some power in the family due to having paid work that made an important contribution to their survival. Through their work, and the importance it held for the family, they were able to negotiate their childcare and household responsibilities with their husband, and shift the expectation that they had to the primary nurturer just because they were the mother.

Similarly, women in Amrita Pande's research on gestational commercial surrogacy in India, were contesting assumptions about what motherhood entailed. Rather than it being based on biological ties alone, the surrogates regarded themselves as the mothers of the children they were carrying due to the blood, sweat and labor they were putting into their work. The surrogates expressed that they would feel sadness when they had to give up their child to their lawful parents, just as a mother would when giving away a daughter in marriage, as Johri explained in her article. Since many of the surrogates were married and mothers themselves, their work also changed the dynamic in their own relationships, as they were carrying a child that was not their husband's, and they were being financially compensated for it. Like the women in Maitra's study, since their income was vital to the family's financial security, their husbands were forced to play more of a role in childcare, and give their wives more autonomy.

Both of these authors expose how South Asian mothers are reconstructing cultural norms and values through their work and through pushing back on expectations that are placed upon them. For the mothers who are home-based workers this means ensuring that their work and time are valued despite the fact that they are working from home. For the surrogates it means acknowledging the emotion and bond they have with the baby they are carrying and that through their work, they are mothering a child.

CONCLUSION

It is hoped that this chapter has been able to offer insight on South Asian Mothering and will initiate dialogue on the question, "*What Do South Asian Mothers Need?*" As scholars in this chapter have outlined, South Asian cultural constructions of motherhood influence how South Asian mothers understand themselves, their role as mothers, and their relationships with their children. However, *how* culture is embedded in their mothering practice and to *what* extent it shapes or constrains their mothering practice is varied and complex. For some South Asian mothers the pressure they experience to fulfill cultural norms pertaining to motherhood can lead to a decline in mental health, while for others it can lead them to push back and resist patriarchal assumptions that undermine their mothering. For most South Asian mothers their experience lies somewhere between two contrasts. In this way, South Asian mothers negotiate culture, family and selfhood through the manifestation of their motherwork and their subsequent attempts to validate their motherwork, nurture their autonomy and strengthen their voices.

WORKS CITED

Bains, Satwinder Kaur. "South Asian Mothers With Special Needs Children." *South Asian Mothering: Negotiating Culture, Family and Selfhood*. Eds. Jasjit K. Sangha and Tahira Gonsalves. Bradford, ON: Demeter Press, forthcoming 2013.

Gonsalves, Tahira and Jasjit. K. Sangha. "South Asian Activists Speak Out About Politics, Sexuality, Health and Mothering." *South Asian Mothering: Negotiating Culture, Family and Selfhood*. Eds. Jasjit K.

Sangha and Tahira Gonsalves. Bradford, ON: Demeter Press, forthcoming 2013.

Handa, Manavi. "Mothering the South Asian Mother: Stories from Midwifery." *South Asian Mothering: Negotiating Culture, Family and Selfhood.* Eds. Jasjit K. Sangha and Tahira Gonsalves. Bradford, ON: Demeter Press, forthcoming 2013.

Johal, Tarnjit. "Sikh Mothering." *South Asian Mothering: Negotiating Culture, Family and Selfhood.* Eds. Jasjit K. Sangha and Tahira Gonsalves. Bradford, ON: Demeter Press, forthcoming 2013.

Johri, Rachana. "From *Parayi* to *Apni*: Mother's Love as Resistance." *South Asian Mothering: Negotiating Culture, Family and Selfhood.* Eds. Jasjit K. Sangha and Tahira Gonsalves. Bradford, ON: Demeter Press, forthcoming 2013.

Krishnaraj, Maithreyi. *Motherhood in India: Glorification Without Empowerment?* New Delhi: Routledge, 2009.

Pande, Amrita. "The 'Sweat and Blood' of Womb Mothers: Commercial Surrogates Redefining Motherhood." *South Asian Mothering: Negotiating Culture, Family and Selfhood.* Eds. Jasjit K. Sangha and Tahira Gonsalves. Bradford, ON: Demeter Press, forthcoming 2013.

Maitra, Srabani. "Perspectives on Work and Family Lives: Exploring the Lived Experiences of South Asian Immigrant Mothers Working from Home in Toronto." *South Asian Mothering: Negotiating Culture, Family and Selfhood.* Eds. Jasjit K. Sangha and Tahira Gonsalves. Bradford, ON: Demeter Press, forthcoming 2013.

Meiyappan, Soumia and Lynne Lohfeld. "New Mothers in a New Land: The First Time Mothering Experiences of Sri Lankan Tamils." *South Asian Mothering: Negotiating Culture, Family and Selfhood.* Eds. Jasjit K. Sangha and Tahira Gonsalves. Bradford, ON: Demeter Press, forthcoming 2013.

Mucina, Mandeep Kaur. "Lessons of *Izzat.*" *South Asian Mothering: Negotiating Culture, Family and Selfhood.* Eds. Jasjit K. Sangha and Tahira Gonsalves. Bradford, ON: Demeter Press, forthcoming 2013.

Mutta, Baldev. "Empowering Punjabi Mothers Through Integrated Holistic Counselling." *South Asian Mothering: Negotiating Culture, Family and Selfhood.* Eds. Jasjit K. Sangha and Tahira Gonsalves. Bradford, ON: Demeter Press, forthcoming 2013.

Sangha, Jasjit K. *Stepmothering: A Spiritual Journey.* Bradford, ON: Demeter Press, 2012.

Sangha, Jasjit K. and Tahira Gonsalves, eds. *South Asian Mothering: Negotiating Culture, Family and Selfhood*. Gonsalves. Bradford, on: Demeter Press, forthcoming 2013.

Zaman, Sadia. "Mothers and Warriors." *South Asian Mothering: Negotiating Culture, Family and Selfhood*. Eds. Jasjit K. Sangha and Tahira Gonsalves. Bradford, ON: Demeter Press, forthcoming 2013.

3. Mothers, Family, Children and Families: Health and Well-Being

What Do Mothers Need?

Midwives!

BARBARA KATZ ROTHMAN

I HAVE BEEN STUDYING BIRTH for coming up on 40 years now—my oldest child is 38 this summer. I move on to other things, and come back, over and over again, to issues of birth and midwifery as a special kind of sane touchstone. In so much of the work I do, I honestly do not know what the answers are or ought to be, what would be the "right" thing to do, how to connect my politics and my values to my intellectual explorations. But in birth I do actually know exactly what the answers are and what we ought to be doing. We're not doing it, and I haven't made much headway in improving things, but at least I know what I want to see. What I want to see is the return of the midwife.

Early on, when I was first studying midwifery, what interested me was what went on in a midwife's head. I wanted to understand how midwives and obstetricians could look at what appeared to be the same thing, the baby-out-of-vagina sameness of birth, and see such very different meanings there. In the course of doing that work, interviewing many midwives, attending their formal and informal meetings, reading the literature of the newly reviving midwifery and home birth movement in the United States in the 1970s, I came to differentiate what I called the "midwifery model" from the ubiquitous and then-normative "medical model" of perinatal care. Obstetricians saw the endangered product of a man, trapped within the risky confines of a woman, a vulnerable fetal patient needing care and often rescue. Midwives saw a woman's body growing and nurturing and bringing forth her baby. A male-centered vision contrasted with a woman-centered one; a world of separate and discrete beings in ongoing conflict with each other contrasted with the interdependence of us all.

It is not surprising that as a young graduate student in sociology, a woman at a moment of feminist passion and activism, an academic and scholar struggling to find her place in the academy, I would focus on the minds and collective worldview of midwives. My questions today are different. It is not only I who have aged, but feminism, the discipline of sociology, and a society growing world-weary of the excesses of advanced industrial capitalism. New questions arise, new concerns grab our attention. "The Body" is a developing area of work in American Sociology. And the work of the hand, craftsmanship, embodied skill, is being rediscovered in American society.

One of the best examples of this new "turn to the hands" is to be found in Richard Sennett, *The Craftsman*. In that work, Sennett quotes the philosopher Kant, who tells us that "The hand is window to the mind." Sennett examines the work of the hands of musicians, glassblowers, chefs, and other skilled workers, and leads us to an understanding of craftsmanship, of artisanal work.

While I feel as strongly as ever that in order to understand the differences in practice between midwives and obstetricians one must understand the underlying ideology, the conceptual model of pregnancy and birth that they bring to the laboring woman, I now want to follow the reverse path. Let us go not only from the mind and its world view or model to the practice, but from the work of the hands to see into the mind.

I come to this turn to the hand through a rather odd door—the world of Food Studies. Food Studies is a newly developing discipline, which places what we eat, how we grow, gather, prepare and serve our food, at the center of our understanding of social relationships. Food and the acts and arts of its preparation, carefully studied, can tell us a great deal about who we are as individuals and as societies.

When I first learned of Food Studies, guided by my colleague Jonathan Deutsch, what struck my interest were the similarities to be found in the choice of home cooking and the choice of home birth, the decision in each of these areas of intersection between the body and the larger society, to avoid the industrial and seek out the individualized. As different as birth and cooking are, I began to see that people's search for meaning, for authenticity, in home cooking is part of the same larger fabric as the home birth movement, that both express our uneasiness with consumer society. Within the family, within the personal sphere, within the bounds of our homes, we are trying to avoid being swamped with consumerism, to avoid bar-coding everything. There is a sadness there, a deep-seated dissatisfaction with the marketplace as a way-of-life that people are trying to express in places as seemingly disparate as the kitchen and in the birthroom.

In the midwifery and home birth movement the struggle was to hold on to the meaning and place of birth in the context of family rather than medicine, to move birth out of the hospital as a big impersonal institution, and bring it home. (Rothman 1982, 1989; Simonds and Rothman). Birth is at the dramatic end, dinner at the mundane, but in both, I hear much the same concerns being expressed. As we find our lives taken over by huge institutions, industries and media, we try to find a little place that's really and truly ours, where we can be ourselves. We search for something "authentic," something meaningful in life.

Laura Shapiro, in her contemporary history of cooking, said that once we had so many alternatives, dinners out, pre-made foods to bring in, "it was never clear anymore whether making dinner was an honor or an obligation or even a necessity. And if dinner went, what was left?" (214). I have heard midwives say almost the same thing about giving birth. If you can just give birth with an epidural, polishing your nails and reading a book or something at the same time, then what does it mean to have a baby? What about a world that offers us pregnancies for hire, or the proverbial, much-worried about babies out of machines? Who are we, they are asking, if we do not do anything ourselves, make anything ourselves?

A lot of the more serious issues I've been dealing with for years now in the arena of procreation are there in a more playful, less fraught way, in cooking. I know it sounds strange, but: The choices people face in birth—which of the new technologies and tests to use, home births or hospitals, cesareans, epidurals—all seem to be saying something deeply true about oneself. Who *are* you, if you do or don't birth "naturally"? What kind of a woman has a cesarean by choice? What kind of a woman chooses a midwife, let alone a home birth? In cooking—it is much the same, but who cares? That is, in the U.S., someone can brew her own beer and bake her own bread one night, just to see what it's like, grind her own flour even, eat it with the vegetables she has grown in her garden and the yogurt she cultured herself—the whole nine yards. And the next night, one can stop in at a take-out place for dinner because the kids are cranky and it's on the way home, and what the hell, one can bake again tomorrow. With births, it's not like that—people do not feel as free to say "With this one we'll do every prenatal test there is, do ultrasounds every month, plan an elective cesarean section, bottle feed and then use disposable diapers; with the next one, we can go off and do it without any of that, birth unattended on a farm somewhere, breastfeed for years and years, dress the baby in nothing but pure cotton hand-washed in spring water."

Precisely because it is less fraught, talking to people about how they cook, what ingredients they use, what they do in the kitchen, is informative, and sheds some light on the larger issues of who we are in the world, how we negotiate our place. Birth and cooking both explore that interface between the body and the culture. For people who are not food insecure, for people who are deciding what, where and how to eat, not whether they can eat at all, the stakes are understood as lower, so that in the kitchen rather than the birth room, the possibility for creativity is opened up. As the neurosurgeon hero of Ian McEwan's *Saturday* says, "In the kitchen, the consequences of failure are mild: disappointment, a wisp of disgrace, rarely voiced. No one actually dies" (181).

These were the questions that I then brought to the world of food. But when I came to that world, I saw that there were people who had been thinking hard about the meaning and place of food in our lives in the same ways that midwives think about birth.

At the first Food Studies meeting I went to, there was a panel of artisanal food makers—a brewer who was hand-crafting beers, a cheese-maker, and a baker who had resurrected a kind of wheat grain thought to be extinct, having it cloned and growing it again for the first time in a century.

There was a brief self-congratulatory conversation, in which the food makers on the panel were celebrating their contributions, their uniqueness in the mass production society. "It's not like some company with a hundred employees," one said. "Ah, when you count the bottlers and all, I have a hundred employees," said the beer brewer. "It's not like we are using high tech laboratories," the first offered again. "No," said the baker, "think about what we had to do to clone that wheat!" and the cheese maker agreed, "there is much laboratory science I need to use." A brief flurry of talk followed as they quickly sought some common ground: just what was it that made them all artisanal, all so unique? I sat there and smiled to myself—I have heard such conversations over and over again at midwifery meetings. Among midwives, someone might have said "It's not like I'm just working with strangers," and another would have said, "You know, sometimes at my hospital, the elevator door opens and out comes some

16-year-old kid in labor and crying, and even though I never saw her before, I am her midwife." "It's not like we are using high technology interventions!" and another would say, "well, with the high-risk population I am working with, I do often use those." And they too would have worked to find the common "midwifery" vision that they share, what it is that they bring as midwives that distinguishes them from obstetricians who "churn out" birth services. (The chief difference between the many such panels of midwives I have seen and this one with the artisanal food makers was the absence of crying and hugging.)

Barbara Katz Rothman

Both groups have a value system that disdains "mass production" and "industrial-style," whether they are talking about the ways birthing women are treated in hospitals, or the ways foods are made. But both groups are concerned with being "elitist," available only to a few wealthy or very knowledgeable people. In midwifery, that value is often shorthanded as "going where the women are," that it is important to be practicing in hospitals if that's where ordinary women find themselves birthing. I was struck by the way the artisanal food makers faced roughly the same issue: how to make their fine, individualized products more available to more ordinary people.

This discussion among the midwives, as among the food producers I heard at that conference, would have centered eventually on some "personal" quality. The midwives are not mass producing births: each birth is focused on the individual woman, her needs, her life. The process is important, and not just the product. And so it was for the food makers—the making, not just the food, defines the art.

In both worlds, there are shared concerns about "cooption," about losing the essence to people who market the ideology without following through. In birth, we see it in hospitals that offer lovely "home like" birthing rooms which they rarely use, that talk about "family centered" births but have cesarean section rates of 30 percent, about four times what they were as recently as the 1970s. In cooking, we see it in the use of "natural" or "organic" or just pictures of lovely grandmas in their kitchens or traditional food making equipment on the labels of industrial food products.

In both worlds, there is a very real concern with deskilling. Midwives talk despairingly of women "not knowing how to give birth anymore," of having lost the idea of actually *giving* birth to the medical experience of *being* delivered. More particularly, they worry about the loss of the specific midwifery skills: through all of human history, midwives have known how to help birth a breech baby. In contemporary U.S. hospitals, a breech birth will almost automatically mean a cesarean section, and so in short order there won't be anyone around in the states who even knows how to attend a vagina breech birth. In the food world, similar concerns are expressed, as both general and specialized knowledge are lost. I don't think I even know anybody who knows how to pickle things. And both "foodies" and "birthies" face a larger world that says "so what?" Who needs the skills to deliver a breech while we have the skills to do surgery? And who needs to know how to pickle a vegetable when they come that way from the supermarket?

Midwives, I am suggesting, hold much the same position in the world of birth as do the makers of artisanal foods in the world of cooking. Just about every human community has had midwives, just as almost all have people who know how to make certain foods. Consider the baker, or the tofu-maker: each household could be making that product or doing that activity at home, but most often one member of the community comes to specialize, to learn the particular skills of the trade. Similarly, each family could catch its own babies, but it gets complicated, and the body of sophisticated knowledge, the ways of handling problems, come to be located in a select few people. One big oven will suffice for the community, one mill for grinding and a baker comes into being. Women who are called for births come to know more and more about birth, and then pass that knowledge on down to a next generation, and midwifery comes into being. In many languages the word, unlike the English which means "with women," is "wise woman," speaking directly to locating that shared communal wisdom of birth in one member of the community.

With industrialization, birth, like bread-baking, tofu-production, cheese-making, and pickling moved out of the community. And in our post-industrial society, people have sought to recreate the traditional, the natural, the authentic. In birth, as perhaps in food, the focus in popular language is often on the "natural," but people who actually set out to learn the complex skills required for midwifery practice or for artisanal food production, see little that is "natural" there. In birth we speak of avoiding the "technological," or the "technocratic." In food, "industrial" is the object of derision. The artisanal food maker, like the midwife, tries to reclaim old skills and traditions, hone ancient arts.

Midwives and artisanal food makers are the ones who develop an ideology that they then "sell" to "consumers," all the while trying to move beyond the values and limitations of the marketplace for meaning-making. They stand between a technical industrial world on the one hand and the everyday world of shared knowledge on the other. As cooking, like birth before it, moves into the mystification of specialized practice, they are the intermediaries between these worlds of meaning. They hold within themselves a set of skills that the society as a whole fears losing—but hesitates to actually use.

In birth, as in food, the purists are not winning. People certainly talk more knowledgeably about both midwives and "authentic" and "traditional" food than they did 25 years ago. But in the United States, midwifery attended, woman centered home births are probably about as common in the world of birth as artisanal food is in the world of food. How many North Americans even know someone who has had a home birth? And how many *don't* know someone who has had a cesarean? What is called an "epidemic" of cesarean sections is as familiar—and arguably as bad for our collective health—as fast food meals. In this context, people are still struggling, in both arenas, to find a path for themselves.

Because if all this goes, what's left?

Artisanal workers are leading the food movement, from elite food down to school lunch programs, and, I suggest, offering a fine role model for midwives to follow. From Japan to Italy and around the world, the food makers have been convincing to government, to media and to consumers, arguing that their work is a valued part of a nation's cultural heritage.

This is precisely what we would like to see for midwifery—value as well as legitimation.

And what is being valued is expertise, true traditional skills and knowledge, a cultural heritage embodied in the worker. Midwives have been in an interesting position with regard to valuing their own skills. The emphasis many of us in the birth movement have put on the naturalness of birth itself, the awe-inspiring ability of a woman's body to successfully birth without intervention, without medical assistance, has made it hard for people to truly value midwifery skills. In the U.S., when people talk about midwifery care, they often think of it primarily in terms of waiting—midwives permit more time, do not rush birth, do not rush women into cesarean sections when birth goes slowly. But midwives do far more than just wait. Midwives have skills of the hands, the kinds of craft skills that Sennett explored. In midwifery education, we talk about how to teach these skills of the body, how to learn to see, feel, smell, hear, touch and know. The elaborate internships, apprentices, placements and residencies for midwifery students are ways in which we provide safe learning space.

We often find, in the world of midwifery, that there is much made of "instincts" and the "art" of midwifery. I'd like us to think more about the learned skills, the mastery of skills, the true expertise of the craftsman, which comes to look like instinct. This is not offered as an alternative to "evidence based," scientifically grounded practice. Science provides us a set of data, true hard knowledge about how things work. Science, in the world of food, can teach us much about how bread is made, the viscosity of an egg, the cellular life of wheat, the microscopic worlds of yeast. But a skilled baker does more than follow the scientifically developed recipe. The skilled baker feels the dough and knows that yes, this is the proportion of water to flour. But with this flour that was ground in this particular mill, from a strain of wheat that grew in this particular location at this particular time of year, and on this particular day in which it rained, the amount of water will have to be adjusted. Similarly the midwife can understand all of the science and the evidence, and yet say on this particular day, with this particular woman and this particular baby in the position it is, truly knowing and understanding all of what is going on, this is the moment for this particular bit of pressure. Or, in both bread and birth, the answer may well be olive oil!

We know that no amount of reading and learning the science will ever substitute for learning hands-on skills. One can understand everything there is to know about the making of a cello, the composition of the strings, the sound waves involved in each note—and still not be able to play the cello. One can understand everything about glass and heat—and still not be able to blow a vase from a molten lump of glass over a fire. It is claimed that it takes about 10,000 hours of practice to develop expertise—that comes to about three hours a day for ten years. So too, I would suggest for midwifery care. Thousands of hours of practice go into making an expert midwife.

On the other hand, this is a good moment to rethink obstetric skills. cesarean sections? Are those so very high tech and hard to learn? In many other areas of surgery now, surgeons are offering laparoscopic and other truly "high tech" surgeries, and comparing that to the relative barbarism of crude scalpel-based surgery. But cesarean sections can never be done laparoscopically, through the belly button! If we listen to what other surgeons have to say about the skills of obstetricians, perhaps we would be more comfortable talking about the truly advanced skills of midwifery. Faced with a breech birth, the obstetricians now know only to take a scalpel and slice the woman open. Trained midwives know how to ease that baby around or ease it out breech. These are the traditional skills we should be admiring.

Now more than ever, with obstetricians losing hand skills, with surgical births reaching a record high with negative consequences for maternal as well as infant morbidity and mortality, we need our midwives.

WORKS CITED

McKewan, Ian. *Saturday.* New York: Anchor Books, 2006. Print.

Sennett, Richard. *The Craftsman.* New Haven: Yale University Press, 2008. Print.

Rothman, Barbara Katz. *In Labor: Women and Power in the Birthplace.* New York: W.W. Norton and Co., 1982. Print.

Rothman, Barbara Katz. *Recreating Motherhood.* New Brunswick, NJ: Rutgers University Press, 1989. Print.

Simonds, Wendy and Barbara Katz Rothman. *Laboring On.* New York: Routledge, 2007. Print.

Shapiro, Laura. *Something from the Oven: Reinventing Dinner in 1950's America.* New York: Penguin Books, 2005.

DisAbled Mothers in the 21st Century

Finding Empowerment Through Activism

JEWELLES SMITH

ACCORDING TO 2006 STATISTICS CANADA DATA, 15.2 percent of women in Canada live with disabilities. Of these women, approximately 13 percent are of childrearing/bearing age, that is, 464,630 Canadian women (Statistics Canada). Trish Day, a mother with cerebral palsy, who started Parents with Disabilities Online, said the following:

> No human baby I have ever heard of arrives with built-in expectations about how you will parent. You may do things differently, but the baby will not know the difference. The baby is going to accept whatever you do as normal. (qtd. in Hill)

In this paper I will address a few common barriers that parents, in particular mothers with disabilities, experience. I will draw on my own experience as a mother with disabilities to demonstrate how challenging it can be to maintain a household in the face of common misconceptions and outright discrimination. I realize that some of my challenges were exacerbated by the reality of being a single parent but that in itself would be an entire other paper! First I will discuss a little of my beginnings as an activist and a new mom; next I will discuss how these two worlds collided; and finally I will draw out how this life of mothering, living with disabilities and activism has led to empowerment. Or, at least, moments of feeling a sense of empowerment.

I am going to briefly mention a current and very relevant case that has been in the Canadian papers this spring regarding a family that has been faced with possible apprehension of their child (newborn) based not on their skill as parents, but solely on their disabilities and how the prejudice of government agencies and hospital staff perceive their "ability" to parent.

Maricyl Palisoc and Charles Wilton are the parents of a newborn son. Both parents have cerebral palsy or CP. Although both parents are quite capable of caring for their son and have an accessible home and regular support care, the Ontario Children's Aid Society has threatened that they will remove the child unless the child is given 24 hour care in the home by an "able-bodied" person. The disability community is very concerned with this response from a government agency. Although Canada has recently signed and ratified the United Nations Convention on the Rights of Persons with Disabilities, it is clear from this story, many other current situations, as well as my own experiences, that there remains a lot of work to be done in raising awareness before people who are disabled will be able to parent without the interventions and prejudices of government and citizens.

I have not been threatened with the apprehension of my children, but I most definitely have experienced intrusive and unwanted attention from child welfare authorities that was brought on by a school's response to my "well-being," as they framed it. Before I discuss this, I am going to backtrack a little and give you some background on how I became an activist and a parent.

HOW DID I BECOME AN ACTIVIST?

My disabilities came later in life, after I had given birth to my children. I first recognized that I was becoming an activist halfway through my undergraduate degree. I began university in part due to the unexplained intermittent weakness and loss of use of the right side of my body. I had worked for fourteen years in the service industry, culminating in managing restaurants. However, after the birth of my eldest son and second child, my health was seriously impacting my ability to work. When I became pregnant with my second son, I recognized that I had to make some changes. I decided that I would explore higher education, rightly discerning that if my body continued to decline, I would be unemployable in my field.

The second semester I was in university, attending the University of Northern British Columbia, I had a surgery that permanently impacted the use I have of my right hand. I had to go to the disability centre and access support services. To make a long story short, I soon discovered the amazing technology out there and the very limited access to and bureaucracy involved in receiving accommodations. This was a time of severe cuts to many funding sources including childcare, education grants, and other financial supports. Initially, I began to write letters and approach local media to address the challenges that I was experiencing in accessing services I required to pursue higher education. I experienced a very particular sort of backlash from members of the community based on assumptions about my background, my rights as a woman parenting alone, and on my views that childcare and education are basic rights. Very quickly I found myself traveling to attend protests and to speak out about the effects of these cuts on many people, but especially on mothers.

My frustrations lead to my activism and into a community of other women who have found empowerment through activism. I shifted my area of study from psychology to Women's Studies and English Literature. The reality is that my entry into activism and student politics ran parallel to my introduction to mothering. I cannot tell you how hard the road to completion of first my bachelor degree and then my Master's degree was, but I made it. My becoming an activist was due, in no small part, to my children.

MOTHERING AND ACTIVISM

The road to activism is strange indeed. One does not arrive fully formed and defined as "Activist" and in fact, the role and the direction of energy is ever changing and adjusting as life moves forward. I began my own activism focused on access to education for myself (and the future of my children); as well, I focused on childcare and resources. However, when my children began school, I had no idea of the battles ahead. We lived in Burnaby and Vancouver for the first eight years of their school experience.

Beginning in grade one, my eldest son began to experience deliberate exclusionary practices by his teacher. Often she would send him to the office rather than communicate with me on how to manage a situation. At that time, my son had multiple allergies and was struggling at school. He was undiagnosed but also living with Asperger's. According to Dictionary.

com, Asperger's Syndrome is "a developmental disorder characterized by severely impaired social skills, repetitive behaviours, and often, a narrow set of interests, but not involving delayed development of linguistic and cognitive abilities." Asperger's Syndrome is an autism spectrum disorder. The experiences we had in Vancouver were heartbreaking, as I watched my introspective son turn into a bundle of anxiety and lost confidence. Eventually the Vancouver school decided to segregate my son and put him on a list for testing. They took the same measure with my younger son. My youngest son spent three years in a segregated classroom while he waited for psycho-educational testing. I made the decision to move back to Revelstoke, British Columbia (where I had spent many years and completed grade 12).

In Vancouver, too often while I was advocating for my child's needs in the school system, teachers and so called support team members would draw attention to my own health challenges as if these were part of the discussion. I have been an advocate in the past and thought that I would be able to advocate and navigate the system for my children. Eventually, however, I had to call on fellow advocates to accompany me into meetings so that a neutral person could note the moments when the conversation became about single parenting and a child living with a parent who was disAbled rather than about the child and his educational needs.

A LITTLE ABOUT ACCESSIBILITY AND ACCOMMODATION

There can be many barriers to accessing the school and staff members for women who are differently abled. I have encountered a few myself, and have heard countless stories from women with varying visible and invisible disAbilities about access, accommodation, and barriers.

Women who use assistive devices for mobility encounter many barriers to places their children go such as daycares, schools, after school activities or even to homes where their child might wish a play-date. Women who live with chronic fatigue or symptomatic mobility issues, and who are not visibly "disabled" are often unable to access these same places. I had a very real challenge with this myself a number of times. At one point while I was living in Vancouver, my sons attended a school that required two flights of stairs to reach the office (the classroom was another flight up). There was an elevator but it was locked and only opened if someone at the office was alerted to the need for access. Of course, to alert the office, one had to go up the stairs. And when one (such as myself) does not appear to need the elevator, there are gross assumptions made, including laziness. Staff also visibly displayed their annoyance the one time I did request the elevator. Deaf women may experience difficulty when arranging for an impromptu meeting regarding their child. Not to mention that just as with the parents with CP mentioned at the start of this talk, too often deaf women experience discrimination and unnecessary "interventions" from government workers. For those mothers coping with a mental health disease, an entire paper would be needed to simply *summarize* their experiences with accessibility and support.

Suffice to say that there is far too much misinformation and discrimination in DisAbled mother's lives. A key challenge that needs to be addressed in all cases is the fear that parents have in approaching agencies when they do need assistance. According to Laurie Beachell of the CCD, "Often there is an assumption that parents are unable to look after their child, rather than look at what can we do to help the family support the child." Many parents are too afraid to seek help, fearing that they will lose their children. It is clear that the best outcome is for parents and children to stay together with the support they require.

HOW/WHEN DID I FIND EMPOWERMENT?

While I was preparing this paper, I found myself reflecting on the times in my life when I have felt "empowered." It seems like such a nebulous goal, yet, I can tell you there were many nights when I felt less than empowered as I strived to meet the needs of my two sons while struggling with my disabilities at their worst. There are my obvious health and chronic pain issues, but I also live with the sometimes-debilitating effects of PTSD (post-traumatic stress disorder). Too often the manner in which teachers and school staff approach a child with learning disabilities and behavioural issues is to attack the parenting, especially in the case of a single mother. Poverty is also, too often, a vulnerable target.

There was one school in particular where I met the full force of discrimination on many levels. First, the school was an old building with many stairs (I mentioned this above). Second, the school demographic was upper middle class, two parent (two income) plus live-in grandparent (grand-

Jewelles Smith

mother) families. I have two strong memories of the beginning of the fight in that school—in the first instance, I was at work, at Simon Fraser University. I received an *urgent* call from the school. Apparently the boys had the wrong lunches in their respective bags. The school asked if I could please come to the school to rectify the situation. Literally, their classrooms were two rooms apart. I was at least 45 minutes away on a good traffic day. I declined and instructed them to have my eldest son walk over to his brother's classroom and exchange lunches. The second incident actually has become a joke in our family. It is really two part in nature: first, I received a call from the school that my youngest was not wearing underwear (how the heck did they know?) and I replied that I was aware of this, he does not like underwear and I was not going to wrestle them on. He was in grade three after all. The second incident followed a couple days later when the school again made an urgent call when I was at Simon Fraser University and informed me that my son's socks did NOT match! And that if I was struggling so much with clothing the boys that calls could be made to "assist" me. First of all, my first reaction was "at least he has socks on!" but then I recognized that she was quite serious. Unfortunately, my attempt at humour only reinforced her idea of me and my single parent status. I am not joking about this, how I wish I were: the school ended up making a call in to the Ministry of child welfare and I had the agonizing experience of being "investigated." It was clear from the questions of the Ministry representative that the focus was on my "ability" and health status. The call had been made by a "concerned person who felt perhaps parenting was overwhelming my disability and perhaps I would require support or respite."

After the investigation, and the report that identified this as a "ridiculous" complaint, the school informed me that they felt my children would be better served in another school; in fact, in a segregated classroom in another school. This was the beginning of my understanding of the power of wealth, class and ability. I later learned that this school often identified children in single parent families, reported them and ensured that the children moved on to "more appropriate" schools. As I mentioned above, this journey has definitely oscillated between aspects of my ability and my single parent (mother) status.

I believe that year was the turning point in my empowerment/activist journey. Heretofore I had been an activist on campus and for many issues: single parents and parents on campus, students with disabilities, the right to child care, education rights, class/poverty, and women's rights to mention a few. Now I became an activist *parent* for my sons and their right to education and to my right to parent them regardless of my fluctuating health challenges.

I am going to jump ahead a few years to my final frustration with the Vancouver School District and a moment of clarity I had where all of the previous struggles culminated in what I believe is the best decision I have made for my boys since the decision to go to university. In my eldest son's final year of elementary, I was informed that due to his Gifted/Learning Disabled status and the Asperger's, he was being referred to an amazing high school program GOLD—but he would have to write an essay to be accepted (this is in fact where his learning disability shows up—written output). Suffice to say, he was not accepted, the school asked to meet with me and offered him a spot in the behaviour challenged classroom of about ten students. They informed me that they would keep him occupied and hope that he made it to the end of grade nine.

I went home, cried through a very long night and then began to make phone calls. Specifically, I called "home" to Revelstoke where I had not lived since 1995, but where I completed my own grade twelve. The school staff remembered me and put together a great alternative program for my son. We moved and I am happy to say that two years later, he has just begun grade ten, he is almost fully integrated in the classrooms and he has received a couple "A" grades. Grade ten planning is for a fully integrated experience with an occasional scribe for exams and essays. My other son had also been segregated and put on a wait list for testing in Vancouver. He had been on the wait list for three years when we moved. He was tested within three weeks of beginning school in Revelstoke. He was diagnosed as gifted with dyslexia. He is now excelling and has just entered grade eight. I cannot say enough about the different experience we have had here.

CONCLUSIONS: WHAT DO DISABLED MOTHERS NEED?

So about *empowerment* and *mothering*, I wonder sometimes about where the success here comes from: out of my own path to assertion and active advocacy? Or residing in a difference of school district? I am very clear with the school here about my expectations and goals, I do not let my own health and disabilities come into the conversation—*ever*. If I am not well enough to attend a meeting, I make it clear that I need to reschedule and there is no time for the school to condescend or to challenge my parenting. I wonder also about being in a space where I have a history.

What I learned and would like to share with other mothers who either live with disabilities or live within a limited means—don't let the school, daycare, or anyone else change the issues—their job is to teach your child, not to examine your parenting lifestyle, choices, struggles or in fact anything unless there is clear abuse or neglect. I also advise taking an observer/advocate with you on meetings with the school. It is absolutely your right. Have the other person take notes and have a signal to indicate when they might want to mention something forgotten, or to help keep the conversation on track. Be clear, the school has no business in your health, and be aware that "concern" is sometimes a mask for judgment.

In conclusion, living with disabilities can be an exhausting maze of bureaucracy and barriers. Empowerment does not come overnight; rather it is a long and arduous journey. Faced with bureaucracy that appears determined to maintain the barriers to participation in society, too often, it is easier to leave off the fight for basic rights and access than it is to continue that battle. However, becoming a mother and wanting the same opportunities for your children as any other mother wants for her children can reveal a wellspring of resolve that has previously lain dormant. There are so many different challenges that are unique to mothers with disabilities that one short paper cannot begin to address their complexities and particulars. I hope that by sharing my own warbling path that is by no means completed, I have given the reader something to think on, and perhaps enlightened a little on the complex experience of mothering with disAbilities.

WORKS CITED

Brosnahan, Maureen. "Parents with Disabilities want Support, Not False Stigma." CBC News. May 2, 2012. Web.

Hill, Mary. "Mothers with disabilities—Physical limitations are no limitations to loving and Nurturing a Child." *Babyzone*. Web. Accessed: September 11, 2012.

Statistics Canada. "Persons with Disabilities, by Age Group and Sex (2006)." 22/06/2009. Web. Accessed: 7 January 2011.

Toward a Feminist Analysis of Motherhood, Family and Food Allergies

HEATHER HEWETT

FOR SEVERAL DECADES, feminist scholars have been studying the ways that gender inflects the division of labor in individual households. Sociologists such as Marjorie DeVault brought attention to the centrality of food preparation in the social reproduction of family, and a wide range of scholars working in the fields of feminist mothering studies and food studies have begun to look more closely at the complex relationships between gender, food, culture, and family in the U.S. and globally. To date, however, the increasing prevalence of food allergies and sensitivities, and the challenges of feeding families in which one or more children have chronic and/or life-threatening conditions, remains unexamined within these discussions.[1]

Food allergies not only complicate and heighten the labor involved in feeding children but also transform food itself into something that threatens rather than nourishes. The resulting anxiety can heighten the emotional labor experienced by parents—a burden that still tends to be disproportionately shouldered by more mothers than fathers. In this paper, I provide an overview of some of the issues and offer some preliminary observations about the impact of children's food allergies on mothers—who I define as the person engaged in the work of mothering, or what Sara Ruddick calls "maternal thinking," regardless of gender—based on my experiences as a mother of a daughter with severe food allergies, asthma, and Celiac disease.

The experience of living with and managing food allergies has implications not only for our understanding of families and food but also for our understanding of caregiving in the context of disability, chronic disease, and illness—experiences and conditions familiar to most if not all of us. At some point, all mothers provide care to children, parents, partners, or themselves in the context of one or more of these issues. Many scholars, writers, and activists have done tremendous work in the realm of articulating what it means to care in the context of disease and disability (see Kittay). I would like to add to this discussion by suggesting that food allergies provide a particular experience of disease and disability: as chronic conditions, they require medical management to prevent allergic reactions; and although some children grow out of their allergies, many do not. Thus my reflections in this paper may well apply to a larger group of conditions that also need to be medically managed such as asthma, epilepsy, and diabetes.

OUR STORY

My nine-year-old daughter has what doctors call "IgE-mediated food allergy" to seven foods (dairy, eggs, peanuts, tree nuts, fish, shellfish, and sesame seeds), six of which are on the top eight list of allergens. She also has anaphylaxis, which means that two (or more) of her body's systems react when she eats one of these foods. For example, when she accidentally ingests milk—even a small bite of muffin with milk baked in it—she immediately reacts with hives, vomiting, and a swelling throat. To use simple language (as I have learned to do with adults responsible for her care): if she is not immediately given epinephrine by injection, she will die. Like many children with food allergies, she has asthma (plus eczema, as an infant—what Sandra Beasley calls the "holy trifecta" of allergy, asthma, and eczema) (Beasley 211). One year ago, she was diagnosed with a separate autoimmune disorder, Celiac disease, which further restricts her diet.

At this point, the only treatment for her food allergies is avoidance. When she was younger, my husband and I exerted a tremendous amount of time and energy making sure that her environment was safe—in other words, making sure that she didn't come into contact with any food allergens, including foods that might be cross-contaminated. We still spend a lot of time on the logistics of feeding her. For example, we bake everything ourselves, we make all of her school lunches, we bring all of our food when we travel, we shop at multiple grocery stores in order to buy specialty allergy- and gluten-free foods, and so on. We also have to make sure that all adults who care for her know how to treat her in case of emergency. Admittedly, managing her allergies is becoming a bit easier now that she's older. This had given me some breathing space in which I've begun to reflect upon the anxiety I've grown accustomed to living with over the past nine years. While it has dissipated a bit now that she's older, it's still there; and I know it will come back in a new form when she becomes a teenager. And while I don't wish to make unfounded generalizations based on my experience alone, I would like to use our experiences as a basis for theorizing some of the larger issues, suggesting areas for further research, and offering some tentative thoughts about the overarching question guiding the May 2012 MIRCI conference: what do mothers need?

ANXIETY AND FOOD ALLERGIES

The parenting advice I've heard from child therapists specializing in food allergy is that parents need to learn to manage their anxiety. The advice goes something like this: you don't want too much, which is dysfunctional and leads to paralysis and overprotection; but on the other hand, you don't want too little, which can lead to risky behavior and dangerous exposures (Greenberger). You need to live with a "necessary anxiety" in order to make sure your child stays safe. In my experience, this advice accurately reflects what's often called for—though I would add that it hasn't always been easy for me to "manage" my anxiety when my child has gone to the emergency room in an ambulance multiple times because of accidental food ingestion. I would also note that this "necessary anxiety," or vigilance, is different from the anxiety associated with both "overparenting" and "intensive mothering," both of which have been critiqued by feminist scholars and writers as well as cultural scholars more generally (Hays; Warner; Stearns; Nelson; O'Reilly). Of course, it's quite possible that a parent of a food allergic child who by necessity engages in vigilant parenting also finds herself (or himself) practicing "overparenting" or experiencing "too much" anxiety. The two are not always mutually exclusive. At the same time, some people sometimes interpret medically necessary vigilance as overparenting—as when columnist Joel Stein called food allergies a "yuppie invention" in a 2009 article in the *Los Angeles Times*. This broader backlash against food allergic kids and their parents takes on a gendered cast when it dovetails with the mother blame that scholars such as Paula Caplan have critiqued. It also parallels

Heather Hewett

other "ableist" biases and discrimination against individuals with disabilities whose accommodation is sometimes viewed with suspicion, resentment, and/or hostility.

Furthermore, the psychological advice to parents of children with food allergies—to accept, manage, and even cultivate a "necessary anxiety"—doesn't consider the way this labor is frequently gendered. When mothers perform more of the daily tasks of parenting, they can experience a psychic toll from the extra work, food preparation, and emotional labor of caring for a child with food allergies. (Not to mention the time for extra doctor or hospital visits associated with medical management.) This labor can extend beyond psychological/emotional work and the tasks of medical management to encompass self-education and advocacy. For example, in spring of 2012, I went to a food allergy conference sponsored by the nonprofit organization FAAN, the Food Allergy and Anaphylaxis Network; not surprisingly, most of the attendees were mothers. And while the conference was excellent, no one there questioned the gendered dimension of caring for children with food allergies—perhaps because the stakes can be so high. Why question the gendered dimensions of food allergy-related care and the psychic toll of anxiety when your child's life and well-being are at stake?

Historically in our culture, and still today, the ultimate responsibility for a child's safety and well-being rests with mothers. Mothers bear this responsibility, and they are blamed for any failures. This "mother blame,"

Paula Caplan argues, "pervades our culture" (3), and both "good mother" myths and "bad mother" myths work to generate a "narrow band of acceptable behavior for mothers" (136). When we apply Caplan's observations to food allergy, we can see how both too much anxiety and too little anxiety can be deemed as "bad mothering." So too, effective advocacy work that asks schools not to discriminate against food allergic kids can be seen as pushy or overbearing—also "bad mothering" (which might also be viewed as "overparenting"). I have sometimes wondered whether others have viewed me as being "pushy" or "overly involved" or "overly sensitive" about food allergies; and particularly when my daughter was younger, I struggled with managing my own fears about her safety. Given her extreme sensitivity to dairy, present in multiple forms in the diets of so many kids, I was constantly aware of the ever-present possibility of accidental contamination and death. This fear fueled my vigilance.

Psychologist Janna Malamud Smith provides insight into the impact of fear on mothers, observing that the "one powerful, recurrent theme [in mother's stories] is the mother's fear of child loss" (8). In *A Potent Fear*, she writes that:

> you cannot grasp the long, robust endurance of gender inequality without exploring the ways mothering affects women, heightening their sensitivity to varieties of threat, awakening new and more profound fears of loss, intensifying focus, and inexorably drawing them toward personal choices and accommodations that seem to enhance their children's safety. (7)

She further argues that society uses this fear to disempower mothers: that "[e]ach place and time, each society, jury-rigs ways of addressing and mediating fears about the survival and well-being of children—yet often at a high price to mothers" (7). The fear of an allergic reaction, and the possible loss of one's child, is precisely the fear that mothers of severely allergic children face in the most mundane of decisions. Is this package of cereal okay for my daughter to eat? Can she eat those fries? Can she do this or that activity safely? Fear can propel mothers forward to vigilance and advocacy—but it can also cause mothers to pull back because of the worry of being perceived as being a "bad mother." Caplan puts it in this way:

> ...consciously and, particularly, preconsciously, many women anticipate and fear, often with very good reason, that should they challenge their social role, should they defy the explicit or implicit rules of their environment, they might unwittingly damage their children. (26)

Why challenge the scripts of "good motherhood" when the safety of one's food allergic child might seem to depend upon adhering to its dictates?

I also wonder about the following question: to what extent is the "necessary anxiety" shouldered by many parents of food allergic children a coping strategy that, at least partly, arises from the fact that our society generally expects that families, often without much help from schools or other institutions, will do the work of keeping food allergic children safe? To be sure, in the U.S., we have improved matters greatly by passing legislation that has resulted in better food labeling practices, making it easier to detect the presence of allergens in the food we buy at the grocery store. Even so, the person responsible for food preparation at home—often, of course, mothers—must frequently become a detective, calling companies to inquire about production lines and the possibility of cross-contamination for particular items. Not all companies are as careful as is necessary. And parental vigilance must somehow protect food allergic children everywhere—even when mothers aren't present. We haven't yet changed all of our institutions to accommodate children with severe allergies. Schools, camps, daycares, and other institutions designed to care for children vary tremendously in terms of how food allergy-aware or even accepting they are. As a result, in January 2012, a seven-year-old girl named Ammaria Johnson died at her school in Virginia when a classmate gave her a peanut and her school did not give her a shot of epinephrine, because she did not have a prescribed epi-pen at school. As a mother and a feminist, I am enraged and devastated by a death so easily prevented. Why have we not changed all of our institutions to accommodate food-allergic kids? Her death also terrifies me, as do news stories about the deaths of other food-allergic children. Would mothers still carry around the same amount of anxiety—either "necessary" amounts, or excessive amounts—if all institutions and adults were adequately trained and prepared to identify allergic reactions, administer epinephrine, and prevent bullying by including food allergy in diversity educational initiatives? If we took all that extra food out of classrooms?

If we thought carefully about how to make cafeterias safe for all kids? Perhaps not.

Finally, I'd like to point out that the "necessary anxiety" that I have heard child psychologists call for in parents is not necessarily accessible to all parents. The model of advocacy that we depend on (mothers as advocates for their children) assumes certain privileges of education, class, race, language, and time. What of the Spanish-speaking, recently immigrated mother whose food allergic son shares a classroom with a friend of my son's? What of access to affordable and quality healthcare, doctors and allergists, and medication such as epinephrine? The FAAN conference attendees sitting around me were, not surprisingly, mostly white, middle- or upper-middle-class mothers. I don't wish to generalize from one conference, as FAAN is committed to reaching out to an economically, geographically, and racially diverse group of people. But those conference attendees unwittingly contribute to the perception that food allergies are somehow a middle-class phenomenon. As medical research suggests, this is not at all the case (Wang et al.). Further research is needed; but I wonder whether mothers and families struggling with other issues, socioeconomic or otherwise, have fewer resources to deal with either the advocacy or the medical management necessitated by food allergies.

The feminist analysis of food allergies thus leads to three observations—that the work of parenting food allergic children (and children with similar chronic conditions) and the attendant "necessary anxiety" is gendered; that it might be lessened if society changed; that the model of individual advocacy is not available to all mothers and families. So what do mothers of food-allergic children need? A short list suggests that they need what many mothers need: feminist/gender-aware understanding and support; more understanding and research about the work of parenting children with food allergies, which is still not fully understood; support that doesn't assume that mothers alone should be the ones to keep their children safe; support that includes changing the cultures and structures of schools, camps, and other institutions to meet the needs of all kids and keep them safe; support that ensures access to healthcare and medications such as epinephrine for all families; commitment to teaching about diversity and inclusion to all kids, including those with food allergies and chronic disease; money towards buying healthy, safe food (as allergen-free processed food tends to be quite expensive); money towards research to find an answer to why food allergies are on the rise in industrialized countries. These steps should go a long way towards easing the burden on mothers and addressing the full range of needs of families living with food allergies.

[1]No one yet understands the reasons, but rates of food allergy among children are rising in the U.S. and other industrialized countries. A 2008 report issued by the Centers for Disease Control and Prevention tracked an 18 percent increase of reported food allergy between 1997 and 2007 among children under 18 in the U.S. (Branum and Lukacs). A more recent *Pediatrics* study put the number of food allergic children in the U.S. at eight percent of all kids under eighteen (Gupta et al.). That's two children out of every 25, the size of many public school classrooms.

WORKS CITED

Beasley, Sandra. *Don't Kill the Birthday Girl: Tales from an Allergic Life.* New York: Crown, 2011. Print.

Branum, Amy M., and Susan L. Lukacs. *Food Allergy Among U.S. Children: Trends in Prevalence and Hospitalizations.* NCHS Data Brief. Hyattsville, MD: National Center for Health Statistics, 2008. Web. 12 Apr. 2012.

Caplan, Paula J. *The New Don't Blame Mother: Mending the Mother-Daughter Relationship.* New York: Routledge, 2000. Print.

DeVault, Marjorie L. *Feeding the Family: The Social Organization of Caring as Gendered Work.* Chicago: University of Chicago Press, 1994. Print.

Greenberger, Brett. "The Emotional Impact of Food Allergies." The 19th Annual Food Allergy Conference. The Food Allergy and Anaphylaxis Network. Westchester Marriott, Tarrytown, NY, 28 April 2012. Conference presentation.

Gupta, Ruchi S. et al. "The Prevalence, Severity, and Distribution of Childhood Food Allergy in the United States." *Pediatrics* 128.1 (2011): 9-17. Web. 12 Apr. 2012.

Hays, Sharon. *The Cultural Contradictions of Motherhood.* New Haven: Yale University Press, 1996. Print.

Kittay, Eva Feder. *Love's Labor: Essays on Women, Equality and Dependency.* New York: Routledge, 1998. Print.

Nelson, Margaret K. *Parenting Out of Control: Anxious Parents in Uncertain Times*. New York: New York University Press, 2010. Print.

O'Reilly, Andrea. "The Motherhood Memoir and the 'New Momism': Biting the Hand That Feeds You." *Textual Mothers/Maternal Texts: Motherhood in Contemporary Women's Literatures*. Ed. Elizabeth Podnieks and Andrea O'Reilly. Waterloo: Wilfrid Laurier University Press, 2010. 203-213. Print.

Ruddick, Sara. *Maternal Thinking: Toward a Politics of Peace*. Boston: Beacon Press, 1995. Print.

Smith, Janna Malamud. *A Potent Spell: Mother Love and the Power of Fear*. Boston: Houghton Mifflin, 2003. Print.

Stearns, Peter N. *Anxious Parents: A History of Modern Childrearing in America*. New York: New York University Press, 2003. Print.

Stein, Joel. "Nut Allergies: A Yuppie Invention." *Los Angeles Times* 9 January 2009. Web. 7 Jul. 2012.

Wang, Julie, Cynthia M. Visness and Hugh A. Sampson. "Food Allergen Sensitization in Inner-City Children with Asthma." *The Journal of Allergy and Clinical Immunology* 115.5 (2005): 1076-1080. Web. 16 August 2012.

Warner, Judith. *Perfect Madness: Motherhood in the Age of Anxiety*. New York: Riverhead Books, 2005. Print.

4. Mothers, Education and Social Change

(Cheesy) *Mami* Issues and Representations

MELISSA MALDONADO-SALCEDO

> *...the home is not jeopardized when the woman contributes with her talent and activities to the development of nations."*
> —Luisa Capetillo (1918)

IN 2012, KRAFT LAUNCHED A SERIES OF CAMPAIGNS, which revealed a Latina mother attempting to negotiate her son's American identity. In the mother-son exchange, the son (re)produces his (Americanized) *Latinidad* for the viewers (America).[1] The mother prepares the food and the son consumes it. Because of this give-and-take, they make each other happy. Kraft's summary of the commercial is, "A mom and son secretly try to make each other happy. She cooks him some Kraft Mac & Cheese and he stays as Latino as he can."[2] The son's efforts to "stay Latino" are exhibited in his choice of side dishes; for example, he accompanies his Mac & Cheese with (spicy) chicken. While at the dinner table, he wears a *chuyo* (a wool Andean hat) after playing a maraca. The mother has the typical "Latin Look," whose attributes cultural anthropologist Arlene Davila describes as including, "olive skin, long dark hair, brown eyes, and a Spanish accent." Her son appears racially ambiguous, which further accentuates his "Latino" costumes and props.[3]

"Staying Latino," according to this commercial necessitates undermining dominant American norms and social cues. In order to make his mother happy, the son must compromise his true self by dressing up and sounding like what viewers identify as Latino. These signifiers of *Latinidad* prove critical. In the process of attempting to make his non-assimilated mother happy, the son deceives her into preparing him Kraft Macaroni and Cheese. This (product) is what will make him as happy as his mother, who wishes

to inherit her culture. It is clear that despite living and raising a son in the United States, the mother remains linguistically and socially isolated. This historical trope of a non-assimilated mother and an Americanized son remains popular and familiar. The father appears as an accomplice to the son's "secret." For example, father and son are seen enjoying a Hip-Hop video together, but rapidly change the channel as the mother walks by. They are then seen "acting" as if they enjoy listening to what sounds and looks like Mexican music.[4] She smiles and nods in approval. Despite the numerous awkward attempts of the mother to "understand" her son's American-ess, she fails. What is particularly attention grabbing is how this commercial conveys that the onus of maintaining "Latino" culture is on the mother. She however is frozen in time and space.

The mother gives the impression she has very little interaction with the public sphere. Yet she is an outsider in her own home, whereas father and son bond over American culture.[5] She is just a *"mami"* who speaks very little English, and frequently embarrasses her (Americanized) son before his non-Latino friends. This (cheesy) representation is problematic and indicative of historical attitudes and contemporary ideas of Latina mothers in the United States. It is important to unpack the media's role in shaping ideas about citizenship and national identity in order to critique how it affirms what communication theorist Isabel Molina-Guzman identifies as, "traditional notions of the United States as white, Anglo-Saxon Protestant nation" against the "inherently exotic, foreign, and consumable" Latinas (2010a: 7). This symbolic colonization reproduces dominant norms around ideas of belonging and visibility and discloses mainstream anxieties about the growing presence of Latinos in America (9).

COMMERCIALIZING ASSIMILATION: CHILDREN BEWARE

This Kraft campaign emerges at a very contentious time for Latina mothers in America. For instance, undocumented Latina mothers are being detained by immigration and subsequently they lose custody of their American children ("Illegal immigrant loses custody"). This is in part due to the aggressive the criminalization of immigrants, and the inextricable framing of their reproductive capability as a "threat to the nation" (Chavez). These children are adopted by American parents and thus into American culture. They are then saved from their criminal (Latina) mothers. If they are pregnant, detained women are forced to give birth shackled to their beds (Constantini). This particular performance of childbirth is loaded with many historical ideas of race concerning Latina bodies. This view is developed extensively in Molina-Guzman's discussions on global commodity culture in her work *Dangerous Curves* (2010b). She explains, "Latinas inform how the bodies of ethnic women are used to discipline definitions of race, ethnicity, nation, and national identity" (Molina-Guzman 2010b: 115). The attack on Latina immigrant mothers is grounded on the notion that their children must be "American." In current debates around immigration *and* education, it appears as if being American is fundamentally incompatible with Latino culture. For this reason our broken immigration system should not be examined separately from the urgent need for educational reform. Staggering numbers show that Latina high school and college students are dropping out. Latinas living in poverty are enslaved and oppressed by draconian welfare reforms, which systematically limit opportunities to obtain a college education. They are then stuck in low-wage paying jobs with few possibilities to create a different type of future (Hays; Collins). These circumstances beg the following question, how do we as community stakeholders empower Latina mothers and daughters to break these cycles of (silencing) poverty? Furthermore, how can we intervene, when the media representations of Latina mothers are subject to the racialized and gendered tendencies of institutional "modern power?" After all, the function of the media is to uphold ideas of "dominance and subordination?" (Foucault 61). While this question is specific to Latinas, it concerns all of America because of the leadership role Latinas are undertaking (privately and publically) within the United States. Joseph Villescas writes that our social landscape conveys the ways in which "the growing pool of talent in the Latino population is becoming increasingly compromised of multidimensional Latinas...." While Villesca's observation is incredibly promising, it further fuels anxieties about Latina bodies within the nation and the need to "discipline" them (Molina-Guzman and Validivia).

Latina mothers and daughters are often compelled to negotiate what it means to be a Latina in America, and American as a Latina. As popular media suggests, these identities cannot coexist harmoniously in one home, much less in the greater United States. Leo Chavez posits in the *Latino Threat Narrative* that this circumstance is a "contradiction of citizenship and belonging." For this reason the Kraft campaign and other similar representations in the media read challenging. As Chavez notes, they assume that Latinas are on the whole "unchanging and immutable...not subject to history and the transforming social forces around them; they reproduce their own cultural world" (51). Latinos have been historically subject to stereotypical representations in the media. Robert Amundson and Daniel Lichter write that most Latino characters on television "come from a generic background without reference to national origin...." as if these specificities are irrelevant. Absent from these representations are the cultural, historical, and economic differences among different groups within Latino communities (397). The conflation of all countries, peoples, and communities within Latin America and the Caribbean is intensely contrived. This flattening out of important differences enables constructing (all) Latina mothers as (threatening) outsiders, originating from a similar place of disorder and criminality down South.[6] Their wombs, as Chavez notes, become a site of (potential) national insurgency due to dominant discourses around immigration, welfare, and sexuality. The intersection of these discourses animate media depictions of Latinos and they also inform policies. Since Latinas alter the demographic makeup of the (white) nation, their reproduction is conceived as a form of resistance. After all, Latinos are the fastest growing group in the United States. The assumed fertility of Latinas makes them responsible and culpable for the "browning" of the Nation (Molina-Guzman 2010d: 163).

MOTHERHOOD IN TRANSLATION

According to a 2009 report released by the Mexican American Legal Defense and Education Fund (MALDEF) and National Women's Law Center, young Latinas expressed that they were deeply affected by the persistent discrimination they encountered in school by teachers and classmates alike. Classrooms are a volatile site of sociopolitical and cultural struggle. For most Latinas, an education still is the best option for attaining social mobility within America. Writing rather dynamically on this issue in 1918, Luisa Capetillo succinctly argued that mothers need to become educated in order to be the best possible mothers to rear their children. She wrote, "Education means cultivating patience, tolerance, a sweet disposition, harmony, abnegation, and temperateness. Anyone who cultivates these virtues is truly educated" (Capetillo 150). Her glaringly obvious point was that if you were trapped in a job where you were overworked and underpaid, this would inevitably take a toll

Melissa Maldonado-Salcedo

on all aspects of your personal life. In her view an education must be available to everyone in order to engender progress. This ideal remains exceptionally relevant. Education is the "ladder" to success in America, particularly for Latinas who often feel compelled to negotiate cultural expectations of gender against ideas of (capitalist) progress.[7] No greater example of this message exists than in the 2004 film, *Spanglish*. The all too familiar plotline centers on a young mother, Flor Moreno, who emigrates from Mexico with her daughter in search of a "better life." In Molina-Guzman's analysis of this film included in "Maid in Hollywood: Producing Latina Labor in an Anti-immigration Imaginary," she cites a thread on the Internet Movie Database (IMDB) that communicated the overall distress about the implications of immigration in a "white" America per this film. Interestingly enough, the thread denotes how Flor's initial inability to learn English was interpreted as a political strategy of resistance. It read, "Damn if I'm not annoyed by immigrants who make the USA their home and find every excuse to not become Americans or learn English" (2010d: 162). Anti-immigrant sentiments are pervasive and therefore certain viewers personalize these filmic depictions of immigrants. To see a Latina immigrant succeed without completely abandoning her culture and "becoming American" like in the film incited personal attacks on Latino immigrants. Evidence of these interpretations and retaliations exist in the debates around the controversial legislation known as the *DREAM Act* (Development, Relief, and Education for Alien Minors), which would provide a path towards permanent residency for undocumented high school graduates who have grown up American. This proposed and challenged Federal law exposes a strong intersection between education and immigration.

This IMDB thread offers a small glimpse into a larger phenomenon. In Flor's daughter's admission essay to Princeton she prefaces by thanking them for encouraging her to apply and for also informing her of all the available scholarships. She then proceeds to school them, "... as I hope this essay shows, your acceptance, while it would thrill me, will not define me. My identity rests firmly and happily on one fact: I am my mother's daughter." While I can appreciate her "Stay Latina" approach, I remember the Kraft commercial. Both mothers attempt to shield their children from "complete assimilation" by evoking essentialized notions of Latina domesticity. In the Kraft commercial the mother is assumed to be a stay at home mom (considering her very limited knowledge of English.) Flor's character performs the same duties but outside of her own home as a domestica with a similar command of English. Both children keep their mothers "happy" by embracing their *latinidad*, which in the Kraft commercial centers on a product that could be purchased (clothes, music, food), while Cristina's *latinidad* is rooted in her recognition of being her mother's daughter, recognizing her mother's history as part of her own.

A few years after the release of *Spanglish*, Supreme Court Justice Sonia Sotomayor joined the highest rank in the American judicial system by becoming the first Latina to become Supreme Court Justice. In 2009 she echoed Cristina Moreno's gratitude in an emotional homage to her mother, Celina Soyomayor. Justice Soyomayor shared "I have often said that I am all that I am because of her and I am only half the woman she is" (Saul). *The New York Times* (Fernandez and Scott) noted that while Justice Sotomayor moved the audience with this "once classically American" tale of rags to riches, President Obama made specific references to Celina's story of sacrifice and hard work as a single mother. He mentioned that she worked multiple jobs, owned the only encyclopedia in the neighborhood, sent her children to private school, and tirelessly believed in the "promise of a good education." When asked about her role in shaping her daughter's career path Celina responded, "I don't know what I did ... I was just there" (Shane and Fernandez).[8] While I do not question the influential role Celina Sotomayor had on her daughter's life, I must recognize that I know many mothers who do everything that Celina did and have yet to reap the benefits of a "good education."

The existing high school drop-out rates for latinas continues to upsurge in an alarming way. Latinas are the fastest growing ethnic group amongst American women, yet are less likely to graduate High School or College. According to a previous study on latina girls and education released by the American Association of University Women Educational Foundation in 2001, the association's director, Jacqueline Woods noted that they are many financial, social, and cultural resources that are lacking for latina women in comparison to other groups (Hayasaki). Woods identifies this lack as just one of the multiple "pressures and stresses" which restrict the prospects Latina girls can pursue.

MAMI ISSUES

An underlining point that emerges in the aforementioned studies is that most Latinas genuinely understand the importance of an education and its relationship to social mobility. However, as the 2009 report by MALDEF emphasizes, many Latinas remain influenced by both family and societal expectations. These notions are so often based on stereotypes of Latinas as "submissive underachievers and caretakers." These stereotypes are then internalized because of mainstream media and what I identify as, "*mami issues*." In the Latino community, remarks a Latina McNair scholar, "values and traditions" are assumed a marker of social capital, though they are not recognized as the same type of social capital that other ethnic or socioeconomic groups value (Cervantes 28). *Mami issues* become embodied and performed between mother and daughter in what is said and not said; in what is done, and not done. Many of these cultural constructs and stereotypes severely overwhelm Latina identity and become internalized through the very institutions, which as an "assemblage," to build on Jaspir Puar's use of the term, engendered this predicament. The institutions that craft *mami* issues are immigration, family, education, and the media. Each institution shapes the relationship with the other.[9] *Mami* issues look like this from the perspective of a Latina daughter: *"My mother wants me to be like her, but she is not even from here."* This is even if the mother has lived in the United States for more years than the daughter has been alive. *"My mother does not understand that in America people are more open."* This simply means, "*I should be able to stay out as late as my friends and go out where they go."* This might seem like a frivolous issue, but when you are eighteen and still have a curfew as I did, this becomes your biggest cultural clash. Move away? Not a feasible option. Most Latina college students live at home and contribute financially or in other family matters (Hayasaki; Cervantes). A popular viewpoint of Latina mothers, not dissimilar to Celina Sotomayor's view is that an education is the best inheritance. Sobering news; it is becoming increasingly more difficult to leave this inheritance (as statistics show.) Another troubling *mami* issue is the lack of identifiable role models outside of the realm of pop stars, *"I look up to Shakira, Jennifer Lopez, and Sofia Vergara because they are the most popular Latina role models available to me, outside of my mother."* I never took into consideration my hips, booty, or breasts when it came to evaluating my future. Theorist Richard Dryer shares that celebrities, like the abovementioned, represent Westernized ideas of individualism, wealth, desire, and social worth. This therefore influences how Latinas envision their potential for academic and professional success (CNN).

MY MOTHER

My mother experienced her feminist awakening as a child. She explains that my grandmother, who married at thirteen, and had twelve children soon after, treated her daughters incredibly different than her sons. There is a long history of this type of mothering within Latino homes because of how Latina women are acculturated into *marianism.* Latinas within the Catholic culture are expected to be passive and as sociologist Evelyn Stevens explains, "semi divine, morally superior to, and spiritually stronger than men" (Stevens 123). This is why their ability to reproduce is treated as a source of power. Also men learn to perform their masculinity in relation to their superiority to women through machismo (the other side of *marianism.*) These ideas of the inferiority of daughters circulate and often become deeply embedded in Latino understandings of family.

One student in my Latina Women course told me that her parents chose to baptize her brother and not her or her three sisters just in case there was a heaven, he would go. Another Latina student told me that although she had to work and go to school, her older brother did not work, do chores, and received an allowance from her parents so he can go and "socialize" when he was in school.

I recently told my mother that I was happy we did not have a brother growing up because my sister and I would probably have a very different relationship with her now. Although she laughed it off, I am not blind to the privileges and attentions my son receives from her. They are exactly the same ones I wanted as a child. I laugh this off, because I question how different I would be as a mother, had I a daughter.

My uncles roamed the Colombian countryside without restraints or domestic responsibilities. At a young age they assumed their role as breadwinners, working the land from sunrise to sunset alongside my grandfather. The gender roles at home were clearly demarcated to mirror the culture. My grandmother and her daughters would cook for the men in their homes without so much of a thank you in return because they honestly believed that this was all they could do for their families ... care for them.

My mother did not have a "room of her own," nor had she even heard of Latina feminist writers such as Sor Juana Inez, Luisa Capetillo, or Antonia Storni. These *feminista* trailblazers shared the same hemisphere as my mother; some would even argue similar social constraints. They wrote about their ideals over 50 years before my mother was born. They advocated for women's liberation through an education. Growing up, my mother did not have access to their texts but she came to similar conclusions out of experience and circumstance.

My mother shares that as a child, my grandmother frequently made her wash my uncle's white pants by hand under the scorching son. To this day, most of the streets in my mother's village remain unpaved. Dirt roads that lead to nowhere still enclose my grandparent's home. My mother would eventually pave an entrance and replace the clay walls with cement. In the absence of comfort and opportunities, most girls my mother's age cleaned and cooked for their families. My grandmother did it, her mother before. This would prepare them and make them fit to clean and cook for their own family. One day, my grandmother, who still has a fondness for seeing microscopic faults, told my mother she needed to "wash the pants again." Apparently, she saw a stain. My mother watched in horror as my grandmother then threw the seemingly white pants into the mud. Defiantly, my mother refused to wash those pants again or any other ones for her brothers. "I'd rather die than wash another pair of pants." I imagine that at that point, whatever notion of a childhood she had was washed away. She picked herself up, left the dirty pants behind, and all of the baggage she believed held her back. Her details about what happened afterwards are unclear, but what I do know is that at age twelve she left to the big city to work as a *domestica*. She remembers envying the girls who paraded their uniforms on their ways to school. She said that even if she had had the economic means she would have not been allowed to go to school. Many Latino families (until this day) choose to educate boys over girls. My cousin Kelly was never enrolled in school, but her older and younger brother were. As a child she exhibited a lot of intelligence and creativity. However, my uncle (the same one whose pants my mother threw in the mud) would not "educate a girl so that she can then just be a wife." Needless to say, the last time I heard, Kelly is now a 26-year-old single mother who still lives in extreme poverty with her four children. She cannot read or write. She has had problems keeping her daughters in school, while simultaneously sets money aside for her son's future education. He has yet to enter preschool. My mother shared that as a child she envisioned her prince charming to have a washing machine. My father told me that it was one of the first things they purchased as a couple.

Since my mother was unable to go to school, she was limited in her employment prospects. She transitioned from working as a *domestica* to working at a factory. By the time she was 18, she was unofficially a manager but could not be hired or paid as one, because she did not have a diploma. This motivated my mother to look up North for opportunities. She left for New York City when she was only 20. She had me when she was 30 and at the time, owned a successful hair salon in midtown Manhattan. She gave it all up for me when I was born with hip dysplasia. She became my own 24 hour nurse. I asked her if she could have been anything in the world, what would she choose? "A teacher."

At the end of my first year of doctoral studies, one professor left me a note that in a one-two punch patted me on the back, but also put a lot of my personal turmoil into perspective. She wrote, "You are a force of life but, maybe anthropology is not your cup of tea ... it requires work." She left this message to me on a post-it with my final paper for her class. This was the only feedback that I had received all semester. I tried hard not to personalize it and see the hidden lesson. Although, what I really wanted to do was agree. I thought to myself, "They are on to me; I do not deserve to be here." I soon discovered I had an acute case of imposter syndrome.

Nonetheless at that moment, I was forced to consider in what way(s) did I "appear lazy." I never turned in a paper late. I always did my work and actively participated. I had a job, and a two-year-old son at home. I never complained or asked for special consideration. I rarely if ever participated in the social activities that most of my cohort did. Although I recall on two occasions cooking and preparing up a spread for one of the Friday departmental parties practically alone. Mothers and Lazy rarely go in the same sentence. I looked inward to answer this question, though I soon realized that what I experienced had more to do with what I represented as a person, than with who I really was as a scholar. Though, how can one ever divorce these identities?

Interestingly I had gone through a lot of schooling never feeling intimidated or demobilized by my identity as a Latina. The stakes felt higher when I became a mother. I considered dropping out, but I kept thinking about how I fought my whole life to not be that stereotype, that statistic, to exceed that expectation. I grew up in the 1980s. I had a fourth and sixth grade teacher tell my mother, "Your daughter is just going to end up pregnant before high school ... like they all do." My music school teacher had told my mother when she requested a scholarship, "Why do you bother, Latinos don't even care about education." I thought if I dropped out, what would be my legacy? My mother's life of strength inspired me to stay strong. I went to her house to talk to her about my feeling of self-doubt. I sat on the washing machine as she cooked for me. My mother never taught or expected my sister and I to cook or maintain any aspect of a house. All she wanted was for us to bring home good grades. So like many times before, I asked her if she thought I should quit. She broke it down (like she always has). She reminded me that I have something to say that comes from a place of experience, and is informed by more than observations and questions. I have a history of strong Latina warriors in my own genealogy ... in me. The classroom, for many Latina mothers and mothers-to-be, represents a battleground for unimagined futures. "*Your place, Melissita, is in the classroom.*"

So then I understood the post-it note for what it was (not), an invitation to challenge myself. Especially when "the other" becomes the ethnographer, that voice can destabilize the paradigms that historically have privileged white cultural norms and values. By dropping out I thought, I sustain this paradigm that has had a silencing effect on Latina histories. Reflecting on her own education, Rita Kohli writes that, "...Many of us have been socialized through racially biased educational systems and carry skewed perceptions of ourselves, our communities, and other non-White racial or ethnic groups" (180). I felt confident that in a very real way I was a hard worker. However, this personal knowledge did not dissipate my self-doubt. One hardly ever walks around with a sign that testifies to one's competency. And sometimes, just being in a classroom should have this effect, but it does not.

During my second year of doctoral studies, I was offered the opportunity to teach a course entitled, "Latina Women." I soon came to realize that my role as a Latina professor was special. For many of the Latina women in my class, I was the first educator at the college level that looked like them, came from where they came from, sounded like them, and was a mother. I am always asked about my relationship with my mother. Did I have "*mami* issues?" A slew of them.

I was the first in my family to cut her hair short, to leave the church, to drink and smoke, to be "of this world," and for this reason every visit to my mother's house feels like a coming out experience. I live across the street from her, still spend every holiday with her, and respect her role as matriarch. We come from two very different political spectrums, but she is my mother. Her hands sold fruit, cleaned homes, sewed clothes, and reared other people's children, so that I would not have to, if I did not want to.

She recently told me she admired me as a mother because I wanted my son to always know the best possible version of me. Whispering she said, "You and your sister are enhanced versions of me." And that became our secret. I knew I was very much like my mother, while being very different. I broke the cycle of our shared history through an education that she worked so that I could have. My first semester teaching Latina Women was challenging because I learned more about myself than I could ever teach in one semester.

This essay has helped me reflect on these learnings that came out of teaching about my own "*mami* issues." I feel empowered by just being able to share this story, which I can only hope repeats itself over and over again. When I stand in front of my classroom the first day, I introduce myself the way I feel matters to me and my Latina sisters, "*I'm a first-generation Colombi-rican, born and raised in the projects and proud of it. I am a mother who was educated on how to live and be by the most incredible person I know...my mother. She has a post-doctoral degree from the school of hard knocks.... And if she or my son calls on my phone, I have to pick up.*" I caveat to my Latina scholars that an education and motherhood are not incompatible. Sometimes, having credentials does not necessarily mean that you know everything that matters to you. Sometimes, we want to be like our *mamis,* despite our *mamis*. Sometimes, we become our *mamis*, or enhanced versions of them and that's more than okay. *Gracias,* Mom!

[1]Cultural anthropologist Arlene Davila describes this notion of Latinidad as the "out-of-many, one-people process through which 'Latinos' or 'Hispanics' are conceived and represented as sharing one common identity" (16).

[2]The full description on YouTube for this commercial is, "A mom and son secretly try to make each other happy. She cooks him some Kraft Mac & Cheese and he stays as Latino as he can."

[3]Interestingly, the macaroni and cheese which traditionally is served as a side dish in American cuisine, becomes the main dish, while the Latino dishes are sides.

[4]The "overtly Mexican" representation is seen in mariachi dressed tex-mex singers dancing up and down.

[5]More so, the mother is an outsider in America, a non-American.

[6]The 2003 film, *Maria Full of Grace* examines the circumstances that lead a seventeen year old Colombian mother to become a drug mule and immigrate and stay in the United States to have her child. While incredibly provocative, the film supported ideas that construct Latinas as dangerous border crossers.

[7]In the 2012 Presidential debates, Obama referred to education as America's "ladder." This term is reminiscent of American's use and application of the term "boot straps."

[8]An interesting parenthetical comment that is important to note is that in the same *New York Times* article that highlighted the mother-daughter story of Celina and Justice Sonia Sotomayor, a photo of the duo was printed. On May 30, 2009 a correction on the story was printed to note that the original photo caption was not of Justice Sotomayor and her mother but of Justice Sotomayor and the former office manager at her former law firm.

[9]For example, my immigration status and that of my mother's influences the way I engage with my studies. The media produces stereotypes that (mis)inform classmates and educators about my abilities as a Latina.

WORKS CITED

Amundson, Robert S. and Daniel R. Lichter. "Distorted Reality: Hispanic Characters in TV Entertainment." *The Social Construction of Differences, and Inequality: Race, Class, Gender, and Sexuality*. Ed. Tracy E. Ore. Durham : Duke University Press, 2003. 386-399. Print.

Capetillo, Luisa. *A Nation of Women: An Early Feminist Speaks Out*. Houston: Arte Publico Press, 2004. Print.

Cervantes, Andrea Gomez. "Breaking Stereotypes by Obtaining a Higher Education: Latinas' Family Values and Tradition on the School Institution." *McNair Scholars Journal* 14 (1) (2010): 23-54. Print.

Chavez, Leo. "Latino Sexuality, Reproduction, and Fertility as Threats to the Nation." *The Latino Threat: Constructing Immigrants, Citizens, and the Nation*. Leo R. Chavez. Stanford: Stanford University Press, 2008. 70-95.Print.

CNN. "Survey: Latinas Face Challenges that Hinder their Education." 04 September 2009. *CNN Living* Web. 21 September 2012.

Collins, Jane. *Both Hands Tied: Welfare Reform and the Race to the Bottom in the Low-Wage Labor Market*. Chicago: University of Chicago Press, 2010. Print.

Constantini, Cristina. "Undocumented women forced to give birth shackled while in police custody." *Huffington Post* 30 November 2012. Web.

Davila, Arlene. *Latino Inc.: The Marketing and Making of a People*. Berkley: University of California Press, 2001. Print.

Dream Activist. Web.

Dryer, Richard. *Heavenly Bodies: Film Stars and Society*. New York: St. Martin's Press, 1986. Print.

Fernandez, Manny and Shane Scott. "A Judge's Own Story Highlights her Mother's." *New York Times* 27 May 2009. Print.

Hayasaki, Erika. "Latinas Face Obstacles in Education, Study Says." *The Los Angeles Times* 25 January 2001. Print.

Hays, Sharron. *Flat Broke: Women in the Age of Welfare Reform*. Oxford: Oxford University Press, 2006. Print.

"Illegal immigrant loses custody of five-year-old son as judge allows

American foster parents to adopt him." *The UK Daily Mail* 12 July 2012. Print.

Kohli, Rita. "Breaking the Cycle of Racism in the Classroom: Critical Racial Reflections from Future Teachers of Color." *Teacher Education Quarterly* (2008): 177-188. Print.

Lopez, Iris. *Matters of Choice: Puerto Rican Women's Struggle for Reproductive Freedom.* New Brunswick: Rutgers University Press, 2008. Print.

Maria Full of Grace. Fine Line Pictures, 2004. Film.

Mexican American Legal Defense and Education Fund (MALDEF) and National Women's Law Center. "Listening to Latinas: Barriers to High School Graduation." 2009. Web.

Molina-Guzman, Isabel. "Introduction: Mapping the Place of Latinas in the U.S. Media." *Dangerous Curves: Latina Bodies in the Media.* Isabel Molina-Guzman. New York: New York University Press, 2010a.1-22. Print.

Molina-Guzman, Isabel. "Becoming Frida: Latinidad and the Production of Latina Authenticity." Isabel Molina-Guzman. *Dangerous Curves: Latina Bodies in the Media.* New York: New York University Press, 2010b. 86-118. Print.

Molina-Guzman, Isabel. "Disciplining J.Lo: Booty Politics in Tabloid News." Isabel Molina-Guzman. *Dangerous Curves: Latina Bodies in the Media.* New York: New York University Press, 2010c. 51-86. Print.

Molina-Guzman, Isabel. "Maid in Hollywood: Producing Latina Labor in an Anti-Immigration Imaginary." Isabel Molina-Guzman. *Dangerous Curves: Latina Bodies in the Media.* New York: New York University Press, 2010d. 151-174. Print.

Molina, Isabel and Angharad N. Valdivia. "Disciplining the Ethnic Body: Latinidad, Hybridized Bodies, and Transnational Identity." *Governing the Female Body: Gender, health, and Networks of Power.* Eds. Paula Saukko and Lori Reed. Albany: State University of New York, 2010. 206-232. Print.

Saul, Michael. "Sonia Sotomayor Pays Emotional Tribute to her Mother." *NY Daily News* 26 May 2009. Print.

Stevens, Evelyn P. "Marianismo: la otra cara del machismo en Latino-América." *Hembra y macho en Latino-América: Ensaios.* Ann Pescatelo Mexico: Edicion Diana, 1977. Print.

Villescas, Joseph P. A. "Latinas, not Latinos, Hold the Future in their Hands." *News Taco: The Latino Daily* 4 December 2012. Web.

Influencing Evolution Through an Evolving Revolution

LORRI P. SLEPIAN AND LAURIE N. SYLLA

MOTHERS NEED MANY THINGS. Mothers need....
•a less violent and dangerous world to send their children into;
•to be able to send their children to school or the candy store without fear of their being bullied or killed;
•an environment of peace and freedom in which to raise their children;
•and a world that does not call upon its children to sacrifice themselves on the altar of war.

Mothers need....
•breathable air and drinkable water and eatable food and access to basic medication;
•food and shelter and warmth for their children and themselves;
•and social and economic structures and policies that support them as mothers and as income generators.

Mothers need...
•societies that honor, truly honor, mothering;
•and societies that value, truly value, children;
•cultures that will allow their children to unfold in their own way to their full potential.

Mothers need...
•to learn they can trust themselves, and trust themselves as mothers;
•to learn to listen to and to trust their voices of inner knowing;
•to forgive themselves for their mistakes, for being who they are and who they aren't;

•to forgive their partners if they have them, and to forgive their children for their mistakes, and for being who they are and who they aren't;
•to break free of isolation and self-doubt;
•And they need friends who are mothers—to be embraced in a community of mothers.

Mothers need...
•the opportunity to evolve individually and collectively;
•to recognize their inherent maternal rights;
•to feel entitled to the full expression of these rights;
•and to develop a maternal consciousness and a maternal revolution.

In short, mothers need a transformed society. How does that happen? It happens through an evolving revolution rooted in a strong mothers' movement—a movement of mothers individually and collectively working together for needed services, structures, and policies—empowered by consciousness, awareness, empathy, entitlement and a sense of sisterhood as mothers. It happens over generations of both incremental and radical change, guided by a vision of transformed humanity. It happens through shared commitment to create a world that is more peaceful and less violent, and through a willingness to turn away from violence, to turn away from nurturing hate, to turn away from creating conditions that cause us to kill each other. It happens when we are willing to walk that path, even knowing that it will take a long time to get there, even knowing that the path may be longer than our time to walk it.

Everything evolves. Everything changes. We can influence changes in humanity by using intention and consciousness. To change the world we have to work to reach toward humankind's potential and promise. If we utilize our inner knowledge, our empathy, our maternal wisdom and conscious intention, if we begin to really know ourselves and each other, then we can influence the development of humanity. We have that power. The future of humanity is literally in the hands of mothers. Mothers, focused and conscious and empowered, can influence changes in humankind. It is through mothering that we can elevate consciousness and elevate the societal culture, and thereby elevate the world. Although it sounds big, accepting that mission can bring forth the best in each of us—in all of us. Accepting that mission creates an urgency and an obligation to give mothers what they need. Accepting that mission causes us to look, learn, and lead through a maternal perspective.

So, how do we get there? How do we create societies where mothers get what they need and are able to mother in ways that lead to the transformation of humanity? We start where we are with what we have. We begin with the internal. We validate. We make connection. We wake up. We join together. We make demands. We take action. We build a mothers' movement.

We begin with the internal. New mothers, awestruck with new responsibility and a new, vulnerable being to care for may find their internal world now includes new levels of fear and doubt, self-criticism and ambivalence, guilt and anger, resulting in loss of self-esteem. The critical voice can be very hard to silence. But there is more to that internal world. There is love and vulnerability, compassion and creativity. There is the learning and insight gained from mother-work. Paying attention to our feelings and our inner-world brings wisdom. Noticing, tolerating and understanding our feelings can ultimately lead to thoughts and actions that are compassionate and creative. This paying attention is our best tool for knowing and learning, for developing our children, ourselves, and human kind.

Sara Ruddick, a well-known transformative author focused on mothers' issues, used the phrase "maternal thinking" to describe the thinking she did as a mother and Toni Morrison used the phrase "conscious mothering" to describe the deliberate attention black mothers give to developing their children's emotional resources to counteract growing up in a racist society. Conscious mothering is intentional, growth-promoting, ethical, character-shaping mothering; conscious mothering increases the likelihood that the next generation will have the emotional resources and the commitment to humanity and to themselves that could raise up humankind. And it grows out of the internal.

Yet, it takes more than the internal to achieve conscious mothering; it takes connection and it takes empowerment. It is through connection with other mothers that mothers find their power. It is through connection that mothers learn from their own lived experiences as mothers and validate what they know. It is through speaking the truth with other mothers about the mothering experience that the critical voice is silenced.

This connection is a crucial part of an empowerment process. Empowerment can be broken into five phases:

First comes becoming aware, paying attention and noticing. Women notice and become aware of what happens inside them, what they are feeling, what their physical responses are, and they learn from these as they listen to others.

Second comes validation. In speaking together, women receive validation for their own thoughts, feelings, and experiences. Validation is most important because without it you can feel alone and crazy in your mothering journey. Such aloneness diminishes mental health and allows the critical voice too much power.

Third comes gaining understandings. Understandings emerge when you reflect on what you hear in a setting of non-judgmental connection and compassion. With gained understandings, the sense of self deepens and the view of the world enlarges.

Fourth comes entitlement. At this point women are stronger and feel entitled to different and better responses to their needs, wants and rights as mothers.

Fifth is taking action. Because they feel entitled and are informed, they are able to take action and make changes in their families, in their schools, in their communities. They make changes in the way doctors, elected officials, and public institutions respond to them. They, aware and strong and connected to each other, become part of the Mothers' Movement.

One model for empowering mothers and growing a mothers' movement began in the U.S. in the early 1970s. Recognizing the needs mothers had for places to build knowledge, experience respite, give and receive validation, nurture and be nurtured, heal and be healed, share wisdom, gain understandings, develop abilities, forge friendships, be leaders, and explore their needs, a small group of mothers created the first Mothers' Center. It took root in the vision of creating ethical, growth-promoting environments for mothers where they could safely speak the truth of their maternal experience to each other.

The purpose of the original Mothers' Center, as envisioned by Patsy Turrini, LCSW, was to create a space where women could take a deep look at the impact of pregnancy, the birth experience, adoption, and child-rearing on themselves and to serve women at all stages of mothering. The founders wanted a space where mothers could study and understand their work as mothers, learning from experts, from themselves, and from each other. The Centers were places where mothers came to respect mother-work as a source of knowledge and could speak their truths without fear of disapproval. They became places where mothers would grow to understand that they had inherent rights and where they could safeguard their right to mother in healthy ways.

These mothers' centers grew into the National Association of Mothers' Centers (NAMC), a national organization that pioneered the creation of a mothers' movement, connected by Mothers' Centers, and rooted in Mothers' Center culture. This was a movement and a culture that respected and valued the entrance into motherhood, that profound unfathomable experience of love, ecstasy, anguish, despair, pleasure, commitment, rage, doubt, compassion, deep vulnerability, joy, and fulfillment. It was a movement and a culture that was, and still is, ethical, growth-promoting, nurturing, respectful, empowering, and responsive to the emotional, informational, social, practical, economic, and political needs of mothers. The NAMC created an actual Mothers' Declaration of Rights, which was most recently updated in 2004.

NAMC Mothers' Declaration of Rights

The work of mothering can have enormous benefits; the beneficiaries of this work are not only the mother and child, but families and society as well. The work of mothering also creates enormous demands. It requires inordinate physical and psychological energy, and is often performed with limited social support and access to historical wisdom and current research. It may have long term and often unanticipated negative economic repercussions for the woman and her family. We believe that mothers have the right to perform this vital and essential work in a supportive environment, one that acknowledges the value of her work and accounts for her economic, social, educational, psychological and physical needs. Every mother, every child, every family deserves nothing less. Therefore, we believe in the following rights:

Economic

•To have unpaid caregiving conceptualized as work and valued accordingly by society (i.e., included in the census, accounted for in GDP calculations, counted in welfare rights, credited toward social security benefit calculations...)

•To pursue occupational goals as well as family ones (i.e. availability of good part time jobs, childcare subsidies, workweek reduction/flexibility, ...)
•To have training to upgrade or optimize her skills as well as childcare provisions to facilitate utilization of training opportunities

Social
•To have a Mothers' Center in every community—comfortable and safe community space
•To have safe, affordable childcare options available to any family that needs it
•To be entitled to parenting support services
•To lead a life free from violence and discrimination

Educational
•To have more influence/voice in the areas of maternal health, birthing practices, women's health and research
•To be entitled to information about maternal and child development
•To have the information about the work of women/mothers who went before us

Psychological and Physical
•To value mother knowledge gained from the attunement to self and child
•To acknowledge the value of maternal experience to the growth and development of the mother
•To support the emotional health of pre- and post-partum women
•To have access to adequate health and mental health care before, during and after pregnancy and child birth to ensure optimal outcomes for infant and maternal health.

NATIONAL ASSOCIATION OF MOTHERS' CENTERS © 2004

The philosophy of the Mothers' Center movement and of the NAMC was and still is centered on the belief that, in an atmosphere and culture that values women, children and families; fosters deep connections among women; embraces ambiguity and diverse viewpoints; and raises the voices of women, mothers can become the experts on the developmental and societal needs they and their families have. This philosophy is operationalized in the Mothers' Center settings through: consensus decision-making, where the goal is to have everyone feel her voice has been heard and respected, even when there is not universal agreement on a decision; encouragement of members to approach and receive each other with an assumption of the other's integrity and good intentions and to respond to each other with empathy; maintenance of a spirit of inquiry that supports peer-professional intellectual exchanges between recognized experts and expert women/mothers; a commitment to empowerment by validating women/mothers as they become aware, gain understanding, and take action to claim the inherent maternal rights they are entitled to.

This Mothers' Center culture is one in which women do a radical thing. They speak and tell the truth. This culture has had a profound impact over the years, trickling down the generations from Mothers' Center members to their children, their sisters, and their families. It changes the way people relate to each other. Mothers' Center culture allows us to learn that a mother has an intrinsic right to discover what gives her life meaning, both within and alongside her role as mother. It is a culture that supports the right to mother in healthy ways and supports our children's right to grow in healthy, loving families. It is a culture that insists that the world must pay attention to the needs of women/children/families. It is a culture that builds the individual and collective mother voice.

The NAMC exists to promote the development of a movement where mothers together work to institute the changes that would lead to a less violent and transformed world where parenting is done within a caring society. The v exists to support and assist in replicating both Mothers' Centers and Circles, and to advocate for women's social and economic empowerment throughout the U.S. The NAMC's vision is a society where the work of taking care of others is valued, supported, at the center of public discussion, and a priority in public policy.

Since the creation of the NAMC and the early days of the mothers' movement, society has evolved. Additional organizations have sprung up around the globe supporting mothers and a mothers' movement. Motherhood and the needs of mothers are common topics of public discourse, even if that discourse is often structured in fallacious dichotomies that ask the wrong questions: Better to work or be a stay at home mom?

Lorri P. Slepian

Better to build a career or to have your children before it's too late? Can you have it all or do you have to give it all up to mother? Many of the goals of the feminist and mothers' movements are now so integrated in society that they are no longer perceived as feminist. The internet is available as a source of information and a means of virtual connection to other mothers. In many countries including the U.S., most mothers work outside the home, and many mothers are single parents, creating new need for structural changes to adequately support today's mothering realities. Men are playing larger roles in parenting and the importance of how men father is increasingly recognized. Social policy has improved, with developments such as the *Family Medical Leave Act* that requires employers to allow time for caregiving without penalty. Yet, there is so much more to be done.

The question we need to answer is how do we create societies where the differing needs and differing desires of different mothers are met in ways that allow them to fulfill their mothering responsibilities in the best way possible. We need to create work structures and economic incentives that allow time and space for caregiving and for economic self-sufficiency. Countries such as France and England offer examples of these types of policies. They provide months of paid maternity leave and weeks of paid paternity leave. France provides economic supplements for additional children and allows mothers to take up to three years of time off with employers guaranteeing the right to return to the same or similar position; England requires employers to do their best to meet flexible work schedule requests of parents of young (under age six) or disabled children. England provides tax credits and France provides low cost day care. Collectivist social structures, such as the Kibbutz in Israel, or inter-generational extended family networks living together as commonly seen in more traditional societies are other alternatives that assure children are cared for and economic needs tended to. In contrast, laws in several countries in Africa that prohibit women from owning their own property or inheriting their own homes and possessions upon their husband's deaths assure their impoverishment and impede their ability to adequately care for their children.

Mothers need access to reproductive health care that includes family planning that allows them to control the spacing and the number of their children and quality pre and post natal care for themselves and their offspring. They need sanitary conditions and access to health care. They need access to education for themselves and their children. They need freedom of movement without fear of attack. They need their basic needs taken care of so they can focus on the socio-emotional development of their children. They need intellectual stimulation and emotional support and interpersonal connection. They need partnership that supports parenting. They need validation. They need societies that pay more than lip service to valuing motherhood—that actually invest in motherhood. They need societies that recognize and are committed to the profound, transformational impact that can be achieved when mothers are enabled to mother in healthy and conscious ways.

We, as mothers, need to support each other in efforts to bring the maternal into the work of constructing a society, a different kind of civilization. We need to understand and accept that we have not only the responsibility, but the RIGHT to mother in healthy ways. Recognizing this right, this entitlement, and claiming it, demanding the environment and the social support and the economic support and the emotional support to allow us to mother in healthy ways, can transform society and will create the conditions for our collective Mother Force to evolve a more highly developed human-kind, a caring society, and a more peaceful, less violent world.

Portions of this chapter have previously appeared in L. Slepian, L. Sylla, and R. Weston, "A Radical Hope: The Birth and Evolution of the National Association of Mothers' Centers," in Andrea O'Reilly (Ed.), The 21st Century Motherhood Movement: Mothers Speak Out on Why We Need to Change the World and How to Do It *(Demeter Press, 2011).*

In the Scholarly Way

Making Generations of Inroads to Empowered Indigenous Mothering

JENNIFER BRANT AND KIM ANDERSON

WHAT DO MOTHERS NEED? As scholarly Indigenous[1] mothers, we have often been called upon to answer this question as it pertains to our peoples. In this paper we could present the basic, the urgent, the statistical, and that would probably be enough. As a young mother and student presenting at a conference in 2011,[2] for example, Jennifer (co-author of this paper) began with the following:

> The Royal Commission on Aboriginal Peoples tells me I can anticipate a life-expectancy rate that is ten years less than that of other women in Canada. Data from the Canadian Population Health Initiative tell me that I belong to the unhealthiest group in the country (Harper 179). As an Aboriginal woman, I am likely to earn 30 percent less than non-Aboriginal women. I am three times more likely to contact HIV, and five times more likely to die as a result of violence (Amnesty International). Further, as an Aboriginal mother it is reasonable for me to be fearful of my children being taken away through state intervention. I belong to a group in which my position is exceedingly disadvantaged "by every common measure of poverty, such as income, educational attainment, incidence of disease and life expectancy" (Amnesty International 7).

Jennifer's short introduction harbours plenty of material to unpack about "what Indigenous mothers need," and we want to put it out there so that we don't lose sight of the basics. The fact is that after over five hundred years of contact and colonization, Aboriginal peoples in Canada continue to find themselves at the bottom of every health, social and economic indicator in this country, and too many of our mothers struggle to raise children in conditions of poverty and abuse.

So what do Indigenous mothers need? Food, shelter, safety and security; let's not forget! But this paper focuses on a different kind of critical need, and one that is not visible in statistics or indicators. We have written about the experience of what we are calling "the eachother." For as Jennifer and Kim—two Indigenous moms—our story is about how we found ourselves in eachother, as well as through the greater web of relationships that has been critical to rebuilding an empowered Indigenous motherhood. And how, in particular, we have done this through what is often experienced as a colonial, western and foreign institution: academia.

As a pair we represent successive generations of mothers/scholars. Kim is a 48 year-old Cree/Métis woman and Associate Professor at Wilfrid Laurier University and has been doing research and writing about Indigenous families since the mid 1990s. Jennifer is a 30-year-old Mohawk woman and Ph.D. student at Brock University and is currently doing research on the needs of Indigenous mothers in post-secondary education. We met in 2009 at a consultation held by Brock University and organized by Jennifer to look at programming that would assist Indigenous women to achieve at Brock. We'll begin with our own stories and then show how our lives are connected to a larger web of Indigenous mothers using the academy as a means of reclaiming empowered Indigenous mothering.

KIM'S STORY

I first became a mother in 1995, with the birth of my son, Rajan. At the time, I was a thirty year-old woman who had been working in community based Aboriginal organizations in Toronto, and I had a commitment to re-learning the cultural and "traditional" ways that had been stripped from so many of our peoples as part of colonization. I was eager to learn how to decolonize as a mother, and had a hunger for learning what "traditional Native parenting" or "Indigenous mothering" might look like.

There were no books on this in the parenting section of my local bookstore, or at any of the specialty Indigenous booksellers for that matter. As with most traditional knowledge, the place to go looking was among older women who were able to speak about their own experiences and the knowledge they had gained from oral tradition. I remember making one such request while pregnant with Rajan; humbly offering tobacco[3] to a woman who was an "auntie" or (othermother) to me in the urban Aboriginal community of Toronto. Of course, she chuckled at my request for "teachings" about "Indigenous parenting styles," for she didn't have some kind of neat package she could provide. And now, eighteen years later, I realize the obvious—that knowledge about parenting, any style, comes through the messy stuff of practice and reflection. But further to that, my understanding of the complexity of Indigenous mothering would involve years of study about the histories of our peoples, and research into the physical, mental, emotional and spiritual needs of our present. By now I have a few things to say about Indigenous parenting and mothering, but it has taken awhile. Ultimately, the interest I had as a young mom propelled me through two graduate degrees as well as scholarly, consulting, and community-based research so that I could produce the kind of literature I had once wanted to read myself.

It's important to note that my academic focus on Indigenous families did not start out so clearly. I had decided to go back to university when I first became pregnant because I felt it would be good to upgrade my research and writing skills in the interest of supporting a family. I started a Master's degree at OISE/University of Toronto when Rajan was four months old, with the intention of writing a thesis about gender in First Nations politics (an area where I had been working). But when one of my courses required that I do qualitative research I ended up interviewing Aboriginal women who were involved with the child welfare system because this was a research area of need identified within the Toronto Aboriginal community.

Although I was familiar with the kind of inequities described by Jennifer above, this was the first time I had considered the lives of disadvantaged Aboriginal families from the standpoint of a *mother*, and it hit me like an emotional tsunami. I finished that project wanting to know why so many Indigenous women, who are purportedly *sacred* by virtue of their status as "lifegivers" in our communities, were in such dire and often abusive situations. More than anything, I needed to feel a sense of hope, especially as a new mom. And so for my next course, I interviewed a number of Aboriginal women across Canada about identity re-construction and empowered Indigenous womanhood, and wrote a paper, which grew into a thesis, which grew into my first book, *A Recognition of Being: Reconstructing Native Womanhood.*

Kim Anderson

My work since the Master's degree has often involved listening to stories by and about Aboriginal women, and has been built out of a web of relationships that spreads across Turtle Island (North America). Starting with the stories I collected for that first paper, I learned from the power of "the eachother"; a power that comes from listening and telling. But writing can be such a solitary activity, and once you finish the work and put it out there you don't really think about how it might go on to have a life of its own. I didn't realize that my storywork would connect me to other generations of women, who, as readers, would discover themselves in the stories I had heard. This is now part of Jennifer's story, which she tells later in this paper.

For me, meeting and working with Jennifer has been a critical part of building empowered Indigenous motherhood. I can see what is useful in terms of the stories I have gathered, and I can listen and learn from her about what is important to the next generation. There is healing in seeing that we have similar needs and interests, such as reclaiming ceremonies or culture-based ways of parenting. Jennifer has also helped me with what I need as an Indigenous mother by moving me into that "auntie" role. Jennifer is a generation younger than me, so I have life experience as well as academic experiences that allow me to be the auntie, but it is worth mentioning that many of our women go back to school later in life—many as moms of adult children—so there are other mentoring possibilities and relationships I can build with women who are entering academia at my age or even older. Academia has thus given me one place to be an auntie, and all of the relationships, roles and stories in "the eachother" we develop together along the way are critical to our health as Indigenous moms.

One key element of "the eachother" is that it flows forward and backward in time. It is not a line, but a circle. And so while writing this paper my thinking came back around to the late Patricia Monture, a formidable Mohawk woman, mom, activist and scholar of Indigenous studies, law and sociology. I'll finish with a story about what I learned from her when I was a young mother and student.

I first met Trish when she came to speak at the Native Women's Resource Centre of Toronto where I was working in the late 1980s, and I was amazed with her courage and energy. She wasn't much older than me, but had already accomplished so much. A number of years later—the year my son Rajan was born—Trish published her first, and seminal collection of essays, *Thunder in My Soul: A Mohawk Woman Speaks.* Among other things, this book spoke to her experiences as an Aboriginal woman in the academy, and it made those of us with similar experiences not feel so alone. Trish is also notable for generously encouraging those who were starting out in academic careers. We were only acquaintances at the time, but when I told her I was working up a book out of my Master's thesis, I remember an outburst of genuine excitement ("You go girl!"). I carried this enthusiasm like a torch inside me over the years it took to write that book.

Perhaps what impressed me most about Trish was the way she incorporated children and mothering into every part of her life. Watching her do things like give a keynote with her five-year-old playing on the floor beside her gave me permission to bring my children to places like the Congress of Social Sciences and Humanities. I'm not saying it is easy or always possible to have our children with us—or that it's easy for *us* to be present for our children as we work through graduate degrees and academic careers. But Patricia's practice taught me something about Indigenous parenting styles and philosophies of childrearing. That is, children in "traditional" Indigenous societies were always present in adult work environments, because that is how they learned, took on responsibility, and contributed to community. This was also how they learned to be attentive and respectful, which was a discipline that was required in our land-based communities. Perhaps most important, it gave our children a sense of purpose and belonging.

I finish with this story about Trish because it demonstrates one of the

Indigenous parenting practices that I can now articulate after years of observation, study and reflection. It is also central to the work that Jennifer is doing with Indigenous mothers at Brock University, which starts with a story about Jennifer's experiences as a student.

JENNIFER'S STORY

> When someone with the authority of a teacher, say, describes the world and you are not in it, there is a moment of psychic disequilibrium, as if you looked into a mirror and saw nothing. Yet you know you exist and others like you, that this is a game with mirrors. It takes some strength of soul—and not just individual strength, but collective understanding—to resist this void, this non being, into which you are thrust, and to stand up demanding to be seen and heard. (Rich 199)

Much of my university experience can be described in these often-quoted words of Adrienne Rich. I began my studies in 2002 at the age of 20. At this time I was just over three months pregnant with my first son, Jayden, who was born only two weeks before my final exams. Needless to say, my entrance into undergraduate studies came with many challenges as I also embarked upon my new journey into motherhood. Despite these challenges, I was determined to succeed not only for myself, but also for my son who became intertwined and inseparable from my role as a student. With a focus on sociology, I immediately became immersed into areas that focused on child development and socialization. Everything became about my infant son, who brought about new purpose and meaning in my life. I was a single mother and in many ways I lost myself in caring for my son.

My earlier days at university can be described, at best, as an alienating experience. As both an Aboriginal woman and a single mother, it was difficult to find a sense of belonging among my peers. I quickly became familiar with the challenges of balancing my roles of mother and student along with the other challenges I faced as an Aboriginal student positioned in a Eurocentric education institution. I came with a different reality than the typical university student and without the supports to navigate this unknown and unfamiliar territory; I experienced the university as a scary, unwelcoming place. Naturally, as a young mother, I felt isolated

Jennifer Brant

and lonely having nothing in common with the other students. The curriculum, course design, and delivery only furthered these feelings of alienation.

It wasn't until my third year of university that I became involved with the Aboriginal student supports and attended their social and cultural gatherings. It was here that I found a sense of belonging within the university. There were other women like myself who were also raising young children. Within this environment, I found a paradigm shift away from the mainstream tendency to de-compartmentalize student and family responsibilities. As Kim has pointed out in her story about Patricia Monture, it is not uncommon to have children attend all manner of events in Indigenous contexts. Thus, with the on-campus events organized by the Aboriginal student services, children were always welcomed, and, in fact, encouraged to participate. It was incredibly refreshing that for once I did not have to experience the usual tension of leaving my maternal responsibilities at the door when I entered the university. This allowed the university to become a familiar place for my children, who now think of the university as a friendly place where they come to drum, dance, and listen to our traditional teachers. I am hopeful that the university will continue to have this appeal and these few cultural events that take place on campus will grow.

My experiences as an Aboriginal mother on campus speak to the interconnectedness between mother and child and the need for building community and "the eachother." Through the new connections I developed, and the friendships I made, I was able to envision my university experience as more of a decolonizing journey; one in which I was finally able to bring my whole being (mother, student, and community member). While my program of study itself remained culturally irrelevant, and my experiences as an Aboriginal woman and single mother left me positioned at the margins, I now had a venue where I could make sense of this and connect with others like myself.

Those experiences of undergraduate student life as a mother inspired me to pursue graduate studies with a focus on the barriers Aboriginal women face in universities. Well aware of the multiple challenges I had faced, I sought out to explore the university experiences of other Aboriginal women and use my findings to advance a holistic model of Aboriginal women's educational access and academic success.

In graduate school I began to explore the need for curriculum that would help me with my path to empowered Indigenous mothering. Early on I enrolled in a course on Maternal Pedagogies, and the text was Andrea O'Reilly's *Maternal Theory: Essential Readings.* As I went through the required course readings I was not surprised by the usual lack of Indigenous content, but when I went home and read through the table of contents I noticed Kim Anderson's article, "Giving Life to the People: An Indigenous Ideology of Motherhood." I asked my professor if we could add this article to our required readings list, and when she agreed, the article became my course focus. I was drawn to the idea of incorporating an Indigenous ideology of motherhood into an academic context. How might we use the theory in the article to develop a curriculum and program specific to Aboriginal women? In response to my direction, my professor asked me how I might set up the notion of an Indigenous ideology of motherhood in contrast to "the dominant scary view of Aboriginal mothers beset by being responsible for a generation of children suffering from, say, fetal alcohol syndrome." She challenged me with "How do you shatter that trope?"

At first, I was offended by this statement. I felt the stigmatization attached to being a young Aboriginal Mother, and it touched on how I have had to learn to work through this stigmatization every day as I balance the roles I carry as a mother and student. But I knew I also come from a community where "children are the hearts of our nations" and where I feel my position as a young Aboriginal mother is always welcomed and embraced. So my professor's comment prompted me to reflect on this further.

I was lucky because I was able to draw from the small but growing body of literature written by Indigenous scholars about the experience of mothering in our communities. While Kim Anderson's (2007) work on the Indigenous ideology of motherhood could perhaps been seen as idyllic, she had written other work that offered critical assessments of the state of our families today. I discovered her (2003) article, "Vital Signs: Reading Colonialism in Contemporary Adolescent Family Planning," which begins with the following:

> *Children Are the Hearts of Our Nations* and *Our Children Are Our Future* are familiar sayings that adorn Aboriginal organizational logos and letterhead, T-shirts and bumper stickers. We adopt these sayings as powwow or conference themes and print them on banners to welcome participants. But after the meetings, the speeches and the MC's platitudes at the powwow, where do our children really stand? If children are the heart of our communities, I think we need to take a serious look at our heart condition. (2003: 173)

Throughout this article, Kim draws attention to the crisis that Aboriginal families face as our families are becoming younger and larger, with limited economic resources and a lack of the traditional family practices that were once prevalent. While it is beyond the scope of this article to discuss the reasons why negative views of Aboriginal motherhood (such as those noted by my professor) exist, it is important that these experiences are understood through a decolonizing framework. The work of Anderson and other Indigenous scholars is helpful as it frames contemporary challenges within historical contexts.[4]

I was thus able to draw from the literature to articulate an informed response to my professor, and as I dug deeper I saw that beneath the messy colonial debris there is profound beauty and power. In Kim's article, "Giving Life to the People: Indigenous Ideology of Motherhood" (2007), for example, I was drawn to the description of motherhood as grounded in spirituality. I saw power in the maternal body, as she referred to traditional teachings that connect a woman's body and her ability to procreate with the power of creation and the ability of Mother Earth to sustain life. Through other work, I learned about things like the importance of rites of passage ceremonies such as the Berry Fast or traditional family planning practices, and I also learned why these traditions have not been as accessible to me as they should have been.[5] As Kim points out, understanding the way colonization has repressed these traditions helps us to understand some of the current disheartening realities our communities face. Her work attests to the need to restore them as a way to bring the balance back to our families and communities. All of this is built into the stories of the women she has worked with along the way.

The empowerment I experienced from reading academic literature about Indigenous motherhood made me realize the value of incorporating it into maternal based curriculum to support the educational experiences of other Aboriginal women, many of whom are also raising families. This material can also support our learning experiences at the community level. For example, as I was struggling to complete my final paper for the maternal pedagogies course, I had the opportunity to participate in my first Full Moon Ceremony. During this ceremony, I received an oral teaching about the Berry Fast. This was very important for me because this experience validated much of what I had read about in the literature.[6]

As I move along my journey, I intend to continue participating in ceremony and learning about the traditional family practices embedded in my own culture. This will guide me as I contribute to the emerging literature on the experiences of Aboriginal women in education, and work to shatter the tropes of Aboriginal mothering as my professor encouraged me to do. It will also guide me as I raise my own children, honour them as gifts from the Creator, and instill in them a strong Aboriginal identity.

NEW INROADS AND GENERATIONS

> *When the women heal the family will heal. And when the family heals, the nation will heal.*
>
> —Margaret Lavallee (qtd. in Kenny)

This quote speaks to the critical role of women in Aboriginal communities. As mothers, Aboriginal women are the first teachers of future generations, but they also are viewed as 'Mothers of the Nation' by way of their political, activist and organizing roles within their communities. With education being essential to improving the social and economic realities that are faced by Aboriginal peoples, improving the educational opportunities of young Aboriginal women and mothers is a must. Thus, it is important to promote Aboriginal women's access into universities as a way to respond to the current realities of Aboriginal women, and, by extension, to heal Aboriginal families, communities, and nations. This was the premise that inspired individuals at Brock University to start a transition program for Aboriginal women and mothers.

Jennifer's experiences as an Aboriginal mother and student brought her together with these individuals, and into the team at the Tecumseh Centre for Aboriginal Research and Education at Brock that created the *Gidayaamin Aboriginal Women's Certificate Program.* Gidayaamin is a transition year program now in its second year, offering the culture-based student and academic supports that Aboriginal women/mothers might need to be successful in university. It was built from stories that Jennifer and colleagues gathered from Aboriginal women. These women's narratives, along with the literature, pushed the university to go beyond simple notions of access towards a more community-driven approach in which the voices of young Aboriginal mothers become central to culturally responsive programming, and their experiences as both Aboriginal and mother become embraced as educational opportunities rather than barriers.

One of the main themes that came out of consulting with the women was that they wanted to center their children in the educational experience. Many women expressed the desire to provide a better life for their children as a key motivating factor in their decision to pursue post-secondary education. Beyond this, they expressed a vision that defined core elements needed to make their intersecting roles as mothers and students seamless. This included a support circle of women to encourage one another and assist in childcare responsibilities. Their vision included a space for families akin to an Aboriginal Head Start program that could provide access to culturally relevant childcare onsite while they attended classes. This was also described as a welcoming centre for families where they could be involved in the childcare between class and study time.

Interestingly enough, much like Kim had described in the lessons she had learned from Trish, one of the women brought her infant son to the mothers' consultation gathering, while another woman was pregnant. As they shared their visions of centering their children in their educational experiences, the visibility of the children at the gathering provided a synergy that drew attention to the importance of this vision. This synergy continued when the program started, as children have been welcomed into Gidayaamin in a variety of ways. For example, while child care placements are encouraged so that women can attend to their academic work, children are also welcome in the classes and contribute to the overall community environment of the class. Beyond this, children and families are invited to all of the Gidayaamin social events, so that much like Jennifer described in her experience, children can get to know the university as a friendly place where the whole family can participate.

The women that were consulted toward the development of a transition year program also expressed a desire for a decolonizing curriculum that embraces women's roles as mothers. Like Jennifer and Kim, they were seeking culture based knowledge and teachings as well as academic knowledge about mothering, women's issues, spirituality, and parenthood. One woman simply stated she wanted to learn about "women's stories, you know, just stories." They asked to have Aboriginal men as role models involved in university programming so their boy children could have access to traditional teachings as well. The Gidayaamin program responded to these culture and community based knowledge needs by bringing the Aboriginal community into the university setting through social and cultural events. By bringing in the drum, the heartbeat of Mother Earth, participants were reminded of the maternal connection between Aboriginal mothers and their children. These connections take place at the social and cultural events where Honour Songs are shared for the women, their families, and community.

In thinking of overall design of the program, the team knew that solutions towards healthier families, communities, and nations are embedded in the development of strong cultural identity formation, and the reclamation of Indigenous ideologies of motherhood is key to that process. Jennifer knew that what she needed as an undergraduate student was to see her culture and pieces of her own story reflected in academic material. She had found some of this in Kim's book *A Recognition of Being: Reconstructing Native Womanhood* (2000), which offers a theory of identity formation for Aboriginal women. This theory posits that we resist negative stereotypes, reclaim culture and tradition, reconstruct it into our modern lives, and act on it with a renewed sense of responsibility to community. Jennifer went back to this theory to guide the development of a holistic framework for the Gidayaamin program. Thus, while the women's narratives informed the vision, the literature provided the theoretical grounding. Within the program, then, women learn to resist negative stereotypes through critical thinking and reading; they have opportunities to reclaim Indigenous culture through the literature, guest speakers, and on campus activities; they are encouraged to be creative and think about how to reconstruct traditional and academic learning into their lives, and to share these connections through written assignments, creative works and presentations; and, finally, the women are encouraged to act on the new identities and responsibilities they discover as part of the learning journey.

While the Gidayaamin program is only in its second year, initial feedback from the students shows that the curriculum is indeed empowering. Students have begun to draw strength from maternal histories such as those advanced in the literature.[7] They find the resilience of Aboriginal motherhood as described in the literature inspiring, and Jennifer has seen this resilience grow within them as they move through the curriculum. It is a curriculum that empowers, is inclusionary rather than exclusionary, and the women, for once, see themselves reflected in course delivery, design, and material. They have been able to do all this in a culturally safe space which allows them to learn and explore from traditional knowledge and practice.

Looking back to Adrienne Rich's comment cited earlier about the need for strength of soul, collective understanding and resistance, we can reflect on how this might be accomplished through the academy with Gidayaamin as an example. Gidayaamin includes maternal histories curriculum coupled with community support to foster a collective understanding and develop a support network by welcoming Aboriginal families and community. It is one example that demonstrates how culturally relevant programming can be designed in a way that allows Aboriginal women to blend their experiences of schooling and mothering, tasks that were rendered incompatible under residential school programs. Moreover, this is a program that has grown out of the collective and "the eachother" experiences of Indigenous women through dialogue, storytelling, literature, academic study and relationship building.

FINAL WORDS

As Indigenous women, some of us are faced with more challenges than others, but watching the women in the Gidayaamin Program has given Jennifer the confidence that Indigenous based maternal pedagogy can inspire Indigenous women on the whole to share in common understandings, and walk down a winding path together, supporting, and drawing strength from one another. Jennifer is now a second year doctoral student who continues to face significant challenges along the way, but the work of Aboriginal women who have already planted seeds and laid down pathways has been invaluable. Kim continues to learn as she listens to stories of other Indigenous mothers and collaborates on mothering work, such as co-writing this paper. There are many ways of seeking out empowered Indigenous motherhood, but the two of us have done it through the academy and by connecting with other women through our writing and organizing. We continue to find ourselves in the eachother, and, to our surprise, in the scholarly way.

[1]There are many ways to refer to the first peoples of Canada and worldwide. In this chapter we use both Indigenous and Aboriginal. "Aboriginal" is used to refer to first peoples within Canada, which include First Nations, Inuit, and Métis as recognized in Section 35 of the Canadian Constitution. The term "Indigenous" (as used here) is inclusive of first peoples on the whole; to indicate and be inclusive of a broader category of first peoples internationally.

[2]Jennifer Brant's comments presented at the Motherhood Initiative for Research and Community Involvement International Research Conference on Mothering, Motherhood and Education, Toronto, Ontario, October 2011.

[3]Tobacco is offered as a gift in exchange for the sharing of knowledge.

[4]For example, many of the chapters in D. Memee Lavell-Harvard and Jeanette Corbiere Lavell, eds., *"Until Our Hearts Are on the Ground": Aboriginal Mothering, Oppression, Resistance and Rebirth,* draw attention to the colonial impact on Aboriginal motherhood, but also bring us back to a time when women were honoured for their roles as mothers.

[5]For example, Kim Anderson describes how traditional family planning has "been attacked and suppressed to the point that it is now hard to find" and points out that these understandings were replaced by a "Western medical paradigm that gave birth, pregnancy and female sexual reproductive health matters over to male doctors" (2003: 181).

[6]For example, Kim Anderson writes about the empowerment that comes from participating in the Berry Fast in "Honouring the Blood of the People: Berry Fasting in the Twenty-first Century" (2000b). While the Berry Fast ceremony has been lost through colonization, Anderson asserts that

it is making a comeback in Aboriginal communities through reclamation of an Indigenous ideology of motherhood. Further, she indicates that it is now being offered in a way that reflects the contemporary needs of Aboriginal youth. This demonstrates a revisioning of traditional Aboriginal ceremonies as a way to address the distinct needs of Aboriginal youth. Anderson advises that through these ceremonies young women learn about patience, sacrifice, and taking the time to learn about and build relationships. She also demonstrates how the Berry Fast is helping women to learn about respecting their bodies. Through empowerment, the Berry Fast allows women to learn about how to say no and withdraw from unhealthy situations. Anderson describes sacrifice, self-discipline, and a sense of responsibility as lessons that young women learn by participating in the Berry Fast.

[7]In addition to the work in Kim Anderson, *A Recognition of Being: Reconstructing Native Womanhood* (2000a) and Kim Anderson's article, "Giving Life to the People: An Indigenous Ideology of Motherhood" (2007), there are many relevant stories presented in Dawn Memee Lavell-Harvard and Jeannette Corbiere Lavell's anthology, *"Until Our Hearts Are on the Ground": Aboriginal Mothering, Oppression, Resistance and Rebirth;* Gail Guthrie Valaskakis, Madeleine Dion Stout and Eric Guimond's *Restoring the Balance: First Nations Women, Community and Culture;* and Patricia Monture and Patricia McGuire's, *First Voices: An Aboriginal Women's Reader.* These stories provide evidence of the hardships many Aboriginal mothers have faced and overcome, offering stories of strength, determination, and resilience.

WORKS CITED

Amnesty International. *No More Stolen Sisters: The Need for a Comprehensive Response to Discrimination and Violence against Indigenous Women in Canada.* Ottawa: Author, 2009. Print.

Anderson, Kim. *A Recognition of Being: Reconstructing Native Womanhood.* Toronto: Sumach Press, 2000a. Print.

Anderson, Kim. "Giving Life to the People: An Indigenous Ideology of Motherhood." *Maternal Theory: Essential Readings.* Ed. Andrea O'Reilly. Toronto: Demeter Press, 2007: 761-781. Print.

Anderson, Kim. "Honouring the Blood of the People: Berry Fasting in the Twenty-First Century." *Expressions in Canadian Native Studies.*

Eds. Ron F. Laliberte et. al. Saskatoon: University of Saskatchewan Extension Press, 2000b. 374-394. Print.

Anderson, Kim. "Vital Signs: Reading Colonialism in Contemporary Adolescent Family Planning." *Strong Women Stories: Native Vision and Community Survival.* Eds. Kim Anderson and Bonita Lawrence. Toronto: Sumach Press, 2003. 173-190. Print.

Harper, Anita Olsen. "Sisters in Spirit." *Restoring the Balance: First Nations Women, Community, and Culture.* Eds. Gail Guthrie Valaskakis, Madeleine Dion Stout and Eric Guimond. Winnipeg: University of Manitoba Press, 2009: 175-199. Print.

Kenny, Carolyn. "When the Women Heal: Aboriginal Women Speak about Policies to Improve the Quality of Life." *American Behavioural Scientist* 50 (4) (2006): 550-561. Print.

Lavell-Harvard D. Memee and Jeannette Corbiere Lavell, eds. *"Until our Hearts are on the Ground": Aboriginal Mothering, Oppression, Resistance and Rebirth.* Toronto: Demeter Press, 2006. Print.

Monture, Patricia. *Thunder in My Soul: A Mohawk Woman Speaks.* Halifax: Fernwood Press, 1995. Print.

Monture, Patricia and Patricia McGuire, eds. *First Voices: An Aboriginal Women's Reader* Toronto: Inanna Publications, 2009. Print.

Rich, Adrienne. "Invisibility in Academe." *Blood, Bread & Poetry: Selected Prose, 1979-1985* New York: W. W. Norton, 1986. Print.

Valaskakis, Gail Guthrie, Madeleine Dion Stout and Eric Guimond, eds. *Restoring the Balance: First Nations Women, Community, and Culture.* Winnipeg: University of Manitoba Press, 2009. Print.

Ripe for Revolution

GWEN LEWIS

WORKING FOR *HIP MAMA ZINE* over the last two and a half years, I have read the gamut of heartbreaking essay submissions. Stories of homelessness with kids written from places of fear and desperation; tales of utter failures within our healthcare and education systems. When the institutions put into place by society begin to fail, families, particularly poor families, are the first to feel these failures. Through my own experiences and research, I have seen cracks in the foundations of the social constructs we rely on for civilization as we currently enjoy it. In the United States of America, our educational system is falling apart from lack of funding, and poor structure. The insurance based healthcare system is a perfect image of evil—no health care decision should be made by a corporation; profiting off of denying health care should be a crime. (To the point where "denying healthcare" shouldn't even be a thing that happens!) With the current "economic slowing" we've seen a significant loss of the middle class, meaning that more people have joined in the struggle to just survive in a system that requires money to attain our most basic survival needs of water, food and shelter. With its level of open, unapologetic corruption, our current political system makes a mockery of the spirit of government, which should be to serve the people. The problem with allowing these corruptions is that they are at the root causes of so many of our problems and our politicians would rather keep us distracted with a big show of bipartisan bickering over hot-button issues than actually working together, as public servants should, towards a better future for us all. I come to activism rather unwillingly, there are so many other things that I would prefer to be doing with my time than having to stand up against this system but I have seen too many problems and too many connections to be quiet. We have gotten to the point where we are going to need to enact huge social change if we want to continue to survive at all and we have also come to the point where we really need social change to benefit the people.

As a civilization, we've been going in a certain direction for a long time and avoiding any signs of danger ahead. We've done this in terms of our treatment of the environment, allowed it within our politics, our economic systems and the treatment of the lower classes. Big issues of political, economic and social origins are coming to boiling points all over the world. As a person on this planet and a mother of the next generation, the first and biggest problems that I believe we need to address are the ones that will affect us all at the level of survival. We need to be working towards solutions in the problems of food and agriculture, population, water and energy. These issues are intricately interwoven and I will try to address them as thoroughly as I can.

Food, one of our most basic survival needs, is at the core of so many of our problems. There is so much wrong with our current food system that we need to rethink everything within it starting with how it's grown. Agriculture, as we're practicing it, is the number one polluter on this planet. We are destroying our water, air and soil with chemicals and we are losing one of our most valuable resources, soil, through massive erosion and desertification. Only three percent of our planet's surface is productive, arable land and we lose a hectare of that agricultural land every 7.67 seconds to urbanization and desertification. With a rising global population, we will have more mouths to feed than ever and less soil to procure food from. If we want our children to have places to grow their food, we are going to need to start changing the way we look at agriculture.

Today's generation is the first to have shorter life expectancies than the last and it is because of the food we are eating. After picking, each time a food is processed it loses 90 percent of its nutrients. The foods we're buying in boxes at the stores contain next to nothing of the nutrients found in the original food. Most of the foods available to us are processed beyond nutrient recognition and rounded out with sugar and salt. The food that is grown for processed foods is grown as cheaply as possible, even subsidized by our tax dollars to keep it cheap and the other corners cut usually further degrades the quality of the food. The meat that the majority of people in the USA consumes is positively disgusting. Grown in feces-choked feedlots and dark cages, the disgusting and inhumane practices of our meat industries produce meat of poor quality and significantly depleted nutritional value. The regulations over these processes have been skewed in such ways that they actually favor these practices, excluding small farmers from competition. Those who may want to produce high-quality meat in a sustainable way and try to forge forward in the practices of clean, safe meat are met with regulations skewed towards the larger, corporate sized process, problems with availability of slaughtering units, high fees and strict regulations on selling practices. In the end with the fees involved with slaughtering and butchering and the increased cost of doing meat sustainably, clean meat has a hard time competing with the cheap stuff that everyone is used to. The thing is, that cheap meat is only artificially cheap. The corn grown to feed the cattle is subsidized by our tax dollars, the oil for moving the corn isn't factored in and the shipping of the animal and then the actual meat isn't accounted for in the price we pay either. If all of the costs of the "cheaper" meat model were accounted for, it would show that it actually costs a lot more money to create that low quality meat and I'm not even exploring the cost in land and soil degradation or the fact that we're feeding corn to animals that aren't designed to process corn or all the problems associated with that. This system simply can not go on this way.

Even the fresh fruits and vegetables that we have access to at the super market have huge problems associated with them. Usually grown far away in massive monocultures, they're picked early and coated in wax or chemically ripened on their long trip to the grocery store. The exploitation of workers in other countries, the carbon footprint for shipping, the poor tasting, poor quality fruits and vegetables just aren't worth it. Furthermore, vast monocultures are beginning to cause problems for bees. Bees are the great pollinator, it takes around 2 million blossoms worth of nectar to produce a pound of honey. For each pound of honey that's potentially 2 million berries or squash or melons or apples. There are some monocrops so vast that the lack of diversity can't support bees year round so bees don't live in these areas. These monocrops require bees to be driven in from all over the country in order to pollinate them. The problem with this is that our bees have been suffering from something called Colony Collapse Disorder, the cause of which is hard to nail down. There are several theories as to what causes Colony Collapse Disorder, theories of viral combinations and environmental elements that we introduce like pesticides. With the trucking of bees all over the country to pollinate certain crops, however, we're seeing a more rapid spread of these cases. Trucking bees is a waste of resources and having them mingle in this way is further endangering them at a delicate time for them. We do not want to see a world without honey bees so we should be taking the time to take better care of more of them now. This could be a good reason for some monocultures to start planting polycultural crops so that we can sustain more bees year round in more places.

Our food system has grown massive and far-reaching in an age of cheap oil. In this time, most of us have lost the ability to cook food from fresh ingredients. This process started when women like my grandmother decided to work to help sustain the family income. Women really entering the workplace and striving for careers of their own is, without a doubt, a huge step forward for women. The negative side to this wonderful step forward is that processed food is what stepped into the kitchens of most homes as the women stepped out. The problem here is that our grandparents didn't teach our parents to cook or eat fresh, and they didn't teach us, and now there are children who grow up who can't identify broccoli or carrots. In this time that we have been losing our food preparation skills, food processors have refined their techniques, cheapened their processes and grown larger. Their food is easy, it's what our parents fed us and at the end of a long day of work it is fast and filling. It's hard to say no to that. Except when it's not. The amount of calorically dense, nutritionally poor, processed foods that we are consuming is out of control. The processes involved in growing, processing and shipping these artificially cheap, barely-foods are depleting more resources than the world can sustain and these foods are only succeeding in making us sicker, fatter, and dead earlier. We need to be growing our food more locally and should be encouraging this trend world-wide. We should still continue encouraging global trade where it is necessary, there are some places that will always need to import food and for some foods there are only certain places they will grow. These long-range foods should be considered specialty items however. We should be leery of whatever practices give us bananas all the way from South America at consistently cheap prices year round. Something about that reeks of exploitation. I think it is more important that people around the world plant food to feed themselves, however, before growing crops to send abroad. We need to be learning how to grow and cook fresh food again. Re-learn a respect for seasonality. I

Gwen Lewis

have heard some rhetoric about the movements that have come out in favor of cooking fresh as being anti-feminist. As if women are the only people capable of working in the kitchen! It is my firm belief that if everyone requires food to live than *everyone* should know how to feed themselves and be involved in the kitchen, man, woman and child. My husband and I share our kitchen, and involve our three and a half year old daughter wherever we can; working together, we can play into each other's cooking strengths. As we have learned more about food nutrition, we strive only to work with the freshest ingredients and with practice our food has only become more delicious. We hardly see the point in going out to eat any longer as the food we make at home is guaranteed to be just as delicious (or usually better), it's certainly cheaper, and we are better in control of where our ingredients come from.

There are ways to produce enough food sustainably, for everyone. We need to be encouraging more people to go back into farming, break up the subsidized mono-cultures and plant polycultures, permacultures, silvacultures! We need to be raising our meat outside in the sun, practicing animal husbandry and rotational grazing to build our soil back up and we need to be doing this closer to the market. People should know their farmers and see the conditions in which their food is grown, we simply can't sustain the massive way in which we are currently shipping our food.

Water depletion is another huge issue that we're coming up against. Water rights are spurning intense conflicts around the world. Between water pollution, abuse of and over pumping our groundwater, improper agricultural practices and the degradation of our watersheds through deforestation, water depletion is a terrifying reality for our very near future. If there wasn't enough evidence for this already than the terrifyingly predatory way that large water corporations are conducting their businesses should be a clue. Water is absolutely necessary for our survival, we cannot live without water, it is something that everyone has a right to. We need to be cleaning it up and restoring it now, fixing our policies and the so-called rights to it because if we wait too long we will find ourselves dying of thirst.

Energy depletion is a big problem. With the discovery of crude oil and fossil fuels, we were able to create tons of cheap energy and resources. Nearly all of our modern innovations and technologies are sourced from oil and when oil isn't a direct part of the process it is always a part of the global shipping network. Peak Oil is a reality and it doesn't matter when it happens, we are hopelessly dependent on oil, nothing can take its place as far as an energy source is concerned. Since the discovery of this source of energy the population of the world has soared, growing exponentially. Sure there are other innovations involved in our population growth but they have all been fueled by oil. Now the bloated population of the world is utterly dependent on this energy source that is absolutely going to run out. Our last administration tried to "secure" this resource for us with a big war but there is nothing we can do to keep us in oil forever and the oils that will be left to gather after peak oil will be only the dirtiest, most expensive, land and earth degrading oils to gather, it won't be worth it. Look at the exploitation of Northern Alberta's oil sands! How much oil is wasted in the process of extracting that? How much water is polluted? How much land is destroyed? It's NOT worth it … and we're doing it, right now, anyway. We need to work seriously on alternative energies and start preparing ourselves now for a world without oil.

A lot of these problems are tied intrinsically to large corporations and large amounts of money and when we go to fix these problems we will assuredly run into the most resistance from corporations who are benefitting from the dysfunctions in these systems that we have allowed. There's a whole lot of government corruption involved with what large corporations like oil/energy, food and water companies are allowed to get away with in terms of pollution and waste. I do not consider myself a religious person but I have come to believe that greed is the deadliest sin of all because corporate sized greed is at the root of so many of our problems. The liberties that have been taken with resources like soil and water that are necessary for everyone to live, are astounding and disheartening. If this civilization is to come to a close it will be at the hands of corporate sized greed. Regulations have been slowly manipulated to turn corporations into mindless greed machines that consume without thought and whose only laws are geared towards the bottom dollar and profit for the investors. It is on this loose moral ground that we allow for horrible monstrosities to be committed against our world, the environment, people all around the world both locally and internationally, people whom are just struggling to make ends meet are utterly exploited by large corporations whether it be because they are the only employer in town or because they are the only money in a country. We allow for this to happen and we continuously vote for it with our dollars every day. Of course even when you're trying not to fund a horrible corporation with your money it's extremely hard to figure out the web of connectivity and monopolization that has become of our global marketplace. Huge amounts of greed are at the base of so many of our problems and yet people will defend a corporation's "right" to make money and there is a fear that if we try to raise taxes or hold them accountable they will leave. Good! It's a backwards way of thinking that we need the corporations to sustain us, in truth they need us to continue their money ballooning and if they want the continued benefit of our moneys they better shape up or ship out. We shouldn't accept any corporation that makes a profit while it is actively polluting or otherwise knowingly contributing to problems of the future.

As I mentioned before, we lose a hectare of arable land every 7.67 seconds. At the same time we are also losing our access to fresh water. We are teetering unsustainably on this planet at seven billion people and this number is expected to soar to nine billion within the next 40 years. We will have more people to sustain and far less of an ability to do so. The only way we grew to such numbers and came to be sustained here is through the energy provided by oil, a resource that is sure to run out and with our rate of consumption it will run out sooner than later. There's a lot of worry out there about how we're going to sustain 9 billion people on this planet and there should be! Yet there's almost no discussion about an attempt at not going there. We absolutely need to be discussing population control at this time. I'm tired of hearing about China and India and Africa and how they're the "main culprits" for population growth;

this is a cop-out. The population of the world should be regulated by the population of the world and "first world" babies are contributing to that unsustainable population growth just as much as any other baby; and as far as energy consumption goes, babies in the first world are far larger consumers. It is all of our responsibilities to educate on this and consider the overcrowded future that we are currently bringing children into. In the future our children or grandchildren could go hungry or thirsty simply because we decided to bring too many of them into this world. I am not calling for anything as dramatic as forced sterilization or saying that we need to impose laws on anybody's bodies. I'm saying that we need to increase our education on these issues and increase our access to contraceptives. With education and access to contraceptives, women naturally tend towards spacing their births. We especially need to be educating people on the risks of having an out of control global population because the general populace seems to be alarmingly unaware of most of the issues I've discussed in this essay and this epidemic of ignorance is distressing. If people were only AWARE of these issues, they would certainly desire less children. My husband and I have chosen to stop at one child. At times this is a difficult decision because babies *are* adorable and our bodies are evolutionarily predisposed towards making us desire more of them. This is a decision that we are absolutely in agreement on, however, as we do not want to contribute any further to overpopulation. People who would have upwards of two or three children *today* and going forward from now need to be educated and should carefully examine their motives. Those who want many children out of genuine love of children should perhaps consider adoption so that we can take care of the unwanted children we already have rather than birthing more.

Part of moving towards having less children is that we'll want to be making sure to take even better care of the children we do have. Addressing any of the problems I've been discussing is going to take huge amounts of social change. We're going to need a degree of social change *just* for people to accept that these are issues that we need to be focusing on at all, as our current mindset still seems to be that the earth is limitless. If we continue in this mindset we will find out that it is not true and it may be too late. When I say these are the issues "that will affect us all at the level of survival," I mean that *separately*, each of these things has the ability to end us and we're seeing major depletion in all areas at once.

The ways we do things are going to have to change significantly. It is my hope that while we are adjusting to cultural shifts as far as consumption goes that we will be able to figure out ways to raise the standard of living for everyone as well. There is a great deal of disparity in what we call the first world. Sure, we have "first world problems" now that are absurd when compared to "third world problems" but within the countries that we're referencing when we make these generalizations, there still exists a huge amount of disparity, starvation, and oppression.

I'm starting work on a project this fall where the end goal is to create a space for open democratic debate amongst the people. For too long we have been consuming our news and our opinions from a broken media system; a system that has a precedent that shows that "news" is not required to be factual and whose more subtle socializations are likely to be far more disturbingly efficient. This country, and the entire world for that matter, has a lot of problems coming to it and if our politicians aren't going to take their jobs seriously and actually strive for improvement or work together towards solutions than we need to start these discussions among the people. I believe that the people should be educated on these issues and that we should be educating each other because we have a whole lot of problems and the more people we have thinking about the solutions the more likely we are to find them. The problems that I have discussed above are necessary to address for the survival of our children in the nearer future than we'd like to believe, and this is why I have discussed them as the topic of what mothers need most. I have a three year old daughter and I can say with certainty that what I need most in the world is for her to have a future where she can do whatever she wants and doesn't have to worry about clean water to drink or starvation or the end of civilization. While we're addressing these problems however, I'd like to talk about all of our social structure issues that I see as having the most significant day to day effects on family. Together we can tackle the problems of universal health care, education, child care, an out of skew work culture and bridging the disparity gap. There are a lot of hot button issues that are being used as political distraction and the maddening thing is that they are all issues that are fueled by ignorance, issues that I believe can be solved with logic and critical thinking. I can't wait to start having these conversations. I'm excited because I think that we're capable of better ideas when we come together.

As a mother, a lot of this comes down to the world that I want to leave to my child and I confess that I spend a lot of time thinking about utopia. As a society we've gotten extremely cynical of the idea of utopia. At the same time that our governments ideally want us to display patriotism and loyalty, if things are so bad for the lower classes and minorities that we can't even humor the idea of utopia or speak about it in polite company, then this is the time when we need to be talking about it the most. The truth is that we have swallowed a lot of bi-partisan rhetoric on the way government and economic systems work but neither of the idealistic views of these systems really work, it is my opinion that this is because neither ideologies account for greed. We need to take a look at the ways things really work and come up with and implement new systems. Our education system is bankrupt and broken? Let us discuss the problems and come up with solutions. Healthcare is a mess of corporate profit and manipulation? Let us come up with a new system. Who knows, perhaps the ultra-rich will consider conceding the money for health care and education to the public, give us a truly equal playing field for success before they find themselves in an uproar of the citizenry. I don't claim to know how it is going to happen but we shouldn't say that we can't improve things and use that as a reason to never try. All wealth is earned through labor and if we are going to come to bring our civilization to a level of utopia it is going to take a lot of our labor.

> Mankind are more disposed to suffer, while evils are sufferable, than to right themselves by abolishing the forms to which they are accustomed.
>
> —Thomas Jefferson

5. Mothers, Partners and Parenting

Shared Parenting and Challenges for Maternal Autonomy

SUSAN B. BOYD

WOMEN HAVE LONG STRUGGLED to achieve social, legal and economic supports for their activities as mothers, as well as to achieve some measure of autonomy in relation to reproduction. Yet the institution of motherhood (Rich) raises a conundrum for women. As mother-caregivers, women provide essential support for their children in their process of growing towards autonomous adulthood. The very caregiving that mothers provide to children, however, simultaneously constrains women's own autonomy. In this chapter, I argue that despite changes allowing women far greater control over their reproductive capacity and encouraging increased participation by men in child care, mothers still face serious challenges to their autonomy in the twenty-first century.

These challenges arise as a result of conflicting socio-legal policies. This chapter will show that, on the one hand, mothers are still expected to assume primary responsibility for the care and well-being of their children. On the other hand, family law stresses the importance of children having a relationship with "both parents" and places pressure on mothers to ensure that children have meaningful relationships with their fathers, too often emphasizing quantity of time and not quality of relationship. Not only does this latter trend reinforce the dominance of the heterosexual, patriarchal family, but it constrains the ability of women to make decisions about, or take control over, their own lives. I will conclude that economic self-sufficiency is fundamental to women's ability to achieve relative autonomy as mothers and suggest that the emphasis on shared parenting is related to the privatization of economic responsibilities, which in turn compromises women's economic and reproductive autonomy.

WOMEN'S STRUGGLES FOR AUTONOMY AS MOTHERS

It may seem counter-intuitive to argue that women's autonomy is compromised in relation to motherhood, given the changes that have occurred over the past few decades. In Canada at least, women have achieved greater control over their reproductive lives as a result of the legalization of birth control and the decriminalization of abortion (Brodie, Gavigan and Jenson; McLaren and McLaren). As well, due to the diminished socio-legal stigma associated with both illegitimacy and divorce, more women are raising children outside marriage (DeParle and Tavernise). Some women now actively plan to raise children on their own and access to reproductive technologies allows some to conceive without the assistance of a male partner (Kelly 2012). Maternity and parental leave offer some women the ability to have children while retaining labour force attachment (Madsen). These changes, while beneficial, tend to benefit only certain women, with access being constrained by factors such as poverty and race.

In family law, which is my focus, we have also seen mixed results. The patriarchal system that gave legal guardianship to fathers of children born within wedlock shifted to a focus on the best interests or welfare of children during the twentieth century (Boyd 2003). For some decades, this shift meant that mothers were awarded legal custody of children far more often than fathers, in part reflecting the primary responsibility that most mothers held for children's care. However, the rationale for the shift towards maternal custody rights was also problematically rooted in essentialist notions about women's special capacity for care. Mothers who departed from the normative expectations of white, middle class, heterosexual motherhood were often viewed as unfit to care for children. Mothers who were marginalized as a result of poverty, race, aboriginality or sexuality were especially vulnerable to being labeled as "unfit, resulting in loss of their children to either the state or to other family members (e.g. Millbank; Kline; Roberts). Mothers who worked outside the home were also often viewed as less worthy candidates for custody (Boyd 2003). Overall, women's autonomy as mothers was heavily constrained by the expectation that their mothering be situated within traditional, heterosexual, nuclear family forms.

In addition, throughout the twentieth century, the law reform movement to abolish the laws on illegitimacy resulted in the removal of most legal distinctions between children born within and outside marriage, arguably a progressive move for all concerned. The obligations of fathers to pay child support were increasingly enforced even in relation to children born outside marriage. Indeed, the slow but steady erosion of the status of illegitimacy mainly reflected a concern with who would financially support a child: the public purse or the father (Boyd 2011). "The legislation was not conceived so much to aid the illegitimate child as to relieve the public of the obligation to support a child likely to become a public charge" (New Brunswick 11). Although the removal of illegitimacy as a legal status in the 1970s and 1980s was justified mainly as an affirmation of the rights of children, it positioned birth fathers as potentially equal parents, regardless of whether they had a caregiving relationship with a child. The abolition of illegitimacy came, in fact, just as the lobby to give fathers equal rights in family law commenced.

During the last two decades of the twentieth century, challenges were made to the image of mothers as selfless caregivers and fathers as breadwinners, including by mothers themselves. Perhaps the most radical challenge to these highly gendered images was the legal recognition of same sex relationships, and same sex parenting (Kelly 2011b). But the expectations of fathers also changed during this period, with complicated consequences for mothers. Early second wave feminists optimistically emphasized men's potential to share equally in parenting and care work, contributing to the liberal, formal equality discourse that influenced parenting law reforms in the 1970s and 1980s. Advocacy in favour of fathers' equal rights to children is also embedded in this approach (Boyd 2003; Crowley).

As a result of the rise in fathers' rights as well as the recognition of same sex parents, family laws became largely gender neutral, symbolizing the equality of, or lack of difference between, men and women as parents. The notion of mother love became an increasingly "exhausted script" (Smart 1991: 486) and claims about father love and fathers' rights prevailed, often justified by reference to children's best interests. That is, to be healthy and well-adjusted, children must have relationships with their fathers. Fathers' claims to "care about" children were received positively, whereas mothers' claims and their demonstrated "care for" children was regarded as self-interested (Smart 1991). Although many fathers did not contribute much to child care when relationships were intact, after relationships fell apart, mothers were expected to encourage and support fathers in building relationships with their children. Maternal labour was therefore actually increased, not decreased, for many mothers as a result of the push towards joint custody and shared parenting.

Although it is clear that men have the capacity to engage in care labour (e.g., Doucet), any idealistic vision of the ease with which fathers might actually take up this challenge in heterosexual families has given way to a more pragmatic realization of the intransigence of the sexual division of labour (both public and private). Given the unequal sharing of child care labour in most homes, the equal and gender-blind treatment of mothers and fathers in parenting laws problematically masks the greater role that most mothers play in relation to children's care. It also obscures the constraints that mothers' childcare responsibilities place on their ability to participate in the labour force, thus compromising their potential for economic autonomy. Generally, this economic problem for mothers is only unmasked on separation or divorce, when women's economic dependency becomes apparent (Gadalla).

Many feminists have challenged the ways in which the legal system has taken up arguments for equal parenting—for instance, through law's increased emphasis on joint custody, shared parenting, and the importance of maximizing contact between fathers and children (e.g. Boyd 2010). While equal parenting norms can work well for some separated families, they can also generate very difficult scenarios for mothers and children in circumstances involving conflict, power dynamics or, worse still, abuse (Fehlberg, Millward, and Campo; Rhoades; Trinder). Liz Trinder's review of studies on shared residence (ranging from 30 percent to 65 percent of overnights and still common only in a minority of separated families) found that studies generally fail to distinguish between different types of shared care families, "lumping" together co-operative and litigating or high conflict families, as well as those in between. This is a problem because the research raises questions about the impact of shared parenting arrangements where there are concerns about safety, fears of violence, or conflict and litigation. Moreover, it appears that any legal presumption in favour of shared care can deflect attention away from violence or inhibit a parent from raising concerns about violence (Trinder 493). Given the extent of violence in the separating and divorcing population, and the fact that it tends mainly to be directed by men against women, this latter finding is troubling (Statistics Canada; Brownridge). When children's rights to a meaningful relationship with fathers are prioritized within the legal

Susan B. Boyd

system, protection from harm seems to take a back seat (Kelly 2011a). In an Australian study, some women reported that their ex-partners tried through shared care arrangements to control their and their children's lives (Fehlberg, Millward, and Campo 266).

Lest it be thought that it is problematic to focus on maternal interests in a field that prioritizes children's interests, research shows that legal norms that emphasize shared parenting and that are inattentive to women's disproportionate responsibility for care of children do not even serve children well, reflecting a focus on equal rights for fathers rather than recognition of children's interests or needs (Smart 2004). Smart's research showed that children in the UK who have lived in an "equal shares" arrangement were unhappy, even miserable, when an equal shares approach was taken by their parents without listening to and consulting with the children, recognizing them as separate beings, and acknowledging their changing needs (Smart 2004). A study by Jennifer McIntosh et al. found that children in rigid arrangements were most likely to be dissatisfied and that children in shared care were also more likely than those in other arrangements to report wanting a change. The move toward shared parenting rests on a political desire for fathers to be as engaged with children as mothers are. Yet there is little evidence that law can make this happen or that the amount or frequency of contact is either better or worse for children; instead, the quality of parent-child relationships has a more significant effect on the well-being of children (Trinder 488).

The push for shared parenting rights also has an economic impact, which does not serve all mothers well. In much fathers' rights advocacy, the argument for equal rights as parents is rooted at least partly in resentment about child support obligations. These obligations fall more heavily on fathers because most women continue to earn less than men and to make career sacrifices in order to care for children (Crowley 106-144). Fathers' rights advocates often argue that equal parenting would obviate the need for money to change hands between parents (Crowley 144). This argument overlooks the impact on women of their childcare responsibilities and the fact that shared parenting does not necessarily diminish costs such as housing. Fathers' rights advocates also argue that if a father must pay child support, he should have rights to see his children, even though in law, child support and child custody rights are viewed as separate. It is no accident that, in Canada, efforts to enforce child support obligations in the late 1990s resulted in a review of the laws on child custody and proposals for some form of shared parenting (Boyd 2004: 54). Canada's *Federal Child Support Guidelines* state that when parents both spend at least 40 percent of the time with a child over the course of a year, the Guidelines do not apply as strictly (s.9). As a result, there is an incentive for fathers to push for at least 40 per cent of parenting time in the hopes of reducing child support payments.

While many mothers and children have no doubt benefitted from the child support law reforms (Canada Dept. of Justice), the changes to child support went hand in hand with moves towards shared parenting becoming a norm. This normative framework has, as we have seen, generated other challenges for women's autonomy and, sometimes, their safety or the safety of their children.

WHAT DO MOTHERS NEED?

Despite women's ongoing disproportionate responsibility for child care and the negative impact it can have on their autonomy, both economic and otherwise, the main impetus within the legal system is now to encourage shared parenting (Boyd 2010). This model is premised on the notion of the importance to children of having two, presumably opposite sex, parents. (Although shared parenting laws can also be applied to lesbian parents, it is premature to say how they play out in that context.) Efforts within the legal system to disrupt the emphasis on equal treatment of mothers and fathers, for instance where there is a history of abuse, tend to be trumped by the emphasis on the importance of contact between children and fathers. As we have seen, research raises serious concerns about the well-being of women and children in a system that makes shared parenting the norm or starting point for negotiation.

What do mothers need in the face of this normative push for shared parenting? Clearly they need advocates to assert their interests and, where appropriate, to resist shared parenting within the family law system. This issue is significant in an era of cutbacks to legal aid for family law issues (Sarophim). Beyond advocacy though, I suggest that the root of the problem lies in a deeper issue.

Many feminist scholars have shown that the traditional, nuclear, "anti-social" or privatized family plays a particular role within capitalism as a socio-economic institution and as an ideology (e.g., Barrett and McIntosh). Notably, this family is expected to provide ostensibly "free" reproductive labour by women in relation to the care of children and other family members. In turn, productive labour in the "public" sphere, which is often framed on a male model, can be pursued on the assumption that the "private" sphere is handling the fundamentally important care work. Clearly, this family form generates problems for mothers who are attached to the labour force by choice or necessity.

Despite the modern focus on "work-family balance" and reinforcing paternal responsibilities for children (Collier and Sheldon), the material basis of the privatized family has not been challenged. Indeed, many would argue that it has been reinforced during the recent neo-liberal decades, which emphasize privatized and individualized responsibility (e.g., Gavigan and Chunn). For most women, this means that they remain primarily responsible for their children and at least somewhat reliant on a partner for economic support, especially in a shrinking welfare state. As Martha Fineman (161-164) puts it, as a result of the costs of "inevitable dependency" (for example, the dependency of children on their parents) being privatized within the family, a "derivative dependency" arises in mother-caretakers.

Even when they participate in the labour force, mothers tend to earn less than other women and fathers because "being a mother is incompatible with being an ideal worker" (Becker 68). The sexual division of labour prevails not only in families but also in workplace practices that favour workers who are not impeded by care responsibilities. The depression in mothers' wages has lifelong consequences, including poverty in older women (Becker; Crittenden).

Moreover, under the restructuring of welfare law in most liberal states, single mothers have been rendered undeserving of public support, instead being viewed as employable market citizens with responsibility for their own support (Gavigan and Chunn). Mothers' unpaid labour goes unrecognized. Even though planned single motherhood is on the rise (Kelly 2012), many governments continue to insist on the importance of "finding fathers" for children, not least because this is a way of providing financial support for children in the private rather than public sphere.

Some feminists suggest that gender equality in the future relies on men sharing equally in child rearing (Hirschmann). As we have seen, some fathers' rights advocates argue that if real shared parenting existed, child support would not be needed (Boyd 2004; Crowley). These arguments for equal parenting may be persuasive for mothers in heterosexual relationships who feel burdened by their greater responsibilities for child care, but I suggest that they are too narrowly framed. Instead, we need public and economic supports for "transgressive" mothers (Boyd 2012) who do not have or do not want partners who share in childcare. Making it feasible for all women to undertake mothering outside of traditional couple relationships contributes to the empowerment and autonomy of all mothers.

Even women who have chosen to parent with a child's father at some point in time need to be shielded from an unthinking imposition of shared parenting norms. After relationships fail, most children still live primarily with their mothers, who typically continue primary care responsibilities that they had prior to relationship breakdown (Robinson 9). Gender asymmetry in adult parenting relationships has proven difficult to alter via the introduction of new legal norms. Studies have shown that pre-separation parenting patterns are highly relevant to post-separation possibilities (Smart and Neale; Fehlberg, Millward, and Campo 263). That is, if equal parenting does not exist prior to separation, it is unlikely to be easily achieved afterwards. Mothers' responsibilities for children can be especially onerous after separation, and this asymmetry needs to be recognized within the legal system, not obscured by gestures towards equality for fathers.

What, then, do mothers need? They need financial security and funded daycare that enables them to make meaningful choices about when and how to have children and how they will care for them. They need to be able to exercise some autonomy over their lives even after they separate from the fathers of their children and especially when they must negotiate a parenting arrangement with a father who is un-cooperative, conflictual or abusive. Mothers' stories need to be listened to within the legal system and they need to be believed when they identify evidence of abuse or power dynamics in their past relationships. The evidence seems quite clear that such dynamics do not bode well for any form of shared parenting and do not produce good results for children, let alone mothers. The trend towards shared parenting as a norm in the legal system needs to be tempered. Offering mothers economic and social and reproductive autonomy will benefit children as well.

Research for this chapter was supported by the Social Sciences and Humanities Research Council of Canada. Jennifer Flood (JD 3, UBC Law) assisted in its final preparation through research and editing.

WORKS CITED

Barrett, Michèle, and Mary McIntosh. *The Anti-Social Family.* London: Verso, 1982. Print.

Becker, Mary. "Care and Feminists." *Wisconsin Women's Law Journal* 17.1 (2002): 57-110. Print.

Boyd, Susan B. "Abolishing Illegitimacy: The Contradictions of Law Reform." Unpublished paper on file with the author, 2011.

Boyd, Susan B. "Autonomy For Mothers? Relational Theory and Parenting Apart." *Feminist Legal Studies* 18 (2) (2010): 137-58. Print.

Boyd, Susan B. *Child Custody, Law, and Women's Work.* Don Mills, ON: Oxford University Press, 2003. Print.

Boyd, Susan B. "Demonizing Mothers: Fathers' Rights Discourses in Child Custody Law Reform Processes." *Journal of the Association for Research on Mothering* 6 (1) (2004): 52-74. Print.

Boyd, Susan B. "Motherhood." *A Research Companion to Feminist Legal Theory.* Ed. Margaret Davies and Vanessa Munro. Aldershot: Ashgate, forthcoming 2013. Print.

Brodie, Janine M., Shelley A. M. Gavigan, and Jane Jenson. *The Politics of Abortion.* Toronto: Oxford University Press, 1992. Print.

Brownridge, Douglas A. "Violence Against Women Post-Separation." *Aggression and Violent Behavior* 11 (5) (2006): 514-530. Print.

Canada. Dept. of Justice. *Children Come First: A Report to Parliament Reviewing the Provisions and Operation of the Federal Child Support Guidelines*. Ottawa: Dept. of Justice, 2002. Web. 18 May 2012.

Collier, Richard, and Sally Sheldon. *Fragmenting Fatherhood: A Socio-Legal Study.* Oxford: Hart Publishing, 2008. Print.

Crowley, Jocelyn Elise. *Defiant Dads: Fathers' Rights Activists in America.* Ithaca: Cornell University Press, 2008. Print.

Crittenden, Ann. *The Price of Motherhood: Why the Most Important Job In the World Is Still the Least Valued.* New York: Metropolitan Books, 2001. Print.

DeParle, Jason, and Sabrina Tavernise. "For Women Under 30, Most Births Occur Outside Marriage." *The New York Times* 17 Feb. 2012: n. pag. Web.

Doucet, Andrea. *Do Men Mother? Fathering, Care, and Domestic Responsibility*. Toronto: University of Toronto Press, 2006. Print.

Federal Child Support Guidelines. SOR /97-175. Canada. Department of Justice. Web.

Fehlberg, Belinda, Christine Millward, and Monica Campo. "Shared Post-Separation Parenting in 2009: An Empirical Snapshot." *Australian Journal of Family Law* 23 (2009): 247-275. Print.

Fineman, Martha. *The Neutered Mother, the Sexual Family, and Other Twentieth Century Tragedies.* New York: Routledge, 1995. Print.

Gadalla, Tahany M. "Impact of Marital Dissolution on Men's and Women's Incomes: A Longitudinal Study." *Journal of Divorce & Remarriage* 50 (2009): 55-65. Print.

Gavigan, Shelley A. M. and Dorothy E. Chunn. "From Mothers' Allowance To Mothers Need Not Apply: Canadian Welfare Law As Liberal and Neo-Liberal Reforms." *Osgoode Hall Law Journal* 45 (4) (2007): 733-72. Print.

Hirschmann, Nancy J. "Mothers Who Care Too Much: What Feminists Get Wrong About Family, Work, and Equality." *Boston Review* 35 (4) (July/August 2010): n. pag. Web. 22 Jan 2012.

Kelly, Fiona. "Autonomous From the Start: Single Mothers By Choice in the Canadian Legal System." *Child and Family Law Quarterly* 24 (3) (2012): 257-283. Print.

Kelly, Fiona. "Enforcing a Parent/Child Relationship At All Cost? Supervised Access Orders in the Canadian Courts" *Osgoode Hall Law Journal* 49 (2) (2011a): 6-38. Print.

Kelly, Fiona. *Transforming Law's Family*. Vancouver: University of British Columbia Press, 2011b. Print.

Kline, Marlee. "Complicating the Ideology of Motherhood: Child Welfare Law and First Nation Women." *Queen's Law Journal* 18 (2) (1993): 306-42. Print.

New Brunswick. *Status of Children Born Outside Marriage: Their Rights and Obligations and the Rights and Obligations Of Their Parents: A Working Report*. Fredericton: Law Reform Division, Dept. of Justice, 1974. Print.

Madsen, Lene. "Citizen, Worker, Mother: Canadian Women's Claims to Parental Leave and Childcare." *Canadian Journal of Family Law* 19 (2002): 11-74. Print.

McIntosh, Jennifer et al. *Post-Separation Parenting Arrangements and Developmental Outcomes For Infants and Children. Collected Reports.* Three Reports Prepared for the Australian Government Attorney-General's Department. Victoria: Family Transitions, 2010. Web. 18 May 2012.

McLaren, Angus, and Arlene Tigar McLaren. *The Bedroom and the State: The Changing Practices and Politics of Contraception and Abortion in Canada, 1880-1997*. Toronto: Oxford University Press, 1997. Print.

Millbank, Jenni. "Lesbians, Child Custody, and the Long Lingering Gaze of the Law." *Challenging the Public/Private Divide: Feminism, Law, and Public Policy*. Ed. Susan B. Boyd. Toronto: University of Toronto Press, 1997. 295-303. Print.

Rhoades, Helen. "The 'No Contact Mother': Reconstructions of Motherhood in the Era of the 'New Father.'" *International Journal of Law, Policy and Family* 16 (1) (2002): 71-94. Print.

Rich, Adrienne. *Of Woman Born: Motherhood As Experience and Institution*. New York: W. W. Norton & Company, 1976. Print.

Roberts, Dorothy E. "Racism and Patriarchy in the Meaning of Motherhood." *American University Journal of Gender and the Law* 1 (1993): 1-38. Print.

Robinson, Paul. "Parenting After Separation and Divorce: A Profile Of Arrangements For Spending Time With and Making Decisions For Children." *Juristat* 29 (4) (2009). Ottawa: Statistics Canada, 2009. Web. 18 May 2012.

Sarophim, Jaime. "Access Barred: The Effects of the Cuts and Restructuring of Legal Aid in B.C. on Women Attempting to Navigate the Provincial Family Court System." *Canadian Journal of Family Law*

26 (2010): 451-472. Print.

Smart, Carol. "Equal Shares: Rights For Fathers Or Recognition For Children?" *Critical Social Policy* 24 (4) (2004): 484-503. Print.

Smart, Carol. "The Legal and Moral Ordering of Child Custody." *Journal of Law and Society* 18 (4) (1991): 485-500. Print.

Smart, Carol, and Bren Neale. *Family Fragments*. Cambridge: Polity Press, 1999. Print.

Statistics Canada. Canadian Centre for Justice Statistics. *Family Violence in Canada: A Statistical Profile*. Catalogue no. 85-224-X. Ottawa: Statistics Canada, 2011. Web. 18 May 2012.

Trinder, Liz. "Shared Residence: A Review of Recent Research Evidence." *Child and Family Law Quarterly* 22 (4) (2010): 475-98. Print.

What Do Mothers Need?

Not to Give Up on Their Own Ambitions and Persistence in Securing Partner Participation in Family Life

D. LYNN O'BRIEN HALLSTEIN

AS I PREPARED THE TALK that is the first draft for this chapter, I was told that I was granted tenure at my university. This is the second time I have secured tenure, because I gave it up the first time due to family-life decisions my partner and I made. And, now that I have tenure again, I can finally say publicly that part of the reason why I gave up tenure the first time was because I was so confused about how to manage my own ambition in tandem with a male partner who had very little doubt that he had the right to be a high-achieving professional with ambitious career goals, and that it was my job to be the primary parent, even though I had my own career and ambition. Indeed, as scholars (Pyke; Stone; Williams) have shown, my husband's sense of entitlement to his own ambitions is not unique; even when married to ambitious or high-achieving women, many men still feel professional ambition is their unquestioned right. And, what makes this worse is that my husband was and is one of the especially "good guys": he was attracted to me and admired my ambition; he wanted and wants me to be successful. But, like many contemporary men, without reflection and persistence and left to his own devices, he was willing to hold on to his own sense of entitlement to his ambitions and assumption that primary parenting was my job. Fortunately, my partner and I have made an enormous effort to make our family work in relation to both of our ambitions, but it was a hard, long fight, which took much time to understand fully, work on, and continues to be challenging.

As a result, this chapter addresses the culmination of my thinking and intellectual struggle to make sense of what I advocate: remembering that our personal lives are also political allows contemporary mothers to hold on to their own ambitions while also persisting in securing partner participation at home in the private sphere, as they live with and within the successes of second wave feminisms in their public lives. Indeed, in this chapter, I want to argue that mothers must re-remember the rallying cry of our second-wave feminist foremothers: "the personal is political." We must do so because, as contemporary women's public lives are becoming more and more similar to men's, we seem to have "forgotten" that our personal lives and family relationships are also political and, often but not always, deeply implicated in patriarchy and patriarchal relationships. In fact, I contend that we must re-remember just how much the personal is political in two specific ways: first, we must re-focus on both our right to and need for our own personal ambitions and, second, we must refuse to engage in normative wife roles in our private lives and family structure. If we do not do so, then, maternal empowerment in the twenty-first century will continue to elude contemporary mothers, even though contemporary women's lives are more similar to men's lives in the public sphere.

Before I make this case, however, I want to be as clear as possible about whom I am speaking about. When I talk about "mothers" and "women" I am both talking about myself and primarily about women of privilege: women who have the various sorts of race, class, and heterosexual privileges that allow them to make the kinds of choices I discuss in this chapter. Equally important, I want to be unambiguous that, when I argue in a few minutes that women seem to be losing or sidetracking their ambition, I am neither judgmental about nor blaming women. Indeed, my own decision to resign tenure the first time could have been seen by others as my own loss of ambition. While I now understand that my decision to resign was the result of a complex set of issues that made resigning seem like the best way to "make it all work," until mothers have a better understanding of the complexity and difficulty of maintaining their own ambitions after becoming mothers, misreading mothers as somehow less ambitious will remain quite easy for others. Thus, in this chapter, rather than blame women or myself, I am trying to make sense of a complex set of factors that encourage women and mothers to see their own ambitions as secondary to their partner's and family.

ARE WOMEN LOSING OR SIDETRACKING THEIR OWN AMBITION?

I want to begin making my case by addressing this issue of women and ambition. Before I do so, however, I want to clarify how I understand ambition. When I use the word *ambition*, I mean an ardent desire to achieve a particular goal or end. And, in the context of this chapter, I am primarily talking about women, as Pamela Stone puts it, who are high-achieving professional women who have graduated from leading colleges, earned graduate degrees, and pursued successful careers in their chosen fields prior to motherhood (22). Also, as does Stone, I am interested in what happens to high-achieving women's ambition (both professionally and as women) after they become mothers. With this framing in mind, I now ask and answer the following question: Are contemporary women losing or sidetracking their ambition?

On one hand, we all know that most young women today are ambitious. Indeed, Kathleen Gerson reports in a recent CNN online article, "In a headline that calls out for attention—'A Gender Reversal on Career Aspirations'—the Pew Research Center reports that two-thirds of young women now say 'being successful in a high-paying career or profession' is one of the most important goals in their lives" (par. 1). Moreover, the same article also reveals that, "While it may not be surprising that these women express more ambition than their mothers and grandmothers, it is surprising when they also display more ambition than their male peers" (par. 2). Moreover, as many professors—myself included—know, when we talk to our women students, especially undergraduates, most just assume that they will someday have both a career and a family. In fact, Andrea O'Reilly argues that most educated and class-privileged mothers either lay the groundwork for a career or establish a career before they become mothers. As O'Reilly puts it specifically, "Today, for the majority of middle-class women, motherhood is embarked upon only after a career is established, when the woman is in her thirties" (2004b: 9). Equally important, most young women seem to ground this decision in the post-second wave choice to "do it all." As Susan Douglas and Meredith Michaels' work suggests, today, educated women are taught the post-second wave middle-class premise that contemporary women now have the choice to "do it all" or "have it all," as long as they make good choices in terms of timing and planning when to become mothers (5).

On the other hand, both recent studies and anecdotal evidence suggest that contemporary women seem to be becoming less ambitious. In fact, Anita Bruzzese recently reported in *USA Today* online that:

> A women and workplace survey from *More* magazine shows that 43 percent of the women surveyed say they are less ambitious now than they were a decade ago. And only a quarter of the 500 women ages 35 to 60 say they're working toward their next promotion. And forget about the corner office: three out of four women in the survey—73 percent—say they would not apply for their boss' job. Almost two of five—38 percent—report they don't want to put up with the stress, office politics and responsibility that often go hand in hand with such positions. (par. 5-6)

First, it is important to point out that there are so many things we don't know about these women interviewed—their economic, race, and/or sexuality locations in culture[1]—and, equally important, it is not clear that all the women interviewed were mothers. However, as Joan Williams tells us in *Unbending Gender*, 90 percent of women will become mothers during their working lives (2). It is likely, then, that many of these women are also mothers. Thus, even though I use this study with some caution, I do feel comfortable arguing that this study does reveal something quite significant. The women surveyed are women between 35 and 60, and, consequently, these are likely the kind of women O'Reilly (2004b) describes as establishing a career before becoming mothers. So, this begins to raise the question: is there something about motherhood that diminishes women's ambitions?

In addition to the study just noted, I think that there is some anecdotal evidence that would appear to suggest that motherhood diminishes women's ambitions. My middle- to upper-middle-class neighborhood, for example, is filled with women with advanced degrees who are at home full time or work only part time, so that they can be the primary parent. Moreover, when I talk to my female friends whom I attended graduate school with, many of them also report that their middle- to upper-middle-class neighborhoods are also filled with many mothers at home[2] who earned advanced degrees before becoming mothers. So, what is going on here? Rather than lose ambitions because they become mothers, I believe that it is what happens to women's lives *after they become mothers* that is the problem. More specifically, I am suggesting that what is going on is a life-stage issue where mothers are compromising and/or sidetracking their own professional ambition because their lives are split between the post-second wave feminist gains they have enjoyed as young women without children in the public sphere and ongoing gender oppression and pre-second wave gender roles in the private sphere, at home, once they become mothers.

CONTEMPORARY MOTHERS' SPLIT SUBJECTIVITY

A brief discussion of what I call "contemporary women's post-second wave split subjectivity" helps to clarify further my argument. Today, young women and mothers live and mother within a complex and contradictory gender world. Indeed, feminist writers and scholars (Crittenden; Hayden and O'Brien Hallstein; Hirshman; O'Brien Hallstein 2008a; O'Brien Hallstein and O'Reilly; O'Reilly 2004b, 2010; Orenstein; Warner; Williams; Wood) have all shown that, even though second wave feminism opened up access to educational and professional contexts for at least already privileged women, women still have primary responsibility for childcare and childrearing once they have children. Popular writers (Crittenden; Hirshman; Wolf), for example, all argue that this is the case even when women work and across class lines. As Linda Hirshman puts it: "the assignment of responsibility for the household to women applies in every social class" (11). Ann Crittenden also reveals that women's responsibility for childrearing and care also emerges even if a couple shared household labor before the arrival of a child. As she puts it: "Before the arrival of the first child, couples tend to share the house work fairly equally. But something about a baby encourages the resurgence of traditional gender roles" (25).

Ironically, then, many women today, particularly those who are college educated, heterosexual, middle-class and professional, may not actually encounter overt gender discrimination until they become mothers. As Crittenden puts it, "Many childless women under the age of thirty five believe that all the feminist battles have been won" (88). But, as Crittenden puts it so well, "once a woman has a baby, the egalitarian office party is over" (88). Contemporary women's lives, then, are split between newfound gains as unencumbered women (women without children) and old gendered expectations when they become mothers. Thus, at the core of women's split subjectivity and lives is a key tension between women's post-second wave freedom from key pre-second wave gender discrimination as unencumbered "young" women in the public sphere and ongoing gender-based discrimination once "older" women become mothers in the private sphere. I contend that true empowerment for mothers is not going to be realized until we recognize and utilize this understanding of women's contemporary lives because two things are true at once today: unencumbered women's lives—women without children—are more and more similar to unencumbered men's lives in the public sphere, while simultaneously, once women become mothers and adhere to normative caretaking roles and responsibilities, their lives remain unequal in relation to men's lives in the private sphere.

One result of contemporary mothers' post-second wave split subjectivity is that a "new" normative family configuration is emerging, a family arrangement that Miriam Peskowitz describes as a *neo-traditional family*. Neo-traditional families appear to be new and even progressive because many contemporary, privileged heterosexual families have both an educated and professional mother and father. This family configuration continues to be problematic, however, since the basic foundation of pre-second wave family roles and responsibilities still hold once children arrive: mothers continue to be primary caregivers of children in this "new" family type. In other words, while unencumbered women have benefited in real and important ways from second wave feminism, once high-achieving women become mothers, many of those women adopt neo-traditional family configurations that continue to place the primary responsibility of household labor and caregiving on them. In new and complex ways, then, while contemporary women's lives have been freed from a *domestic destiny* as mothers, women's lives have not been freed from *domestic responsibility* in their homes. Equally important, neo-traditional families are the new norm for many privileged heterosexual families, and this "new" family structure creates complexity and tension for "making it all work."

WHEN "IT JUST DOESN'T WORK": THE HEGEMONY OF THE MALE CAREER

Within the private sphere, at home, then, is where this split subjectivity creates complex difficulties for heterosexual couples who try to maintain two careers after children arrive, particularly in terms of "having it all" or "juggling it all." When couples have difficulty trying to make two-career-families-with-children work, it is mothers who most often quit careers. Stone's recent study of 54 high-achieving women who chose to leave their professional careers to stay at home full time after becoming mothers, for example, reveals that even formally high-achieving women are the ones who quit their professional careers when "juggling it all" becomes too much. Drawing on Pierre Bourdieu's notion of habitus—the idea of embodied history that is so internalized that it becomes "second nature," and so it is forgotten—Joan Williams addresses why this is the case and is worth quoting in length:

> "It just wasn't working"—this formulation encodes as choice an economy with work schedules and career tracks that assume one adult in charge of caregiving and one ideal worker, men's felt entitlement to work "success," and a sense that children need close parental attention. It encodes a habitus structured by domesticity, with default modes that set up powerful force fields pulling women back toward traditional gender roles. (38)

Clearly, Williams reveals that a multilayered number of factors make it difficult to make juggling two careers and children work, while simultaneously cultivating traditional gender roles in the private sphere. Others in this volume and O'Brien Hallstein and O'Reilly's recent edited volume on academic motherhood address further the challenges ideal worker norms and intensive mothering raise for two-career-families-with-children and the barriers to mothers' empowerment that Williams describes above. As a result, here, I want to address further "men's felt entitlement to work success," the connection between this entitlement and women's supposed lack of or changing ambition, and then link both to the importance of re-remembering just how much the personal continues to be political. Specifically, I want to flesh out further the habitus of men's felt entitlement to career success and ambition by addressing the following question: Why do men believe they have the right to their own career and ambitions?

In addition to Williams' argument that men feel entitled to career success because of ideal worker norms and domesticity, upper class men in particular benefit from the hegemony of the male career. Karen Pyke, in fact, argues, "The supremacy of the male career is most apparent in the marital arrangements of the middle to upper classes" because men are generally freed from the day-to-day responsibilities of childrearing and care (533). Moreover, drawing on the early work of Arlie Hochschild,

D. Lynn O'Brien Hallstein

Pyke argues, as does Williams, that the supremacy of the male career is founded on a patriarchal notion of gender differences, which "provides a rationale for husbands' entitlements that obscures the underlying gendered power structure. The logic is this: Because husbands are the main providers in their families, they ought to have certain privileges and rights that enable them to perform their duties" (533). Although Pyke was writing in 1996, Stone's more recent work in 2007 also confirms that contemporary research, "consistently reveals another pervasive pattern: in addition to shouldering the work of family, women defer to or accord privilege and priority to their husbands' careers over their own (and by extension often shield or exempt their husbands from household responsibilities)" (64). Moreover, in detailing why high-achieving women "opt out" of their professional career in two-career couples, Stone suggests "The fact that men's careers came first was the underlying and unspoken 'reason' women quit, but men's careers almost always come first; they come first in couples in which women continue working" (78).

Because upper-class professional men feel entitled to their own careers, it has become habitus: the default mode for many professional men is to never even question their right to have a career, most especially for upper-class men. In the families of the 54 women she studied, Stone, for example, also reports that, "few husbands were willing to step off the career track to allow women to continue theirs" (70). Talking about a high-powered consultant and a partner in her firm who quit her career in deference to her husband's career, Stone writes, "her response is yet another and especially compelling illustration of the deference women accorded their husbands' careers, which they appeared not to recognize and did not acknowledge as such" (70). The consultant, however, was one of many high-achieving women who deferred to their husband's career. As Stone concludes, "...one can see in this story [the consultant's] how women repeatedly, and simultaneously, exalted their husband's careers, deferred to them, and sheltered them from household responsibilities, all of which, in combination, redounded to the detriment of their own careers" (72). Thus, both Stone's and Pyke's work clearly show a pervasive habitus or "default" pattern in high-achieving women's personal lives that obscures the underlying gendered-power structure that continues to impede mothers' empowerment at home.

FINDING EMPOWERING SOLUTIONS FOR MOTHERS

Understanding mothers' contradictory lives within men's felt and, often, realized entitlements and the hegemony of the male career, then, allows me to answer the following questions in more complex ways—Why does it seem that so many women have lost their ambition when they become mothers? And, Why is it that so many women sidetrack or make their own ambitions or careers secondary to either their family or their male partner's ambitions? One more complex answer to these questions is: because women's public lives and expectations are contradicted by the habitus of their private lives, many women believe that the best solution to "make it all work" is to render their own ambitions secondary to their partner's and/or family. To put it another way, because our everyday habits and practices in our private lives is linked to *what has not happened* in our public lives—real structural changes to make having a family and a career manageable *for both* men and women—many women scale back their expectations as the only solution to "make it all work."

But, is this the solution that we want to accept as the answer to the ongoing need for large-scale social change to accommodate family life? I do not think so, because making the choice either to scale back or eliminate entirely women's own ambitions in the public sphere preclude rather than support mothers' empowerment. The primary reason why is because empowering mothers today means that we still have *both* private-sphere gender-power structures and norms and large-scale social changes, particularly in terms of ideal work norms and professional expectations, to enact in order to secure mothers' empowerment. While much of what we need today is different from what second wavers advocated for, that does not mean that we need to throw out the second wave focus on women changing their personal lives as means to continue to empower women and mothers.

Indeed, from the beginning, second wavers understood the need for both personal and large-scale struggle. As Bonnie J. Dow writes specifically within the context of the sometimes acrimonious relationship between some second and third wave feminists:

> Second wavers didn't think they could change the world without changing women—they tried to do both, and fought hard for childcare, by the way. Perhaps third wavers committed to personal acts of resistance, when they reach that life stage when they want to work and mother, could consider the rejection of postfeminist guilt and romanticized motherhood one of those "localized struggles" that are "linked to broader, structural kinds of change." (6)

Thus, rather than scaling back our expectations and agreeing—either explicitly or implicitly—to privilege and support men's entitlement to career and ambition over our own, we need to remember that, *in order to continue to change the world to empower mothers*, we need to continue to change both ourselves and broader social structures.

CONCLUSIONS

So, what's a mother to do? My answer to this question is quite clear: be ambitious women, empowered mothers, and super bad or non-normative wives. How can we do that today? First, mothers must re-assert their right to have lives separate from mothering, to maintain their commitment to their own ambitions. For the mothers who O'Reilly (2004b) notes—women who lay the foundation of a career before having children—and those whom Douglas and Michaels describe as wanting to be both good mothers and good professionals (12), these women must allow themselves the ambition that they once felt when they were younger. Of course, aging usually comes with more wisdom, so that ambition may be different from a young woman's ambition. But, most importantly, as with men, women have the right to maintain their own ambitions after children—even when it gets hard and difficult—and must persist in securing what they need at home to realize their right to continue to be high-achieving women. Moreover and related, remembering that the personal is political in relation to securing partnerships at home is especially important *now* because ongoing gender-divisions of labor at home continue to be tied to gender inequalities in the public sphere. As Rosanna Hertz suggests, "Gender inequalities in the labor market are intimately tied to gender inequalities in the home because the time women spend in unpaid work—particularly child care—reduces their availability for employment" (241).

Second and related, the neo-traditional, heterosexual family structure must be eradicated. The neo-traditional family structure will only be eradicated if women and mothers continue to insist on securing partnerships at home. Most immediately, we need to refuse the normative wife and "good" mothering roles that are supported by the neo-traditional family structure. This does not mean, however, that we have to be bad mothers. Rather, being non-normative or bad wives creates the possibility for empowered mothering. Why do we need to be non-normative or bad wives to be empowered mothers? At the most basic level, being bad wives is a strategy that can challenge the habitus of the private sphere and the neo-traditional family. In William Hanks' review of Bourdieu's work in relation to anthropology, Hanks argues, "the stability of the habitus is not expressed in rules, which Bourdieu rejects, but in habits, dispositions to act in certain ways, and schemes of perception that order individual perspectives along socially defined lines" (69). In other words, habitus is experienced in everyday life and practices; people are formed in their everyday actions and practices. One core organizing structure of neo-traditional families is the normative wife role and we must, as did I, learn how to challenge the everyday practices and actions of this role.

Again, O'Reilly's (2012) work is helpful here to explain further why the normative wife role is so pivotal to the neo-traditional family structure. O'Reilly writes and is worth quoting in length:

> The normative wife role assumes and expects that 1) the family will be organized around the career of the husband; 2) that

> the career of the wife, should she have one, will be necessarily secondary to that of her husband; 3) that the wife is to support her husband's career and its advancement; 4) that the woman is responsible for and performs the many and varied tasks of maintaining the household and home making. (2012: 198)

Clearly, O'Reilly reveals how the normative wife role reproduces and regulates neo-traditional families and women's ongoing caretaking responsibility for childrearing, while also requiring women to sidetrack their own ambition for their husband's. Thus, refusing the normative wife role and accompanying assumptions also helps eradicate neo-traditional family structures.

Refusing the normative wife role also helps to secure maternal empowerment at home. This is the case because, while family-friendly government policies and workplace practices are certainly desired and needed, they will only serve to empower mothers if their progress is matched in the private sphere. As a matter of fact, based on her large qualitative study of mother academics, O'Reilly (2012) also argues that gender inequity in the home is more often a determinant to employment success than family-friendly policies in the workplace. When asked what enabled them to achieve success in academia, for example, the overwhelming majority of respondents identified not workplace policies but the support of their partners. Moreover, O'Brien Hallstein and O'Reilly note that historian Jodi Vandenberg-Davis also suggests that non-normative family structures "may prove to be more important than the rather minimal institutional adaptations" to challenge ongoing gender inequality and secure maternal empowerment for mothers (38). Hertz also argues that resisting gender inequality at home is vital, when she suggests, "Unless something drastic changes [in professional expectations], the more difficult battle for gender equality will be found not in the nation's factories and corporate high-rises but in its private homes" (243). Thus, securing maternal empowerment today requires mothers' refusals to engage in the everyday practices of the normative wife role by being "bad" wives.

I want to stress, however, that being bad wives does not mean that we have to be bad mothers or bad partners. Rather, non-normative wife roles, in addition to challenging the habitus of neo-traditional families and opening the space for women's own ambitions, can also create the possibility for maternal empowerment in the private sphere. Maternal empowerment, whether it be termed feminist (Gordon; Glickman; Green 2004b; O'Reilly 2004b), outlaw (O'Reilly2004b; Rich), radical (Cooper), rebellious (Douglas and Michaels), or hip (Gore and Lavendar) seeks to confer to mothers the agency, authority, authenticity and autonomy denied to them in patriarchal motherhood (O'Reilly 2004a, 2004c, 2006a, 2006b, 2007, 2008). Erika Horwitz's (2003, 2004) study on empowered mothering reveals that the practice of outlaw motherhood may be characterized by seven themes: The importance of mothers meeting their own needs; being a mother does not fulfill all of a woman's needs; involving others in their children's upbringing; actively questioning the expectations that are placed on mothers by society; challenging mainstream parenting practices; not believing that mothers are solely responsible for how children turn out; and challenging the idea that the only emotion mothers ever feel toward their children is love. In short, when we no longer persist in securing partnerships and we "forget" our early ambitions, then, we may be giving up the most important place to secure empowerment for mothers: familial configurations that allow for empowered mothering, happy women, and more equitable partnerships.

I want to conclude by drawing on the wise ideas of Sara Ruddick in *Maternal Thinking*. She suggests that some mothers acquiesce and are obedient to the norms that devalue women and privilege men, but other mothers mother with a consciousness that resists inauthentic norms and values (104). Here, then, I have tried to suggest that mothers who mother with the second wave consciousness that the personal is political will be better able to be high-achieving women after they become mothers, while also continuing to resist the inauthentic norms, values, gender-power dynamics, and family structures that prohibit maternal empowerment in the twenty-first century.

[1]The article does suggest the following, "Polling Company Inc./Woman Trend surveyed women who had at least a college degree, were employed in a professional position and had at least a $60,000 annual income if single and $75,000 if married" (Bruzzese par. 11). So, it is clear that the women interviewed were the professional women I am interested in, in this chapter, which also means the women are at least middle-class and above.

[2]I want to be especially clear that I am in no way engaging in the so-called "mommy wars" here when I am comparing mothers who work and those who are at home full time. Rather, with Stone, I am trying to complicate our understanding of why so many mothers feel like opting out is the only solution to making family life work today. Thus, I am only pointing out that there are high-achieving women who have opted out, and I am doing so without judgment or evaluation.

WORKS CITED

Bruzzese, Anita. "Survey: More Professional Women Choosing Time Over Money." *USA Today* October 30, 2011. Web. Retrieved 06/04/2012.

Cooper, Baba. "The Radical Potential in Lesbian Mothering of Daughters." *Maternal Theory: Essential Readings*. Ed. Andrea O'Reilly. Toronto, Demeter Press, 2007: 186-193.

Crittenden, Ann. *The Price of Motherhood: Why the Most Important Job the World is Still the Least Valued*. New York: Henry Holt and Company, 2001.

Douglas, Susan J. and Meredith Michaels. *The Mommy Myth: The Idealization of Motherhood and How It Has Undermined Women*. New York: Free Press, 2004.

Dow, Bonnie J. "Does the Postfeminist Generation Have an Authentic Voice?" Paper presented at the National Communication Association Annual Conference, New Orleans, LA, November 17-20, 2011.

Gerson, Kathleen. "Why Are Young Women More Ambitious Than Men?" *CNN Online*, April 26, 2012. Web. Accessed 04/26/2012.

Glickman, Rose L. *Daughters of Feminists: Young Women with Feminist Mothers Talk About Their Lives*. New York: St. Martin's Press, 1993.

Gordon, Tuula. *Feminist Mothers*. New York: New York University Press, 1990.

Gore, Ariel, and Bee Lavender. *Breeder: Real Life Stories from the New Generation of Mothers*. Seattle Washington: Seal Press, 2001.

Green, Fiona. "Feminist Mothers: Successfully Negotiating the Tensions Between Motherhood and Mothering." *Mother Outlaws: Theories and Practices of Empowered Mothering*. Ed. Andrea O'Reilly. Toronto: Women's Press, 2004. 31-42.

Green, Fiona J. "Developing a Feminist Motherline: Reflections on a Decade of Feminist Parenting." *Journal of the Association for Research on Mothering* 8 (1&2) (Winter/Summer 2006): 7-20.

Hanks, William F. "Pierre Bourdieu and the Practices of Language." *Annual Review of Anthropology* 34 (2005): 67-83.

Hayden, Sara and D. Lynn O'Brien Hallstein. *Contemplating Maternity in an Era of Choice: Explorations into Discourses of Reproduction.* Lanham, MD: Lexington Press, 2010.

Hays, Sharon. *The Cultural Contradictions of Motherhood.* New Haven: Yale University Press, 1996.

Hertz, Rosanna. "Book Review: The Contemporary Myth of Choice." *American Academy of Political and Social Science.*" 596 (Nov. 2004): 232-244.

Hirshman, Linda R. *Get to Work: A Manifesto for Women of the World.* New York: Viking, 2006.

Horwitz, Erika. *Mothers' Resistance to the Western Dominant Discourse on Mothering.* Ph.D. Thesis. Simon Fraser University, 2003.

Horwitz, Erika. "Resistance as a Site of Empowerment: The Journey Away From Maternal Sacrifice." *Mother Outlaws: Theories and Practices of Empowered Mothering.* Ed. Andrea O'Reilly. Toronto: Women's Press, 2004. 43-58.

O'Brien Hallstein, D. Lynn. "Public Choices, Private Control: How Mediated Mom Labels Work Rhetorically to Dismantle the Politics of Choice and White Second Wave Feminism." *Contemplating Maternity in an Era of Choice: Explorations into Discourses of Reproduction.* Eds. Sara Hayden and D. Lynn O'Brien Hallstein. Lanham, MD: Lexington Books, 2010: 5-27.

O'Brien Hallstein, D. Lynn. "Second Wave Silences and Third Wave Intensive Mothering." *Mothering and Feminism in the Third Wave.* Ed. Amber E. Kinser. Toronto: Demeter Press, 2008a. 107-116.

O'Brien Hallstein, D. Lynn. "Second Wave Successes and Third Wave Struggles." *Women's Studies in Communication* 31 (2) (Summer 2008b): 143-150.

O'Brien Hallstein, D. Lynn. *White Feminists and Contemporary Maternity: Purging Matrophobia.* New York: Palgrave, 2010.

O'Brien Hallstein, D. Lynn and Andrea O'Reilly, eds. *Contemporary Motherhood in a Post-Second Wave Context: Challenges, Strategies, and Possibilities.* Toronto: Demeter Press, 2012.

O'Reilly, Andrea. "Between the Baby and the Bathwater: Some Thoughts on a Mother Centered Theory and Practice of Feminist Mothering."

Journal of the Association for Research on Mothering 8 (1&2) (Winter/Summer 2006a): 323-330.

O'Reilly, Andrea. *Feminist Mothering*. Albany: SUNY Press, 2008.

O'Reilly, Andrea. "I Should Have Married Another Man; I Couldn't Do What I Do Without Him: Intimate Heterosexual Partnerships and their Impact on Mothers' Success in Academe." *Contemporary Motherhood in a Post-Second Wave Context: Challenges, Strategies, and Possibilities*. Eds. D. Lynn O'Brien Hallstein and Andrea O'Reilly. Toronto: Demeter Press, 2012. 197-213.

O'Reilly, Andrea, ed. *Maternal Theory: Essential Readings*. Toronto: Demeter Press, 2007.

O'Reilly, Andrea, ed. *Mother Matters: Motherhood as Discourse and Practice*. Toronto: ARM Press, 2004a.

O'Reilly, Andrea, ed. *Mother Outlaws: Theories and Practices of Empowered Mothering*. Toronto: Women's Press, 2004b.

O'Reilly, Andrea. *Toni Morrison and Motherhood: A Politics of the Heart*. Albany: SUNY Press, 2004c.

O'Reilly, Andrea. *Rocking the Cradle: Thoughts on Motherhood, Feminism, and the Possibility of Empowered Mothering*, Toronto: Demeter Press, 2006b.

O'Reilly, Andrea. *Twenty-First Century Motherhood: Experience, Identity, Policy, Agency*. New York: Columbia University Press, 2010.

Orenstein, Peggy. *Flux: Women on Sex, Work, Kids, Love, and Life in a Half-Changed World*. New York: Double Day, 2000.

Peskowitz, Miriam. *The Truth Behind the Mommy Wars: Who Decides What Makes a Good Mother?* Emeryville, CA: Seal Press, 2005.

Pyke, Karen D. "Class-Based Masculinities: The Interdependence of Gender, Class, and Interpersonal Power." *Gender and Society* 10 (5) (Oct., 1996): 527-549

Rich, Adrienne. *Of Woman Born: Motherhood as Experience and Institution*. 2nd ed. New York: W.W. Norton, 1986.

Ruddick, Sara. "Maternal Thinking." *Maternal Theory: Essential Readings*. Ed. Andrea O'Reilly. Toronto, Demeter Press, 2007. 96-113.

Stone, Pamela. *Opting Out? Why Women Really Quit Careers and Head Home*. Berkeley: University of California Press, 2007.

Warner, Judith. *Perfect Madness: Motherhood the Age of Anxiety*. New York: Riverhead Books, 2005.

Williams, Joan. *Unbending Gender: Why Family and Work Conflict and*

What To Do About It. Oxford: Oxford University Press, 2000.

Wolf, Naomi. *Misconceptions: Truth, Lies, and the Unexpected on the Journey to Motherhood.* New York: Anchor Books, 2003.

Wood, Julia T. *Gendered Lives: Communication, Gender, and Culture.* 7th ed. Belmont: Wadsworth, 2007.

Beyond Baby Mama Drama

What Black Single Mothers Expect from the Fathers of Their Children

WANDA THOMAS BERNARD

MANY RESEARCHERS HAVE LOOKED at relationships between Black women and men. However, few have specifically examined the relationships between Black mothers and fathers from their own perspectives, what we call *First Voices*. Standards and expectations are often set for Black men according to how men rate themselves on an imaginary scale of masculinity (Stoltenberg 188). In addition, hegemonic masculinity, racist, and sexist stereotypes set boundaries for the expectations which Black women presumably set for Black men. In their study on how Black couple relationships are affected by negative racial stereotypes and Afrocentricity, Shalonda Kelly and Frank J. Floyd found that racism adversely affected black male-female relationships when couples internalized negative images of themselves portrayed by society. There was also the belief that negative stereotyping may threaten trust, which is thought to be essential to a viable relationship. Looking at the impact of economic instability and neighborhood security, Carolyn Cutrona et al. found that neighbourhood level economic disadvantage was positively related to financial strain, which impacted negatively on marital quality for both Black men and women. However, higher neighbourhood level economic advantage was associated with higher marital quality.

In recent years, there has been a shift in family structure, formation, and an increase in the number of single parent families or female-headed families. In a society in which the nuclear family is normally assumed to be a prerequisite for the social and economic success of children, Black community patterns of family formation—which are perceived as fundamentally different from those of whites—are often viewed as responsible for a number of disadvantages experienced by Black children (Ricketts 32). Very little research has been conducted about Black single mothers, and Bette Dickerson states that research about them has been pursued through conventional paradigms based on models and concepts of the dominant culture resulting in many myths and distorted portrayals.

Although North American societies are now more multicultural and acknowledge the existence of diverse family structures and formations, the tendency still exists to revert to the 'ideal' conjugal, nuclear unit as the universal model of comparison in determining the extent of familial stability and productivity (Dickerson). As a result, the experiences of Black single mothers and other families that do not fit the "ideal" or norm of a nuclear family are sometimes not validated and are generally perceived as problematic. Thus, it is important to redefine "family" to reflect and represent the social realities of Black single mothers and their families as well as other single parent families.

This chapter speaks of Black single mothers, sometimes referred to as *Baby Mamas,* and presents their views of what they expect from the fathers of their children. Moving beyond the drama of broken hearts and failed relationships, this paper explores some of the experiences of Black single mothers with the fathers of their children, and the factors that influence their relationships as co-parents. I conclude with a discussion of the types of supports Black mothers say they need to parent successfully as they negotiate the '*rocky terrain of baby mama drama*' and some suggestions for how they might gain better access to those supports.

UNDERSTANDING SINGLE MOTHERHOOD

Single motherhood has become more common in society today not only among Black families but whites as well. Although single motherhood is usually associated with teenage pregnancies or births out of wedlock, other factors are often overlooked. These include divorce, marital separation, widowhood, formal and informal adoption, with divorce being cited as the leading factor (Dickerson). The increase in the rate of incarceration among Black men also contributes to single motherhood among Black women. With the lack of research on single Black mothers in comparison to other groups, Dickerson asserts that Black women may not create the majority of out-of-wedlock births in the United States overall, but there is a staggering growth in the number of Black single mothers.

CHALLENGES FACED BY BLACK SINGLE MOTHERS

Black single women face many challenges, among them the most salient and debilitating are: negative stereotypes, employment, poverty, and racism, each of which is examined below. These women live with the multiple jeopardy of being Black, single women living in poverty, and when they become parents, they live with multiple stressors dictated by their social location.

Stereotypes About Single Black Women

Deeply entrenched and misleading misconceptions lead to a negative portrayal of Black families, Black single mothers and their children. They are stereotyped as inferior, non-productive, and dysfunctional for themselves and society (Dickerson). There are more stereotypes attached to those on social assistance and these stereotypes are sometimes perpetuated and reinforced by the media, politicians and scholars (Davis 41). "Black women then are seen as unworthy users of welfare—they are considered to be chiselers, brood mares, and lazy matriarchs" (Mink; Roberts; Jewell cited in Davis 42). In other words, they are perceived as cheats or swindlers who do nothing but give birth to children. Moreover, Black single mothers are often portrayed as "dependent" rather than "independent," as "lazy" rather than "hard working" and as "unworthy" and "undeserving." These labels create obstacles and barriers for them (Sidel), which are burdensome and difficult to overcome.

Single mothers are often defined as deviants who are dangerous to their children, to the well-being of their family and the wider society (Sidel 22). Ruth Sidel adds that portraying them as deviants has a dual function: it makes explicit the norms of the culture and pressurizes members of the society to conform to those norms, and draws closer together others in the population who may further stigmatize or discriminate against those individuals who have been branded as deviants.

In addition, branding Black single mothers as deviants prevents others from seeing the strengths, individual characteristics, and positive traits they possess. According to sociologist Kai Erikson, "when the community nominates someone to the deviant class, it is shifting a few important details out of the stream of behaviour he *[sic]* has emitted and is in effect declaring that those details reflect the kind of person he *(she)* really is" (7). Sidel notes that while a single mother may be kind, hardworking, honest, devoted to her children and God-fearing, having a child outside of marriage, especially if she is a teenager, causes her to be labeled deviant. This label may have a negative impact on her self-esteem, and the self-esteem of her children.

Furthermore, Black single mothers are labeled "irresponsible" for having children as teenagers, having children without being married and/or getting involved with irresponsible men who are not present in the lives of their children. In the case of divorced single mothers, they are blamed for subjecting their children to divorce and selfishly putting their needs above the needs and well-being of their children (Sidel 26). They are blamed for getting involved with "irresponsible" men, rather than "responsible" men, and men with no jobs or few or no prospects (Sidel 26). This therefore implies that the decision of a father to walk away from his children and his refusal to pay child support or be involved in nurturing his children is shifted from the father to the single mother. Single mothers are forced to take the blame for choices made by the fathers of their children, and it is assumed that they should be able to distinguish which men will get married to them and become responsible fathers. They are also criticized for having children when they lack the social and economic resources to care for their children and this sometimes impacts their eligibility for social assistance.

Black single mothers and fathers have the same sole and primary role or responsibility—to provide shelter, feed, clothe, and nurture their children. Black single fathers are commended and admired immensely for taking care of their children. There are very few or no negative stereotypes attached to single fathers. While Black single mothers have the same responsibilities single fathers have, and are in the same position—being single parents—they are penalized for this role and have many negative stereotypes attached to them. "Precisely the same role that won him praise and commendation earns single mothers hostility and condemnation" (Sidel 21). For Black single mothers, the responsibility of taking care of their children is more challenging due to low wages arising from discrimination in employment, perpetuated by stereotypes. They are forced to live and function in a society that constantly stigmatizes them, making their lives and the lives of their children more challenging. Thus, while Black single mothers are condemned, Black single fathers are viewed as "exemplary citizens, acting in ways that far exceed society's expectations of them, thereby meriting honor and respect in the community" (Sidel 23).

Employment

As stated in the previous section, Black single mothers are often stigmatized. These stereotypes have negative effects and affect employment opportunities for them. A research study that explored the employment needs of employers revealed that employers described Black single mothers in the workforce as "single mothers whose difficulties lead them to be either poor workers or desperate yet reliable workers" (Durr and Hill 202). The study further revealed that such stereotypes are meant to keep Black single mothers in the lowest paid positions. Employers tend to focus on women's childcare responsibilities or potential conflicts in their paid work but fail to notice the same childcare responsibilities of single fathers (Durr and Hill 202).

Whether employed full-time or part-time, single mothers may also face interruptions in employment due to their care giving responsibilities as well as difficulties in establishing careers, acquiring requisite education and updating their skills (Erera 109). These factors make it more difficult for them to get better employment opportunities and better wages. As such, single mothers mainly participate in labor markets as low-skill workers (Mills and Hazarika 144). There may also be a constant fear of being laid off due to conflicts in their paid work and childcare responsibilities.

Poverty

Black single mothers are one of the poorest groups in society. There are a number of factors contributing to the impoverishment of Black single mothers. As women, they are discriminated against because of their gender and are subject to low wage discrimination (Erera 110). As Black women, the discrimination is two-fold as they experience racial discrimination in employment and are also discriminated against because of their gender and single motherhood, thereby leading to more challenges and stressors in their lives and the lives of their children. As parents, Pauline Erera asserts that single mothers are disadvantaged in having to reconcile paid work, childcare responsibilities and domestic work—unpaid work—and are therefore likely to have interrupted work histories (109).

Black single mothers are also discriminated against because of their low socio-economic status. According to Erera (2002), their poverty places them at risk of being considered negligent by state courts for living in sub-

Wanda Thomas Bernard

standard conditions (104). "Instead of receiving sufficient government support to maintain adequate living standards, they risk having their children removed from the home and placed in foster care" (Steinbock cited in Erera 105).

The high cost of childcare is more problematic among Black single mothers who may be unable to afford it due to poverty, and are also faced with the dilemma of reconciling paid work and caring for their children at home (unpaid work). As a result of this conflict and the lack of affordable childcare, Black single mothers may have to engage in part-time employment, and the revenue they earn may not be sufficient for them to care for their children. "It is possible that Black women face constraints from childcare responsibilities more times over the course of a year compared to white women" (Durr and Hill 202).

In addition, the culture of poverty is sometimes blamed on the culture of single motherhood. This culture has been held accountable for poverty and its associated problems (Dowd 18). Single mothers are blamed for not making better choices and not working hard enough to get out of poverty; poverty is viewed as a personal choice. According to this view, "single mothers are moral and economic hazards that produce environmentally impaired children" (Dowd 19).

Furthermore, not all fathers who are court ordered to pay child support do so and those fathers who do pay child support pay very little (King; Seltzer cited in Erera 110). This contributes to the impoverishment of Black single mothers. In cases where single mothers sue the fathers of their children in an attempt to collect child support, they are often perceived as vindictive and greedy (Walters and Abshire cited in Erera 110).

Racism

People of African descent face various forms of racism and oppression, and for Black single mothers the challenges are multiplied. They struggle with negative stereotypes about Black people, negative stereotypes about single mothers, discrimination in employment, and poverty. All these factors combine to create multiple layers of oppression, and their children are impacted negatively.

Black women do not perceive the enemy to be Black men; the enemy is considered to be oppressive forces in the larger society that subjugate Black men, women and children (Lander). Hence, the challenges experienced by Black single mothers are not only caused by the absence of the fathers of their children but also by a "complex combination of entrenched gender roles" and the "debilitating consequences of racism" (Dowd).

My colleagues and I have stated elsewhere that the impact of racism on the everyday lives of people of African descent in general, and that of Black women in particular, is alive and well in Canada (James et al.; Etowa, Wiens, Bernard and Clow; Bernard and Bernard; Bernard, Lucas-White and Moore). Yet, despite the challenges of navigating a world where race, gender and class still matter a great deal, we have also noted the incredible resilience that these women demonstrate as they not only survive, but succeed, in hostile and unwelcoming environments.

Resilience and Strengths of Black Single Mothers

Black single mothers live in an environment where they are expected to fail as parents. Amidst all the challenges, however, many are very resilient and find step-by step ways to nurture and care for their children.

> In spite of a culture that has failed to meet the needs of single mothers because of weak child support enforcement, prohibitive child care cost, schools that are slow to recognize the single mother's schedule, most single mothers are doing a very good job. They are showing that self-reliance is the key to a joyful and productive life. (Engber and Klungness 3)

Dhyana Ziegler asserts that Black single mothers are usually portrayed as problematic, in need of national action, and suggest that they lack appropriate family values (cited in Erera 115). In reality, this picture is both inadequate and ironic as research suggests that Black single mothers or Black single parent families are more successful in coping with single parenthood than whites (Erera 115). "Their relative success is attributed to their strong social support networks, close communities and the help and presence of multiple parental figures" (Dickerson 115). Black families are usually made up of extended family members and grandparents who are willing to step in and take on the parental role or support Black single mothers and their children. As Claudine Bonner and Wanda Thomas Bernard assert, this helping tradition is multigenerational, and continues today.

Black communities tend to be very close knit and community members rely on each other for support. Therefore, neighbours sometimes help Black single mothers by either encouraging them or providing childcare when the need arises. Moreover, within Black communities, Black single mothers are not subject to stigma the way that white single-parent families are within the white communities (Jarrett cited in Erera 115). This lack of stigma within the Black community makes it easier for Black single mothers to go about their daily responsibilities.

Black single mothers successfully teach their children—especially sons—to be responsible and independent. Sons learn from their mother's struggles and consider their own relationship (or lack of relationship) with their fathers, and do things differently by being devoted fathers to their own children (Lamanna and Riedmann 262). Black single mothers help their children appreciate their parents' hard work and learn to assume more responsibility at home thereby helping them in their future endeavours. Nancy Dowd states that, "the families that have the most to teach are arguably those who have faced and overcome the greatest obstacles, those led by African American women" (104).

WHAT BLACK SINGLE MOTHERS EXPECT FROM FATHERS OF THEIR CHILDREN

Our review of the literature offers some insights regarding what Black single mothers expect from the fathers of their children. It is a widely held belief in western societies that mothers and fathers have equal responsibilities to nurture their children and ensure their safety, health and overall well-being from infancy to their transition into adulthood. Civitas (Institute for the Study of Civil Society) notes, "people often say that the most important thing in raising children is to give them lots of love, something that all parents can do, regardless of whether they are a mother or a father" (1). Although there are fathers who are absent in the lives of their children and Black single mothers have to work twice as hard to take care of their children alone, they have some expectations they would like fathers of their children to meet.

Black single mothers expect the fathers of their children to be involved in their upbringing. Civitas states that children with both parents involved in their lives benefit from increased richness of care and a variety of caring styles. They also expect fathers to be involved in their children's lives because fathers and mothers provide "bridges to the world" as children are exposed to important aspects of the outside world. "Through their fathers and mothers, children have access to a vast network including grandparents, cousins, aunts and uncles, friends of the family, work colleagues, community organisations, faith communities, and even personal histories." Learning more about the personal histories of both parents, and the exposure of children to their grandparents and other immediate and extended family members gives them an opportunity to form relationships, develop a sense of belonging and identity, and provides them with more family members to support and care about their well-being. Furthermore, children grow up knowing their fathers and do not have to ask who their fathers are or ask why their fathers do not want them. This may lead to enhanced self-esteem which may impact them socially and psychologically. Children are also exposed to more experiences and practical opportunities such as job possibilities (Civitas).

Black single mothers expect fathers of their children to contribute financially in the care of the children. Considering the fact that on average women earn less than men, reliance upon the income of fathers will enable Black single mothers to better provide for their children. Louie Burghes, Lynda Clarke, and Natalie Cronin note that the earnings of fathers are uniquely linked to many positive results for children, even when the earnings of mothers are taken into consideration. The financial support of fathers therefore lessens the stressors experienced by Black single mothers and decreases the likelihood that children will grow up in poverty.

While it is important to support children financially, Black single mothers also expect their children's fathers to be there for their children in order to provide them with a sense of security, especially when they are young. Civitas states that babies need predictability and security from their mothers and fathers, and they develop attachments with parents who respond to their every need. While babies rely more on their mothers, many children come to prefer playing with their fathers as they grow older because fathers provide unpredictable, stimulating, and exciting interactions for them (Clarke-Stewart). This interaction and involvement of fathers fosters the social, emotional, and intellectual development of children.

Although they are non-resident fathers, Black single mothers still expect the father of their children to spend "quality" time with their children and be involved in their lives. Black single mothers expect fathers to assist their children with their homework or class projects and ensure that their children adhere to established rules. According to Frank Furstenberg and Andrew Cherlin, when non-resident fathers use their time with their children wisely by helping with homework, setting and enforcing rules, and supervising their children, the children tend to benefit emotionally, physically, and psychologically and tend to do better in school.

Regardless of gender or age, children need positive male and female role models in their lives, and the first people children look up to are their parents. Black single mothers therefore expect the fathers of their children to be positive role models. As children grow older, they tend to pick up new habits—both negative and positive—from peers and other people in their environment. Black single mothers want their children's fathers to be very active in the lives of their children, promote positive behaviour by setting good examples that children can learn from and emulate, and discourage negative behaviour.

As Black children grow older, their experience of racism may damage self-esteem, lead to poor performance in education, and impact other areas of their lives. Hence, Black single mothers expect their children's fathers to provide emotional support in dealing with racism as well as other problems they may encounter as they grow older. Fathers who are active in their children's lives listen and support their children when they experience joy, sadness, anger, fear, and frustration. Furthermore, fathers who are emotionally supportive tend to raise children who are more in tune with the needs of others (Horn, Blankenhorn and Pearlstein). In addition, it is natural for children to be very curious as they grow older and to ask a lot of questions. The involvement of fathers therefore gives children not only mothers who can answer their questions, but also fathers who will impart valuable information and help them learn more about their environment.

With the increasing rates of juvenile delinquency among Black teens, Black mothers expect the fathers of their children to help instill in them a sense of right and wrong, so that they grow up with good moral values and standards. Every child needs a "moral compass" when they are faced with challenges or conflict, and both fathers and mothers need to help children develop a sense of right and wrong that serves as a foundation for establishing the moral character which will serve them through to adulthood (Horn et al.).

Although children get a lot of advice and support from mothers, there are times when they want to discuss some of their dreams and aspirations with a male figure to get an alternative perspective. Black single mothers want fathers to be active in their children's lives to provide an alternative perspective on life. Men and women have different parenting styles. This does not necessarily mean that the parenting style of mothers is better than that of fathers and vice versa. However, having alternative parenting styles can be healthy for children as they will be exposed to different perspectives through each parent (Horn et al.).

The mentorship of children should not be left in the hands of others because parents hold the primary responsibility for nurturing and mentoring their children. As such, Black single mothers expect fathers to act as mentors for their sons and daughters and provide guidance in educational and career choices as well as encourage and support their goals and aspirations. Diana Kahn noted that because the abilities of women in society are often devalued, daughters value the counsel of their fathers and need encouragement from them. Kahn added that daughters experience the adolescent process of separation-individuation from mothers and thus are favorably inclined toward their father's advice. Black single mothers also want fathers to help their sons develop a healthy gender identity by imparting a positive sense of what it means to be male (Horn et al.). Sons therefore grow up with respect for women and understand their role in the family and the society at large. Black single mothers also expect fathers to contribute in teaching their children survival and other life skills so that they can become responsible, hardworking adults.

In conclusion, Black single mothers face a number challenges because of their race, gender, status as single mothers, and negative stereotypes. These lived realities bring various forms of discrimination, and contribute to multiple forms of oppression for these women. As mothers with the sole responsibility of taking care of their children, they experience poverty and its related challenges. While struggling on a daily basis to provide the best quality care for their children, Black single mothers have some expectations from fathers of their children in order to ensure their health and well-being. Although a lot of focus has been placed on the negative effects of single motherhood, single mothers are resilient and amidst all the struggles, many still succeed in raising hardworking, responsible, and independent children with strong moral values.

THE RESEARCH STUDY

As part of a larger study of Black men and the strategies they use to survive in societies where they are expected to fail, we organized two conferences, one in Sheffield, England and one in Halifax. A workshop on Black Women's Expectations of Black Men was held at each conference. During these workshops, Black women shared their expectations of their Baby Fathers, and some of their voices are shared below. There were six workshops on this topic, three at each conference. They were over-subscribed—an indication of the desire to talk about these issues. There were a total of seventy participants, all between the ages of 18-55, and 90 percent of them were women.

VOICES OF BLACK WOMEN IN ENGLAND AND HALIFAX

Participants stated that they want "more open communication" between Black men and women. They want dialogue about things that really matter in their relationships, with each other, and with their children. Essentially, these women were calling for a "cease fire" with the fathers of their children, in order that they could more effectively co-parent their children. They noted that the best way to do this was through more open communication without barriers of unfilled expectations or mediocre parent-child contact. This is similar to Civitas findings that Black single mothers want the fathers of their children to be actively involved in their upbringing. Essentially, their message is that parenting from both parents can and should happen whether you are in a relationship with the partner or not.

Participants also talked about wanting "love, respect and trust" from Black men. They stated that they want a sharing of responsibilities when parenting, whether they are living together or not. Many of the women shared that the thing that made them feel most disrespected was the realization that they were "one of several Baby Mamas," or that their former partner was using his relationship with his child or children as a way of 'managing' or controlling what she did. Most of the women who participated in these sessions carried a lot of anger about their failed relationships, however, through voicing their concerns, they felt supported in their desire to let go of the anger to move forward. Their call for love, respect and trust from Black men generally, and the fathers of their children more specifically, was identified as a call for them to redefine Black masculinity.

One of the most fundamental *wants* identified by the women in this study was that Black men take responsibility for their children. There was recognition of the impact of racism, and systemic discrimination on Black men, including the legacy of slavery, and how that impacts life chances. However, there was a simultaneous call for them to "deal with those realities" and shake the stereotypical masks of what Black masculinity should be. They issued a "call to action" especially to Black fathers, asking them to take the parenting role of their children more seriously, whether they were in a relationship with the *Baby Mamas* or not.

Participants also called for those Black men that can be positive role models to 'step up' and be role models and mentors for children, especially boy children, who were being raised by single mothers. Essentially, they were asking for Black men who *could*, to stand in for those fathers who were absent, to be "otherfathers" to the children who needed them most. "Otherfathers" were identified by Wanda Thomas Bernard (2009) as significant contributors to the survival of Black men, especially in cases where birth fathers were absent. These findings are also consistent with those of Wade, Horn, David Blankenhorn and Mitchell Pearlstein who assert that Black men and women both have much to offer children as they transition through life stages. In this study there was an assertive call for otherfathers to take a more active role in the lives of those children who are the victims of *Baby Mama Drama*.

CONCLUSION

While not all Black single mothers are poor, those defined as *Baby Mamas* are more likely to live in poverty, to be high school dropouts, and are more likely to have problems with employment, if they have employable skills. They face racism and sexism and live at the intersection of race, class and gender oppression, with many barriers to overcome to succeed in a world where the odds seem stacked against them. However, despite the challenges, many of these women are very resilient and many empower themselves as they break free from the oppression that could engulf them. They want to get beyond the *Baby Mama Drama*.

Black men who are not in relationships with the mothers of their children often feel immobilized by their inability to be providers and caregivers. However, rather than address the real issues, many blame the mother for the drama in their lives—hence the term *Baby Mama Drama* that was coined by the Hip Hop generation. We see it appearing in rap music, pop culture, and spoken word poetry. Yet, there appear to be few efforts aimed at challenging this damaging stereotype.

The most salient point raised by the women in this study was that they want to get beyond the *Baby Mama Drama*. The children are the most important part of the relationship in question, and even if the relationship does not work the children deserve the very best from both parents. Black women want "...the fathers of their children to be 'fathers' and not just sperm donors." What does this mean? It really means redefining what it means to be a Black man—redefining Black masculinity. It means challenging those negative stereotypes of Black masculinity. It means parenting Black sons differently—from a pro-feminist perspective. It will make a difference if parents teach their sons to respect women; we will see a difference when society views Black men differently and when they perceive themselves differently; there will be a difference when society makes a real change in male and female gender roles and gender role expectations; when society dismantles sexism, we will see a difference.

But where do we begin? Participants in this study called for more dialogue between Black women and men. They also called for the creation of new visions of Black masculinities, by us and for us, rooted in an Afrocentric value system that is gender neutral. Can we get beyond *Baby Mama Drama*? Absolutely yes! The answers lie in a redefinition of Black masculinity, and a redefinition of what it means to co-parent a child effectively when parents are no longer living together. Such re-definitions can only occur when women and men clearly articulate their wants and expectations to each other.

WORKS CITED

Bernard, Wanda Thomas. "Black Men in the Diaspora: Resilient and Surviving but Still Catching Hell." *International Social Work*. Ed. G. G. James, R. Ramsay and G. Drover. Toronto: Thompson Educational Publishing, 2009. 81-102. Print.

Bernard, Wanda Thomas and Candace Bernard. "It Takes A Village: Building Networks of Support with African Nova Scotian Families." *Valuing the Field.* Eds. Marilyn Callahan, Sven Hessle and Susan Strega. London: Ashgate, 2000. 116-130. Print.

Bernard, Wanda Thomas, Lydia Lucas-White, and Dorothy Moore. "Triple Jeopardy: Assessing Life Experiences of Black Nova Scotia Women from a Social Work Perspective." *Canadian Social Work Review* 10 (2) (1993): 256-274. Print.

Bonner, Claudine and Wanda Thomas Bernard. "Labouring for Change: Narratives of African-Nova Scotian Women, 1919-1990." *Women in the Promised Land: New Essays in African Canadian History.* African Diaspora Cultural Series. Ed. N. Reid-Maroney. Ottawa: University of Ottawa Press, forthcoming. Print.

Burghes, Louie, Linda Clarke and Natalie Cronin. *Fathers and Fatherhood in Britain*. London: Family Policy Studies Centre, 1997. Print.

Civitas. *How Do Fathers Fit?* London: The Institute for the study of Civil Society, 2012. Print.

Clarke-Stewart, Allison. "The Father's Contribution to Children's Cognitive and Social Development in Early Childhood." *The Father-Infant Relationship: Observational Studies in a Family Setting*. Ed. F. A. Pedersen. New York: Preaeger, 1980. 111-146. Print.

Cutrona, Carolyn E., Daniel W. Russell, Todd W. Abraham, Kelly A.Gardner, Janet N. Melby, Chalandra Bryant and Rand D. Conger. "Neighborhood Context and Financial Strain as Predictors of Marital Interaction and Marital Quality in African American Couples." *Personal Relationships* 10 (2003): 389-409. Print.

Davis, Dana-Ain. *Battered Black Women and Welfare Reform: Between a Rock and a Hard Place.* New York: State University of New York Press, 2006. Print.

Dickerson, Bette. *African American Single Mothers: Understanding their Lives and Family.* Sage Publication Series on Race, Ethnicity and Ethnic Relations. Vol. 10. Ithaca: Sage Publications, 1995. Print.

Dowd, Nancy. *In Defense of Single-Parent Families*. New York: New York University Press, 1997. Print.

Durr, Marlene and Shirley Hill. *Race, Work and Family in the Lives of African Americans*. Maryland: Rowman & Littlefield, 2006. Print.

Engber, Andrea and Leah Klungness. *The Complete Single Mother: Reassuring Answers to Your Most Challenging Concerns*. Avon, MA: Adams Media, 2006. Print.

Erera, Pauline. *Family Diversity: Continuity and Change in the Contemporary Family.* Thousand Oaks, CA: Sage Publications, 2002. Print.

Erikson, K. *Wayward Puritans: A Study in the Sociology of Deviance*. Don Mills: Pearson/Allyn & Bacon, 2005. Print.

Etowa, J., J. Weins, W. T. Bernard and B. Clow. "Determinants of Black Women's Health in Rural and Remote Communities." *Canadian Journal of Nursing Research* 39 (3) (September 2007): 56-76. Print.

Furstenberg, Frank F., Jr. and Andrew J. Cherlin. *Divided Families*. Cambridge, MA: Harvard University Press, 1991. Print.

Horn, Wade F., David Blankenhorn and Mitchell B. Pearlstein, eds. *The Fatherhood Movement: A Call to Action*. New York: Lexington Books, 1991. Print.

James, Carl, David Este, Wanda Thomas Bernard, Akua Benjamin, Bethan Lloyd and T. Turner. *Race and Well-Being: The Lives, Hopes and Activism of African Canadians*. Halifax: Fernwood Publishing, 2010. Print.

Kahn, Diana G. *Fathers as Mentors to Daughters*. Radcliffe Institute Working Paper, 1981. Print.

Kelly, Shalonda and Frank J. Floyd. "The Effects of Negative Racial Stereotypes and Afrocentricity on Black Couple Relationships." *Journal of Family Psychology* 15 (1) (March 2001): 110-23. Web.

King, Valerie. "Variation in the Consequences of Nonresident Father Involvement for Children's Well-being." *Journal of Marriage and the Family* 56 (1994): 963-972. Print.

Lander, Jayce A. *Tomorrow's Tomorrow – The Black Woman*. New York: Anchor Books, 1972. Print.

Lamanna, M. A. and A. Riedmann. *Marriages, Families and Relationships: Making Choices in a Diverse Society*. Belmont, CA: Wadsworth Cengage Learning, 2010. Print.

Mills, Bradford F. and Gautam Hazarika. "Do Single Mothers Face Greater Constraints to Workforce Participation in Non-Metropolitan

Areas?" *American Journal of Agricultural Economics* 85 (1) (2003): 143-161. Print.

Mink, G. *Welfare's End*. Ithaca: Cornell University Press, 1998. Print.

Ricketts, E. (1989). "The Origin of Black Female-Headed Families." Institute for Research on Poverty. University of Wisconsin-Madison. 1989. Web.

Roberts, Dorothy. *Killing the Black Body: Race, Reproduction, and the Meaning of Liberty*. New York: Vintage Books. 1997. Print.

Sidel, Ruth. *Unsung Heroines: Single Mothers and the American Dream*. Berkeley: University of California Press, 2006. Print.

Stoltenberg, John. *Refusing to Be a Man. Essays on Sex and Justice*. New York: Penguin Books Ltd., 1989. Print.

"Blurred Lines and Grey Flecks"

Breadwinning Mothers, Caregiving Fathers and a Dilemma of Gender "Equality" in Care

ANDREA DOUCET

> This is a Photograph of Me
> It was taken some time ago
> At first it seems to be
> a smeared
> print: blurred lines and grey flecks
> blended with the paper;
>
> then, as you scan
> it, you can see something in the left-hand corner…
>
> —Margaret Atwood

I BEGIN MY DISCUSSION[1] of the dilemma of equality in care with four "photograph(s) of me" and their stories.

STORY 1: TWO GENERATIONS OF WORK AND CARE

The first is a photograph of my parents, Clarence and Norma. The photo was taken just a few days before they were married in a small town in northern New Brunswick in 1956. Then and for most of the years after that, my father worked as a labourer at the local pulp and paper mill. When I was growing up in that small town in the 1960s and 1970s, my days began with the shrill call of the eight o'clock whistle at the mill calling the men to their work shifts. Along with hundreds of other men—the fathers of the children I went to school with—my father would enter the mill through a front gate that was staffed by the mill's only female employee, have his work card punched, and then work eight to twelve hours in

the papermaking plant. He worked at the paper mill for nearly forty years. Clarence was the breadwinner. When he arrived home from the mill, often covered in sawdust and smelling of sulphur, no one expected him to do any domestic work; his care work consisted of teaching each of us children to ride a bike, being there for holidays and special events, and offering words of wisdom when he could. Indeed, what was expected of him once he arrived home was to simply be there.

My mother was expected to be there as well, but hers was an active presence—a job; she was the primary caregiver to six children. The house and the children were her responsibility. She had worked at the Royal Bank on Main Street, but when she gave birth to her first child in 1958, she quit and dedicated herself to housework, community work, and childcare. My mother's days were filled with the routine family chores of housecleaning, cooking all meals from scratch, making and sewing our clothes, washing all those clothes in an old-fashioned wringer washer in our basement, hanging out loads and loads of laundry, and organizing, monitoring, and driving us to various activities. She volunteered at church and school events, diligently brought our old clothes to the "low-rental houses" just down the street from the paper mill, and worked tirelessly to accommodate the countless relatives who drove down from Ontario to visit their New Brunswick homestead each summer.

I admit that for most of my life I never thought about whether my parents were equal in parenting or in life. I saw them both as overworked, equally invested in different forms of care (directly and indirectly), and often tired.

This is a photograph of me and my husband, Derek. It was taken by my mother, Norma, exactly 50 years later as the first photo, in the same small seaside town in northern New Brunswick and just a few miles down the road from where my mom and dad stood. We are, metaphorically speaking, also standing on the shores of a major upheaval in gender patterns of caregiving and breadwinning that had happened in the course of those fifty years. Enormous changes had occurred in many countries, including Canada and the United States—changes that continue to this day. One need only look at the rising rates of breadwinning mothers[2] and fathers' increasing commitment to caregiving—stay-at-home dads, single dads, gay father households, and an overall increase in men's take-up of parental leave.[3] The ways in which these massive changes play out in the everyday lives of women and men has been the focus of my research for twenty years. It has also been part of my own life as a breadwinning mother.

STORY 2: TWO KITCHENS

The third is a photograph of me standing in my mother's kitchen in the mid-1960s. It surprises me now to think that we always called it our "mother's kitchen," but, then, I don't remember my father ever stepping

into the kitchen. My father's usual routine was to come home from the mill and sit at the head of the table in the dining room just next to the kitchen. It was only recently that my sister Lyse sent me this photo and she said, "Andrea, you could do a sociological analysis of mom's kitchen!"

What would it mean to do such an analysis? (Rose). The objects in the photograph can be seen as ordinary family objects. Yet, if you look more closely, you can see intersections of class, domestic technologies, religion, and history. *The laundry basket.* Six kids and a husband's mill clothes: laundry every day. *The fabric.* My mother sewed most of our clothes. *The sugar.* She did all the baking, and lots of it. *The Catholic calendar.* My parents, as practicing Catholics, did not use birth control. Six children was normal (even small) for working-class Catholic families in my town.

The fourth is a photograph of me in our kitchen. Already there is a difference because it isn't *my* kitchen at all. It is just one of many kitchens my husband and I knew together, as we moved several times to accommodate my job changes. In contrast to my mother's kitchen, this is a shared kitchen. It is normal for us, but it seems it is still newsworthy as this is

a photograph that appeared in *Maclean's* magazine (Canada's national news magazine) in March 2012 for a cover story about breadwinning mothers. I was interviewed for the article because I am writing a book on this subject, but when the writer found out I was also a breadwinning mom, she sent a photographer to our house. It was Tuesday afternoon. Derek cooks on Tuesdays. But, on average, I spend as much time in the kitchen as my husband does, both cooking and cleaning. And reading and writing. And, for many years, doing homework with our oldest daughter and our twins. On paper, I am the primary breadwinner and he is the secondary earner, but we have been shared caregivers for twenty-two years of our three daughters.

When I think about this issue of *primary* and *secondary* and *sharing* and *equality*, I think of what a woman named Sally in upstate New York told me three years ago as I sat in her kitchen. She is a pharmacist; her husband worked in advertising but then became a stay-at-home dad when he lost his job. She put the issue as succinctly as anyone could: "We have men who are primary breadwinners. And now we have more and more women who are primary breadwinners. But *there really is no socially acceptable model for a mother who wants to be a secondary caregiver.*"

After two decades of ethnographic work on breadwinning mothers and caregiving fathers in three countries and after having personally interviewed over three hundred men and women, including a small group of couples whom I have followed for ten years (in Canada) and five years (in the United States), I have come to see that seeking gender equality in care work is not as straightforward as I thought it was.

What do I mean by this? Am I against gender equality? Not at all. As a feminist scholar, all of my work has been theoretically and politically aimed at gender equality. Indeed, my research program on what supports and facilitates those who are seeking to challenge gender norms began with the insights of Sara Ruddick, a leading mentor of the Motherhood Initiative for Research and Community Involvement (MIRCI), and her provocative statement that "the most revolutionary change we can make in the institution of motherhood is to include men in every aspect of childcare." I was also moved by her view that mothering work, when taken up by both women and men, would lead to "radically recasting ... the power-gender roles" (Ruddick 1982: 89). Part of what Ruddick was advocating was gender-free parenting, a call that has been taken up by most feminist researchers who study care. I also took up this call, but in the course of writing my book, *Do Men Mother?*, I came to a different position. I have come to draw theoretical parallels between my work on care and that of feminist sociologist Barrie Thorne's ethnographic research on children. Thorne argues that gender differences in everyday life and practice can be ignited at a moment's notice and then fade away just as quickly. In a similar manner, I have argued that gender differences in care work are embodied, relational, and fluid identities and practices that shift and change over time and within complex webs of social and institutional relationships; they can appear suddenly in particular contexts and be irrelevant, mute, and inconsequential in others.

The dilemmas of equality in care work are really dilemmas of theorizing equality in relation to care and conceptualizing care as something measurable and knowable from evidence. Thus, my approach is not only theoretical, but also informed by the entanglement of theory with ontology, epistemology, and methodology. In this chapter, I look at how gender equality has been constituted in my field of gender divisions of domestic labour and care, as well as in the fields of mothering/fathering. It is rooted in a research program that has consistently addressed the puzzling and persistent link between women and domestic *responsibilities* as well as what impedes or facilitates active father involvement. My work has increasingly moved from questions of what to questions of how; that is, I have turned more and more of my focus toward scrutinizing the theoretical, methodological, epistemological, and ontological underpinnings of this field, as well as the taken-for-granted concepts that guide research, constitute data, and produce findings. I have also moved toward the invisible aspects of everyday life that could matter in our scholarly understandings of gender and care work. Two of these aspects include the specific concept of care and the interactions between gender equality and gender differences in care.

DEFINING CARE

Indeed, many feminist theorists have provided useful conceptualizations of care with attention to its articulation in public and private settings, its place as both paid and unpaid work, its intersections with neo-liberal programs, and its varied articulations across class, ethnicity, and sexuality (Braedley and Luxton; Grant et al.). As many theorists of mothering and care work have reconfirmed, parental care is produced, reproduced, governed, and constituted simultaneously and relationally at both structural and everyday levels, as Adrienne Rich demonstrates in her well-known distinction between the experience and the institution of mothering and as Selma Sevenhuijsen notes in her distinction between the institutions of motherhood and fatherhood. Bluntly put, there are massive gender inequalities in the taking on of care work, and the costs of motherhood and maternal care have been very high (Crittenden). Indeed, a great deal of feminist ink has been spilled over the "costs of caring" for the very young, the very old, the elderly, the sick, and the disabled in all societies (Folbre 1994; Ruddick 1995).

My research has focused on a particular unit of analysis with regard to care, which is unpaid family care of dependent children and parental responsibilities for that care. This care encompasses skills, feelings, dispositions, activities, and practices that are rooted in social relationships of interdependence that change across time and spaces. This care is both labour and love (Graham); it is oppressive and joyful, burdensome and life enhancing. It implies knowing what must be done based upon identified needs and acting to fill, or find others to fill, those needs (Sevenhuijsen; Tronto). It is interactional, inter-subjective, and is located in the social world of relationships between one parent or caregiver and one child, between two parents or multiple caregivers and their child/children, and between parents and other people who are involved in caring for children.

In terms of the everyday practices of care, parental care can be viewed as a set of at least three overlapping *responsibilities* (emotional, community/social, and moral) (Doucet 2006a; Ruddick 1995). The *emotional* dimension of care refers to attentiveness and responsiveness, careful "knowledge about the needs of others" (Tronto 141) and the steady process of "thinking about" children or "parental consciousness" (Walzer). The *community* part of care recognizes that parenting is not only domestically based but also community-based, inter-household, and inter-institutional (Doucet 2006a). Incorporating a community dimension into domestic care recognizes all the social networking, coordinating, balancing, negotiating, and orchestrating of all the other people and institutions who are involved in children's lives. Finally, care is also comprised of a *moral* component, or what Ruddick calls "social acceptability." This component considers how parents and care workers feel they "ought to" and "should" act in society (Daly; Finch and Mason; McMahon). This is well-expressed by Joan Williams who notes that "masculine norms create workplace pressures that make men reluctant or unable to contribute significantly to family life," as well as her provocative point that women face "hydraulic social pressure to conform to societal expectations surrounding gender" (Williams 149).

My work, and the work of many others, has pointed to how, in spite of dramatic shifts in men's taking up of care work, there have been smaller shifts in the *responsibility* for care, especially in heterosexual households (Fox). Systemic gender differences in care are created partly through interactive relations with persistently gendered social institutions, community norms, and ideologies (Luxton); they are reproduced through gendered *habitus* (Bourdieu), which pulls women towards care and men towards paid work especially in infant care (Doucet 2009); and they find a foundation in hegemonic masculinities (Connell), which include a devaluation of activities and identities that have strong connections with traditional femininity. Notably, I have also found they recur because of occasional social surveillance of close embodied relations between men and children (e.g., at playgroups, on the playground, at extracurricular activities) (Doucet 2006b, 2009, 2006a, 2013).

But how do we make sense of these differences? For me, it means thinking carefully about my conceptualization of care. This is not easy, as care is not only an object to be theorized. Ontologically speaking, care is an intrinsically relational concept; that is, it cannot be known simply as an object to be defined and measured, but must be viewed within complex sets of relationships. In other words, it cannot be pulled out of the relations that constitute it. But is this then a dead end? Is parental or "affective" care (Lynch) a Gordian Knot that defies measurement? And is it possible to deal with issues of gender equality and gender differences in care?

THE THEORETICAL DILEMMA OF GENDER EQUALITY IN CARE: WHAT TO DO WITH DIFFERENCES?

Most social science and feminist studies on gender and parenting and domestic divisions of labour are still underpinned by the view that gender differences in care work and domestic labour are to be avoided; gender equality is considered the gold standard toward which couples should strive. In earlier studies of gender divisions of domestic labour, an egalitarian household was defined as one where the man and the woman within it do "share(d) housework equally" or "whose contributions are roughly equal to one another" whether measured by minutes and hours or task division (Brannen). Whatever the terms used, the overwhelming consensus by many researchers remains that a fifty–fifty or egalitarian division of domestic labour is the ideal or most successful pattern (Brannen; Deutsch; Ehrensaft; Hochschild; Kimball).

It was fifteen years ago that I first voiced my concerns about the terms of equality (Doucet 1995), a concern that feminist scholars writing critically about care work have reiterated: "the employment of equality as a concept and as a goal supposes a standard or a norm which, in practice, tends to be defined as what is characteristic of the most powerful groups in society" (Meehan and Sevenhuijsen 38; Young). The result is that equality *in* household life often ends up being that which enables gender equality *outside* household life. Equality in care is viewed, then, in terms of a traditional masculine norm of minimal participation in housework and childcare and full participation in continuous employment. Does gender equality permit gender differences?[4] The question challenges us to think about changing and fluid versions of maternal desire, autonomy (Boyd) and maternal empowerment as well as to consider how things might look different in paternal terms.

The fluidity of parental care suggests that equality does not have the same meaning in all spaces. Specifically, there is sporadic, but consistent, articulations of community surveillance of men who take on care work. While there has been significant change over time, there is still a recurring thread of suspicion about the proximity between male bodies and children, especially the children of others, which impedes efforts to measure and achieve equality. Instances of strong community scrutiny can occur when men enter female-dominated childrearing venues (e.g., daycares or playgroups) (Doucet 2006a),[5] when men are baby-sitting the children of others, when single fathers are raising teenage girls (especially when teen sleepovers occur), and when men in heterosexual households are primary caregivers of infants (Doucet 2009).

Another important question to ask is whether we can aim for equality in care at all times of a child's life. In countries where fathers have access to paternity leave and parental leave, for example, including Sweden and Norway, and yes, Canada, the number of men who take leave and the amount of time they take it is still very small. Resistance comes from all fronts: tradition, community norms, *habitus*, ideology, and issues of embodiment (Doucet 2009). Couples find pressure coming from workplaces and neighbours and even from themselves. I interviewed Brent and Anna, for example, in 2006 and asked how they negotiated the sharing of parental leave in the first year of triplets. Anna replied, "We really bartered. He wanted six and six and I wasn't really ready. I wanted the whole year, but I thought we should share it. He was so keen. It only seemed fair. So we went to *nine* for me and *three* for him" (McKay and Doucet). My work has pointed to the critical importance of men taking parental leave and the tremendous benefits accrued to women, men, and families when they do so. But the dismantling of hegemonic masculinity in the workplaces where this occurs has been very slow.

Given the complexity of care—its terms and its fluid nature across spaces and times—is it even possible to measure care? It is tremendously difficult to define and measure domestic life and labour (e.g., washing dishes, maintaining the car), and even more challenging, in my view, to measure equality in care work (e.g., playing in the backyard, discussing the day's events at bedtime). While equality in employment may be measured and tested by factors such as pay, promotions, and the relative status of women and men, equality within the heterosexual couple's home is less straightforward. Does equality in the family mean that women and men

Andrea Doucet

perform the *same* tasks or an equal amount of *time* performing such tasks? Does it mean doing all domestic duties even if it means forcing a partner to perform a task that he or she dislikes but the other quite enjoys? Should a father go to playgroup sessions where he feels uncomfortable as the only man in the room? Should a mother spend as much time coaching soccer or baseball as fathers typically do? Should fathers share all childcare tasks equally with mothers from the first day of their child's life? Simply by asking the questions, it is clear that the issue is a complex one.

After several decades of research on care, there have been only small pockets of attention given to how we define and measure care (Lynch; Folbre), mainly because it is so difficult to do. Kathleen Lynch points to the particularities of "affective equality" and how there are different kinds of care. Specifically, she writes, "While certain care tasks are commodifiable, and there is a case for substantially improving the conditions of its commodification to preclude exploitation ... love labour cannot be commodified in the same way" (Lynch 565).

This is not a theoretical issue about defining care. It is an ontological issue. Care is intrinsically relational. It is largely invisible (and, thus, often taken for granted). It is embodied. And it is highly subjective in terms of what it means and how those meanings shift over time. I would argue, and I am aware that this is a controversial point, that it cannot—and should not—be measured in tasks and time allocations. Care cannot be stuffed into minutes and hours. I do not believe that you can add up care points and come up with an equality quotient.

If we say that care is difficult to measure, does that mean that we stop studying divisions of labour? No, not at all. Rather, my argument is that we should move the focus to the structures that constitute these divisions: the ideologies and discourses, the lack of childcare that affects women's ability to go back to work, the workspaces that will not support men taking parental leave, all the "hydraulic pressures" on women and men, as while also "shifting attention away from women's identities onto the gender dynamics within which identities are forged" (Williams 5). We move the emphasis from trying to divide, measure, and to "know" the inside of what are personal, private, intimate, potentially joyful, potentially oppressive, possibly celebratory, possibly violent, riddled with emotion and memory, deeply embodied, and identity-producing and saturated sets of relations. Instead, we listen to the stories of what women and men need and what they want and what supports them to have lives of "human flourishing" (Cornell 182). We value what feminists have called the power of testimony and narrative (Code; Fricker) and humbly take on the responsibility and the power invested in re-telling those stories (Code; Mauthner). We stop measuring that which is not measurable.

My position on gender equality and gender differences in care is rooted in feminist theory which calls for the constant interplay between gender equality and gender differences; a focus on how context (space, time, and relationships) matters in how equality and differences interact; and analytical shifts from equality to differences, from differences to disadvantages, and to "the difference difference makes" (Rhode 1989: 313).[6] My thinking about theorizing gender equality and differences has also been aided by Joan Williams's theory of "reconstructive feminism" (115) and her view that gender differences should not be viewed as "real differences" (128; Minow). Gender differences, if and when they occur, are socially located, contextual, and time and spatially dependent: "People have thousands of 'real differences' that lack social consequences. The question is not whether physical, social and psychological differences between women and men exist. It is *why* these particular differences become salient in a particular context and then are used to create and justify women's continuing economic disadvantage" (Williams 128). Building from this point, my work attends not only to *why* but to *how* gender differences become salient in particular moments and social settings.

In thinking about how we theorize gender equality in care, I would argue that we need to attend to the rich interplay between gender equality and gender differences. Indeed, we should shift the focus from measuring gender equality in care towards making sense of gender differences in care. Shifting from equality to differences means, as Barrie Thorne has noted, seeking to make sense of "how, when, and why does gender make a difference—or not make a difference" and "when gender does make a difference, what sort of difference is it?" (36). Notably, the issue is not differences *per se*, but rather why, how, where, and when they recur in parenting; how they affect people's opportunities outside of the domestic sphere; and the interconnections between equality in the workplace and gender symmetry in the home.

CONCLUSIONS: "BLURRED LINES AND GREY FLECKS"

In this chapter, I make two brief arguments. First, I argue that, ontologically speaking, care is a deeply relational concept; that is, it is not an object to be defined and measured but exists within complex sets of relationships. Second, I argue that even when seeking gender equality as a theoretical goal, the issue of what to do with gender differences remains a thorny one. I thus maintain that gender differences need to be considered and discussed when we think about gender equality in care. Together, these two arguments—an argument about care and an argument about gender differences—point to the "blurred lines and grey flecks" (Atwood) that appear in our conceptions of equality/differences and our conceptions of care.

There has been a small revolution in care work in the past half century, but there remains the resilient problem of women's continuing responsibility for care work (even when they are breadwinners) and the puzzle of how we can aim for an overall goal of gender equality in the face of recurring gender differences. I suggest that we need to attend not only to the question of *what* and *why* gender differences occur in care work, but also *where* and *how* differences manifest in social life. To do this, we must accept that gender differences in parenting are elastic, constantly in motion, embodied, relational, and variable according to time and spatial contexts, and that gender equality in care work does not necessarily translate into an absence or erasure of gender differences in the everyday identities, practices, and responsibilities of parenting. Thus, we need a way of theorizing and working with the interplay of gender differences and gender equality in care work and in domestic life.

I have slowly come to believe in an approach that focuses less on gender equality in care and more on making sense of differences and whether, where, and how those differences matter. Indeed, the concept of "symmetry" may be a more apt one here than that of "equality." The concept of symmetry allows for a combination of different and equal elements; it allows for change; and it recognizes that elements can be variable, invisible, and can move in and out of view. Symmetry is the foundation of proportion and balance across time and space; it is the mainstay of great art; it refers to complexly rich theories in quantum physics which include notions of constant movement, flow, "parallelism" and "reciprocity" (Hon and Goldstein). It is, I would argue, a concept that can respond to the dilemma of gender equality in care work.

Thanks to Andrea O'Reilly, Judith Warner, and Heather Hewett for their insights. Thanks to Stephanie Halldorson for editing and comments.

[1]I begin with these lines from Margaret Atwood's poem "This is a Photograph of Me" for two reasons: the first is that I believe that stories that social scientists tell are often dryly empirical but, in fact, are deeply personal, reflexive, and poetic; the second is that these lines have always haunted me, as they point to the shifting meanings of life, of photographs, of surfaces across biographical, generational, and historical time.

[2]In spite of variations in measurement, the numbers for this phenomenon have fluctuated between 20 and 66 percent. According to the 2010 Pew Research Center Report, in 20 percent of American married couples, wives earn more than husbands do; this represents a huge shift compared to 40 years ago when this was the case in just four percent of American marriages. The Shriver Report, which includes single mothers, reveals that "women are half of all U.S. workers and mothers are the primary breadwinners or co-breadwinners in nearly two-thirds of American families" (Boushey and O'Leary). Statistics Canada has reported the Canadian numbers since 2006 as being somewhere between 25 and 30 percent (Sussman and Bonnell).

[3]Men now constitute about 13 percent of stay-at-home parents in Canada.

Stay-at-home father households have increased 25 percent over the past decade and are particularly high in some parts of Canada (in Maritime provinces, they can be as high as 25 percent) (Statistics Canada Labour).

[4]It is important to note here that it is understandable why gender *equality* has been the dominant framework for studying divisions of domestic labour and care. The weighting of the balance of household labour on the side of women has been very costly to many women. These costs can include occupational downgrading; loss of earnings; loss of pensions and benefits; economic vulnerability in cases of divorce; and long-term poverty for women. However, while we know that gender differences within household life do often lead to disadvantages outside of household life, this does not necessarily ease the challenges of delineating what an "equal" division of care looks like.

[5]What one father termed "estrogen-filled worlds."

[6]See also Bono and Kemp; Rhode 1990. For an overview, see Doucet 2006a, 1995. For context and differences, see Thorne.

WORKS CITED

Atwood, Margaret. "This Is a Photograph of Me." *Selected Poems.* Toronto: Oxford University Press 1976. Print.

Bono, Paola , and Sandra Kemp, eds. *Italian Feminist Thought: A Reader.* Oxford: Blackwell, 1991. Print.

Bourdieu, Pierre. *The Logic of Practice.* Cambridge, UK: Polity, 1990. Print.

Boushey, Heather , and Ann O'Leary. *Our Working Nation (Policy Roadmap).* Washington, DC: Center for American Progress, 2010. Print.

Boyd, Susan B. "Shared Parenting and Challenges for Maternal Autonomy." (this volume). Print.

Braedley, Susan and Meg Luxton, eds. *Neoliberalism and Everyday Life.* Montréal and Kingston: McGill-Queen's University Press, 2010. Print.

Brannen, Julia , and Peter Moss. *Managing Mothers: Dual Earner Households after Maternity Leave.* London: Unwin Hyman, 1991. Print.

Code, Lorraine. *Ecological Thinking: The Politics of Epistemic Location.* Oxford: Oxford University Press 2008. Print.

Connell, Robert W. *Masculinities.* London: Polity Press, 1995. Print.

Cornell, Drucilla. *At the Heart of Freedom: Feminism, Sex, and Equality.* Princeton: Princeton University Press, 1998. Print.

Crittenden, Ann. *The Price of Motherhood: Why the Most Important Job in the World Is Still the Least Valued.* Vol. 10th Anniversary Edition New York: Picador, 2010. Print.

Daly, Kerry. "Time, Gender, and the Negotiation of Family Schedules." *Symbolic Interaction* 25.3 (2002): 323-42. Print.

Deutsch, Francine M. *Halving It All: How Equally Shared Parenting Works.* Cambridge, Massachusetts: Harvard University Press, 1999. Print.

Doucet, Andrea. "Can Parenting Be Equal? Rethinking Equality and Gender Differences in Parenting." *What Is Parenthood? Contemporary Debates About the Family.* Eds. McClain, Linda and Daniel Cere. New York: New York University Press, forthcoming 2013. Print.

Doucet, Andrea. "Dad and Baby in the First Year: Gendered Embodiment." *The Annals of the American Academy of Political and Social Sciences* 624 (1) (2009): 78-98. Print.

Doucet, Andrea. *Do Men Mother? Fathering, Care and Domestic Responsibilities.* Toronto: University of Toronto Press, 2006a. Print.

Doucet, Andrea. "'Estrogen-Filled Worlds': Fathers as Primary Caregivers and Embodiment." *The Sociological Review* 24 (4) (2006b): 695-715. Print.

Doucet, Andrea. "Gender Equality and Gender Differences in Household Work and Parenting." *Women's Studies International Forum* 18 (3) (1995): 271-84. Print.

Doucet, Andrea. "'It's Not Good for a Man to Be Interested in Other People's Children': Fathers and Public Displays of Care." *Displaying Family: New Theoretical Directions in Family and Intimate Life.* Eds. Esther Dermott and Julie Seymour. London: Palgrave MacMillan, 2011. Print.

Ehrensaft, Diane. *Parenting Together: Men and Women Sharing the Care of Their Children.* London: Collier Macmillan Publishers, 1987. Print.

England, Paula, and Nancy Folbre. "The Cost of Caring." *The Annals of the American Academy of Political and Social Sciences* 56.1 (1999): 39-51. Print.

Finch, Janet, and Jennifer Mason. *Negotiating Family Responsibilities.* London: Routledge, 1993. Print.

Folbre, Nancy. "Measuring Care: Gender, Empowerment, and the Care Economy." *Journal of Human Development* 7 (2) (2006): 183-99. Print.

Folbre, Nancy. *Who Pays for the Kids? Gender and the Structures of Constraint.* London: Routledge, Chapman and Hall, 1994. Print.

Fox, Bonnie. *When Couples Become Parents: The Creation of Gender in the Transition to Parenthood*. Toronto: University of Toronto Press 2009. Print.

Fricker, Miranda. *Epistemic Injustice: Power and the Ethics of Knowing*. Oxford: Oxford University Press 2007. Print.

Graham, Hillary. "Caring: A Labor of Love." *A Labor of Love: Women, Work and Caring*. Eds. Finch, Janet and Dulcie A. Groves. London: Routledge and Kegan Paul, 1983. 13-30. Print.

Grant, Karen R., et al., eds. *Caring for/Caring About: Women, Home Care and Unpaid Caregiving*. Aurora: Garamond, 2004. Print.

Hochschild, Arlie. R. *The Second Shift*. New York: Avon Books, 1989. Print.

Hon, Giora, and Bernard R. Goldstein. "How Einstein Made Asymmetry Disappear: Symmetry and Relativity in 1905." *Archive for History of Exact Sciences* 59 (2005): 437-544. Print.

Kimball, Gayle. *50-50 Parenting: Sharing Family Rewards and Responsibilities*. Lexington, MA: Lexington Books, 1988. Print.

Luxton, Meg. *More Than a Labour of Love: Three Generations of Women's Work in the Home*. Toronto: The Canadian Women's Educational Press, 1980/2009. Print.

Lynch, Kathleen. "Love Labour as a Distinct and Non-Commodifiable Form of Care Labour." *The Sociological Review* 53 (3) (2007): 550-70. Print.

Mauthner, Natasha. "'Accounting for Our Part in the Entangled Webs We Weave': Ethical and Moral Issues in Digital Data Sharing " *Ethics in Qualitative Research* Eds. Miller, Tina, et al. Second Edition ed. London Sage 2012. Print.

McKay, Lindsey, and Andrea Doucet. "'Without Taking Away Her Leave': A Canadian Case Study of Couples' Decisions on Fathers' Use of Paid Leave." *Fathering* 8 (3) (2010): 200-320. Print.

McMahon, Martha. *Engendering Motherhood: Identity and Self-Transformation in Women's Lives*. New York: The Guilford Press, 1995. Print.

Meehan, Elizabeth M. and Selma Sevenhuijsen, eds. *Equality, Politics, and Gender*. London: Sage, 1991. Print.

Minow, Martha. *Making All the Difference: Inclusion, Exclusion, and American Law*. Ithica, NY: Cornell University Press 1990. Print.

Rhode, Deborah L. *Justice and Gender: Sex Discrimination and the Law*. London: Harvard University Press. 1989. Print.

Rhode, Deborah L. *Theoretical Perspectives on Sexual Differences*. New

Haven and London: Yale University Press. 1990. Print.

Rich, Adrienne. *Of Woman Born: Motherhood as Experience and Institution*. Second Ed. New York: W.W. Norton & Company, 1986. Print.

Rose, Gillian. *Doing Family Photography: The Domestic, the Public and the Politics of Sentiment.* London: Ahsgate Publishing 2010. Print.

Ruddick, Sara. "Maternal Thinking." *Rethinking the Family: Some Feminist Questions.* Eds. Barrie Thorne and Marilyn Yalom. London: Longman, 1982. Print.

Ruddick, Sara. *Maternal Thinking: Toward a Politics of Peace.* Second ed. Boston, Mass.: Beacon, 1995. Print.

Sevenhuijsen, Selma. *Citizenship and the Ethics of Care: Feminist Considerations on Justice, Morality and Politics.* London: Routledge, 1998. Print.

Statistics Canada. "Unpublished Data from the Statistics Canada Labour Force Survey (Lfs), 2009." Ottawa: Statistics Canada, 2009. Print.

Sussman, D. and S. Bonnell. "Women as Primary Breadwinners." *Perspectives on Labour and Income* 7 (8) (2006): 10-17. Print.

Thorne, Barrie. *Gender Play: Girls and Boys in School.* Buckingham, UK: Open University Press, 1993. Print.

Tronto, Joan. *Moral Boundaries: A Political Argument for an Ethic of Care.* New York and London: Routledge, 1993. Print.

Walzer, Susan. *Thinking About the Baby: Gender and Transitions into Parenthood.* Philadelphia: Temple University Press, 1998. Print.

Williams, Joan C. *Reshaping the Work-Family Debate: Why Men and Class Matter*. Cambridge, MA: Harvard University Press, 2010. Print.

Young, Iris Marion. *On Female Body Experience: "Throwing Like a Girl" and Other Essays.* New York: Oxford University Press, 2005. Print.

6. Mothers and Work

Thoughts on the Implications of "Opting Out" for Motherhood and Mothers' Movements

PAMELA STONE

THE DECISIONS OF PROFESSIONAL WOMEN to take time out of their careers for motherhood have been the subject of extensive media coverage from as early as the 1980s, just as educated women were entering the professions in significant numbers (Kuperberg and Stone). Since being given the name "opting out" in an influential article published in the *New York Times* (Belkin), the phenomenon has attracted considerable attention, much of which challenges both the extent and magnitude of the so-called trend (see, for example, Boushey; Percheski) as well as the widespread interpretation that it represents a normative or preference shift in favor of traditional notions of domesticity and family (Williams, Manvell, and Bornstein; Stone).

Much commentary has focused on the presumed adverse economic consequences of this decision for the women making it, such as economic dependence on their husbands, uncertain employment prospects in the future, diminished lifetime earnings, and slowed promotional trajectories (see, for example, Hirshman; Bennetts). Moreover, because educated, professional women are opinion leaders and role models and disproportionately the subject of media attention, alarms have been sounded that their decisions potentially reverberate beyond their own lives to create perceptions (such as "they'll only leave anyway") that harm working mothers and women workers more generally.

While these economic, market-focused concerns are critically important, less frequently raised are questions about what the decision to "opt out" means for the family side of the equation, in particular implications for the performance of, and attitudes about, motherhood. In this paper, I begin a preliminary exploration of these issues by examining aspects of the domestic lives and identities of women at home, after they have "opted out." The paper is descriptive and speculative, and organized as follows. First, I briefly outline the research design of my in-depth study of women fitting the "opt-out" profile who had previously worked in professional careers and were currently at-home mothers. Second, I summarize my key findings with respect to the reasons women "opted out," which show that these women were less pulled home by motherhood than they were "dispossessed" from the workplace—shut out by the paucity of flexible work options and the stigma attached to those which were available. Third, I describe the development of major coping mechanisms by which women deal with the loss of their professional identities. These involve what I term a "professionalization" of motherhood and domesticity through which they create what is, for them, a new and heightened identity as mothers. I conclude by suggesting several implications of this process of emergent identity for the women themselves and for larger cultural conceptions of motherhood. This group of mothers, I argue, is particularly important in defining contemporary motherhood, and I sound a cautionary note about their possible role in maintaining class-based practices of intensive mothering that might potentially slow the adoption of a gender egalitarian work-family policy agenda that supports women of all backgrounds. Alternatively, I suggest, their experiences give them a special vantage point and, coupled with the resources available to them, the potential for exercising significant leadership in issues affecting women and their families across the board.

RESEARCH DESIGN AND SUMMARY OF RESULTS REGARDING REASONS FOR "OPTING OUT"

Research Design

As I describe in my book (Stone), my study of women who "opted out" began before that term existed and was informed by my own observation of fellow mothers in my children's school community who were currently at home. As I got to know these fellow mothers better, I realized that many had once had significant professional careers. My interest in this group sprang from my larger interest in gender inequality and specifically from the seemingly counterintuitive turn their lives had taken. Finding virtually no academic research on this phenomenon, I relied instead on a relatively large

Pamela Stone

popular literature to help me define the type of women to include in my sample. These turned out to be married, white, college-educated women in their 30s and 40s with children living at home who had formerly worked in a variety of professional and managerial fields. Using these demographic criteria for guidance, I interviewed a sample of women fitting these parameters identified using snowball or referral sampling from a variety of starting points that included informal alumni networks of four highly selective colleges and universities and an organization representing mothers at home. My sample numbered 54 women, residing in cities across the U.S., with the largest share coming from the Northeast Corridor. See the appendix of Pamela Stone for details of the study methodology.

The women I interviewed had a median age of 41 (by design, roughly half the interviews were with women in their 30s, half with those in their 40s, with a handful in their early 50s). They had an average of two children, the youngest in the sample being three months, the oldest 16 years. They were highly educated, with half possessing an advanced degree. Their husbands were fellow professionals and managers, and in a few cases business owners. The sample was primarily white, with a few women of Hispanic or Asian descent. Their previous occupations included a variety of professional and managerial jobs. The largest share (67 percent) had worked in male-dominated specialties such as law and finance, with 20 percent having worked in transitional or mixed-gender fields (such as accounting), and the smallest share (15 percent) having worked in traditionally female-dominated specialties such as teaching and counseling.

Because there was so little research on this group of women, my study was exploratory and I relied on the qualitative methodology of in-depth interviews to learn more about these women and their decision to take time out from their careers. Interviews were semi-structured, using a life-history narrative approach. Topics covered included the following: (1) background and demographic information, (2) family and work histories, (3) reasons for quitting their most recent (and in almost all cases their only) job, (4) aspects of the process of quitting, (5) their lives at home, post-quitting, in terms of identity, activities and adjustment, and (6) their future plans with regard to work and family. In this paper, I focus primarily on the interview material gleaned about the fifth topic, women's lives at home following the decision to "opt out."

Key Findings

The larger media framing of the decision to "opt out" characterizes it as a decision that is primarily motivated by motherhood. By this view, women's decisions reflect eschewal of the feminist vision of combining work and family ("doing or having it all") in favor of an avowed neo-traditional preference for domesticity and a household division of labor in which they willingly take on domesticity as a full-time role (Belkin; Kuperberg and Stone). Thus, motherhood per se and notions thereof, including but not limited to a preference for parental care, lead to the decision to quit one's career. Diagrammed causally, the media account looks like this (Figure 1):

Figure 1. Media Depiction of Motherhood and "Opting Out"

Motherhood → Career Exit

In fact, as Arielle Kuperberg and Pamela Stone discover in their content analysis of popular articles on women who have "opted out," it is motherhood, virtually only motherhood, that women are reported to invoke to explain their decisions to quit their jobs. When women even talked about their jobs, they are repeatedly depicted as having had only very positive comments about them.

My study revealed something different. While motherhood certainly figured in women's accounts of their decision to quit, its role in the decision was much less central and operated indirectly. Nine out of ten women in my study aspired to combine career *and* family simultaneously. For the vast majority of these women, work and careers were a central and long-held part of their identities, as the following two quotes exemplify: From a 43-year-old former health care executive: "I had always assumed that I was going to work when I had children. And I didn't understand why somebody wouldn't." And from a 40-year-old former management consultant: "But I had never really envisioned myself being a stay-at-home mom. I think it's just not part of the persona that I ever had."

Unlike the media narratives, in which women (typically speaking on-the-record) had only positive things to say about their jobs, I discovered in my interviews (in which women's identities were not revealed) that features of their jobs were a major reason in their decision to quit, specifically long hours and the penalties attached to motherhood and to working flexibly (typically part-time) as many of these women attempted to do prior to quitting. See Pamela Stone for an extended description and analysis of the way in which workplace "pushes" operated in women's decision-making with regard to leaving their careers. A major conclusion is that while motherhood played a role, it was not a direct one, nor was it for the reasons typically cited in the mainstream media. Rather, as shown in the diagram below in Figure 2, motherhood was a distant, not a proximate or immediate cause of women's quitting.

Figure 2. The Workplace-Mediated Effect of Motherhood on "Opting Out"

Workplace Inflexibility
Motherhood → Marginalization → Career Exit
Mommy-tracking
Stigma

Even though at-home mothers are seemingly the most "traditional" of women, surprisingly, neither motherhood per se nor women's particular notions of what kind of mother they wanted to be, nor their preference for a neo-traditional household arrangement played a determinative role in their decision to quit their careers. Instead, motherhood was important because it "marked" them on-the-job. Becoming a mother stalled women's careers and resulted in their being assigned less interesting and less important job responsibilities. It led them to try out innovative work practices such as part-time and job-sharing (innovative in a professional context) that they discovered, often to their surprise, carried their own penalties. For those who could not arrange reduced hours, it also led to a zero-sum time crunch, in which the long hours demanded of their jobs meant very little time left over for their family and children.

COPING WITH THE RESULTS OF "OPTING OUT"

Finding themselves at home full-time, without paid employment, was a new and unanticipated experience for the women in this study, most of whom had envisioned lives in which they pursued both careers and family. Reflecting their long-held aspirations, the decision to quit was conflicted, difficult, and protracted, belying the ease and facility connoted by the term "opting out." Since these women were not going home to realize aspired-to ideals of motherhood, nor to become the mothers they wanted to be, but rather were heading home as a result of lack of options on the job, once they found themselves at home, even with the children they loved, the faced an identity crisis that was twofold: the loss of their professional identity and the assumption of their new, unanticipated identity of at-home mother. To cope with this dual identity crisis, they developed an array of coping mechanisms.

First, despite not being formally in the workforce, they continued to self-identify as professionals. When asked how they would describe themselves to a new acquaintance, the majority of women (approximately 60 percent) who, it should be noted, had been out of the labor force an average of five years when I interviewed them, continued to identify themselves with reference to their profession. Thus, for example, Lily, a 38-year-old who had been home for six years, when asked this question, replied:

> *I don't think of myself as homemaker or housewife...definitely as a lawyer and mother.... Stay-at-home mom? I'm not totally comfortable with it. I'm glad I made the decision, but I'm not comfortable being described that way.*

Women frequently commented on the challenges of being home, especially how much they missed the collegiality, feedback, positive evaluation, and sense of accomplishment they had at work. While they recognized that they could not change the features of household work and childcare which were so challenging for them—its isolation and taken-for-granted and never done nature—they coped with these challenges, and with their loss of professional identity, by repositioning caregiving work as a profession. Typical of this perspective were remarks like this one by Nan, a 36-year-old former editor: "I have a second career, and it's my children, it's my family." Women often conferred corporate titles on their role, as did Kate, a 39-year-old former marketing executive, who called herself the COO (chief operating officer) of her household.

This professionalization of motherhood also extended to women's volunteer activities in their communities. Thus, Stephanie, a 37-year-old former management consultant, described her search for volunteer work in terms analogous to that of a job search: "I am also searching and making much better decisions about the kinds of [volunteer] activities I do in lining them up with areas I really am interested in, that push me intellectually, that cause me to use the skills that I obtained professionally."

By imbuing motherhood and related unpaid volunteer work with the aura of professionalism, women also invoked the high performance standards they had brought to their former careers. Interestingly, the desire to be especially good at mothering appeared to have been heightened by their perceived sense of loss in having reluctantly given up their careers. Thus, rather than prompting women's decision to quit, high or extreme mothering standards emerged and escalated *after* they were home. Lily, the 38-year-old former lawyer, captured this especially poignantly:

> *If I'm going to put my career on hold and be a full-time mom, I better do it with a lot of enthusiasm, energy, and time.... My new job now is to be a mother, make my child happy, content, pick him up when he cries—he doesn't sleep and neither do I.*

Women thus held on to their former professional self-identity while at the same time repositioning their new identity at home in a more professional light. But, since most of them had never aspired to be full-time, at-home mothers, another problem arose. Many had to deal with their own relatively negative perceptions of the group of which they were now a member. They did this through a conscious process of re-valuation, voiced by about 40 percent of the sample, in which they talked about their increased appreciation of mothering and associated values. A good example of this comes from Meg, a 41-year-old former trader who had been home three years:

> *I am learning to value activities that I never valued before.... I am working hard to attribute value to things that I didn't value before about my life. Working hard to find the value in being home.... A lot of moral guidance and developmental guidance for my children, if I weren't here and accessible to them, someone else would either be doing it or missing the cues they're giving me that they want to talk.*

Through the linked processes of professionalization and re-valuation of motherhood, women were able to accomplish several things. First, by holding on to their original professional identity, they were able to maintain dual identities, something the workplace had not afforded them. They could be professionals at home (like the lawyer taking some time out) even though their experiences at their former jobs had suggested they could not be mothers at work. Second, by framing even the unpaid, least "professional" aspects of their work at home in quasi-professional language, they could somewhat temper or deflect their loss of professional identity and the rewards and accomplishments it had brought them. Third, through a process of re-valuation of the traditional roles of mother and homemaker, they raised the status of their newfound roles in their own eyes. While these strategies may ease the transition of identities required by their decision to interrupt their careers, there is also a suggestion that part of this re-formation of identity may entail some amount of over-compensation, by which women apply the same high performance levels of professional careers to the work of mothering.

POSSIBLE IMPLICATIONS OF THE COPING STRATEGIES SURROUNDING "OPTING OUT"

As Sharon Hays has shown, mothering standards are embodied in widespread cultural norms that are widely shared across class and race. Contemporary standards conform to what she calls "intensive mothering," a style of mothering that requires considerable hands-on interaction between mother and child. The intensive mothering ideology identified by Hays translates to a childrearing practice that Annette Lareau labels "concerted cultivation," emphasizing not only extensive commitments of time, but also resources in the form of educational, cultural, and athletic enrichment. As Lareau's research demonstrates, this mode of mothering is especially characteristic of upper middle class households, whether the mother is working outside the home or at home full-time.

The upper middle class mothers in my study desired to have both career and family, and most were able to realize that combination for some portion of their careers. They did not quit their jobs to become model mothers. To the extent that their decisions are misconstrued by the popular media as being "all about motherhood," they are set up, however unwillingly and incorrectly, as role models for "the good mother," reinforcing the idea that good mothers devote themselves exclusively to their children and do not work outside the home. It is after they have left their job, in their efforts to professionalize motherhood and perhaps justify their loss of career, that they become hands-on, high-touch mothers and participate in a process of professionalization of motherhood that carries with it the potential to reinforce intensive mothering norms and further valorize mothering practices that are inaccessible to all but a small elite group.

This raises a cautionary note for women who "opt out" to not allow themselves to become pawns and poster girls for the resurgence of a neo-traditional, separate spheres notion of work and family that, among other things, creates the inhospitable workplaces that gave rise to their own reluctant decisions to exit their careers. To the extent that "opting out"—a decision open only to a privileged few—balkanizes mothers along class and race lines, it prevents solidarity around a host of women's issues that are at the intersection of work and family, issues like childcare, paid leave, equal pay, and flexible workplaces.

Yet mothers who have "opted out," however privileged, have also seen both sides firsthand. Their negative experiences on the job, coupled with their eye-opening experiences of being home, give them a dual consciousness that creates the potential for a new empathy for, and a new appreciation of, motherhood, traditional "women's work" and the caring values attached to it while at the same time holds fast to former professional identities and attendant skills and values. This new awareness, if acted on proactively by women at home, can foster a broad mobilization of mothers on behalf of an agenda that integrates, rather than divides, work and family. In fact, organizations founded by mothers (many at home or having had a period of time away from work) like Moms Rising, A Better Balance, and Mothers and More, to name but a few, exemplify this possibility, as they mobilize mothers around a range of policies affecting women and their families across the socio-economic spectrum.

WORKS CITED

Belkin, Lisa. "The Opt-Out Revolution." *New York Times Magazine* 26 October 2003: 42-47, 58, 85-86. Print.

Bennetts, Leslie. *The Feminine Mistake.* New York: Hyperion. 2007. Print.

Boushey, Heather. "Are Women Opting Out? Debunking the Myth." Center for Economic and Policy Research ,Washington, DC, 2005. Print.

Hays, Sharon. *The Cultural Contradictions of Motherhood.* New Haven: Yale University Press, 1996. Print.

Hirshman, Linda. *Get to Work.* New York: Penguin Books, 2006. Print.

Kuperberg, Arielle, and Pamela Stone. "The Media Depiction of Women Who Opt Out." *Gender & Society* 22 (4) (2008): 497-517. Print.

Lareau, Annette. *Unequal Childhoods.* Berkeley: University of California Press. 2003. Print.

Percheski, Christine. "Opting Out? Cohort Differences in Women's Employment Rates from 1960 to 2005." *American Sociological Review* 73 (3) (2008): 497-517. Print.

Stone, Pamela. *Opting Out?* Berkeley: University of California Press. 2007. Print.

Williams, Joan C., Jessica Manvell, and Stephanie Bornstein. "'Opt Out' or Pushed Out? How the Press Covers Work/Family Conflict." Center for WorkLife Law, University of California, Hastings College of the Law (San Francisco). 2006. Print.

Mothers on a Tightrope

Finding Balance with Everything on the Line

KUAE KELCH MATTOX

WHEN I WAS A CHILD I loved the circus. The brave ringmaster taming his lions and tigers. The regal horses galloping in circles. The daring acrobats soaring through the sky. The silly clowns climbing out of cars. The smell of popcorn and peanuts wafting lazily through the air. When the live circus music reached its crescendo, our hearts would dance. But when the bare chested man and the sequined woman took to the high wire, the audience hushed, the drums began to roll and we held our collective breath. We all knew it was a balancing act that required strength, focus and nimble feet. One wrong move and they would drop. But we also took comfort in knowing that a safety net would soften their fall below.

Take that net away and you see a portrait of today, with mothers like me, walking our own personal tightrope. Mothers, managing a delicate balancing act against the devastating backdrop of a global recession, an erosion of jobs, industries, and assets. Our minds are spinning, in circles and spheres and shapes with sharp points and angles, trying to balance making money, doing what's best for our children, advocating for our children in school, managing our own careers and taking care of our personal self. There is much at stake. Yet, the safety nets that mothers could once rely upon are no longer there—the value of our college and graduate degrees, our wealth of experience, the allegiance of employers, professional networks, government programs and even the incomes of our spouses have diminished and faded. Now more than ever, anything that upsets the balancing act can launch a trickle down effect that throws the family system into chaos.

I am mother to three beautiful, bright-eyed children, ages nine, thiretteen and fifteen, a veteran journalist who has covered schools as an education reporter for the *Miami Herald*, brought Oprah her daily coffee and learned the ropes as a producer trainee for *The Oprah Winfrey Show*, and produced segments for the award winning *Dateline NBC*. I've also been a PTA president, fundraiser, nonprofit board member, grassroots community organizer, magazine editor in chief, self confessed exercise fanatic and mommy blogger. But my claim to fame these days, at least with my husband and children, is as a stay at home mother and national president of Mocha Moms, Inc., a nonprofit organization founded in 1997 by four mothers in Maryland to support stay-at-home mothers of color. Today, we have grown to 100 chapters in 29 states, which meet weekly, monthly, and participate in a wide range of community service. We are mostly African American, professional women with college and advanced degrees who have worked for some period of time and made the choice to stay at home to focus on the raising of our children, and we've decided that one of the best ways to do that is to lend an ear, a shoulder or hand and support each other along the way. We also want the world to know that two parent African American families, in which marriages are celebrated, actually exist.

The choice to stay at home, for most African American mothers, is unprecedented. Historically, large numbers of African American mothers have not had that opportunity, and the path to success in the black community has been through economic empowerment. Our mothers worked, probably more out of necessity than desire, to keep the family afloat and food on the table. Years ago, we were the cooks and seamstresses, the factory workers and maids, the women who cared for other people's children. Fast forward to the steady growth of the black middle class and greater educational and professional opportunities of the 1980's and 1990's, and some of the children, now married, of the very mothers who worked found themselves able to stay at home to care for their own, a luxury that many had previously thought of as reserved only for white women.

The women who are attracted to the support that Mocha Moms offers have some interesting stories to tell. Many mothers say that they never grew up with the notion of staying at home because in their minds it was simply unattainable. Their mothers didn't stay at home. There were no role models. There was no blueprint. Some mothers say that making the choice to stay at home is difficult because many of their parents, the ones who had fought in the Civil Rights movement for equal rights and for their children to have the opportunities that they did not have, who had big dreams for their daughters, said to their children, you are simply out of your mind. You are throwing it all away. Mothers also lament an educational system that has by and large failed our children, and express a fear that their own children would fall through the proverbial "gap." They want greater control over their children's destiny. Some say they didn't have the opportunity to make the choice. They have been laid off or turned off by an unfriendly workplace and an unforgiving boss who didn't understand the need for flexibility, and who frowned upon anyone who wanted to go home at any decent hour to their family.

In my television world, it was commonly known, and accepted, that women who were pregnant would be "mommy tracked" and not given the plum assignments. Many of us waited until the last possible moment to share that we were pregnant. I was fortunate to have the opportunity, and yes the luxury, to become a stay at home mother 12 years ago at a point in my life when I needed it and wanted it the most. My mother had devastatingly passed away at age 60 nearly three years before, 12 days before Christmas in 1997. I was pregnant with my second child, my son, and I was a producer for *NBC News*. I had spent the past 13 years as a professional journalist working for high profile news organizations, the *Miami Herald*, *The Oprah Winfrey Show, ABC News* and now NBC, and that fire that burns in every good journalist's belly was starting to wane. On my six-month maternity leave, the first three months paid and the last three unpaid, my husband and I discovered that we could survive, and maybe even thrive, on one income. I wanted very much to be home with my children. So I left and I didn't turn back.

It didn't dawn on me that I had stripped myself of my identity, the journalist who enjoyed telling people that I worked for those news organizations, until I was pushing my son one day in a shopping cart down the aisle in Kmart and a syrupy sweet worker came over and said "oh that's so sweet, you're a stay at home mom." I wanted to tell her what was on my resume. *Girl, do you know who I am? I'm a journalist you know. I used to work for the* Oprah Winfrey Show*!* But with a lump in my throat, I found myself struggling to acknowledge my newfound identity. In fact, it took me a good two years to reconcile that I had effectively stripped myself of my professional identity, and needed to somehow recreate or reinvent the person I was to become.

Little did I know that I was writing my next chapter when I gathered a group of mothers that I had met in all the hot mommy spots in and near my town of Montclair, New Jersey, from Shoprite and the Little Y to Barnes and Noble story hour and Gymboree. I gravitated toward a small handful of mothers who looked like me and asked them to help me form a chapter in my area of the national organization that I now lead called Mocha Moms.

Our very first gatherings more than a decade ago were at the homes of very dynamic women, some with Ivy League degrees and most with many professional accomplishments. Everyone had big dreams for their children. I remember the mathematician who said she loved to spend her spare time solving complex mathematical equations, the mother who was a commercial airline pilot, only one of a handful of African American airline pilots in the country, and the African American history scholar, with degrees from Harvard and Princeton, who was a former research assistant to the noted philosopher and professor Dr. Cornel West. These women had made the choice to stay at home, and as I looked around the room I realized it was profound. Sitting in those living rooms and getting to know those women helped to shape my newfound vision of stay at home motherhood and why we were all united in the belief that we needed to support each other.

In those early days in 2002, we met weekly with our children just to touch base, to let our hair down so to speak, to share ideas and exchange information. Not only did we talk about breastfeeding and getting our children to sleep through the night, we talked about positive and negative images on television, books to read to our children, and ways to keep them comfortable in their own skin. We also delved into the personal. Our marriages, our friendships, our feelings, our fears. Stay-at-home motherhood, while rewarding, we confided, can also be a lonely and isolated existence. So our new sisterhood of mothers, who were experiencing the same things, was comforting and welcome.

On a monthly basis, we met for moms-only get-togethers without our children. Sometimes we met at a restaurant, but mostly it was potluck at someone's home. That usually meant foods like grilled fish, baked chicken, rice and beans, baked macaroni and cheese, salads and desserts galore. *Oh, those desserts!* We picked topics and discussed ideas, shared our hopes, supported each other and planned for our chapter's future. There was laughter and yes, some tears. When one of our mothers became ill or came home from the hospital after delivering a baby, we set up a food chain and made food for their families, delivering a dependable daily meal for the first two weeks, just to give the mother and the family a chance to breathe. We often watched each other's children so one mother could run to the supermarket or take a shower or spend a few moments pampering themselves, and as part of Mocha Moms we participated in community service, including hosting educational forums, marching for babies, donating to women's shelters, adopting foster families and purchasing gifts for children of incarcerated parents.

It was, for some time, a very comfortable existence. Our husbands were climbing the corporate ladder, we had our college and graduate degrees tucked in our pockets, our careers on hold, we maintained connections to our professional networks and became heavily involved in our children's schools and in their daily lives. Quite a few mothers, fed up with this country's educational system, started homeschooling their children. For many of us, our focus was so much on our children that we began to neglect ourselves. But the safety nets were there, and the village that we had created was thriving.

But the recession that began at the end of 2007 dealt a harsh blow to our reality, and as quickly as some African American mothers had attained stay at home status, a worsening economy forced many of them to reexamine their lives and reprioritize. High unemployment and job losses disproportionately affected African Americans, including our family and friends, especially our husbands. At the start of the recession, the unemployment rate for African Americans on a quarterly basis was 8.6 percent. In the two years that followed, the unemployment rate rose 7.2 percentage points to 15.8 percent. Young African Americans' unemployment rose 4.8 percentage points annually since the start of the recession, resting at 26.4 percent at the end of 2009 (Reidenbach and Weller). The numbers today have not gotten much better, and African American women have been particularly hard hit. Since the start of the recession, from December 2007 through June 2011, black women lost more jobs than did black men ("Employment Crisis Worsens"). This as studies show that black women continue to bear a heavier responsibility for family and friends than their white counterparts, yet have more trouble paying their bills or getting a loan than white women (Mui and Jenkins).

The effects of the recession on our economic security were devastating. Home ownership declined precipitously among African Americans. The percentage of African Americans with health insurance declined even further. The wealth gap widened substantially between white and black and white and Hispanic households. In 2005, the typical white household held seven times more wealth than the typical Hispanic household and 11 times more than the typical African American household. In 2009, these gaps stood around twice as wide, 18 times between white and Hispanic households, 20 times between white and black. According to the Pew Research Center, the primary source of the growing wealth gaps between white and minority households was the collapse of the housing bubble ("The Racial Wealth Gaps").

And so with the recession, our mothers began to walk a tightrope that they had never walked before, trying to maintain the delicate balancing act of doing what was best for their children and what was best for the financial well being and survival of the family, and also, what was best for ourselves. It added an extra burden of worry. Our children no longer had the safety net they once had, because if dad wasn't out of work, he most assuredly was working and worrying round the clock just to make ends meet, and mothers like us, who used to meet our fellow moms for breakfast on Fridays or for jaunts to the playground were spinning their wheels trying to figure out what's next. *How can I advocate for my children in school, give back to my community, serve as CEO of my household, take care of myself and generate revenue for my family? Is it time to return to work? Why can't I find work? How can I compete? Start a home-based business? Demand a flexible workplace?* We discovered that what was once good for our families before may not be good any more. Mothers, walking a tightrope that is wavering and loosening with every step, and for African American mothers, there is much on the line. The future of our children's education, their health and well-being, our savings, our legacy. All on shaky ground.

The U.S. Department of Education says that inequity in schools is really no better than it was many years ago. Still today, black students, particularly our boys, are disproportionately more likely to be suspended or expelled, they have less access to rigorous high school curricula and more are often taught by lower-paid and less experienced teachers ("New Data from U.S. Department of Education). In the 2008 National Assessment of Educational Progress, eighth grade reading scores of

African American boys were barely higher than the scores of white girls in fourth grade. In math, 46 percent of African American boys demonstrated "basic" or higher grade-level skills, compared with 82 percent of white boys (Kirp).

These are the kinds of devastating numbers that we hear. They are dismal and scary. *Not my son. Not my daughter. Oh no.* But as African American mothers, we know we can't sit idly by. Our children need us and we need to do our part to close the gaps, at home and in school. Through our Mocha Moms, Inc. community service initiative, "Closing the Gap on Minority Health, Prosperity and Achievement," we have been setting up reading nooks in barbershops and beauty shops throughout the country, more than 100 so far, as part of a cutting edge literacy initiative created by a university professor, called *Boys Booked on Barbershops*. Its purpose is to foster a love of reading by taking advantage of naturally occurring opportunities in the neighborhood. We are also hosting community educational summits, healthy moms symposiums and financial literacy workshops, and we've partnered with a wide range of organizations, including America's Promise, Susan G. Komen for the Cure, Be The Match, the EPA and the Girl Scouts to help promote their *Girls in STEM* initiative. This fall we launch a new movement called Occupy Schools™, triggered in part by reading the dismal results of a Department of Education report that found that students of color across America continue to suffer. African American parents, we decided, need to Occupy Schools™. Not the pitch a tent, sit-in, chain yourself to the doors type of occupy, but the literal occupy. Our parents need to be more active, involved and engaged in the schools. That means communicating with teachers and administrators, asking tough questions, holding them accountable, volunteering in the classroom, showing up at PTA meetings, sitting down at the homework table, making a commitment to being a partner in our children's education. And if they show up at their child's school wearing an Occupy Schools T-shirt, well, that helps too.

Despite this difficult balancing act, I know from talking to mothers in our organization that increasingly African American stay at home mothers want to advocate for the many causes in which they believe. They want to push for greater accountability in the classroom. They want to fight to reduce infant mortality, which for African Americans is 2.3 times the infant mortality rate as whites ("Infant Mortality and African Americans."). They want to reduce the rate of asthma, which has reached epidemic proportions in our communities. But the "life" that we are dealing with these days often gets in the way. Many mothers in our organization are going back to work full time, part time and flextime. Some are starting home-based businesses and becoming "momprenuers." *Love that term.* Others are getting separated and divorced. But everyone is looking for the elusive "balance."

Those who are trying to get back to work are finding their own set of obstacles in a world that doesn't quite know where they fit in, and hearing this question a senior producer at a television network that shall remain nameless once asked me during a job interview: *"So you left the workforce to become a stay at home mom? What exactly have you been doing all this time?"*

Here's what mothers need: A working world that values, really values, the work of mothers at home, actually mothers everywhere, so much so that their good work is heralded, not scorned. And I don't mean lip service. I mean companies putting their money where their mouth is.

Probably one of the biggest side effects of these trying times, for mothers, and in particular the African American stay at home mothers that I know, is the stress. Nearly three-quarters of black women worry about not having enough money to pay their bills. Fewer than half of black women believe they have the necessary skills to be competitive in the current job market (Mui and Jenkins). This can take a huge toll on our bodies, both physical and mental. The depression rate among African American women is estimated to be almost 50 percent higher than that of Caucasian women. African Americans account for approximately 25 percent of the mental health needs in this country though we only make up 11 to 12 percent of the national population (Leary). Health disparities are rampant. African Americans are more likely to develop cancer than people of any other race, suffer from heart disease and stroke, and from a higher incidence of diabetes and HIV/AIDS ("What are Health Disparities").

I say all this not to present a picture of doom and gloom, but to let you know that there is much to contend with and for African American parents, much on the line. African American mothers cannot walk this tightrope walk alone, without the love and support of family and friends, and without networks of support like my dear Mocha Moms. There are definite rays of hope, promise and optimism ahead, and for those of us who have made the choice to stay at home, we need look no further than

Kuae Kelch Mattox

the laughter and smiles of our own children to know that our lives have been blessed beyond measure.

So what do mothers need? They need to be educated, about how to be better parents, how to keep their kids healthy, what opportunities and resources are available for their families. They need to be loved and respected and feel valued by their family and their friends and the world around them. They need to be validated and supported for the choices that they make, and if those choices happen to be bad ones, they need to be mentored and guided and yes, from someone, understood.

Mothers need to strengthen and support each other. Forget about the so-called "Mommy Wars" and keeping up with the Joneses. Really support each other. Lift each other up. We're all in this big boat together, muddy water and all. Regardless of race, politics, religion or creed, we have so much more in common than most people think.

Mothers need to be greater advocates for themselves and their children. They need to know when to raise their hand and stand up, to push for what's right and to fight for what they believe. They need to ask the tough questions, be prepared for the answers, and stand their ground. When a teacher or authority figure disparages your child and damages his or her self-esteem, mothers need to call them on it and let them know that they are watching and listening.

Years ago I volunteered with a fabulous organization called Girls, Inc. Their focus through their programs is to promote a girl's "right to be herself." The powerful words in their motto, "Inspiring Girls to be Strong,

Smart and Bold," speak volumes. That's what I've always thought that mothers need, to be strong, smart and bold, and they should look to the very people who make them feel that way.

"African American mothers need organizations and resources that encourage them to step out of their comfort zone, take risks, grow, succeed and sometimes fail, all within a nurturing environment," said my dear friend Maria Roach, who is blazing trails as an online social activist these days.

"Women of color need what all people need—a network of other people to share concerns with and get ideas from. Of course there are more practical things, but for me, anytime I have a challenge, being able to reach out to others in the same boat or who have been in my boat is always a good place to start," said Dionne Ford, a fellow writer.

Mothers need to be a cheerleader to their children and to themselves. It's ok to toot your own horn, because there's enough noise out there to muffle the sound. But be loud and be proud. Stand on the sidelines and cheer on your children. Cheer them for trying, cheer them for working hard, even if the result is not what you had hoped. And for goodness sake, share their good news. Yours too.

For my friend Geraldine Moriba, a busy executive for a major news network, what she needs as a mother is deeply personal.

"To be around people who are positive influences and help me keep perspective; time to be alone to clear my thoughts; time and energy enough to exercise; the patience to be calm and present for my children; enough job flexibility to make time to manage personal tasks during my business day and the comfort of knowing I won't be judged as less dedicated; a special pursuit, project or challenge that I am pursuing for my own satisfaction and growth; sensual attention and alone time with her husband."

Mothers need to exhale, and not feel guilty about it. They need to have fun, to smile and laugh and wallow in the joys of motherhood. Who knows? Maybe that tightrope walk won't seem so daunting after all.

WORKS CITED

"Employment Crisis Worsens for Black Women During Recovery." National Women's Law Centre. 3 August 2011. Web.

"Infant Mortality and African Americans." United States Department of Health and Human Services. 3 July 2012. Web.

Kirp, David. "The Widest Achievement Gap." *National Affairs* 5 (Fall 2010) .n.p. Web.

Leary, George. "Black Women and Mental Health." BlackWomensHealth.com. Web. 8 August 2012.

Mui, Ylan Q. and Chris L. Jenkins. "For some black women, economy and willingness to aid family strains finances." *Washington Post* 5 February 2012. Web.

"New Data from United States Department of Education Highlights Educational Inequities." United States Department of Education. 6 March 2012. Web.

Reidenbach, Luke and Christian Weller. "The State of Minorities in the Economy." Center for American Progress. 15 January 2010. Web.

"The Racial Wealth Gap's Great Recession Surge." Inequality.org. 29 July 2011. Web.

"What are Health Disparities." The Medical News from news-medical.net. Web. 31 August 2012.

At the Core of the Work/Life Balance Myth

Motherhood and Family Dinners

AMBER E. KINSER

THE DISCOURSE OF "BALANCE" is tightly interwoven with discussions and conceptions of family life. Adults employ this discourse in their efforts to navigate the demands of work and family, and in their struggle to pursue goals and interests that ground their identities beyond home and work. We put great store in the idea of balance and the individual's ability to achieve and hold fast to it when in fact, in addition to it being a very slippery thing, it also is something that is beyond the scope of what many, perhaps most, individuals can reasonably be expected to pull off. The demands of contemporary life are so numerous and so at odds with each other that we would do better to examine those demands at their institutional sources than to wait until they have complicated people's lives and then invoke a dream of the balanced life, thus directing attentions away from the sources of those complications and impeding our ability to mediate them.

There are reasons, very real and concrete reasons which we can readily point to, that explain why people feel destabilized and overwhelmed in these times. Some parents report not even attempting a goal of balance or stability (Blake et al. 717), and even among already empowered mothers, balance is elusive (Horwitz 105). Mothers and families are compelled toward the impossible management of work demands, intrusions of school demands into the homeplace, troubled economies, technologies that allow us to connect with greater breadth but shallower depth, and more. They confront general invasions of the family by a multitude of institutions, persons, and products, and the perhaps surprisingly consistent ideology behind them: "the language and logic of impersonal, competitive, contractual, commodified, efficient, profit-maximizing, self-interested relations" (Hays 417). They defend against or accommodate intrusions of the state into their time (as with school projects and homework) and intrusions of the workplace likewise, the loss of the 40-hour work week and the reasonable school week in the "boundless time cultures" they must maneuver (Kvande), and the expectation coming from *everywhere* that they must be accessible to scores of people *all the time*. And in any case, some research suggests that "balance" *per se* doesn't necessarily promote the good life; some parents in fact prefer to live out of balance if the greater proportion of their time and energy is spent on family rather than work (Greenhaus, Collins and Shaw).

It is these larger, social, institutional variables that are at the center of the struggle for some sense of balance rather than smaller, individual, personal choices. Pegeen Reichert Powell argues that women in particular should be suspicious of "balance" discourse, because it wrests agency away from women by charging them with responsibility for acquiring what is impervious to their efforts because it is shaped by variables well beyond their control. Given that it is largely mothers who continue to be given, and assume, responsibility for ensuring family well-being, the discussion of balance is likely to weigh most heavily on them. Indeed, as Christine Blake and her colleagues have shown, while fathers seek a stable work schedule that allows them predictable family time, if anyone prefers work-life balance it is mothers. As with the interrelationship of stress discourses and mothering discourses, which assigns the task of managing stress in motherhood to women themselves (Horwitz and Long), balance discourse renders individuals culpable for outcomes that are rooted far outside of them and that are, as such, beyond their capacity to manage. These problems sit at the societal, not the individual, level but dominant discourses privatize and individualize them nevertheless. Take for example the way that even research discourse weights the impact of, even as it privatizes, the matter:

> *Why should the happy, healthy, productive worker make it a priority to effectively balance the demands from his or her family and work? Quite simply, because so much is at stake when we* fail to manage *these often-competing demands.... There are key consequences that accompany the* failure to effectively balance *the two domains for the employees themselves, their families, and organizations. As a result, not only does the individual*

> *suffer from pressures associated with work-family conflict, but the impact extends to spouses, children, bosses, subordinates, etc.* (Quick, Henley, and Quick 426, emphasis added)

Carrying this larger-than-one's-life obligation, needless to say, sets mothers up to feel frustrated, inadequate, exhausted, and ineffectual in their lives, which serves certain ideological purposes, to be sure, but also exempts social institutions (like the workplace and its "bosses," or a gendered institution of family care) from any culpability, freeing them from the charge of finding, facilitating, and funding solutions.

Then, positioned squarely at this busy and congested intersection of home, work, school, balance, and a score of other institutional discourses, is *food*: its securing, its preparation, its complex role in family relations, its relentless demands on family time and (typically) maternal energies, its conflicts with schedules and finances and bodies. The difficulty of food and meal management, coupled with the insistence that these are private, individual family matters, sit at the core of the work/life balance myth. There are many complex variables related to food for families—food insecurity as one example and the industrialization of food systems as another (Mintz and DuBois). In this essay, I am looking at another dimension of food, one that is different from, but nevertheless interrelated with, such examples.

Specifically, my attention here is directed at over a decade's worth of research on "the family meal" and, more specifically, the emphasis in public health, mental health, and educational attainment arenas on frequent family dinners (FFDs), with Columbia University (CASAColumbia) and University of Minnesota (Project EAT) as two of the most recognized sites of such research, as reference points for subsequent research, and as recipients of many years of enamored media attention. I have examined this subject area largely as it relates to the U.S. and have recently received a major grant from my home (East Tennessee State) university's Research Development Grant Committee for its study.

In short, years of studies have identified strong connections between families who frequently share meals together and positive psychological and health outcomes for children, especially adolescents. Associations have been found between how frequently families share a meal together and adolescent substance use/abuse, healthful eating, depression, asthma, academic performance, self-esteem, eating disorders, enhanced vocabulary, disorderly behavior, and a host of other outcomes. Social policy interventions have focused largely, and myopically, on disseminating information to help families emphasize shared family meals several nights a week and prepare food quickly that is healthy for family members.

This literature does little to address food security, or barriers to frequent meal provision that are situated outside the family, or emotional or psychological variables within the family, or changes in social policy that might help mediate any of it. Nor does it attend to the primary role that mothers continue to play in family meal provision (Allen, Shockley and Poteat; Bianchi, Milkie and Sayer; Bugge and Almas; DeVault; Jacob et al.; Ochs et al.; Owen et al.), to the fact that in most families, whether or not there are children, it is women who primarily act as the "food gatekeeper" (Coveney 114). Such focus on dinners with little regard for who is providing them or how these persons view the meal provision for which they assume responsibility leaves important questions unexplored and prevents us from helping families to actually execute the very thing that researchers claim will make a difference. With comparatively few exceptions, what we see in the research is an abstract focus on how "families" or "parents" ought attend more acutely to frequent family meals. This focus obscures the primary and persistent role that mothers play in meal provision, despite the likelihood of their paid employment outside the home, and conceals the enormously influential roles that school, work, transportation, socio-economic status, child care, athletics, media, food access, psychological special needs, the hegemonic discourse of motherhood (Horwitz), and discourses of child development, the health professions, and normative families (DeVault 136) play in shaping the context of family meal frequency. Further, such a focus grossly misrepresents the limited impact that all of the effort that "parents" or "families" could muster would have against these enormous influences.

Most of us probably have heard plenty of talk over the years, and a good bit of it recently, lamenting the decline of family meals, and distressing over what this portends for the future of the institution of the family, despite the fact that the available evidence for this claim is tenuous at best (Murcott). When interlayered with equally worrisome FFD research, the public dialogue on family dinners reaches frenzied proportions. Little of this talk explores the institutional reasons why a sit-down meal with multiple bowls of steaming food passed between family members seated together in the dining room amid lively and joyful conversation may be elusive for many families; or may prove to be an immense amount of work with very little gratification; or may end up being, at various family stages, just too difficult or impeded to execute with any regularity. To hear many—innumerable academic researchers, politicians, health care professionals, public health administrators, policy makers, children's teachers—tell the tale, the nightly sit-down dinner is the answer to most adolescent and teen problems. And what's even more amazing, goes the tale, is that this answer is fully within reach for each and every family. It is "simple," they say. It is the "easiest way to engage," they say; something "magical" happens around the table, they say (Ferrigno; Forrester; Gibbs; Goldschmidt; "Frequent Family Meals"). Why it's a veritable "magic bullet," they say (Juri).

What most of the research and the subsequent media coverage of family dinners *don't* say, because they don't *have* anything to say, because they haven't *explored* it, is what all this means for *mothers*, who remain primarily responsible for meal provision, despite some societal changes in gendered patterns of family care. In fact, any mention of mothers is disturbingly absent from a great majority of these discussions about frequency of family dinners. The research on the value of families sharing meal times never explicitly states that it is mothers who could solve these adolescent and teen problems, but it doesn't have to. The implication is there just the same. We know from the research cited above and scores more that women continue to hold responsibility for meal provision. And we also know that we have a long and strong history of mother blame for children's outcomes (Caplan; Edmonds; Horwitz; Ladd-Taylor; Thurer) and especially for blame of poor and non-white mothers (Mink). We know that maternal behavior is directed by dominant mothering discourses in ways that paternal behavior is not (Hays; Horwitz; Thurer);we further know that mothers are compelled more specifically in their food provision by public health and nutrition discourses in ways that fathers are not (Devine, Jastran et al.; Owen et al.). And no, as Paula Caplan says, "it's not getting any better—not socially and not in the research arena" (278). Given what we know, it is hardly a stretch to say that it is probably *mothers* who will internalize this research about FFDs and the media attention to it, or that it is *mothers' activities* that are targeted as and understood to be the thing that could save the children from ruin. Comments about meals, whether their sources admit it or not, or claim to intend it or not, are often

Amber E. Kinser

enough comments about what mothers are doing, or not doing, about them. That is, when "parents" hear the question implicitly posed by media outlets, which have taken up the FFD research with fervor—"If solving obesity, alcohol abuse, asthma, and low grades is as easy as the family dinner, then why oh why won't 'parents' do it?"—it is significantly more likely to be heard by mothers than by fathers as either: *No matter how complicated and stressful this is for me, it is comparatively "easy" and "simple" and I should be doing it,* or alternatively though to the same end*: I am a "bad mother" because I am not doing this "easy" and "simple" thing.* I submit that it is not accidental that the "answer" to a whole host of social ills sits right in the lap of the mother. Mother blame is alive and well, even if it is disguised by the rhetoric of "parents" and "families." As Susan Boyd notes about the language of "shared parenting" in family law, for example, these rhetorics function to saddle women with family labor in their refusal to concede the gendered patterns that mark that labor.

The solution to the large number of problems that the family dinner is purported to ameliorate is misrepresented as not only simple and totally fixable, but also totally fixable *by* the family and *in* the family. Whether or not children's academic performance, social skill, physical health, mental health, or future life prospects are at risk is attributed to individual families and what they are or are not providing at the table and whether or not they are "simply" willing to pony it up, serve some supper, and solve their family's problems. Joseph Califano, Jr., former

U.S. Secretary of Health, Education, and Welfare, and former chairman and president of CASAColumbia, one of the longest running research teams focusing on FFDs, stated as much:

> Preventing America's drug problems is not going to be accomplished in court rooms, legislative hearing rooms or classrooms, by judges, politicians or teachers. It will happen in living rooms and dining rooms and across kitchen tables—by the efforts of parents and families. (CASAColumbia 2007: iii)

This focus on social issues as solvable by families means, quite happily for policy makers, the media, health and educational institutions, and a free market economy, that no one will be looking to *those* places for help or solutions. It also means that only families with the greatest store of resources have even a prayer.

We have ample evidence that family dinners are not "magical." If we don't want to ask anyone, anywhere, who is responsible for meal provision if they experience it in this way—a question that would certainly yield abundant data that would quickly put this myth to rest—and if we don't want to trust our own experiential knowledge or very strong gut-level sense that it isn't "simple" or "magical," we could pull from Marjorie DeVault's renowned work to be reminded that "planning a meal is rarely recognized as the kind of intellectual problem it actually is," (47) and to learn that "more than just the provision of edibles, feeding work means staging the rather complex social events that we label meals" (35). We could also turn to a number of researchers, such as Bugge and Almas; Coltrane; Devine, Jastran et al.; and Story and Neumark-Sztainer, to learn that those responsible for family meal provision find it a highly complex undertaking even in its most basic forms. But if we didn't want to look at any of the evidence, and we wanted instead to maintain the cultural myth that the magic in family dinners is what has such significant causal influence on so many social problems, then why oh why—especially given that drug abuse, academic achievement, eating disorders, depression, and the like are in fact social problems, not just individual family ones—are we not looking to larger societal-level explanations for why families find routine shared meals so far out of their reach? *Why are we not assigning highest priority to supporting families* in their orchestration of family meals?

Now. I have no trouble conceding that families sharing meals as a group is a good thing when it works. And—let's go ahead and publicly state it—plenty of times it does not work. Even if a yummy dinner made it magically to the table, sometimes family meals just *do not work*. And in some families, they almost never do; in some families, in fact, they are destructive. But when they work, I can see how frequent family dinners could have some influence on school performance, healthful eating, parent's awareness of and engagement with children's activities, adolescent access to alcohol and other substances, largely because while sitting with children over a meal, parents may be well-positioned to observe children's behavior, learn from and teach through conversation, model or set or clarify parameters for expected behavior, and restrict some access to potentially problematic influences and experiences, especially for adolescents and teens.

But I find no convincing evidence that family meals are either easily within reach or purely positive in influence. Nor do I find any compelling case that if we simply start with current family dynamics and institutional influences as they are, and add FFDs and stir, we will have fixed so much of what ails us. No familial or social problems are solved by simply introducing or increasing one component without regard for how the change will impact or interact with other components. Further, much of the FFD research shows no appropriate regard for issues of causal direction or multiple influences. Paula Caplan's critique of a study in the *American Journal of Orthopsychiatry* is illustrative here. This examination of children's assaultive behavior claims, Caplan explains, that negative interactions with their mothers caused the children's assaultive behavior. The research, she argues, neither seriously considers children's interactions with fathers nor considers the possibility that children who were assaultive were difficult to interact with, thus resulting in negative interactions with their mothers (278-279). Researchers are not asking if children's behavior influences maternal behavior. Similarly, family dinner research with rare exception (Sen; Story and Neumark-Sztainer, as two such exceptions) fails to consider the possibility, for example, that families may in fact be attempting to gather for a meal but are not joined by teens who are engaged in high risk and other potentially problematic behaviors. In these cases, introducing FFDs is not likely to shield children from such behaviors, calling into question the direction of the influence. That is, does family meal frequency impact high-risk teen behaviors, or do high risk teen behaviors impact how frequently families share a common meal as a group? Clearly, the FFD research needs to be significantly expanded to look beyond the simplest of questions and to explore extra-familial and intra-familial influences.

Even so, allowing for the possibility that family dinners are worth facilitating, here is what mothers need if they (we) are going to figure out how to facilitate them. I identify in what follows seven changes—seven to represent dinner for each night of the week—that mothers and their families need if we are going to really and truly support the idea that regular shared family meals is a worthy pursuit.

WHAT MOTHERS NEED TO FACILITATE FAMILY MEALS

1. Mothers need policy makers, health care professionals, and media sources to stop telling them that family dinners are an easy and simple way to protect their families. Mothers need media sources to utilize academic professionals to help them interpret and report family meal research findings accurately, rather than distill them into simplistic news bytes or headlines that do more to perpetuate myths and stereotypes than to inform the public and help families.

2. Mothers need those touting the family meal-as-panacea to acknowledge gendered forms of meal provision so that women's typically disproportionate meal provision labor is not erased and thus can be explicitly supported. Mothers need to be a critical part of the conversation about frequent family dinners.

3. Mothers need government agencies, politicians, advertisers, and media sources to stop treating the issue of healthful food access as synonymous with healthy *recipe* access. Issues of food insecurity and poverty must be a part of the FFD conversation. Policy and other institutional interventions must act from the knowledge that low-income families may not have adequate food or cooking equipment or facilities (Story and Neumark-Sztainer); that geographic location and transportation limitations affect access to affordable and nutritional foods; that instability and work environments of low status jobs, as well as the work demands and stress of those jobs, affect food and meal decisions (Devine, Jastran et al.; Devine, Connors et al.); and that school and work locations impact healthful food access during the day and thus impact health and hunger needs at dinner.

4. Mothers need frequent family dinner campaigners to see that the

orchestration of the family meal is exceptionally more complex than the simple cooking tips and meal planning advice they offer up so freely can address. They need to quit telling mothers that having children in the kitchen is helpful; many families find them wholly unhelpful in fact. Furthermore, children carry with them intrusions of their schools into family life, telling mothers to additionally saddle meal preparation efforts with lessons in math and measurement and basic economics. Social institutions need to stop sending children into the kitchen to fix institutional-level problems, thus further confounding an already complex undertaking. Mothers need researchers and policy makers to explore other interventions that actually support them and to develop incentives beyond health-related ones, which are proving to have limited impact (Owen et al.; Martinasek et al.), especially for poor women (Coveney).

5. Mothers need social policies and institutions to explore what variables are in place that make FFDs more feasible for some families and less feasible for others, and to then commence addressing those variables. We need them to explore how else families might facilitate the touted positive outcomes for their families, since FFDs are so hard to come by for so very many families, and since FFDs are proving to be something other than the "unassailable ideal" they are made out to be (Wilk 429).

6. Mothers need their communities to strategize ways that the *community itself* can facilitate family meals, to deprivatize and deindividualize responsibility for children's outcomes: like scheduling activities around dinner; like a moratorium on certain nights of the week where there is no homework, no sports activities, no lessons, no church activities; like help with homework after school and grade-appropriate school projects that do not require adult-level problem solving; like workplaces that facilitate—versus tolerate, ignore, or impede—the family connections of their employees, and that address the issue of how work schedules interfere regularly and significantly with evening family time; and like organizations and social services that prioritize and facilitate FFDs. We need our communities to recognize the critical role they play in impeding or facilitating family meals.

7. Mothers need someone to conduct research on how frequent family dinners impact the health and psychological outcomes of *mothers,* as well as their aspirations, quality of life, and family relationships, thus moving FFD research beyond monocular child impact studies, even while informing those studies.

Either the family meal really matters in helping to address a variety of social issues, or it doesn't so much, or we're not quite sure either way. It can't matter enormously to policy makers, educators, healthcare professionals and others *but only to the extent* that families bear the burden alone. If it matters, then we need to seek out and amplify the voices of those bearing responsibility for feeding the family. And we need to stop being so narrow-visioned and begin to explore how family patterns are shaped by forces around and within them so that we can direct those forces to help families embody the changes that we claim will make a difference in their lives and in our social world.

WORKS CITED

Allen, Tammy D., Kristen M. Shockley, and Laura F. Poteat. "Workplace Factors Associated with Family Dinner Behaviors." *Journal of Vocational Behavior* 73 (2) (2008): 336-342.

Berge, J. M., M. Wall, D. Neumark-Sztainer, N. Larson and M. Story. "Parenting Style and Family Meals: Cross-sectional and Five-Year Longitudinal Associations." *Journal of the American Dietetic Association* 110 (2010): 1036-1042. [University of Minnesota School of Public Health, Project EAT].

Bianchi, Suzanne, M., Melissa A. Milkie, and Liana C. Sayer. "Is Anyone Doing the Housework? Trends in the Gender Division of Household Labor. " *Social Forces* 79 (1) (2000): 191-228. Web. 10 Aug. 2012.

Blake, Christine E., Carol M. Devine, Elaine Wethington, Margaret Jastran, Tracy J. Farrell, and Carole A. Bosogni. "Employed Parents' Satisfaction with Food-Choice Coping Strategies: Influence of Gender and Structure." *Appetite* 52 (2009): 711-719.

Boyd, Susan. "Shared Parenting and Challenges for Maternal Autonomy." Paper presented at the "'What Do Mothers Need?' Motherhood Scholars and Activists Speak out on Maternal Empowerment for the 21st Century." Motherhood Initiative for Research and Community Involvement, Toronto, Ontario, May 9, 2012.

Bugge, Anechen Bahr and Reidar Almas. "Domestic Dinner: Representations and Practices of a Proper Meal Among Young Suburban Mothers." *Journal of Consumer Culture* 5 (2003): 203-228.

Caplan, Paula. "Don't Blame Mother: Then and Now." *Mother Outlaws:*

Theories and Practices of Empowered Mothering. Ed. Andrea O'Reilly. Toronto: Women's Press, 2004. 275-283.

Coltrane, Scott. "Research on Household Labor: Modeling and Measuring the Social Embeddedness of Routine Family Work." *Journal of Marriage and the Family* 62 (4) (2000): 1208-1233.

CASAColumbia, Columbia University National Center on Addiction and Substance Abuse. "The Importance of Family Dinners," September 2003; "The Importance of Family Dinners II," September 2005; "The Importance of Family Dinners III," September 2006; "The Importance of Family Dinners IV," September 2007;"The Importance of Family Dinners V," September 2009; "The Importance of Family Dinners VI," September 2010; "The Importance of Family Dinners VII," September 2011. Web.

Coveney, John. "What Does Research on Families and Food Tell Us? Implications for Nutrition and Dietetic Practice." *Nutrition and Dietetics* 59 (2) (2002): 113-119.

Devault, Marjorie L. *Feeding the Family: The Social Organization of Caring as Gendered Work*. Chicago: University of Chicago Press, 1991.

Devine, Carol. M., Margaret Jastran, Jennifer Jabs, Elaine Wethington, Tracy J. Farell and Carol A. Bisogni. "'A Lot Of Sacrifices': Work-Family Spillover and the Food Choice Coping Strategies of Low-Wage Employed Parents." *Social Science & Medicine* 63 (10) (2006): 2591-2603.

Devine, Carol M., Margaret M. Connors, Jeffery Sobal and Carole A. Bisogni. "Sandwiching It In: Spillover of Work onto Food Choices and Family Roles in Low- and Moderate-Income Urban Households." *Social Science & Medicine* 56 (2003): 617-630.

Edmonds, Regina. "Maternal Thinking Expanded: A Psychologists View." *Maternal Thinking: Philosophy, Politics, Practice*. Ed. Andrea O'Reilly. Toronto: Demeter, 2009. 204-216.

Ferrigno, Kathleen. "Studies Find that Dinner Makes a Difference; Family Day Spreads the Word." Drugfree.org. Web. 18 Jan 2012.

Forrester, Jeff. "Your Mom Was Right About Family Dinners." TheFix.com. Web. 18 Jan 2012.

"Frequent Family Meals Provide a Host of Benefits." *Internet Wire*, 1 May 2007. *General OneFile*. Web. 14 May 2012.

Fulkerson J. A., D. Neumark-Sztainer, P. J. Hannan and M. Story. "Family Meal Frequency and Weight Status Among Adolescents: Cross-Sectional and Five-Year Longitudinal Associations." *Obesity* 16 (2008): 2529-

2534. [University of Minnesota School of Public Health, Project EAT].

Gibbs, Nancy. "The Magic of the Family Meal." *Time*. 04 June 2006. Web. 14 May 2012.

Goldschmidt, Bridget. "Fewer Family Dinners Lead Teens to Alcohol, Drugs: Study." *Progressive Grocer,* September 24, 2009. *General OneFile*. Web. 14 May 2012.

Greenhaus, Jeffrey H., Karen M. Collins, and Jason D. Shaw. "The Relation between Work-Family Balance and Quality of Life." *Journal of Vocational Behavior* 63 (2003): 510-531.

Hays, Sharon. *The Cultural Contradictions of Motherhood*. New Haven, CT: Yale University Press, 1996.

Horwitz, Erika. *Through the Maze of Motherhood: Empowered Mothers Speak*. Toronto: Demeter Press, 2011.

Horwitz, Erika and Bonita C. Long. "Mothering and Stress Discourses: A Deconstruction of the Interrelationship of Discourses on Mothering and Stress." *Motherhood: Power and Oppression*. Eds. Andrea O'Reilly, Marie Porter, and Patricia Short. Toronto: Women's Press, 2005. 91-110.

Jacob, Jenet I., Sara Allen, E. Jeffrey Hill, Nicole Mead, and Maria Ferris. "Work Interference with Dinnertime as a Mediator and Moderator Between Work Hours and Work and Family Outcomes." *Family and Consumer Sciences Research Journal* 36 (4) (2008): 310-327.

Juri, Carmen. "Family Dinners Help Nourish Relationships." *NJ.com* January 4, 2011. Web. 18 Jan 2012.

Kvande, Elin. "Embodying Male Workers as Fathers in a Flexible Working Life." *Gender, Bodies and Work*. Eds. David Morgan, Berit Brandth, and Elin Kvande. Burlington, VT: Ashgate, 2005. 75-87.

Ladd-Taylor, Molly. "Mother-Worship/Mother Blame: Politics and Welfare in an Uncertain Age." *Maternal Theory: Essential Readings*. Ed. Andrea O'Reilly. Toronto: Demeter Press, 2007. 660-667.

Martinasek, Mary P., Rita D. DeBate, Ashley G. Walvorood, Stephanie T. Melton, David Himmelgreen, Tammy D. Allen, and Robert J. McDermott. "Using Social Marketing to Understand the Family Dinner with Working Mothers." *Ecology of Food and Nutrition* 49 (2010): 431-451.

Mink, Gwendolyn. *The Wages of Motherhood: Inequality in the Welfare State, 1917-1942*. Ithaca: Cornell University Press, 1995.

Mintz, Sidney W. and Christine M. DuBois. "The Anthropology of Food and Eating." *Annual Review of Anthropology* 31 (2002): 88-119.

Murcott, Anne. "Family Meals—A Thing of the Past?" *Food Health, and Identity*. Ed. Pat Caplan. New York: Routledge, 1997. 32-49.

Neumark-Sztainer D., M. E. Eisenberg, J. A. Fulkerson, M. Story and N. I. Larson. "Family Meals and Disordered Eating in Adolescents: Longitudinal Findings from Project EAT." *Archives of Pediatrics and Adolescent Medicine* 162 (2008): 17-22. [University of Minnesota School of Public Health, Project EAT].

Neumark-Sztainer, D., N. Larson, J. A. Fulkerson, M. E. Eisenberg and M. Story. "Family Meals and Adolescents: What Have We Learned from Project EAT (Eating Among Teens)." *Public Health Nutrition*, 13 (7) (2010): 1113-1121. [University of Minnesota School of Public Health, Project EAT].

Neumark-Sztainer, D., M. Story, D. Ackard, J. Moe and C. Perry. "The Family Meal: Views of Adolescents." *Journal of Nutrition Education* 32 (6) (2000): 329-334. [University of Minnesota School of Public Health, Project EAT].

Ochs, Elinor, Merav Shohet, Belinda Campos, and Margaret Beck. "Coming Together at Dinner: A Study of Working Families." *Work Flexibility: Realigning 20th-Century Jobs for a 21st-Century Workforce*. Eds. Kathleen Christensen and Barbara Schneider. Ithaca, NY: Cornell University Press, 2010. 57-70.

Owen, Jenny, Alan Metcalfe, Caroline Dryden, and Geraldine Shipton. "If They Don't Eat It, It's Not a Proper Meal: Images of Risk and Choice in Fathers Accounts of Family Food Practices." *Health, Risk & Society* 12 (4) (2010): 395-406.

Powell, Pegeen Reichert. "Balancing Act: Discourses of Feminism, Motherhood, and Activism." *Feminist Mothering*. Ed. Andrea O'Reilly. New York: SUNY Press, 2008. 257-271.

Quick, Jonathan D., Amy B. Henley, and James Campbell Quick. "The Balancing Act—At Work and At Home." *Organizational Dynamics* 33 (4) (2004): 426-438.

Sen, Bisakha. "The Relationship Between Frequency of Family Dinner and Adolescent Problem Behaviors after Adjusting for Other Family Characteristics." *Journal of Adolescence* 33 (2010): 187-196.

Story, Mary and Dianne Neumark-Sztainer. "A Perspective on Family Meals: Do They Matter?" *Nutrition Today* 40 (6) (December 2005). 261-266.

Thurer, Shari L. *The Myths of Motherhood: How Culture Reinvents the*

Good Mother. Boston: Houghton Mifflin Company, 1994.
University of Minnesota School of Public Health, "Project EAT" (Eating Among Teens). Web.
Wilk, Richard. "Power at the Table: Food Fights and Happy Meals." *Cultural Studies – Critical Methodologies* 10 (6) (2010): 428-436. [University of Minnesota School of Public Health, Project EAT].

What Mothers and Early Childhood Educators Need, But Don't Always Get

Competing(?) Voices on Childcare in Changing Rural Economies

PATRIZIA ALBANESE, MEGAN BUTRYN, LOUISA HAWKINS, AND COURTNEY MANION

ANN RAUHALA AND PATRIZIA ALBANESE (Rauhala et al.) have been doing research mapping childcare coverage from 2000 until 2008, in four Canadian daily newspapers, with particular attention to the unprecedented four federal elections over the period. They found that while politicians were often quoted as "experts" in the area, rarely were the voices and needs of parents and early childhood educators (ECEs) and childcare providers included in the newspaper coverage (Rauhala et al.). In fact, for the most part, the voices of mothers and ECEs/childcare providers have been absent even in academic literature on the topic. This paper presents some of the daily experiences, challenges and views of mothers and childcare providers often absent in other research and writing in this area. It also shows that at times, especially in neo-liberal times, the interests and needs of these key stakeholders appear to be or are made to seem at odds with one another. That said, by highlighting some of these seemingly competing interests and needs, we hope to move closer to providing recommendations that may help shed light on this important social issue and at the same time, remind those who make or shape policy, that the voices of those on the ground are valuable and necessary in policy development.

FRAGMENTED SOCIAL POSITIONS

Feminist discourses have been characterized by theoretical diversity emanating from women's various social position(alitie)s, as they relate to race, ethnicity, social class, age, sexuality, etc. On the ground, women's lived experiences are no less characterized by fissures that result from these and other social and economic circumstances and sets of experiences. In rural Quebec and Ontario working mothers and childcare providers often have much in common—rurality, marital status, social class, gender-segregated jobs, race, age, and sexuality. Both groups typically have husbands affected by job losses in male-dominated industries; are exposed to a shifting economic climate; live a life filled with uncertainty; experience gendered expectations about paid and unpaid work and carry the bulk of family responsibilities. But each has a different vantage point, from which they assess their everyday challenges. And at times, this is manifested as/in opposition to the other. This paper will present some of the differing and at times competing discourses that characterize the experiences of mothers and child care providers. We believe that taken together, though, the two vantage points provide us with a better understanding of the complexity of interrelated social issues. Beyond that, we believe that the recommendations and insight that they provide may help move us forward towards better policies and social services.

THE SHARED ENVIRONMENT: CHANGING ECONOMIC TIMES IN RURAL CANADA

Since the 1970s, rural manufacturing communities in Canada have been negatively affected by globalization and have consequently experienced economic restructuring (McLeod and Hovorka; Albanese 2006; Leach and Winson). Corporations began shifting from domestic manufacturing to manufacturing abroad through the relocation of plants and factories in order to take advantage of cheaper, non-unionized labour around the world (Duffy and Pupo; Leach and Winson). As a result, large numbers of Canadian plants have shut down, leaving significant numbers of men and women out of well-paying, unionized jobs (Duffy and Pupo; Leach; Albanese 2006; Leach and Winson).

Simultaneously, there has been a retrenchment of the welfare state as a result of an emerging neo-liberal political agenda (Duffy and Pupo; Albanese 2011a; Braedley and Luxton; Leach; Luxton). Economic and welfare state restructuring has been gendered and have disproportionately disadvantaged and burdened women (Albanese 2011a, 2007). As the number of manufacturing jobs quickly decline, there has been a stark increase in the amount of service sector jobs—a significant number in female-dominated sectors—associated with the transition to the "new economy" (Leach). The new economy has birthed a bifurcation of jobs and earnings with high paying, high status jobs in technology and finance and low paying, low status jobs in customer service, retail and other consumer services (Albanese 2009; McLeod and Hovorka; Leach and Winson). On top of this, since women are primarily responsible for domestic and caring tasks (Albanese 2011b; Luxton; Albanese 2007), they are often limited to the local economy for employment so that they can fulfill their obligations to the household (Leach; McLeod and Hovorka). As a result, Colleen McLeod and Alice Hovorka conclude that we are witness to complex "gendered economic landscapes" that create an environment where "the needs of women and children have been frequently overlooked" (80).

Although there continues to be the assumption that men are the primary income earners and women work in order to supplement family incomes, declining male wages have made a dual-earner model necessary for many families (Luxton; Albanese 2009). Since many rural women are confined to low-paying, part-time service sector work, multiple job holding has become more prominent among rural women in the labour force (Albanese 2009; Ames, Brosi, and Damiano-Teixeira; Albanese 2006). Multiple job holding has been found to be a strategy for adapting to rural restructuring (Robertson, Perkins, Taylor) in order to top up household incomes deeply affected by the contingent, low-paying and insecure nature of service sector jobs (Albanese and Farr; Leach and Winson).

Downloading of state responsibility onto families and individuals, which is associated with neo-liberal ideologies, has made finding accessible, affordable and flexible services like childcare very difficult, if not impossible to attain (Albanese 2006, 2007, 2011a, 2011b; Ames, Brosi, and Damiano-Teixeira). State retrenchment and neoliberalism have burdened women by making it even more difficult to navigate the needs and requirements of the paid labour market, unpaid household and caring responsibilities, and education—making them seem quite incompatible despite being a growing reality. Canadian family policies don't seem to help matters.

FAMILY POLICIES IN CANADA

Women's experiences with burdens associated with managing paid labour, unpaid caring responsibilities, and education have been heavily

Patrizia Albanese

influenced by some less-than family-friendly Canadian family policies. Canada, as a whole, has been classified as a "liberal welfare state" because it relies on the free market rather than generous state support to families and social programs (Albanese, 2011a, 2011b; Esping-Andersen). Canadian family policies are for the most part, limited, targeted, and not very "family-friendly" (Albanese 2011a; O'Connor, Orloff and Shaver). But due to Canada's jurisdictional complexity (Albanese 2011a), one of its provinces, Quebec, is closer to a social democratic model in its policy intents and gen erosity (Baker; Krull; Albanese 2011a). Since the mid-1990s, Quebec has been transforming its once patriarchal and later pronatalist policies, towards more feminist-informed programs aimed at integrating paid work and family, promoting gender equity, and reducing family poverty (Albanese 2011a; Roy and Bernier; Jenson). Quebec's income tax laws were reformed, removing parents' refundable tax credit for child care expenses (the federal one remains), when it introduced $5/day (increased to $7/day in 2004) child care for children using child care at least three days a week, regardless of family income and employment status (Albanese 2006; Government of Quebec; Tougas, 2002a, 2002b, 2001c; Bégin et al.). It introduced full-time, full-day kindergarten for five-year-olds and for four-year-olds living in "at-risk" neighbourhoods, and expanded school day cares at reduced fee ($5/day/child; later $7) for school-aged children in need of before and after-school care (Albanese 2011a; Japel, Tremblay and Côtè). Quebec also negotiated its withdrawal from the national EI maternity-parental leave benefits program to offer its own system with two options to parents (effective January 2006), both with more equitable eligibility criteria and more generous replacement rates than the national plan (Albanese 2011a; Ministère de l'Emploi, Solidarité Sociale et Famille; Phipps).

At the same time, in the late 1990s and early 2000s, the federal, provincial, and territorial governments were making progress towards improving access to quality child care across the country (through the National Children's Agenda in 1997, the Federal/Provincial/Territorial Early Childhood Development Agreement in 2000 and the Multilateral Framework on Early Learning and Child Care 2003; also see Government of Canada and Government of Quebec). However, after 2006, the Federal Conservative minority government replaced past funding commitments with their own Universal Childcare Benefit, which gives families $100 monthly, before tax, for each child under age six, and professes to provide parents with "more choice in child care." As a result, in most of the country, child care spaces remain expensive and in short supply. Simply finding a childcare space in Ontario has been a challenge for many families, despite new commitments to the establishment of full-day learning for four and five year-olds in the province.

A report released in May 2011, by the Ontario Municipal Social Services Association (OMSSA) warned that in rural Ontario, more than 8,100 children are at risk of losing their child care, including over 500 children with special needs. At least 52 rural child care centres have already closed in the past two years and more than 200 licensed centres with 600 employees face immediate risk of closure, as do 150 home care providers. The report states that, "more than 90 towns and villages across rural and northern Ontario will be left with no local licensed child care options" (OMSSA 1). When child care options exist for parents, most of the work in the sector remains underpaid and undervalued.

UNDERVALUING (INVISIBLE) CARE WORK

Women's emotion and care work, in particular, have been stereotyped, overlooked and/or undervalued (Albanese 2007; James 1992; Staden; Poole and Isaacs; Gannerud). Nicky James (1989) explained that the forms emotional labour takes and the skills it involves leaves women subordinated. Part of the problem lies in the fact that there is often an assumed "naturalness" of women's emotion work—that women care as a matter of course (Albanese 2007). As a result, care and emotion work are treated as innate traits that require no "real" skill(s)—something women inevitably just "do," effortlessly—and this is at times believed to be true, even by other women and mothers. We believe, and argue in this paper, that living in neo-liberal times in parts of rural Canada contribute to women lashing out against or criticizing other women, when the true challenges come from family policies that leave families vulnerable and insecure.

PROJECT APPROACH AND METHODOLOGY

This paper includes first-hand accounts from mothers and child care providers in parts of rural Ontario and Quebec. It draws on interviews from two interrelated studies.

Study 1: Rural Western Quebec[1]

In 2004, Albanese began doing research assessing of the impact of $5 per day ($7) childcare using qualitative interviews with mothers and childcare providers, and a year later, fathers, living in a community located on the Quebec/Ontario border. The study involved a francophone community made up of two adjoining towns in Western Quebec. She interviewed 16 mothers and 17 childcare providers. She conducted follow-up interviews, a year later, with ten mothers and new interviews with ten fathers of children in reduced-fee day care.

The community is in a part of the province that until recently was a prosperous logging region. Almost none of the town's men continue to work in the economically hard-hit (soft-wood) lumber industry—as the last of the remaining paper or lumber mills in the region closed just over three years ago, amounting to three significant mill closures over the course of less than ten years. Many women work in traditional service sector jobs, including sales, food services, health and childcare, others commute to jobs up to one and a half hours away. Many were struggling with cuts to the softwood lumber industry that disproportionately affected this region (Dufour; Statistics Canada). Families increasingly depended on income from women's work, with many entering traditional, low-paid, "pink-collar" service jobs that often required long commutes. One relatively new employer in the region is a customer service call centre that profits from a low-paid, bilingual, female labour force in the area. Despite the low wages, long commutes and irregular hours, most women saw their jobs as necessary for their family's economic well-being (Albanese 2006).

Study 2: Mothers in Western Quebec and Eastern Ontario—Across the Jurisdictional Divide[2]

In the summer of 2009, Patrizia Albanese conducted 55 interviews—22 in Quebec and 33 in Ontario—with mothers of young children living and employed in the Ottawa Valley. This was a non-probability purposive (and snowball) sample of employed mothers working in and around two economically stagnant, small urban centres near the Ontario/Quebec border, in the Ottawa Valley. The interviews were conducted in English in the women's homes, a community centre, or neighbouring locales, in Renfrew County, Ontario, and the Outaouais, in Pontiac County, Quebec. Albanese zigzagged the region, traveling over 5000 kilometres, over a three-month period to conduct the interviews.

All the women in the second project who responded to ads placed in day care centres, social services agencies, in local newspapers and radio, or heard through word of mouth, and volunteered to participate in the study were employed or towards the end of their maternity leave and soon returning to paid work. These women, on both sides of the border, were employed in the service sector, as a lab technician, a free-lance journalist, camp counsellor, in retail sales, in customer service call centres, in office management, child care, health care, and other social and public services. All but one woman in Quebec were either married or living common-law. Six of the women in Ontario were raising their children on their own (and/or with the help of extended family), while the rest had male partners. All but one interview (at the mother's request) were tape recorded, and about one-hour in length. Albanese asked about women's employment history/background, and the impact that they believed that their paid work had on their household work, and their personal relationships. She asked mothers about whether and how their roles and responsibilities at home, at work, and their overlap have changed with paid employment; and about who cares for their children, where, and at what cost. She also asked them who manages their child care arrangements, and about how some of them manage child care in light of their own and/or their partners' non-standard jobs and changing work schedules and shifts.

FINDINGS

The sections below identify some of the themes in which child care providers and mothers both agree and disagree on some of the challenges faced by women as workers (in child care and other fields) and mothers. The themes include: 1) challenges associated with cost of and access to care; 2) the importance and (under)value placed on care work—both parts of life connected to living in insecure, neo-liberal times.

Cost of and Access to Care

i) Cost

Across Ontario and Quebec there are significant differences in what parents pay for child care. In Ontario, parents pay anywhere between $20 and $45 dollars per day per child, and a large number of parents turn to private home care arrangements due to limited spaces and inconvenient location or other access limitations that surround licensed child care facilities. In contrast, in Quebec, parents pay $7 per day (2004), up from $5 per day (1997), for a choice of publicly subsidized, but at times limited, licensed day care centres or smaller, regulated home/family child care settings. One administrator in Quebec explained how the fee structure there worked:

> *So if they had a contract for five days a week, then they get paid their $7 from the parents and then they get the balance from us in form of the subsidy. And we give them, I think right now we're at, total $24.00,* about that.... *For a baby it's a little bit more, they get an extra $9 a day. So it come up to $33 or $34.* (0402001)

Even in a more socially-conscious and more family-friendly policy environment like Quebec, families felt the neo-liberal pinch, and not surprisingly, some tended to turn on the most accessible targets they could find—their childcare providers—to vent their frustrations. For example, when the fee increased in Quebec from $5 to $7 in 2004, some mothers were not happy, but it was childcare providers and not mothers themselves who revealed this in interviews.[3] Childcare providers also explained that there were misconceptions on the part of some mothers that the extra $2 per child was going into the hands of childcare providers. In reality, one childcare provider explained that they actually experienced a cut in funding at the same time that parents received the fee increase.[4]

Not only did some mothers complain about the cost increase to their childcare providers, but childcare providers also revealed that with the price change, some parents seemed to adjust and raise their expectations surrounding service provision. Here is what some childcare providers shared on the matter:

> *Well I had to sit down and tell them that this is not my fault. I have to go with what [government regulation] tell me what to do.... You had to explain to them, and after that they seem ... well it wasn't fair for them too. Some parents didn't like it and that's it. They don't care if we got cut, and they have to pay the $7. It wasn't fair for them.* (0402012)

Another added, with understanding:

> *I find that the parents were really mad. They were used to paying $5 and now they have to pay $7. Cause they said the government didn't respect what they said.... So a lot of parents said well if it goes up it's better to have their kids at home and to have somebody private at home. I was lucky, because we didn't lose nobody* [francophone woman speaking English] *at our daycare, because they (mothers) had to work. And they have pretty good salaries, but the people who don't have a good job well they'll stop work to raise their own kids. There's one there, she took out her daughter of a daycare and it's her papere* (grandfather) *that's raising the child and like he's 70 years old and she's only five, so I find that that is not okay. But sometimes the parent doesn't have no choice. Cause $7 is $7.* (0402017)[5]

Despite recognizing the struggle that families experienced, childcare providers in Quebec identified financial challenges on their end, including concerns about being underpaid for the work they do:

> *Like right now, it's cheap. We're not paid a lot for what we do. It's not a lot of people that work ten hours a day.* (0402009)

> *I don't know how much I'd like to get [paid]. But I know what we're getting right now is not too much. After you pay all your electricity, all your food and pay an assistant there's not too many left.* (0402012)

One did the calculations, to determine that she was indeed severely underpaid for her work:

> *Calculate my hours that I do every day, and calculate the salary after I deduct everything. And we counted, my husband and I, I make three dollars an hour.* (0402015)

That said, despite mothers voicing concerns to their child care providers, there was the recognition that Quebec families were much better off compared to parents in other parts of the country. Of Quebec, one explained:

> *There's a lot more choices and there's so much more understanding of the fact that family is first and work is second ... because Ontario's policy just seems to put the workplace first, and the sacrifices, so many of us have to make for our family, I mean, unreal....* (2-006).

ii) Access/Hours—The Time Crunch, Between a Rock and a Hard Place

"Hours of operation" was a serious challenge that was experienced differently on the two sides of the divide. Both had equally compelling stories; both were trapped between competing demands and challenges surrounding "work-life balance" and the second and sometimes third shift, if you factor in that some women returned to school to upgrade their credentials—an increasingly common phenomenon in "new rural economies."

"Hours of operation" was clearly an area that mothers and childcare providers clashed and struggled with. It was also a topic in which the realities of living in neoliberal times were obvious and extreme. Childcare providers worked a double or even triple shift and needed the children out of their homes and centres at the end of their day, in order to manage the rest of their complex lives. Mothers commuted, worked shifts, managed their own and their families' changing schedules and often had to count on others to help them manage daily demands.

Let us explore this further, in the case of Quebec: home/family child care providers were mandated to remain open and available to families for ten hours per day, however one home childcare provider explained that:

> *[W]henever my ten hours was done, I wasn't done. I had another shift upstairs you know? It was hard, but then we got into it.* (0402002)

Another added that:[6]

> *It's like your work is never finished. Like after five* (p.m.) *you have the cleaning, cause before 5 the kids are not gone, so you can't leave them alone. And then you have to prepare your menus, and your arts and crafts....* (0402010)

Parents arriving late to pick up their children was an especially common and difficult challenge for home childcare providers. One home childcare provider explained:

> *That one parent, I had to remind her that I close at five ... and I go upstairs at five. I want my house back. I started at seven o'clock. That's a problem that they didn't* [have] ... *I have to keep reminding them.* (0402010 and 011)

Similarly, another lamented:

> *Oh yeah yeah, there's no such thing as after hours here...Like I told my parents, when their job is done at 4 o'clock they pack up and leave.... I'd like to too ... you know.... That's another big problem with family daycare. That's a big problem....Of course we have to remind them there. But I tell them. And ... go over with it again. Like my hours, it's quarter to seven to quarter to five.... When four o'clock comes you're out that door. Well, me, I ask for them the kid has to be gone by quarter to five. Of course we gotta keep reminding. You have to.* (0402015)

One childcare provider was sympathetic, but critical nonetheless:

> *I didn't, [charge a late fee] but now I'm gonna start to because I find they're taking advantage of me.... So I have no choice. So I have put it in my contract, but parents are smart sometimes: "Please I'm gonna be late maybe five, ten minutes.... Are you gonna charge me still?" Now you feel bad about it ... she's working hard too, you know ... but we start at certain hours, we have ten-hour day shifts, pick your kids up by five, or pay the fee that you're supposed to pay. Just to make them understand.* (0402012)

Mornings were no less strained for childcare providers. For example, one shared the following:

> *[They think] she'll give him breakfast ... she'll change the diaper, I won't have to change it ... sometimes the kids come in soaking wet. Just dripping. Why don't they take five minutes just to change it. You know?* (0402012)

On the flip side, the reality is that most mothers really did not have a choice as to when they could drop off and pick up their children. Mothers were bound by the constraints of their complex daily lives. But mothers who felt there was flexibility were clearly pleased:

> *For me, well I'm happy with her services, that's obvious.... She's very accommodating for hours, cause I have odd hours, where I have to leave before most of the daycares open, and she's never complained and she adjusted herself to accommodate me from the start. And a lot of people don't, so I'm very fortunate for that. And that's the second main reason that I stayed there. Plus it's really close to my place and convenient.* (0401001)

Those who rushed between work and their childcare provider were much more critical and less happy, for obvious reasons.

> *Sometimes if they close at 4:30 it's hard. Me in the beginning, at first I was like okay, how am I going to work this out at*

> *4:30? Cause when Serge is days he finishes at 4:30, and I work in Shawville (30 minutes away).... So by the time I get home it's 4:30 or quarter to five depending especially in the winter you know? And I was like how am I gonna work this out? So then with my mom and even his mom too, sometimes my mom can't go, his mom will pick her up....* (0401008)

Here is one mother dealing with the same, but also with the added challenge of having to use and pay for, both a home childcare provider and a "baby sitter" to make her childcare needs work:

> *Yeah, cause even me with the shifts that I do, daycare it's mostly for my daughter, cause I have to find babysitters all the time, even though she's in daycare. They only open at 7:00 or 7:30 in morning and I leave at 6:00. So I have to find a babysitter from 6:00 to 7:00 early whose willing to bring her to daycare. And when I finish at quarter to three, that's fine, but if I work evening shifts, it's from 3:00 to 11:00. Well, that's when I have a little bit of a problem as well, cause then I have to bring her in daycare cause you're not allowed to miss. You're only allowed to miss, I think, 16 days in a year. So I have to bring her to daycare, so I don't get go see her all day, then at evening I have to find her a babysitter that's willing to go pick her up at daycare and babysit her 'til 11:00. So I don't see her all that day.* (0401011)

Shift work is a growing reality for many rural mothers, so similarly, another explained:

> *Like, if I work daytime, I have to be at work at a quarter to seven and she only opens at seven. So I have to go and bring him to my mother-in-law, and she'll drop him off. And at night she closes at five, so if I work night shift, she sort of has to pick him up.* (0401012)

Like this mother, many rely on friends and relatives to balance paid work and childcare needs when they try to manage their long commutes, shift work, or working multiple jobs. As a result, it was not surprising to hear echoes on the same theme throughout the interviews with mothers:

> *Well I'm lucky. I have a mother that's always there and a mother-in-law that is always there too. So one drops him off on her way to work and the other one picks him up after daycare. One grandmother can leave in the morning dropping him off, but she's not back fast enough to pick him up, so the other one does.* (0401013)

Others relied on "babysitters" on top of the publicly subsidized child care system. The mother quoted above added:

> *For shift work, daycare is not the best. I have to say. It's not the best, cause we're always running around from daycare to babysitter, babysitter to daycare. And then it ends up costing you cause if you have to pay for the $7 anyway, whether she's there or not, right? Plus a babysitter.* (0401011)

More flexible child care, with longer hours are things that some of the mothers required. On the other hand, when listening to home/family child care providers, it is clear that this would have negative repercussions on their lives. Even larger day care centres that tried to accommodate changing parental needs struggled:

> *It's hard because we've tried that here to extend the hours because one person needs it, and then they don't use it* [due to changing shifts and holiday schedules], *so we're paying the staff to stay, so it's hard with the numbers, like you'd need to have a few people on board that need those hours, otherwise you're paying the staff to be here for nothing.* (2-031)

Shifting shifts caused *some* mothers to need *some* specific arrangements at *some* points in time—but not at others. We see that childcare centres and individual home child care providers could not easily contort to adapt to the changing social and economic reality of the day. The changing economic reality seemed to make it difficult for some childcare providers to accept and understand the struggles of some mothers: running late, arriving early, dropping off children, unfed or in wet diapers, dropping them off late and disrupting the daily centre activities and routines. At the same time, some mothers were intolerant of the same kinds of needs—the need for childcare providers to stop paid work and begin caring for their own families.

Some childcare providers felt taken advantage of, or undervalued by parents. It wasn't so much that mothers using childcare services did not understand the challenges associated with caring for other people's children. Instead, many were consumed by their own struggles and challenges that are so much a part of our current reality in changing and unstable neo-liberal times.

Especially in Ontario there was a sense that mothers worked long hours and very hard, only to pay to keep their children in childcare. One was frustrated with:

> *...Just being tired at the end of the day and then having that portion of my paycheck have to go to pay for the childcare.* (2-031)

This kind of frustration tended to get "dumped" onto childcare providers, who themselves struggled with very similar types of challenges. Both groups of women live in places and economic times that demand a great deal from them: often commuting some distance, working long hours, supporting their often un(der)employed husbands, upgrading their credentials and work-related skills through additional schooling, and continuing to be the ones who manage their childcare needs on a daily basis.

Women working from home—the home childcare providers—were no less challenged, as leaving the housework and carework in one part of the house often meant picking up more of the same on the other. The seemingly unending work, constant instability, and the economic pinch that they felt were products of living in neo-liberal times, in non-urban economies.

The result is that they are at times critical of each other because they are the people closest to themselves—most like them, and most accessible as targets. That said, both groups of women—mothers and childcare providers—recognize the need for the other and both point to the need for better, more family-friendly social policy.

Our goal is not to find flaws within the system, or fissures that may be manipulated and pried open by opponents of subsidized or universal child care, but instead to identify how the lived experiences of different bodies of women are experienced differently depending on which side of their local child care centre gate they stand on. We underscore the fact that both groups of women live in places and economic times that demand a great deal from them. What they want in return are more affordable childcare options that include more flexibility, while at the same time value and fairly remunerate the work that childcare providers do.[6] One mother also concluded by saying: "*having more family friendly employers would be nice*" (2-032), but we're afraid that in the current economic climate, that is far from worker and family friendly, this is a reality that is possible for only a limited few.

[1]This research was funded by two Ryerson University grants: New Faculty Research Fund and SSHRC-Standard Institutional Grant.
[2]This research was funded by the Social Sciences and Humanities Research Council, Standard Research Grant.
[3]Mothers may not have wanted to reveal their displeasure in interviews, because they realized that compared to mothers in the rest of the country, they were significantly better off, even with a $2 increase.
[4]"*Yes. Two dollars yes. They were supposed to give us a raise of two percent, but they didn't give it. We had a letter that it was accepted. They took that out, and they sent us another letter to say we cut $2 each child and it's the parent that pays. So when they gonna put it at 10, they're gonna do the same thing, they're gonna cut on our pay, and it's the parents that are gonna pay us. So we'll never have a raise*" (0402017).
[5]Despite dissatisfaction with the current system and the increase, $7 per day childcare was keeping families with young children in Quebec. "*Yeah of course. I mean we had talked about moving to Ontario, and everything, but because of the daycare [we didn't] ... Cause I work in Ontario*" (0401007).
[5]Another said: "*Like I don't make a lot of money for what I do. And...I don't think I'll have the energy to do this until I'm fifty. You know? Because I work let's say 55 hours a week. I'm open 50. I have to do the groceries. I have to make the food. Lots of times I'll make them [meals] at night or in the morning before I start, but right now I have no problem with it. I have lots of energy. I'm still young. But I can't say I'll be able to do this when I'm 50.*"
[6]"*Probably more flexible childcare like longer hours, and I know it does seem long like 7:00 am till 5:00 p.m. but like I said if I had them there at 7:30 a.m. and something came up and I still had to pick them up at*

*5:00 pm or pay late fees, it's not a long enough day, and more childcare facilities for me that works well, but I don't know if that would work well for everybody, and a childcare centre that provides care for all ages for the after-school children, for the toddler children and more spots for the [153] because your maternity leave ends at a yea*r" (2-030).

"*I think um, having like a, more daycare centers for sure, like more regulated centers where there's you know structure and lots of kids and what not, more part time places, like more part time positions, and the option to do full time or part time, not you lose your spot completely and all those things, and then for workplace, having like emergency daycare, or having an on site daycare*" (2-008).

"*I think more subsidy because of the fact that, they only have so many spaces and if you don't get a space well then you're paying full fee, so to me it leaves a lot of people without, I don't want to say good childcare but sometimes they have no choice but to put them in another home with someone whose cheaper and may not be providing that quality care*" (2-031).

WORKS CITED

Albanese, P. "$7/Day, $7/Hour, 7 Days A Week: Juggling Commutes, Shift Work and Childcare in a Changing ("New") Economy." *Road Blocks To Equality*. Ed. J. Klaehn. Toronto: Black Rose Books, 2009. 26-40. Print.

Albanese, P. "Addressing the Interlocking Complexity of Paid Work and Care: Lessons From Changing Family Policy in Quebec." *A Life in Balance? Reopening the Family-Work Debate*. Eds. C. Krull and J. Sempruch. Vancouver: University of British Columbia Press, 2011a. 130-143. Print.

Albanese, P. "Small Town, Big Benefits: The Ripple Effect of $7/day Child Care." *Canadian Review of Sociology and Anthropology* 43 (2) (2006): 125-140. Print.

Albanese, P. "The More Things Change ... The More We Need Child Care, On the Fortieth Anniversary of the Report on the Royal Commission on the Status of Women." *Reading Sociology*. Eds. L. Tepperman and A. Kalyta. Toronto: Oxford University Press, 2011b. 95-98. Print.

Albanese, P. "(Under)Valuing Care Work: The Case of Child Care Workers in Small- Town Quebec." *International Journal of Early Years Educa-*

tion. 15 (2) (2007): 125-139. Print.

Albanese, P. and T. Farr. "'I'm Lucky' ... to Have Found Child Care: Evoking Luck While Managing Child Care Needs in a Changing Economy." *International Journal of Child, Youth and Family Studies* 3 (1) (2012): 83–111. Print.

Baker, Maureen. *Restructuring Family Policies: Convergences and Divergences.* Toronto: University of Toronto Press, 2006. Print.

Bégin, Loiuse, L. Ferland, G. Girard, C. Gougeon. *School Daycare Services.* Cat. No. 2002-02-00121. Québec: Gouvernement du Québec, 2002. Print.

Ames, B. D., W. Brosi and K. M. Damiano-Teixeira. "'I'm Just Glad My Three Jobs Could Be During the Day': Women and Work in a Rural Community." *Family Relations* 55 (2006): 119-131. Print.

Braedley, Susan and Meg Luxton, eds. *Neoliberalism and Everyday Life.* Montreal: McGill-Queen's University Press, 2010. Print.

Duffy, A. and N. Pupo. "Employment in the New Economy and the Impact on Canadian Families." *A Life in Balance? Reopening The Family-Work Debate.* Eds. C. Krull and J. Sempruch. Vancouver: University of British Columbia Press, 2011. 98-114. Print.

Esping-Andersen, G. *The Three Worlds of Welfare Capitalism.* Cambridge: Polity Press, 1990. Print.

Federal/Provincial/Territorial Multilateral Framework on Early Learning and Child Care. Ottawa: Government of Canada, 2004. Print.

Gannerud, Eva. "A Gender Perspective on the Work and Lives of Women Primary School Teachers." *Scandinavian Journal of Education Research* 45 (1) (2001): 55-70. Print.

Government of Canada and Government of Quebec. "Canada-Quebec Agreement on Early Learning and Child Care, Funding Agreement." 28 October 2005. Print.

Government of Quebec. "Development and Funding Scenarios to Ensure the Permanence, Accessibility and Quality of Childcare Services: Consultations 2003." Québec: Ministère de L'Emploi, de a Solidarité Sociale et de al Famille, 2003. Print.

James, Nicky. "Care = Organisation + Physical Labour + Emotional Labour." *Sociology of Health & Illness* 14 (4) (1992): 488-509. Print.

James, Nicky. "Emotional Labour: Skill and Work in the Social Regulation of Feeling." *The Sociological Review* 37 (1) (1989): 15-42. Print.

Japel, Christa, Richard E. Tremblay and Sylvana Côtè. "Quality Counts:

Assessing the Quality of Day Services Based on Quebec Longitudinal Study of Child Development." *IRPP: Choices – Investing in Our Children* 11 (5) (2005): 1-42. Print.

Jenson, Jane. "Family Policy, Child Care and Social Solidarity-The Case of Quebec." *Changing Child Care: Five Decades of Child Care Advocacy and Policy in Canada*. Ed. Susan Prentice. Halifax: Fernwood Publishing, 2001. 39-62. Print.

Krull, Catherine. "Families and the State: Family Policy In Canada." *Canadian Families Today: New Perspectives*. Ed. David Cheal. Don Mills, ON: Oxford University Press, 2007. 254-272. Print.

Leach, B. "Transforming Rural Livelihoods: Gender, work, and Restructuring in Three Ontario Communities." *Family Patterns, Gender Relations*. Ed. B. Fox. Toronto: Oxford University Press, 2009. 509- 522. Print.

Leach, B. and A. Winson. "Bringing 'Globalization' Down to Earth: Restructuring and Labour in Rural Communities." *The Canadian Review of Sociology and Anthropology* 32 (3) (1995): 341-364. Print.

Luxton, M. "Family Coping Strategies: Balancing Paid Work and Labour." *Family Patterns, Gender Relations*. Ed. B. Fox. Toronto: Oxford University Press, 2009. 453-473. Print.

McLeod, Colleen and Alice Hovorka. "Women in a Transitioning Canadian Resource Town." *Journal of Rural and Community Development* 3 (2008): 78-92. Print.

Julia S. O'Connor, Ann Shola Orloff and Sheila Shaver. *States, Markets, Families: Gender, Liberalism and Social Policy in Australia, Canada, Great Britain and the United States*. Cambridge: Cambridge University Press, 1999.

Ministère de l'Emploi, de la Solidarité sociale et de la Famille. "Quebec Parental Insurance Plan." 2007. Web.

National Children's Agenda. Ottawa: Government of Canada, 1997.

Ontario Municipal Social Services Association (OMSSA). *On the Teeter-Totter: Licensed Child Care in Rural, Northern, and Remote Ontario*. 2011. Web.

Phipps, Shelley. "Working for Working Parents: The Evolution of Maternity and Parental Benefits in Canada." *IRPP Choices* 12 (2) (2006): 1-40. Print.

Poole, Marilyn and Dallas Isaacs. "Caring: A Gendered Concept." *Women's Studies International Forum* 20 (4) (1997): 529-536. Print.

Rauhala, Ann, P. Albanese, C. Ferns, D. Laws, A. Haniff and L. Macdonald. "Who Says What: Election Coverage and Sourcing of Child Care in Four Canadian Dailies." *Journal of Child and Family Studies* 21 (1) (2012): 95-105. Print.

Robertson, N., H. C. Perkins and N. Taylor. "Multiple Job Holding: Interpreting Economic, Labour Market and Social Change in Rural Communities." *Sociologia Ruralis* 48 (4) (2008): 331-350. Print.

Roy, Laurent and Jean Bernier. *Family Policy, Social Trends and Fertility in Quebec: Experimenting with the Nordic Model?* Government of Quebec: Ministère de la Famille, des Aînés et de la Condition Féminine, 2007. Print.

Staden, Helene. "Alertness to the Needs of Others: A Study of the Emotional Labour of Caring." *Journal of Advanced Nursing* 27 (1998): 147-156. Print.

Tougas, Jocelyne. "Child Care in Quebec: Where There's Will, There's a Way." Child Care Advocacy Association of Canada—Parent Voices. 2002a. Web.

Tougas, Jocelyne. *Reforming Quebec's Early Childhood Care and Education: The First Five Years.* Occasional Paper 17. Toronto: Childcare Resource & Research Unit, Centre for Urban and Community Studies, 2002b. Print.

Tougas, Jocelyne. "What We can Learn From the Quebec Experience." *Our Children's Future: Child Care Policy in Canada.* Eds. Gordon Cleveland and Michael Krashinsky. Toronto, University of Toronto Press, 2002c. 92-105. Print.

Universal Child Care Plan. Ottawa: Government of Canada, 2006. Print.

What Mothers Want

Workplace Flexibility

JOCELYN ELISE CROWLEY

MOTHERS IN THE UNITED STATES have entered the workforce in significant numbers over the past 35 years. In 1975, less than half of all mothers with children under the age of eighteen—47.4 percent—were involved in paid employment (BLS 18). Compellingly, by 2010, that number had grown to 71.3 percent (BLS 18). These trends were even apparent for mothers with young children. Over the same time period, mothers with small children ages six and under increased their presence in the paid labor force from 39 percent to 64.2 percent (BLS 19).

While this growth has presented mothers with many opportunities for economic independence and personal fulfillment, these statistics also indicate that these women might be facing new challenges when it comes to balancing their home and paid work lives. More specifically, scholars have noted two significant stressors that these mothers must confront as they map out their lives: role overload and role conflict (Hecht 111). Role overload occurs when individuals experience the pressures of too many tasks to accomplish in a designated period of time. In the case of mothers who work for pay, these are the daily chores of parenting that can vary based on the age of the children involved. With newborns and toddlers, this means feeding, bathing, diapering, clothing, and closely monitoring their playtime activities. With older children and then teenagers, routine care activities might become less pronounced, but the difficult tasks of organizing schedules and guiding character-building behavior become even more important. Added on top of all of these duties are all work-related responsibilities, which can range from light to heavy depending on the hours and commitments of the jobs at stake. In sum, mothers of younger and older children can easily be overwhelmed by parenting and work-oriented obligations.

Role conflict is similar to role overload in that it causes significant stress for mothers. However, it is distinct from role overload in that it pertains to the demands that occur on mothers not in their totality, but rather during the same time blocks (Greenglass, Pantony, and Burke 317). Examples from mothers' everyday lives abound (Erdwins et al. 230). For instance, mothers might be finishing up a project at work, but suddenly receive a call from school that their children are sick and need to be picked up immediately. Or, alternatively, mothers might be required to travel for their jobs while their sons or daughters are starring in a school play. In each of these cases, mothers must choose which task they will complete or event they will attend, which obligation they will have to pass up, and/or how they will coordinate each activity. Regardless of their final decision, they will undoubtedly be left with feelings of doubt, confusion, frustration, and possibly even sadness. With both role overload and role conflict at play, it is not surprising that approximately one-third of mothers choose to stay at home with their children (especially young ones), or are forced into this position because they cannot make affordable child care arrangements (BLS 19). Thus role overload and role conflict explicitly or implicitly affect all mothers, whether currently working for pay or not.

One way to manage both role overload and role conflict is for all mothers to have access to workplace flexibility policies in their current or prospective places of employment. A useful definition of workplace flexibility has been offered by the Alfred P. Sloan Foundation, an organization that provides funding to Workplace Flexibility 2010 at Georgetown University, which does significant research and outreach aimed at interested policymakers in this area.[1] According to this definition, workplace flexibility has three major components:

> (1) **Flexible Work Arrangements (FWAs):** These initiatives include all of those policies that empower employees in the areas of the timing of their work day and their work location.
> (2) **Time Off Options:** These are policies that maximize the ability of employees to take time off under a variety of circumstances, including for planned and unplanned events.
> (3) **Career Flexibility:** These policies focus on facilitating workers' transitions to and from the workforce. More specifically, they

include initiatives that aid workers in exiting the workforce when necessary, help them maintain their skill set while away, and then assist them in re-entering at a later date.

While clearly not a panacea to all of the problems facing mothers who work for pay and mothers who currently stay at home, these workplace flexibility policies could definitely function to help decrease the pressures involved in the double burdens of twenty-first century role overload and role conflict.

METHODOLOGY

In order to study how workplace flexibility might best help mothers across the United States, I selected the only five national mothers' groups located across the country today that maintain centralized lists of their members. These groups are pivotal to the workplace flexibility debate in that they each promote—either strongly or more subtly—certain supports for mothers in their roles in the paid labor force. Depending on the vigor and visibility of their approach, they also attract varying percentages of mothers who currently work for pay versus mothers who stay at home. At one end of the spectrum is MomsRising, which was created in 2006. It is an online advocacy group that champions family-friendly workplaces and operates at both the state and national levels to advance reforms in this area. The four remaining organizations meet in-person on a regular basis. The National Association of Mothers' Centers (NAMC), begun in 1975, provides community support for women either entering the phase of motherhood for the first time in their lives or for those for whom ongoing interaction with similarly-situated mothers has proven to be helpful. Mothers & More, established in 1987, views itself as assisting mothers through the different stages in their lives as well, whether they are currently at-home or working for pay. In addition, created in 1997, Mocha Moms, Incorporated is designed to offer support for mothers of color who are currently choosing not to work outside the home or who have decreased their outside employment obligations at this phase in their children's lives. Lastly, Mothers of Preschoolers (MOPS) began in 1973 with the expressed design of guiding mothers with toddlers along their parenting journey; many but not all of these mothers of young children stay at home. It is also distinct from the other groups

Jocelyn Elise Crowley

in that it has an explicit Christian orientation (Crowley 14-15).[2]

I engaged in a three-pronged data collection effort that included in-depth interviews with 25 members from each of the groups, observational research for each group, and most importantly for my discussion here, a random sample survey of each group's membership from April-June of 2009. The number of survey-eligible[3] members in each group were as follows: MomsRising: 168,786; NAMC: 885; Mothers & More: 5,534; Mocha Moms: 2,853; and MOPS: 84,584.

In order to execute the study, I first obtained each group's membership list, which consisted only of members' names and email addresses. For the three less populous groups—Mocha Moms, NAMC, and Mothers & More—I conducted a census of the membership, i.e., all survey-eligible members were asked to participate. For MomsRising and MOPS, the largest groups in the study, I selected a random sample of 5,000 members. All members were approached up to five times with an advance notice, the initial invitation to participate, and three follow-up requests.

I asked all survey respondents about their involvement in their own mothers' groups, their current arrangement of participation or nonparticipation in the paid labor force, their opinions about workplace flexibility, and their perspectives on if and how to promote flexibility across American workplaces. Web surveys present their own problems in terms of generating a high number of responses (Porter and Whitcomb 580); however, the response rate here was a solid 19.3 percent for the survey, and the overall cooperation rate for all groups was 98.2 percent. Recent research that has explored the propensity of respondents to engage with web-based surveys has documented that response rates approximating 20 percent (and lower) are common (Kaplowitz, Hadlock, and Levine 98). Unfortunately, since each group only provided its members' names and email addresses in order to guarantee their privacy, I was unable to determine the extent of nonresponse bias (Crowley and Weiner 50).

SURVEY RESULTS

In this analysis, I first discuss the basic sociodemographic characteristics of mothers who join these types of groups. At the time of the survey and as indicated by Tables 1-2, the 3,327 group mothers who responded were on average 37.72 years old and had approximately two children under the age of 18. There was also a good mix of mothers who both work for pay at 51.1 percent and those who stay-at-home, at 48.9 percent.

Notably, group mothers were relatively advantaged when considering a variety of other important characteristics. In terms of education, all mothers reported being at least a high school graduate (see Table 3). The remaining mothers can be broken down as follows: while 7.3 percent had "some college" and 5.9 percent had an associate's degree, about one-third of the respondents—34.6 percent—had a bachelor's degree and about 9.3 percent had some graduate training. Most compellingly, a full

Table 1. Age and Total Number of Children: Pooled Survey Data

Characteristic	All Group Mothers
Current Age	37.72
Total Number of Children	2.02
Total Sample Size	3327

Table 2. Employment Status: Pooled Survey Data

Working Status	All Group Mothers
Employed for Pay	51.1 percent
Stay-at-Home	48.9 percent

Table 3. Educational Attainment: Pooled Survey Data

Educational Attainment	All Group Mothers
Less than High School (Grade 11 or less)	0 percent
High school diploma (including GED)	1.1 percent
Some college, but did not graduate	7.3 percent
Associate's degree (two-year degree) or specialized technical	5.9 percent
Bachelor's degree	34.6 percent
Some graduate training	9.3 percent
Graduate or professional degree	41.8 percent

41.8 percent held a graduate or professional degree. In terms of race as indicated by Table 4, the overwhelming majority of group mothers were white, at 76.1 percent.

About one in five members were Black non-Hispanic (18.2 percent); the remaining members were white Hispanic (2.6 percent), Black Hispanic (.9 percent), Asian (2.1 percent), or Native American (.2 percent).

Although not demonstrated in the table, survey respondents from each group were relatively racially homogeneous; for example, almost all of

Table 4. Race: Pooled Survey Data

Race	All Group Mothers
White (non-Hispanic)	76.1 percent
Black (non-Hispanic)	18.2 percent
White Hispanic	2.6 percent
Black Hispanic	0.9 percent
Asian	2.1 percent
Native American	0.2 percent
Other	0 percent

Table 5. Marital Status: Pooled Survey Data

Marital Status	All Group Mothers
Married	93.5 percent
Civil union	0.4 percent
Living with a partner	1.5 percent
Divorced	2.0 percent
Separated	0.8 percent
Widowed	0.5 percent
Never-married	1.3 percent

the Black non-Hispanics came from Mocha Moms. Lastly, with respect to relationship status, as exhibited by Table 5, over nine out of ten group mothers reported being married; the other approximately ten percent fell into other relationship categories, such as civil unions, living with a partner, divorced, separated, widowed, or never-married.

The second part of the study probed areas of commonality with respect to what mothers across all groups—and then separated by paid work status—desire in terms of flexibility when they think about their "ideal jobs." More specifically, the survey asked all mothers how important certain categories of flexibility would be to them in their "ideal job" if they were to obtain it. Their options were as follows: very important, somewhat important, somewhat unimportant, and very unimportant.

Table 6. Importance to Ideal Paid Job: Flexible Work Arrangements

Possible Flexible Work Arrangements	**Flexible Work Arrangements with over 50 percent Pooled Group, Employed, and Stay-at-home Support in "Very Important" Response Category**
1. Flexible starting and stopping times	1. Flexible starting and stopping times
2. Compressed workweeks	2. Compressed workweeks
3. Advance notice of overtime	3. Advance notice of overtime
4. Advance notice of shift schedules	4. Advance notice of shift schedules
5. Control over break time	5. Part-time work
6. Part-time work	6. Telecommuting from home*
7. Job shares	
8. Part-year work	
9. Telecommuting from home	
10. Telecommuting from an alternative workplace	

*This option received less than 50 percent support among stay-at-home mothers only.

Ideal flexible work arrangements represented the first category of inquiry. The survey asked about the importance of flexible starting and stopping times, compressed workweeks, advance notice of overtime, advance notice of shift schedules, control over break time, part-time work, job shares, part-year work, telecommuting from home, and telecommuting from an alternative workplace. Table 6 demonstrates that mothers aggregated across the groups and regardless of whether they were currently employed or staying at home valued specific forms of flexible work arrangements the most. With 50 percent and over expressing support of the option as "very important," all of these mothers favored flexible starting and stopping times, advance notice of overtime, compressed workweeks, advance notice of shift schedules, the option of part-time work, and telecommuting from home (although this last option received less than 50 percent support among stay-at-home mothers). Conversely, access to control over break time, job shares, part-year work, and the option of telecommuting from an alternative workplace were less important to these mothers.

In addition to flexible work arrangements, mothers were also asked about their opinions of time off options and career trajectories in thinking about their ideal jobs (see Table 7). Compellingly, here, too,

Table 7. Importance to Ideal Paid Job: Time off and Career Assistance

Time off and Career Assistance Options	Time off and Career Assistance Options with over 50 percent Pooled Group, Employed, and Stay-at-home Support in "Very Important" Response Category
1. Unpredictable needs 2. Regular time off for recurring needs 3. Extended time off 4. Career Reentry*	1. Unpredictable needs 2. Regular time off for recurring needs 3. Extended time off

*This option received less than 50 percent support among all group and employed mothers.

we saw high levels of agreement (50 percent and over) across the pooled groups and for both employed and stay-at-home mothers as to what types of policies are very important to them. Clear majorities of these mothers argued that short term time off for unpredictable needs, regular time off for recurring needs, and extended time off were very important. The only difference pertained to assistance with career transitions, which less than 50 percent of all pooled group and employed mothers supported.

In summary then, in thinking about their ideal jobs, mothers pooled across groups and mothers who currently work for pay and those who stay at home agree that certain aspects of flexibility could be important to them if they had the opportunity to restructure their lives. One crucial and outstanding question is the extent to which they envision a role for the government in advancing this type of flexibility. Is there any agreement across aggregated mothers' groups, as well as between mothers who currently work for pay and mothers who stay at home as to the proper role of the government in championing flexibility?

The third part of this study offers answers to this question. In brief, the survey inquired of all respondents their opinion of the government's role in promoting flexibility. There were four statements in total, and respondents could simply agree or disagree with each statement. The first statement reflected the most minimal level of governmental intervention, and read, "The government should educate employers and employees about the benefits of flexible work arrangements and best practices regarding how to implement flexible work arrangements." According to Table 8, the majority of pooled group mothers agreed, as did both employed and stay-at-home mothers. The next statement presented in the survey represented a higher level of governmental intervention in workplace flexibility policy: "The government should encourage employers to voluntarily increase access to flexible work arrangements, by, for example, providing grants, awards, and tax incentives." Notably, support stayed constant, with the majority of all group mothers, employed, and stay-at-home mothers agreeing.

The final two and strongest statements presented in the survey asked about *requiring* the government to become involved in promoting flexibility. The two statements were as follows: "The government should *require* employers to establish a process under which employees can request flexible work arrangements and employers must consider those requests," and

Table 8. Support for a Governmental Role in Advancing Workplace Flexibility

Statements	Pooled Group, Employed, and Stay-at-home Support?
1. "The government should educate employers and employees about the benefits of flexible work arrangements and best practices regarding how to implement flexible work arrangements."	1. YES
2. "The government should encourage employers to voluntarily increase access to flexible work arrangements, by, for example, providing grants, awards, and tax incentives."	2. YES
3. "The government should *require* employers to establish a process under which employees can request flexible work arrangements and employers must consider those requests."	3. YES
4. "The government should *require* employers to grant a certain number of requests for flexible work arrangements per year."	4. NO*

*Only employed mothers supported this statement at 50 percent.

"The government should *require* employers to grant a certain number of requests for flexible work arrangements per year." Interestingly, the majority of the pooled group mothers still supported establishing a process to request flexibility; so did a majority of employed and stay-at-home mothers. Only the final statement, which would require that employers actually grant a certain number of flexible work arrangements per year, produced a serious loss of support among mothers, with less than half of all pooled group and stay-at-home mothers agreeing. Only employed mothers reached the threshold level of 50 percent support here.

CONCLUSIONS

Mothers today have many options regarding the future of their life course. Some mothers choose to engage in paid work, as they are seeking personal fulfillment and have strong career aspirations. Other mothers are in the paid labor market because they have to be; economic realities necessitate that they earn money to directly contribute to their families' financial well-being. Still other mothers remain at home, believing this to be the best arrangement for their children, while others stay at home because they cannot afford child care expenses if they were to return to paid employment. Yet mostly all mothers, regardless of their employment status, worry about doing the best for both themselves and their children.

This brief analysis demonstrates that one of the most important ways to resolve the tensions that both sets of mothers face in their daily lives is to promote workplace flexibility. In considering their ideal jobs, pooled group mothers, mothers who are currently working for pay, and those who are currently staying at home value important aspects of flexibility that might be offered to them by their employers. They also share strong views that the government could be doing more right now to advance this goal of flexibility, at least in the areas of employer education and incentives. Clearly, the United States has faced significant challenges in recent years due to the downward spiraling of the economy. But as the country moves out of the Great Recession, hopefully more attention can be paid to policies designed to help all mothers maximize their potential as both workers and parents. A key issue in moving these ideas forward, however, is leadership on at least two fronts.

The first area is leadership in ideas. The federal government, chiefly through the efforts and voice of Michelle Obama, has made workplace flexibility a critical issue for the President's Administration. In fact, the First Lady hosted the first White House Conference on Workplace Flexibility in March 2010. This conference attracted a variety of people with different perspectives on these issues, including business leaders, labor organizers, and academic experts. This effort aimed to reinforce and extend the robust federal history of promoting such policies as telecommuting among governmental workers. In addition, many states have moved in the same direction of promoting workplace flexibility policies, with Arizona and North Carolina, for example, devising plans so their own workers can more effectively complete tasks at home rather than strictly at the office.

The second area where leadership is paramount relates to the groups themselves. The majority of mothers join these groups for friendships and social support. Public policy achievements in the area of workplace flexibility are therefore not always on the forefront of these groups' agendas. The leaders of these groups, then, can play a pivotal role in raising this issue as one of critical importance to mothers across the board, whether currently employed or staying at home. In addition, as these groups presently tend to attract mothers of a higher socioeconomic status, these organizations can and should do a much better job of targeting mothers from all different backgrounds into their membership bases. It is only in this way that a true collectivity of interests can develop, one that becomes representative of mothers from a variety of perspectives who all share the desire to improve the quality of their daily work and family lives.

[1]See http://workplaceflexibility2010.org/index.php/policy_components/

[2]The percentages of mothers who stay at home in MomsRising, NAMC, Mothers & More, Mocha Moms, and MOPS are 26.2 percent, 47.3 percent, 47.7 percent, 48.2 percent, and 65.6 percent, respectively.

[3]"Survey eligible" does not equal each group's total membership at the time of the study. Names removed from the total membership statistics were as follows: (a) duplicate records within groups; (b) duplicate records across groups; and (c) corrupt records, which resulted in a net set of unique membership records. Also removed were members who (d) had no chapter affiliation; (e) were not female; (f) were not residing in the United States; (g) had left the group subsequent to the delivery of the gross set of presumptively unique member records; and/or (h) with no valid email address.

WORKS CITED

Bureau of Labor Statistics (BLS). *Women in the Labor Force: A Databook*. Washington, DC: Department of Labor, 2011.

Crowley, Jocelyn Elise. *Mothers Unite! Organizing for Workplace Flexibility and the Transformation of Family Life*. Ithaca: Cornell University Press, 2013.

Crowley, Jocelyn Elise and Marc D. Weiner. *What Mothers Want: Workplace Flexibility in the Twenty-First Century*: Report to the Alfred P.

Sloan Foundation at http://policy.rutgers.edu/faculty/crowley/WhatMothersWant.pdf, 2010.

Erdwins, Carol J. et al. "The Relationship of Women's Role Strain to Social Support, Role Satisfaction, and Self Efficacy." *Family Relations* 50 (3) (2001): 230-238.

Greenglass, Esther R., Kaye-Lee Pantony, and Ronald J. Burke. "A Gender-Role Perspective on Role Conflict, Work Stress, and Social Support." *Journal of Social Behavior and Personality* 3 (4) (1988): 317-323.

Hecht, Laura M. "Role Conflict and Role Overload: Different Concepts, Different Consequences." *Sociological Inquiry* 71 (4) (2001): 111-121.

Kaplowitz, Michael D., Timothy D. Hadlock, and Ralph Levine. "A Comparison of Web and Mail Survey Response Rates." *Public Opinion Quarterly* 68 (1) (2004): 94-101.

Porter, Stephen R., and Michael E. Whitcomb. "The Impact of Contact Type on Web Survey Response Rates." *Public Opinion Quarterly* 67 (4) (2003): 579-588.

Contributor Notes

Patrizia Albanese is a professor of sociology at Ryerson University and president-elect of the Canadian Sociological Association. She has published books, articles, and chapters on Canadian families, family policies, nationalism, and on children and youth in Canada.

Kim Anderson (Cree/Métis) is the author of *A Recognition of Being: Reconstructing Native Womanhood* (Sumach/Canadian Scholar's Press, 2000) and *Life Stages and Native Women: Memory, Teachings and Story Medicine* (University of Manitoba Press, 2011). Kim is an Associate Professor teaching Indigenous Studies at Wilfrid LaurierUniversity, Brantford.

Wanda Thomas Bernard, Ph.D., RSW, C.M., has a BA from Mount Saint Vincent University, a MSW from Dalhousie, and a Ph.D. from the University of Sheffield in England. She is a Professor, and Past Director of the School of Social Work, Dalhousie University. Her teaching and research interests are in the area of discrimination, racism, oppression and empowerment. She has conducted research on Black Nova Scotian women and their experiences working as domestics. One of Dr. Bernard's most recent research initiatives included a project funded by the Canadian Institutes of Health Research, that examined the impact of racism and violence, including the violence of racism, on the health and well being of Black men, their families and communities, in Halifax, Calgary, and Toronto.

Susan B. Boyd is a Professor of Law at the University of British Columbia, where she holds the research Chair in Feminist Legal Studies. Until 2012, she was Director of the University of British Columbia Centre for

Feminist Legal Studies. In 2012, she was elected a Fellow of the Royal Society of Canada. She teaches in the fields of Family Law and Feminist Legal Studies. Her research lies primarily in the fields of child custody law and legal parenthood. Her books include *Child Custody, Law, and Women's Work* (2003), *Reaction and Resistance: Feminism, Law, and Social Change* (2007), and *Law and Families* (2006). Her recent research is on autonomous motherhood and single mothers by choice.

Jennifer Brant is a Mohawk woman, mother of two boys, and a Ph.D candidate in Educational Studies at Brock University. She is currently employed at Brock University as the Program Coordinator for the Gidayaamin Aboriginal Women's Certificate Program. Her research focuses on the experiences of Indigenous women in education and their intersecting identity roles as mothers, students, and community members.

Megan Butryn is an award-winning, fourth-year student in the Department of Sociology at Ryerson University. She has a wide range of research interests relating to feminism, women and families. She sits on the Ryerson Research Ethics board.

Paula J. Caplan, Ph.D., is a clinical and research psychologist currently an Associate at Harvard University's DuBois Institute. She was recently a Fellow in the Women and Public Policy Program at Harvard Kennedy School and is author of eleven books, including *Don't Blame Mother: Mending the Mother-Daughter Relationship* and *When Johnny and Jane Come Marching Home: How All of Us Can Help Veterans* (which won three major awards, including best psychology book of 2011 in the Association of American Publishers' PROSE competition), and editor of *a twelfth*.

Jeannette Corbiere Lavell is an Anishnabe woman of the Wikwemikong Unceded Indian Reserve on Manitoulin Island. In 1974, the Supreme Court of Canada ruled against her effort to correct gender discrimination in the *Indian Act*. At that time, the *Act* revoked the status of First Nations women who married non-Indians, yet, allowed men to pass their status on to their non-Indian wives. In 1985, after The Charter was enacted, Jeannette and her children regained their status. She is the 2009 recipient of the Governor General's Award in Commemoration of the Persons Case and former president of the Native Women's Association of Canada.

Jocelyn Elise Crowley is a Professor of Public Policy at Rutgers, The State University of New Jersey. Her books include *The Politics of Child Support in America* (2003, Cambridge University Press); *Defiant Dads: Fathers' Rights Activists in America* (2008, Cornell University Press); and *Mothers Unite! Organizing for Workplace Flexibility and the Transformation of Family Life* (2013, Cornell University Press).

Andrea Doucet is the Canada Research Chair in Gender, Work and Care and Professor of Sociology and Women's and Gender Studies at Brock University. She is the author of *Do Men Mother?* (2006) and is currently completing two books: one on breadwinning mothers and a second (co-authored) on reflexive and relational knowing. Her writing on care has been deeply influenced by caring for three daughters (eighteen-year old twins and a twenty-two-year old).

Estelle Sobel Erasmus is an award-winning journalist, author, and former magazine editor-chief (*Woman's Own*, Hachette Filipacchi's *Body by Jake*, *Esthetique*), and adjunct professor at NYU, who sits on the board of directors of the national non-profit organization Mothers & More. She writes a "Teachable Moments" column and Women's Issues column for examiner.com. She went from Dating Diva to Married Lady to Older Mom in a blink of an eye and writes about her transformative journey through motherhood (and marriage) at her award-winning blog "Musings on Motherhood and Mid-Life" (http://musingsonmotherhoodmidlife.com), which was named one of Circle of Mom's Top 25 Blogs by a Mom for 2012. Estelle was also in the 2012 New York production of *Listen to Your Mother*, where she read an original essay on motherhood. She was one of the 2012 BlogHer Voices of the Year, and had her writing anthologized in the *2012 BlogHer Voices of the Year* book. Estelle can be found on Twitter at <http://twitter.com/mommymusings011> and Pinterest at <http://pinterest.com/mommymusings011>. She is currently writing a play depicting her exploits as a single woman prior to marriage and motherhood.

Pat Gowens is a founder of Welfare Warriors and editor of its 26-year-old international publication, *Mother Warriors Voice*. Gowens researches and promotes the need for guaranteed income, similar to European countries' Family Pensions, for all U.S. children. Gowens raised three sons as a single mom whose only access to child support was welfare.

Fiona Joy Green, Ph.D. is a feminist mother, teaches women's and gender studies, and is the Associate Dean of Arts at the University of Winnipeg. She is the author of *Feminist Mothering in Theory and Practice: 1985-1995* (Mellen Press) and *Practicing Feminist Mothering* (Arbeiter Ring), and is co-editor of *Maternal Pedagogies: In and Outside the Classroom* (Demeter) and of the forthcoming *Chasing Rainbows: Exploring Gender-Fluid Parenting Practices* (Demeter). Fiona's most recent interests include the ethics of Mommy Blogging, and the surveillance and judgement of mothers in social media and on reality TV.

Louisa Hawkins is a graduating student in the Department of Sociology at Ryerson University. She is especially interested in feminist research, feminist on-line ethnography and the social production of knowledge. She sits on the Ryerson Research Ethics Board.

Heather Hewett's work on motherhood has appeared in a range of publications, including *Journal of the Association for Research on Mothering*, *Women's Studies Quarterly*, *Brain, Child* magazine, *Chick Lit: The New Woman's Fiction*, and *Mothering in the Third Wave*. She is an associate professor of English and Women's Studies at SUNY New Paltz.

Amber Kinser is author of *Motherhood and Feminism* (2010, Seal), editor of *Mothering in the Third Wave* (2008, Demeter), and co-editor of the upcoming collection *Performing Motherhood* (Demeter). She is a Professor and Department Chair of Communication and former Director of Women's Studies at East Tennessee State University. She currently leads a research team investigating mothers' experiences of family meals.

Dawn Memee Lavell-Harvard, Ph.D., is a member of the Wikwemikong First Nation, a Trudeau Scholar, President of the Ontario Native Women's Association, Vice-President for the Native Women's Association of Canada, and mother of Autumn, Eva, and Brianna. She is also co-editor of *Until Our Hearts Are on the Ground: Aboriginal Mothering, Oppression, Resistance and Rebirth*.

Gwen Lewis is the editor of *Hip Mama Zine,* which can be found at <www.hipmamazine.com>. She lives in Oregon with her husband and their young daughter. When she isn't working on the magazine or entertaining her daughter, she is actively working on a grass roots public awareness campaign and dreaming about utopia.

Melissa Maldonado-Salcedo is a Colombi-Rican mother, scholar, activist, and artist born and raised in New York City's Lower East Side (Loisaida). A doctoral student at the Graduate Center of the City of New York in Cultural Anthropology and adjunct Lecturer at Hunter College, she teaching courses in "Latina Women" and "Latino Communities in the United States." Her dissertation engages with the Argentine diaspora post the economic crisis and its intersection with Latinidad.

Courtney Manion is a student in the Department of Psychology at Ryerson University. When not studying or involved on a research team, she works on campus. She has a wide range of research interests that span both sociology and psychology.

Kuae Kelch Mattox is National President of Mocha Moms, Inc., a non-profit organization with one hundred chapters in twenty-nine states dedicated to supporting stay at home mothers of color. She is an Emmy-nominated journalist who has worked for *NBC News, ABC News, The Oprah Winfrey Show* and *The Miami Herald.*

Margaret K. Nelson is the A. Barton Hepburn Professor of Sociology at Middlebury College. She is the author of many books including, most recently, *Parenting Out of Control: Anxious Parents in Uncertain Times* (2010).

D. Lynn O'Brien Hallstein is an Associate Professor of Rhetoric in the College of General Studies at Boston University. She is the author of *White Feminists and Contemporary Maternity: Purging Matrophobia*, co-editor with Sara Hayden of *Contemporary Maternity in an Era of Choice: Explorations into Discourses of Reproduction*, and co-editor with Andrea O'Reilly of *Academic Motherhood in a Post-Second Wave Context: Challenges, Strategies, and Possibilities*, and she has published in a variety of academic journals.

Andrea O'Reilly, Ph.D., is Professor in the School of Gender, Sexuality and Women's Studies at York University and is founder and director of The Motherhood Initiative for Research and Community Involvement, founder and editor-in-chief of the Journal of the Motherhood Initiative and founder and editor of Demeter Press, the first feminist press on motherhood. She is editor and author of 18 books on motherhood including most recently *21st Century Motherhood: Experience, Identity, Policy, Agency* (2010); *The 21st Century Motherhood Movement: Mothers Speak Out on Why We Need to Change the World and How to Do It* (2011); and (with Lynn O'Brien Hallstein) *Academic Motherhood in a Post Second Wave Context: Challenges, Strategies, Possibilities* (2012). She is editor of the first encyclopedia on Motherhood. In 2010, she was the recipient of the CAUT Sarah Shorten Award for outstanding achievements in the promotion of the advancement of women in Canadian universities and colleges. She is currently completely an article on National Association of Mothers' Centre and maternal empowerment, a monograph on Academic Motherhood, and beginning a study on the Slut Walk Movement. She is twice the recipient (1998, 2009) of York University's "Professor of the Year Award" for teaching excellence. She is the proud mama of three fabulous and feminist adult children.

Barbara Katz Rothman is Professor of Sociology at the City University of New York, holds visiting professorships in Berlin and in Plymouth England, and at the International Midwifery Preparation Program at Ryerson University in Toronto. Her books include *In Labour; Labouring On; The Tentative Pregnancy; The Book of Life; Recreating Motherhood;* and *Weaving a Family.*

Jasjit K. Sangha completed her Ph.D. from the University of Toronto in The Department of Adult Education and Community Development. She has been working on research related to mothering for nearly a decade, exploring how women engage in transformative adult learning through the process of (step) mothering. She is also interested in arts-informed research, life-long learning and holistic approaches to education. She has recently published two books with Demeter Press: a memoir, *Stepmothering: A Spiritual Journey* (2012) and a co-edited collection, *South Asian Mothering: Negotiating Culture, Family and Selfhood* (2013).

Lorri Slepian, LCSW, clinical psychotherapist, was a founding mother of the first Mothers' Center in the world and a past Co-Director and later Board member of the National Association of Mothers' Centers (NAMC) as well as leadership advisor. She has worked to build a Mothers' Movement since 1973 and was the motivator behind the NAMC's Declaration of Mothers' Rights, a document that advocates for women's economic, educational, physical, psychological and social rights, including women's rights to safe births, supportive environments, information about human development and choices about family lives. Lorri is a founder of the NAMC's MOTHERS Initiative dedicated to improving the economic status of mothers and caregivers and is responsible for making the Mothers' Center non-judgmental, non-hierarchical culture a part of MOTHERS.Lorri was instrumental in promoting and training Mothers' Center leaders and members on the unique Mothers' Center culture and has been instrumental in spreading the Mothers' Center programs and vision to many thousands of women. She was married to her loving husband Dan for 58 years and has four wonderful sons, Ralph, Brian, Eric and Greg.

Jewelles Smith completed her Master of Arts in Women's Studies at Simon Fraser University in 2007. Passionate and articulate about women and disability rights, Jewelles has developed her career as a researcher, writer, and consultant, becoming an expert in gender and disability human rights issues in Canada. She has worked for a number of organizations as both staff and freelance, including the CCPA & DAWN-RAFH Canada. She currently thrives in Revelstoke, BC, with her two sons.

Pamela Stone, Professor of Sociology at Hunter College and Graduate Center, CUNY, is the author of *Opting Out? Why Women Really Quit Careers and Head Home,* winner of the American Sociological Association's William J. Goode Award for best book on the family and named one of *Working Mother*'s "Picks for Moms."

Laurie Sylla has more than three decades of experience in human services as a counselor, program manager, executive director, advocate, and researcher. Formerly affiliated with the Yale AIDS Program, she is now with the King County Department of Community and Human Services in Seattle. She is a published poet and has co-authored peer-reviewed journal articles and a book on AIDS, as well as book chapters on microbicides and the mother's movement. Her current research/ writing project is a book for transnational couples (www.lovehasnoborders.org).

Judith Warner is best known for her 2005 *New York Times* best-seller, *Perfect Madness: Motherhood in the Age of Anxiety*, and *New York Times* column, "Domestic Disturbances." She is currently a contributing writer for the *New York Times Magazine,* an opinion columnist for *Time.com,* and a Senior Fellow at the Center for American Progress.

Gina Wong is a Registered Psychologist, Associate Professor, and Chair in the Graduate Centre for Applied Psychology at Athabasca University, Canada. Gina is a board member with the MIRCI. She is the Alberta Co-coordinator with Postpartum Support International. Gina runs a counselling practice and publishes and presents widely on issues in maternal mental health and wellness from feminist and cross-cultural perspectives. Gina is the editor of *Moms Gone Mad: Motherhood and Madness Oppression and Resistance* published in 2012 with Demeter Press.